Queer Realms of Memory

Contemporary French and Francophone Cultures, 109

Contemporary French and Francophone Cultures

Series Editor

CHARLES FORSDICK
University of Liverpool

Editorial Board

TOM CONLEY
Harvard University

JACQUELINE DUTTON
University of Melbourne

LYNN A. HIGGINS
Dartmouth College

MIREILLE ROSELLO
University of Amsterdam

DEREK SCHILLING
Johns Hopkins University

This series aims to provide a forum for new research on modern and contemporary French and francophone cultures and writing. The books published in *Contemporary French and Francophone Cultures* reflect a wide variety of critical practices and theoretical approaches, in harmony with the intellectual, cultural and social developments which have taken place over the past few decades. All manifestations of contemporary French and francophone culture and expression are considered, including literature, cinema, popular culture, theory. The volumes in the series will participate in the wider debate on key aspects of contemporary culture.

Recent titles in the series:

96 Bruno Chaouat, *Out of this World: Gnostic Encounters in Modern French Literature and Thought*

97 Ashwiny O. Kistnareddy, *Refugee Afterlives: Home, Hauntings, and Hunger*

98 Christopher L. Miller, *Thresholds: A 'Complete' Table of the Borrowings in Yambo Ouologuem's* Le Devoir de violence, *and Why They Matter*

99 Kathryn Robson, *Beyond the Happy Ending: Imagining Happiness in Contemporary French Women's Writing and Film*

100 Louise Hardwick, *Creole Cinema: Memory Traces*

101 Ian James, *Rethinking Literary Naturalism: Proust and Quignard After Life*

102 Khalid Lyamlahy, *Nostalgic Rebels: Politics, Aesthetics, and Selfhood in Postcolonial Morocco*

103 Judith G. Miller, *Race and Theatre by Sylvie Chalaye*

104 Patoimbasba Nikiema, *Exile and Return in African and Caribbean Literature*

105 Jacqueline Couti and Anny-Dominique Curtius, *Women, Theory, Praxis, and Performativities: Transoceanic Entanglements in Francophone Settings*

106 Polly Galis, Ciara Gorman and Julie Rodgers, eds, *Disruptive Discourses by Francophone Women*

107 Sarah Tiede Buchanan, *Emergent Voices of (North) African Immigrant Women and Their Daughters in French Literature and Film: Challenging the Inside, Seeking Outside, Passing Through Walls*

108 Belle Marie Joseph, *Trauma and Meaning in French Concentration Camp Poetry (1943–1945)*

EDITED BY SIHAM BOUAMER,
DENIS M. PROVENCHER, AND
RYAN K. SCHROTH

Queer Realms of Memory

Archiving LGBTQ Sites and Symbols in the French National Narrative

LIVERPOOL UNIVERSITY PRESS

First published 2025 by
Liverpool University Press
4 Cambridge Street
Liverpool
L69 7ZU

Copyright © 2025 Liverpool University Press

Siham Bouamer, Denis M. Provencher, and Ryan K. Schroth have asserted the right to be identified as the editors of this book in accordance with the Copyright, Designs and Patents Act 1988.

All rights reserved. No part of this book may be reproduced, stored in a retrieval system, or transmitted, in any form or by any means, electronic, mechanical, photocopying, recording, or otherwise, without the prior written permission of the publisher.

British Library Cataloguing-in-Publication data
A British Library CIP record is available

ISBN: 978-1-83764-406-3 (hardback)
ISBN: 978-1-83624-586-5 (paperback)
eISBN: 978-1-83764-320-2 (pdf)
eISBN: 978-1-83624-923-8 (epub)

Typeset by Carnegie Book Production, Lancaster

Acknowledgments

The idea for this volume emerged from our conversations at the conference "Contemporary French Civilizations" at the University of Arizona in Tucson, Arizona, in September 2019 and the plenary sessions at the conference, "Postcolonial Realms of Memory: Sites and Symbols in the Modern Francosphere," at the Winthrop-King Institute for Contemporary French and Francophone Studies at Florida State University in Tallahassee, Florida, in October 2021. We would like to thank Dr. Martin Munro at the Winthrop-King Institute for the invitation to participate in the conference, which focused on scholarship from the important volume *Postcolonial Realms of Memory* (2020), edited by our colleagues Étienne Achille, Charles, Forsdick, and Lydie Moudileno. We also thank Chloe Johnson and Charles Forsdick at Liverpool University Press for their enthusiasm and support for this project from the very beginning.

Siham would like to express her heartfelt thanks to all the "feminist killjoys" who continue to inspire her through their activism and writings, as well as the killjoys in her everyday life, including friends. A special thanks to Migena Bregu, Stacy Davis, and Ervin Malakaj for their continuous encouragement. She is also grateful for her parents, whose unwavering support, too often unacknowledged, much like that of many immigrants, has been the cornerstone of all her academic projects. Finally, she would like to acknowledge the University of Cincinnati for providing funding that made part of this project possible.

Denis extends his gratitude to the University of Arizona for a scholarly leave, which provided him the time necessary to devote to the completion of the book proposal, and to North Carolina State University for the financial assistance to help with the simultaneous publication of the paperback version of this book. He is also grateful to Abdellah Taïa for his friendship and for sharing many important ideas related to Denis's chapter on Genet's tomb in Larache. As always, Denis is thankful to his husband and best friend Stephen R. Woods for his love and support and to their fearless companions Rocky and Beau.

Ryan would like to express his thanks to the Dean's office and the Department of French Studies at Wake Forest University (WFU) for their support of the project. He is also grateful to his colleagues in the WFU Humanities Institute Faculty Workshop Seminar who offered early feedback on his chapter included here. Finally, Ryan would like to thank his husband Jason, whose support and compassion inspire him in everything he does.

Finally, we would like to thank each other for the countless meetings, conversations, and exchanges. By editing this volume together, we not only learned about and from each other's important scholarship, but we grew as colleagues and friends in solidarity who continue to advocate for visibility and space for all.

Contents

List of Figures x

Introduction: Queering *lieux de mémoire* 1
    Siham Bouamer, Denis M. Provencher,
    and Ryan K. Schroth

I Institutions and Monuments

1 Presenting the present: Queer memories beyond
   same-sex marriage 27
   Bruno Perreau

2 Queer memory takes a monumental turn: Commemorating
   Bruno Lenoir and Jean Diot 41
   Stephen Shapiro

3 The monument and the anti-monument: Aesthetic
   strategies for remembering two crises from French LGBTQ
   history 55
   Scott Gunther

4 Queer experiences in Parisian *collèges* between 1869
   and 1873 71
   Michael Rosenfeld and Clive Thomson

5 Archiving queer France: Constructing a community at the
   intersection of history and memory 85
   Andrew Israel Ross

II Centers and Peripheries

6 Paris, erotic capital of the nineteenth century: The *tournée des grands-ducs* and the emergence of queer *lieux de mémoire* during the Third Republic 101
 Leslie Choquette

7 From the Marais to collective memory: How to map queer France 117
 Kory Olson

8 Carving out space in the city: LGBTQ+ pride as a queer *lieu de mémoire* 131
 Luke L. Eilderts

9 Queering the *périph'*: New sites for queer memory in contemporary French cinema 145
 James S. Williams

III Icons and Figures

10 Cult graves and queer memory 159
 Melanie C. Hawthorne

11 Abdellah Taïa's *transfilial* memories of Genet's tomb in Larache 173
 Denis M. Provencher

12 The Chevalier d'Eon 193
 Todd W. Reeser

13 (Re-)defining the popular music "Gay icon" in media coverage of Dalida and Mylène Farmer 207
 Chris Tinker

14 Giovanna Rincon and *Acceptess-T*: Living archives of transgender solidarity in an age of homonationalism 219
 Blase A. Provitola

IV Alternative Archives: Literature and Cinema

15 Archives of desire: Viewing *cinéma colonial* as a queer *lieu de mémoire* 237
 Barry Nevin

16	*Le lieu de drague comme lieu de mémoire*, or cruising, cinema, and colonial vestiges Jules O'Dwyer	253
17	A queer rewriting of history: The case of Leïla Slimani's *Le Pays des autres* Maxime Foerster	267
18	Fatima Daas's *La Petite Dernière* (2020): A fugitive *lieux de mémoire* for the undercommons Siham Bouamer	277
19	Emotional geographies, queer realms of memory: Act Up-Paris and *120 battements par minute* (2017) Ryan K. Schroth	297
20	Haunted sites and haunted memories: HIV/AIDS temporalities in the contemporary French cultural memory Daniel N. Maroun	315

V New Technologies as Archive

21	Cases Rebelles: The archipelagic and transnational construction of Black queer sites of memory Michaëla Danjé	331
22	Podcasting as a queer archival method for an intersectional French culture Thomas Muzart	343
23	Bodies, memories, visibility: Élisabeth Lebovici's digital reinscription of lesbians in the French visual arts Cristina Johnston	357
Conclusion Siham Bouamer, Denis M. Provencher, and Ryan K. Schroth		371
Index		379

Figures

2.1 Plaque commemorating Bruno Lenoir and Jean Diot in the rue Montorgueil (Paris), dedicated on October 18, 2014	42
3.1 Toulouse plaque	59
3.2 Mulhouse plaque	59
3.3 *L'Artère, le jardin des dessins*: People dancing the tango on *L'Artère, le jardin des dessins*, Parc de la Villette, Paris, 2023	62
11.1 Abdellah Taïa walking in Larache	182
11.2 Abdellah Taïa sitting at Genet's tomb	183
11.3 Sofiane Hennani sitting at Genet's tomb and hugging the gravestone	184
11.4 Saïd sitting on a wall along the coast in Larache	185
11.5 Men and a dog sitting and swimming on the rocks in Larache	187
11.6 Instagram Hashtags	187
11.7 Facebook comments	188
11.8 Facebook comments	189
12.1 The Chevalier d'Eon outside the train station, Tonnerre, Burgundy	200
12.2 Lycée Chevalier D'Eon, Tonnerre	201
15.1 Saint-Avit imagines Morhange and Antinéa together	242
15.2 A delirious Saint-Avit "sees" Morhange	243
15.3 Two anonymous male characters look ahead in the casino	245
15.4 René and Lucien view Lucien's photograph	247
15.5 René embraces Lucien	248

Introduction
Queering *lieux de mémoire*

Siham Bouamer, Denis M. Provencher, and Ryan K. Schroth

Pierre Nora's concept *lieux de mémoire* [realms of memory] has become arguably the most significant academic point of reference when discussing processes of nation-building and their interconnectedness with history and collective memory. Although his theory and approach have acquired popularity well beyond their application to the French context, his influential seven-volume series (1984–92) is not without its own shortcomings and failures, which have occasionally been exposed over the last two decades.[1] It is not until the publication of *Postcolonial Realms of Memory* (2020) that we see an expansive critique of Nora's own selective memory. In this important volume, Étienne Achille, Charles Forsdick, and Lydie Moudileno argue that Nora's shortcomings reflect "a certain French incapacity and/or unwillingness to engage with the inherent and increasingly undeniable imbrication of the colonial in the *roman national* [national narrative]" (5–6). These authors issue an important corrective by expanding realms of memory to include those pertaining to (post)colonial history in both France and its overseas

---

1 See Achille, Forsdick, and Moudileno for an excellent synthesis of the scholarly critique of Nora's work. Another reference we find most productive and in line with our own volume, specifically on transnational and multidirectional approaches, is Rothberg, Sanyal, and Silverman's special issue of *Yale French Studies* from 2010 on "Noeuds de mémoire: Multidirectional Memory in Postwar French and Francophone Culture".

departments and territories. Our project functions in tandem with their publication and seeks to continue challenging Nora's approach and France's national narrative of republican universalism by providing space to examine queer lives, cultures, and memories. Achille, Forsdick, and Moudileno argue that Nora's omissions on postcolonial identities "have been pointed out sporadically over the past two decades" (1). We contend, however, that those related to queer experiences within France's collective memory have never been systematically addressed.[2]

Scholars in French and Francophone studies and in other fields such as history, literary, and cultural studies have dealt occasionally with queer realms of memory in urban contexts (Sibalis; Caron; Provencher, *Queer French*), whether or not they utilize explicitly Nora's term, fully engage with his concept, or challenge his contributions. Our volume is the first book-length study to question Nora's lack of engagement with queer realms of memory in France's national narrative within and beyond its borders and to illustrate how these realms are central (and not peripheral) to what we see, not as France's monolithic French national narrative of republican universalism, but as France's flexible model of universalism that always and already includes queerness and difference.[3] Challenging Nora's conceptualization of *lieux de mémoire* takes many forms and to varying degrees in the volume. Some contributors directly engage with his work, but others have deliberately chosen to exclude his name, as a form of academic protest and/or to allow for the inclusion of other theorists – queer and/or racialized – of memory, many of whom are mentioned in this introduction and have served to inform the directions of this volume.

This collection critically examines the limitations of Nora's concept of *lieux de mémoire* in accommodating queer memory. Indeed, his understanding of *lieux de mémoire* is premised on a stable, national collective memory, which, as the chapters demonstrate, systematically

---

[2] Nora's volume never engages with homosexuality or LGBTQ identities. Moreover, such a reference only occurs once in *Postcolonial Realms of Memory* in Mireille Rosello's chapter "Jeanne Duval".

[3] For more on this, see Suaudeau and Niang, where they argue that France's universalism is already and always informed by "cracks" of difference in the system that strengthen the coherence of the national narrative. See also Provencher's *Queer French* where he examines two opposing models of citizenship – "good" and "bad" sexual citizenship – where the latter accommodates for a more flexible model of universalism to include cracks and transgressions occurring on the margins of society.

marginalizes queer histories and erases their complexity. The examples we highlight here challenge the fixed, national framework of Nora's concept, advocating for a more flexible, inclusive approach to memory. Some chapters reveal how queer memory disrupts foundational aspects of Nora's conceptualization, including its presumed national coherency, its temporal normativity, and its geographical focus. Williams, in his study of *banlieue* cinema, critiques Nora's framework for its "universalizing heterosexual presuppositions," which fail to account for queer differences writ large. Focusing on the Chevalier d'Eon, Reeser continues to interrogate the nationalism inherent in Nora's model and argues that queer memory does not fit within Nora's understanding of the collectivist, national narrative.

At the same time, other chapters refocus the discussion on temporality as a key dimension of queer realms of memory. Tinker's chapter on Dalida and Mylène Farmer highlights its significance in shaping the queer reception of these two iconic figures. While not explicitly engaging with Nora's framework, Tinker's chapter brings into focus the relationship between past and present. Schroth's chapter similarly engages with this interplay but does so through a different lens. He explores how the film *120 battements par minute* (2017) destabilizes Nora's distinction between history and memory through a hybrid and affective approach to queer remembrance.

Just as temporality unsettles Nora's model, other chapters also challenge its spatial and geographical framework. Olson, for instance, explores the self-mapping of queer France. He examines how queer cartography challenges the fixed territorial logic of *lieux de mémoire* and highlights how spatialized forms of memory complicate the presumed stability of national belonging. Gunther pushes the interrogation of space further by questioning the very idea of permanence itself. In his study of queer memorials, he rejects the assumption that sites of memories must be fixed and permanent and instead suggests that these sites might be better understood as "anti-*lieu de mémoire*." This rethinking of spatiality parallels a broader reconsideration of the *lieux de mémoire*. While some contributors seek to expand or reconfigure the concept, others move beyond it entirely. They propose alternative models to foreground how queer memory functions outside traditional narratives of belonging. Provitola, for instance, interrogates Nora's reliance on a normative form of temporality and demonstrates how "queer time" disrupts the linear chronology so often associated with *lieux de mémoire*. Other contributors turn to alternative theoretical models

– for example, Bouamer's *traces-mémoires* or Maroun's hauntology – to conceptualize queer memory beyond national paradigms. In sum, this volume navigates the tension between extending and outright rejecting Nora's framework, as contributors reconsider the applicability of *lieux de mémoire* to queer memory.

Before turning to some of the key concepts important for the framework of this collective work, let us first contextualize some of the major strides and challenges that have impacted the lives of LGBTQ[4] Francophones in France. While broader transnational contexts are relevant, the French context and the national narrative of republican universalism remain central here, as these are what we attempt to challenge most in this volume.

Strides against the backdrop of queer invisibilization in France

In a similar vein to the authors of *Postcolonial Realms of Memory*, who establish a certain sense of urgency to "make visible the invisible thread that links the colonial to French culture" (1), the three editors of this volume, as scholars committed to queer studies, recognize the pressing need for similar work to challenge the systematic invisibilization of the specificities of queer remembering in the French national narrative, and in doing so hope to (re)define and (re)assess what constitutes queer realms of memory. This urgency resonates with what Charles Morris (2006) identifies as the "struggles against annihilating silence" (146) and what Ann Cvetkovich (2003) describes as the "determination to 'never forget'" (9). The historical events, as well as the more recent changes to queer life highlighted below, underscore the critical need for this reevaluation and commemoration.

In the wake of May 1968 and *Le Mouvement de libération des femmes* (MLF), several groups, such as *Le Front homosexuel d'action révolutionnaire* (FHAR), *Les Gazolines*, and *Les Gouines rouges*, began to insert themselves into national and political narratives, framing homosexuality in terms of collective political struggle. Almost in tandem,

---

4 Throughout this introduction, we use the acronym LGBTQ to refer to the many forms of non-normative sexualities that make up the queer population, but we do so while also recognizing that certain groups, namely bisexual and transgender individuals, have historically and systematically been left out of queer representation altogether.

the Stonewall riots of summer 1969 in Greenwich Village in New York ignited a series of related protests and movements among LGBTQ groups throughout the Global North. In 1982, socialist president François Mitterrand took a bold step by revoking the discriminatory law from 1942 (Penal Code article 334) that had outlawed homosexual acts with minors and had raised the age of consent for homosexual couples to 21, while the age of consent for heterosexual couples remained at 15. More recently, in March 2024, the French government approved a law that aimed to recognize and compensate the victims of this discriminatory law ("France's Assemblée Nationale"). With regard to gender expression, France removed gender identity disorder from its official lists of mental disorders in 2010, which ultimately allowed for legal gender changes without medical sterilization in 2016. Despite these advancements toward equality, reparations, and depathologization, it must be noted that trans women of color and sex workers still face marginalization and violence, highlighting the complex issues of homonormativity with regard to trans rights and issues of inclusivity that continue to persist in contemporary France.

Still, we are able to see the development in France of multi-faceted communities and their ability to create collective cultural meaning and memory over the last four decades. Among other sites and cultural productions, this includes the opening of an increasing number of gay and lesbian commercial establishments in the Marais (Sibalis; Caron; Provencher, *Queer French*), the publication of personal advertisements in print media, like *Gai Pied* and *Lesbia Magazine,* and the creation of *le téléphone rose* (LGBTQ phone sex chat lines) on Minitel 3615. With the AIDS pandemic, this also led to the *affaire du sang contaminé* [the contaminated blood affair], the creation of Act Up-Paris, the founding of newer magazines like *Illico* and *Têtu,* the celebration of World AIDS Day in Paris, with the infamous large pink condom on the Obélisque de Louxor, as well as the tradition of French AIDS fiction by Hervé Guibert, Pascal De Duve, Cyril Collard, and Guillaume Dustan among others. Much more recently, cultural products such as the films of Robin Campillo, Olivier Ducastel and Jacques Martineau, Sébastien Lifshitz, François Ozon, and Céline Sciamma, or the writings of Nina Bouraoui, Fatima Daas, Constance Debré, Virginie Despentes, Paul B. Preciado, and Abdellah Taïa, to name only a few, have come to represent the increasingly globalized queer world, as well as the local and national forces that shape it. Indeed, all of these artists and their works contribute to an expanding national narrative that is under constant negotiation within current contemporary political and cultural contexts. Similar to France's former colonial subjects who were excluded from the "logics that underpin the concept of *lieu de mémoire*" (Achille, Forsdick, and Moudileno 7), LGBTQ folks in France who until the 1980s "possessed reserves of memory, but little or no 'historical capital'" (7), would finally be able to speak up and "sortir du placard et dans la rue" [come out of the closet and into the street] (see the cover of *Têtu*, July–August 1995, inaugural issue).

This newfound visibility was not, however, without its challenges. The project of founding an LGBTQ historical center in Paris has been the center of strong tensions and debates both between activists and the mayor of Paris and also within the LGBTQ community for more than 20 years. Shockingly, there is still no place and no budget for the archives (Gey; see also Gunther, this volume). At the same time, and more recently, with the *Pacte civil de solidarité (PaCS)* [civil solidarity pact, or civil union law] of 1999, the "loi Taubira" [Taubira law] of 2013, or "le mariage pour tous" [marriage equality] (see Perreau, this volume), some significant LGBTQ cultural practices and sites are beginning to disappear or be absorbed by other non-queer practices and sites. For example, some LGBTQ bookstores and public cruising areas have almost all but vanished or been displaced because of the culture of conspicuous consumption that has led to gentrification and increased surveillance in real-life spaces. Paris's iconic LGBTQ bookstore Les Mots à la Bouche, which long resided on the corner of Rue Sainte-Croix de la Bretonnerie and Rue Vieille du Temple, in the Marais district, has been priced out of its own neighborhood and moved in 2020 to 37 Rue St-Ambroise in the 11th *arrondissement*, north of and a bit outside of the revolutionary site of Place de la Bastille. Indeed, with the ushering in of new communicative technologies, including "social networking" and dating/cruising applications for smartphones, new sites of relative queer freedom (see Olson, this volume) have also emerged, allowing LGBTQ people to socialize and connect differently, but not without new forms of social isolation. Stalking and bullying in virtual spaces, alongside continued symbolic and physical violence in real spaces, including increased hatred from French Catholic conservatives and political movements from the right and far right against "American-style" gender and queer theory (Perreau) continue to haunt and undermine LGBTQ quotidian experiences.

The urgency of this current volume cannot be overstated if we also consider the current political climate in France and across the globe as it relates to definitions of citizenship and their exclusionary nature for minority and marginalized groups, and LGBTQ groups in particular. Challenging the selective framework of Nora's *lieux* and the overall national narrative of republican universalism has indeed led to strong reactions from the defenders of the so-called universal values of the French Republic. Achille, Forsdick, and Moudileno, for example, note that the different initiatives that have brought attention to the role of France's colonial legacy to understand French structural and systemic racism have been accused of being, "anti-republican or 'un-French'" (2). They refer here to responses such as the manifesto signed by a certain class of French intellectuals, including Nora himself, and published in *Le Point* in 2018, accusing *Indigènes de la République* and other activist movements of spreading "decolonial thinking," which the intellectuals view as "being a 'shameful' hijacking of the values of liberty, equality and fraternity on which" France's democracy was founded (1). They contend that "These issues are [however] central to discussions of French identity, or what some would call 'Frenchness', especially at a time when the increasing hybridization of France [...] raises questions about current understandings of republicanism and how this ideology fits (or does not fit) the socio-cultural realities of the early twenty-first century" (2). If these scholars highlight the necessity to redefine Frenchness through considering the ethnic, racial, and religious backgrounds of the population, it is also necessary to take account of marginalized groups whose sexualities fall outside the boundaries of heteronormative, homonormative, and cis-gendered citizenship.

Several recent events and movements that suggest France has taken a turn to celebrate its diversity in new ways have continued to advance discussions since then. These developments, which have occurred in both cultural and political contexts in France, prove that our project is timely and essential. For instance, on March 6, 2024, the French government unanimously approved the law that will provide reparations to gay men who were arrested for homosexuality between 1945 and 1982 (Lavau). This also includes a recent photograph exhibition by Roger Viollet on the "diversity" of France, as well as Emmanuel Macron's decision with the assistance of city minister Nadia Hai and historian Pascal Blanchard to recalibrate the naming of streets in France (Gaspar; Blanchard). Historian Pap Ndiaye has also been appointed to direct the Palais de la Porte Dorée – built for the 1931 Paris Colonial Exposition – to retell the story of France's immigrants (Nayeri). Josephine Baker's installation into the French Pantheon on November 30, 2021, is yet another significant milestone in this regard. As the first Black woman and a resistance agent, Baker's pantheonization communicates a "message d'ouverture sur le monde et de diversité des héritages [...] que la France est, et demeure, un pays d'accueil" [a message of openness to the world and to the diversity of heritages (...) that France is and remains a host country] (Flandrin). At the same time, Baker is often implicitly positioned as "straight" in much of this journalistic writing, further erasing queerness in official narratives (Strong). Indeed, there has been progress in recognizing and valuing the diversity of the many people who live in France. But, unfortunately, this progress has been studied by only a small number of scholars and this research has largely excluded LGBTQ communities and identities.

On a related note, in 2021, Pascal Blanchard and fellow historian Yvan Gastaut published an answer to President Macron's call at a commemoration ceremony on August 15, 2019, to all French mayors to address the paucity of public spaces named after African soldiers who fought alongside their French compatriots in World War II. Gastaut and Blanchard responded with *Portraits de France* (2021), published on the French government's website, which includes the photographs and bio-sketches of 318 deceased public personalities of immigrant origin and from the former colonies alongside a list of an additional 100 living figures (10). These well- and lesser-known male and female public figures "ont choisi la France" [have chosen France] as their place of residence, "ont 'rendu service' à la République" [have served the Republic], or "ont contribué à la richesse et à la diversité de notre histoire, de nos cultures, de nos sciences ou de nos destins" [have contributed to the richness and the diversity of our history, our cultures, our sciences or to our destinies] (7). Readers encounter, for example, a first image of Moroccan footballer Larbi Ben Barek (2), which is quickly followed two pages later by one of Josephine Baker (4). The authors admit how difficult it was to compose a comprehensive list and how they had to set aside the names of another 2,000 figures during their compilation. Their goal with this publication, its accompanying exhibit at the Musée de l'Homme, and subsequent traveling exhibits is: "insuffler une part de féminisation des noms et une part de diversification des personnalités retenues pour rééquilibrer un paysage aussi monochrome" [to breathe life into this project with one part feminization of the names and one part diversification of the selected personalities in order to recalibrate such a monochromatic landscape] (7).

At the same time, however, when we conduct a content analysis of this very important and impactful publication, the term "homosexuality" occurs only four times in 318 bio-sketches (58, 80, 89, and 189), and its analogous terms – "gay," "lesbian," "bi," "trans," or "queer" – never appear. What is most interesting about these few occurrences is that they appear in the entries on the sole homosexual figure included in the volume, U.S. writer James Baldwin (58), as well as on Russian–Armenian writer Nina Berberova (80), who dealt openly with Tchaikovsky's homosexuality in her writing, and on Tunisian lawyer and activist, Gisèle Halimi, who fought for women, homosexuals, and anti-colonialism (198). For us, this is not France in "toutes ses diversités" [all its diverse facets], as Gastaut and Blanchard would argue (7). By not including queer French-speaking figures in France, this publication continues to tout France's national narrative that always includes a universalist tone of integration and occults the doubly marginalized LGBTQ and postcolonial figures who are so essential to recent work in intersectionality and French and Francophone studies (Bouamer and Provencher). Moreover, Gastaut and Blanchard's definition of "alterity" (15; 23–24) remains tied to both the symbolic order of gender differences in France (Foerster; Fassin; Robcis) and affiliations associated solely with the administrative and geopolitical spaces of the French regions, the nation, and the former colonial empire. This all runs counter to our important transnational, translingual, and intersectional project where LGBTQ sites, archives, memories, and communities transcend these tempo-spatial constraints and the need to imagine more often than not their "impossible" situations transnationally and transfilially (Provencher, *Queer Maghrebi French*) beyond the Hexagon.

Challenging French republican universalism and reclaiming queer citizenship

The contributions in our volume seek to extend the gallery of the *Portraits de France* to further challenge what it means to be queer French and queer in a Francophone space. While certain French politicians and intellectuals who criticize the approach to the social sciences in the U.S. academy may attack our project as yet one more example of American imperialism, and call it "un-French," "anti-Republican," or an all-out attack on French republican universalism, we argue, in line with scholars working on empire, like Achille, Forsdick, and Moudileno, that queerness has always been part and parcel of the French landscape as well as a constitutive element of French imperialism, as demonstrated by Jarrod Hayes's (2000) groundbreaking work.[5]

Grossly categorized by French president Emmanuel Macron and others as forms of *Islamo-gauchisme* [Islamo-leftism], this project is in fact a simple exercise to reclaim LGBTQ voices and dignity through archiving, commemoration, and memory-making. Reactions to the (re)assertion of queer citizenship into the French national narrative of republican universalism have provoked a similar backlash. Bruno Perreau (2016) examines the French outcry against gender and queer theories, led by conservative opponents of gay marriage in France, and demonstrates how they "see it as a conspiracy hatched in the United States to undermine the traditional family and national identity" (13). Ultimately revealing the transatlantic construction of queer theory, Perreau illustrates how this body of thought emerged from French intellectual criticism and how it remains central to it today.

While Perreau focuses on the proponents and opponents of same-sex marriage and also the reception of gender and queer theory in France, Denis M. Provencher (2007) offers a broader analysis on the attacks on queer socio-political presence and argues that "French republican universalism is always and already queer" (11). He traces the dialectic tension that has long existed in France's national narrative between "good" and "bad" sexual citizenship. Provencher illustrates that the "good" sexual citizens operate in relation to "a French republican model of universalism that blurs all forms of 'difference'" (11) where LGBTQ French citizens, like their heteronormative counterparts, subscribe to normative forms of social reproduction – such as integration into the French family, same-sex marriage, and a bourgeois life of conspicuous consumption.

At the same time, Provencher analyzes a long French tradition of the "bad" sexual citizen, which draws inspiration from the narratives of the archetype "Genet" that blurs (global) gay identity and crafts an alternative "queer" model" (11) informed by the author's transgressive nature and "outlaw" (Bersani, *Homos*) status to the nation. This is a global and alternative queer model that sexual citizens in France and other Francophone contexts can draw upon to illustrate their belonging in or disidentification with the world. We see this alternative queer

---

5 For more works that examine the ways in which sexuality, immigration, and French colonialism intersect, see for example Amari; Shepard; Provencher, *Queer Maghrebi French*.

model at work in the writings of many writers and film directors, such as Moroccan author, Abdellah Taïa (Provencher, *Queer Maghrebi French*), and Québécois author, Kevin Lambert. We also see it in the queer performances of French musician Chris(tine) of Christine and The Queens and the Québécois drag queen Gisèle Lullaby, to name just two.

Ultimately, these notions of alternative models of citizenship help us define queer citizenship in relation to queer memory in our volume. While queer belonging has been excluded from the official French national narrative, as well as from more progressive attempts to expand it, such as *Portraits de France* or even *Postcolonial Realms of Memory*, the contributors to this edited collection identify alternative forms of queer memory-making. Here, we consciously mirror Muñoz's comments on "world-making potentialities" in reference to the "ritualized tellings – through film, video, performance, writing, and visual culture" that "help us carve out a space for actual, living sexual citizenship" (35). Indeed, to capture the essence of queer citizenship, we must first contest the heteronormative sexual structures that have shaped narratives of citizenship and that, as Lauren Berlant (1997) notes, have excluded people – including queer people – who have endured "the violence of their partial citizenship" (19). Following Berlant, we

> do not see why the nation has to have an official sexuality, especially one that authorizes the norm of violent gentility; that narrows the field of legitimate political action; that supports the amputation of personal complexity into categories of simple identity; that uses cruel and mundane strategies to promote shame for non-normative populations and to deny them state, federal, and juridical supports because they are deemed morally incompetent to their own citizenship. (19)

Thus, *Queer Realms of Memory* offers a space where these limitations are exposed in order to denounce the violence queer groups have historically suffered and continue to suffer; in doing so, our project aims to restore the potential for full citizenship to these minoritized groups.

To be sure, the archiving and analyzing of queer realms of memory undertaken in this volume is part of an effort to reestablish queer citizenship as *living* citizenship. As several scholars have noted, the theorization of queerness – of queer lives and experiences – has been largely marked by recurrent conversations about death. Take, for instance, Leo Bersani's influential 1987 essay, "Is the rectum a grave?" or Lee Edelman's provocative work in *No Future: Queer Theory and the Death Drive* (2004). More recently, Jasbir Puar, drawing on Michel

Foucault's thoughts on biopolitics and Achille Mbembe's concept of "necropolitics," or the "living dead," has articulated "queer necropolitics." In *Terrorist Assemblages: Homonationalism in Queer Times* (2007), Puar raises questions crucial to the theoretical orientation of this volume and the reinstitution of a living queer citizenship, asking, for example, "How do queers reproduce life, and which queers are folded into life? How do they give life? To what do they give life? How is life weighted, disciplined into subjecthood, narrated into population, and fostered for living?" (36). The contributions to our volume propose a similar line of questioning but consider memory as an analogous concept to life. Indeed, the chapters here seek to go against what Berlant calls the "abstracted dead citizenship" of queer memory in order to revive "live citizenship," which involves "better ways of thinking about nationality, culture, politics, and personhood" (20).[6]

Many of the contributions to this volume also take into account the intersection between these alternative notions of citizenship and the genealogy of queer affect. Following thinkers like Berlant, Cvetkovich, and Muñoz, Sara Ahmed argues that "[c]itizenship provides a technology for deciding whose happiness comes first" (133). Describing the ways in which happiness and "goodness" converge within queer archives, Ahmed reminds us that:

> A literal reading suggests that the very distinction between happy and unhappy endings "works" to secure a moral distinction between good and bad lives. When we read this unhappy queer archive (which is not the only queer archive) we must resist this literalism, which means an active disbelief in the necessary alignment of the happy with the good, or even in the moral transparency of the good itself. Rather than reading unhappy endings as a sign of the withholding of moral approval for queer lives, we must consider how unhappiness circulates within and around this archive, and *what it allows us to do*. (89)

We thus embrace in this volume the "unhappy" queer realms of memory, as they inevitably allow us to further challenge the "good" and "right" forms of French sexual citizenship while interrogating the memory-making processes that posit some queer realms of memory as "good" and some as worthy of being forgotten.

---

6 For example, Provencher's chapter in this volume on transfilial memory advances this discussion about *living* citizenship and what it means to materially or symbolically "pass on" or "transmit" a heritage to one's imagined or transfilial family members.

The question of what we forget when we remember is perhaps inherent in memory studies at large, but it is certainly central to understanding the memory-making and memorialization processes of marginalized groups who have long received the message that their history is shameful, worthless, or nonexistent. Nancy Wood (1999) theorizes *les lieux d'oubli*, or sites and spaces that "public memory has expressly avoided because of the disturbing affect that their invocation is still capable of arousing" (10). Historian Guy Beiner (2018), who engages with Wood's work, variously refers to these spaces as "realms of forgetting" or "sites of oblivion." Similarly, Sarah Gröning (2016) elaborates on *les lieux de traumatisme* [sites of trauma], which focus not on spaces of remembrance but rather on the effects of national forgetting vis-à-vis minoritized communities. Gröning offers the examples of *le bateau au négrier* [the slave boat] and *le cachot* [the colonial prison cell] in the fiction of Patrick Chamoiseau and Fabienne Kanor as sites that can trigger either individual or collective trauma. Hence, for Gröning, following Glissant, "les communautés antillaises font un effort pour oublier leur passé largement traumatisant" [Antillean communities make an effort to forget their largely traumatic past] (195). While the chapters collected here do not necessarily rely on these conceptualizations, they nonetheless form the backdrop upon which our project was formed. Ultimately, by wresting memory from normativity, these thinkers democratize the practices of remembering, opening it up to populations like the LGBTQ community that have historically been rendered invisible in "official" accounts of national memory. Here, we see how memory-making is intersectional by nature and that in the French national narrative, it always and already involves a universal narrative filled with difference.

Queer realms of memory: Archiving LGBTQ sites and symbols

Drawing on scholarship in queer French and Francophone studies and in LGBTQ studies at large, we define queerness as an anti-normative approach or stance that works against heteronormative organizations of time and space. This lens disrupts the social and sexual norms that reinforce institutions such as marriage, the family, child rearing, and their associated legacies (Duggan; Halberstam). At the same time, in line with José Esteban Muñoz's theorizing in his now classic first book (1999), this stance allows for LGBTQ individuals and communities to work simultaneously in line with and against normative practices and discourses, or what he refers to as forms of "disidentifications." While the contributors to *Queer Realms of Memory* aim to archive and analyze queer memory and forms of belonging that are specific to the communities they reflect, their lives and stories still function in relation to the French national narrative of republican universalism no matter if they stand close to or at a distance from the dominant culture. At the same time, when they stand at a dis-identificatory or queer distance, they are also associated with other global forces discussed below including forms of neoliberalism and Anglo-American forms of queer belonging, particularly those that are situated within a transnational context concerning discourses on universal human rights, coming-out, safe sex and HIV prevention, and more.

While we have chosen to borrow Nora's expressions and their translations into English, we must add that we understand "memory" and "realms of memory" in the broadest of terms and have worked to incorporate diverse forms of representations. However, we remain uneasy with the long-accepted terms "lieu" and "realm" as they undoubtedly reify certain canonized domains, kingdoms, and empires of memory. This, in turn, lends a certain exceptionalism to normative processes of memory-making and memorialization. Following Achille and Moudileno, in *Mythologies Postcoloniales* (2018), we agree that "[l]e quotidien est tout sauf banal" [the everyday is anything but banal] (7) and that "le quotidien est un palimpseste où persistent les traces d'histoire" [the everyday is a palimpsest where traces of history persist] (1). While their work highlights the need for the "quotidian" to be decolonized in terms of race, we contend, drawing on Muñoz's emphasis on the failure of "banal optimism," that such work must take into account non-normative sexualities and non-binary expressions of gender.

Achille, Forsdick, and Moudileno contend that such corrective measures are crucial not only to revise Nora's "chosen entries [that] could have easily teased out the colonial dimensions of the memory practices they describe" (7–8), but also to "underline the urgency of asserting the central place of the colonial in the making of modern France" (2). As such, our volume's complementary approach challenges Nora's line of argument regarding the nationalism, minority exclusion, and historical discontinuity of his *lieux*. As queer people have long been excluded from France's history, our project intentionally conjugates the term "site," exploring its many valences, as a way to redefine history and memory as a non-teleological process where LGBTQ lives and cultures come into focus across multiple temporalities both nationally and transnationally.

Recognizing "[t]he essential need for an understanding of queerness as collectivity" (11), Muñoz (2009) examines processes he refers to as "queer utopian memory" or "queer utopian remembrance." In order to highlight the interconnectedness of queer experiences, history, and memory, Muñoz draws attention to the necessity to consider the concrete rather than abstract nature of this utopia. For him, locating utopia in "a collectivity that is actualized or potential" is essential for reinvesting queer struggles with a certain "historical consciousness" (3) and preventing a narrow focus on "banal optimism" or a single historical case as a framework. Following Muñoz's reflection on "the performance of queer utopian memory" as "a utopia that understands its time as reaching beyond some nostalgic past that perhaps never was or some future whose arrival is continuously belated" (37), we understand queer realms of memory "not as a primary preoccupation with recovering what actually happened in the past" (Achille, Forsdick, and Moudileno 9), but rather as a distinct way of representing the past – one that is firmly grounded in the materiality of the present. Of course, some of the *lieux* discussed in *Postcolonial Realms of Memory* and in this volume are anchored in material and physical spaces. However, while many of the contributors' studies insist on the physicality of various queer realms of memory, we must point out that several chapters also examine the more abstract (see Perreau, this volume), ephemeral (see Eilderts, this volume) and digital *lieux*[7] (see Johnston; Provencher; Muzart; Danjé, all this volume), or, in the words of Achille, Forsdick, and Moudileno, the "events, figures and other tangible entities that transcend the strictly spatial" (9).

To be sure, theorists working in other disciplines have indeed pointed out the transcendence of the strictly spatial *lieux*, and many of our own contributors draw from this scholarship. For instance, Marianne Hirsch's concept of postmemory underscores the transportability of memory. Postmemory, according to Hirsch, "describes the relationship of the second generation to powerful, often traumatic, experiences that preceded their births but that were nevertheless transmitted to them so deeply as to seem to constitute memories

---

7 See for example Cristina Johnston, in her contribution to this volume, who makes an argument to call these sites of memory "landscapes," in order to capture the digital, affective, and aesthetic elements of certain queer realms of memory.

in their own right" (103). Working within the field of Holocaust studies, Hirsch examines the generational transmission of trauma to the "descendants of survivors (of victims as well as of perpetrators) of massive traumatic events" (105) through "stories, images, and behaviors" (107). The specificity of postmemory is thus this distance between the event and its remembrance, as well as the memory's connection to the past that is "not actually mediated by recall but by imaginative investment, projection, and creation" (107).

Conjugating postmemory with queerness, Dilara Çalışkan focuses on mother–daughter relationships created by trans women who do sex work in Turkey. The "narratives of trans mothers and daughters," Çalışkan argues, "remind us that not only memory becomes inheritable through certain modes of family and time, but also alternative forms of family and time can be formed through memories that unexpectedly become inheritable" (271). Çalışkan, echoing Halberstam's notion of the "jigsaw puzzle" and Muñoz's "queer utopian memory," argues that "the concept of 'queer postmemory' [...] aims to open spaces for improvisational practices that play with the predetermined itineraries and directions of memory [...] refusing to position memory and its journey as an outcome of fixed relations and temporal frameworks" (262). Similarly, Alison Landsberg's notion of prosthetic memory expands upon the idea of collective memory, capturing the ways in which "the cinema and other mass cultural technologies have the capacity to create shared social frameworks for people who inhabit, literally and figuratively, different social spaces, practices, and beliefs" (8). Landsberg's understanding of prosthetic memory, by insisting on "the premise that cultural memories no longer have exclusive owners" (18), thus "creates the conditions for ethical thinking precisely by encouraging people to feel connected to, while recognizing the alterity of, the 'other'" (9).

In conclusion, these diverse theoretical frameworks, while not necessarily appearing in each and every contributor's chapter, emphasize the fluid and dynamic nature of memory, challenging traditional, fixed notions of remembrance. By highlighting the transportability and generational transmission of memory, as seen in Hirsch's postmemory, the creation of alternative familial and temporal structures through queer postmemory, and the inclusive potential of prosthetic memory, these scholars demonstrate how memories can transcend spatial, temporal, and social boundaries. This convergence of ideas not only enriches our understanding of queer remembering but also opens up new possibilities for shared and inclusive forms of memory-making.

Building on this idea of shared inclusive memory, the notion of "symbol" in our title is equally as important as the term "site." Indeed, to capture the essence of the queer realms of memory gathered in this volume, it is important to understand the many interplays of materiality and symbolism. Within his own definition, Pierre Nora elaborates on the complex nature of sites of memory. He posits:

> *Lieux de mémoire* are as simple and ambiguous, natural and artificial, at once immediately available in concrete sensual experience and susceptible to the most abstract elaboration. Indeed, they are *lieux* in three senses of the word – material, symbolic, and functional. Even an apparently purely material site, like an archive, becomes a *lieu de mémoire* only if the imagination invests it with a symbolic aura. A purely functional site, like a classroom manual, a testament, or a veterans' reunion belongs to the category only in as much as it is also the object of a ritual. And the observance of a commemorative minute of silence, an extreme example of a strictly symbolic action, serves as a concentrated appeal to memory by literally breaking a temporal continuity. (18–19)

Despite our contention with Nora's conceptualization of *lieux de mémoire*, it is within this complex framework and symbolic flexibility that we invite readers to approach both the individual contributions and this volume as a space where collective memory can converge. While this project's function as an archive is evident, its symbolic value also serves as a commemorative act. In this capacity, it aims to honor and perpetuate the memories of queer individuals and forge a collective remembrance, which, we hope, will transcend these pages.

In spite of the importance of the symbolic, the functional aspect of this volume as an archive of queer memory is central to challenging the normative conceptualization of *lieux de mémoire*, as well as its limitations. In *Postcolonial Realms of Memory*, Oana Panaïté raises this question in relation to Krzysztof Pomian's entry on archives in Nora's original volume. She notes, for example, that "Nora's project does not account for the exclusionary side of the archive, as it is enlisted by state institutions and private organizations to project a collective national ideal" (27). She draws attention here to the nation's role in limiting definitions of what constitutes colonial archives, but the same dynamic is in motion when it comes to the exclusion and the difficulties in documenting and conserving queer narratives and memories. For Panaïté, literature serves as a key site of memory that occupies "an intermediate space between memory and history" and fulfills crucial archival functions: "managing public recollections, salvaging private memories, and conserving, selecting, organizing and transmitting the archives for social, political and cultural purposes" (24).

Panaïté's reflection on literature as a dynamic space that challenges conventional socio-political archiving practices and content resonates with the importance of considering a variety of sources for the preservation of queer memory. For instance, Ann Cvetkovich similarly challenges normative historiography by examining the archival value of "cultural texts as repositories of feelings and emotions, which are encoded not only in the content of the texts themselves but in the practices that surround their production and reception" (7). Echoing Panaïté, Cvetkovich calls for a similar "responsibility of remembering" – "the determination to 'never forget'" (9). As she reminds us, "[t]hat gay and lesbian history even exists has been a contested fact, and the struggle to record and preserve it is exacerbated by the invisibility that often surrounds intimate life, especially sexuality" (242), thus reiterating the importance of the three archival tasks identified by Panaïté.

Like Panaïté and Cvetkovich, who emphasize the need to expand archival practices beyond official institutions, the contributions in our volume present a wide range of ways to approach – and challenge – what constitutes legitimate archival sources. As such, Jack Halberstam's plea (2005) to reject "[t]he archive [as] simply a repository" and instead approach queer archives as "a construction of collective memory, and a complex record of queer activity" (169–70) is of paramount importance to our project. Taking into account this complexity, we did not want, for example, to limit exclusively the contributions to the *lieux* that Nora classifies (an openness we found significant in *Postcolonial Realms of Memory*). We instead invited our contributors to propose their own *lieux* and be, in the words of Halberstam, "the users, interpreters, and cultural historians [that] wade through the material and piece together the jigsaw puzzle of queer history in the making," a method that is crucial according to Halberstam "for the [queer] archive to function" (170). This notion of a "jigsaw puzzle" accentuates the idea that archiving and memorializing queer history must be a collective endeavor.

For this collective work to come together, we selected authors from diverse academic backgrounds who span various career stages and contribute cutting-edge work in queer French and Francophone studies and memory studies.[8] While most contributors focus on examining

---

8   We would like to thank all of our contributors who read an early version of this introduction and provided valuable feedback. We extend special thanks to

specific *lieux* – whether through cultural productions, icons, institutions, or monuments – others take a broader approach and offer critical overviews that serve as useful reference points for further exploring key questions related to queer memory (see Perreau; Olson, this volume). Alongside these approaches, Michaëla Danjé's piece stands out for its conceptual distinctiveness. As a creative work by a community organizer, it challenges conventional scholarly writing and positions itself as an activist's manifesto, which is an approach we, as editors, intentionally welcomed. Danjé's intervention, in its rejection of rigid academic forms, reflects a broader methodological commitment in this volume: a collective assembling of the "jigsaw puzzle" of an otherwise invisible or undocumented set of queer lives, feelings, and memories and their related historical events, archives, monuments, and commemorations.

Moreover, mirroring Muñoz's approach in including what he calls "ritualized tellings, through film, video, performance, writing and visual culture" (35), we did not privilege one cultural form of *lieu de mémoire* over another in the archiving we tackle in this volume. The scholars engage with a wide range of both living and historical figures and icons, as well as diverse cultural products (archives, cinema, digital installations, film festivals, gravesites, letters, literature, maps, marches, media, monuments, memorabilia and ephemera, music, podcasts, social media platforms, websites, etc.). Indeed, all of these elements – from the identities of our individual scholars to the variety of the sites of memory they study – demonstrate the volume's broader goal of critically engaging with intersectionality. And, while no single work can account for all possible expressions of intersectionality, we hope it is clear that many of our contributors do. As such, certain authors in our volume begin to point to the intersectional nature of queer realms of memory (see Bouamer; Danjé; Muzart; Provencher; O'Dwyer, all this volume), where what may begin as a site of memory for LGBTQ citizens can and will eventually overlap with identity formation and commemoration among other non-queer groups of (global) citizens.

As a final note, we have organized the volume thematically to reflect its critical trajectory. The first section, "Institutions and Monuments," has been placed at the forefront to situate the volume's critique of Nora's framework as a foundational intervention and directly challenge his conceptualization of *lieux de mémoire*. In this section, contributors

Blase Provitola for their substantial input, particularly regarding the discussion of trans experiences, which was extremely beneficial.

critique the heteronormative underpinnings of certain institutional landmarks and/or administrative structures. Some of these sites have been classified as *lieux de mémoire* by Nora, while others are reimagined or reinvented as such through a queer lens. The second section, "Centers and Peripheries," challenges the traditional notion of a centralized geography and narrative by highlighting the multiplicity of queer centers and peripheries. In contrast to Nora's volume, where Maurice Agulhon provides a singular focus on "Paris," this section of our volume emphasizes the diverse and intersectional dynamics of queer memory and mapping. The third section, "Icons and Figures," assembles contributions that identify personalities – whether famous or lesser-known to the larger public – that have become key in queer memory-making and (dis)identification. These figures collectively establish a "Queer school of the dead and the living," challenging Mona Ozouf's concept of the Panthéon as "l'école normale des morts." The last two sections move beyond traditional notions of *lieux de mémoire* to open new frameworks for queer archival practices. The penultimate section examines how literature and cinema contribute to queer memory-making. The final section explores the role of new technologies such as websites, podcasts, and digital installations in constructing innovative queer archives. Taken together, these sections comment on and challenge Nora's conceptualizations of *lieux de mémoire* while constituting an archive of French queer realms of memory. Finally, our conclusion to the volume returns to several of the key themes discussed here, addresses the various challenges and limitations to our project, and invites the reader to apply broadly our analytical tools when pursuing their own research in memory studies and not just when applied to LGBTQ sites and symbols.

Works cited

Achille, Étienne, Charles Forsdick, and Lydie Moudileno, eds. *Postcolonial Realms of Memory: Sites and Symbols in Modern France*. Liverpool UP, 2020.

Achille, Étienne, and Lydie Moudileno. *Mythologies postcoloniales: Pour une décolonisation du quotidien*. Honoré Champion, 2018.

Agulhon, Maurice. "Paris: A traversal from east to west." *Realms of Memory: The Construction of the French Past*, vol. 3, *Symbols*, edited by Pierre Nora and Lawrence D. Kritzman. Translated by Arthur Goldhammer. Columbia UP, 1998, pp. 523–53.

Ahmed, Sara. *The Promise of Happiness.* Duke UP, 2010.
Amari, Salima. *Lesbiennes de l'immigration: construction de soi et relations familiales.* Éditions du croquant, 2018.
Baril, Alexandre. "Francophone trans/feminisms: Absence, silence, emergence." *TSQ: Transgender Studies Quarterly*, vol. 3, no. 1–2, 2016, pp. 40–47.
Beiner, Guy. *Forgetful Remembrance: Social Forgetting and Vernacular Historiography of a Rebellion in Ulster.* Oxford UP, 2018.
Berlant, Lauren. *The Queen of America Goes to Washington City.* Duke UP, 1997.
Bersani, Leo. *Homos.* Harvard UP, 1996.
———. "Is the rectum a grave?" *October*, vol. 43, 1987, pp. 197–222.
Blanchard, Pascal. "Ni 'remplacisme,' ni 'effacement': comment nous avons choisi ces noms pour enrichir l'histoire de France." *Huffington Post.fr.* March 29, 2021. Web.
Blanchard, Pascal, and Yvan Gastaut. *Portraits de France.* République française, 2021–22.
Bouamer, Siham, and Denis M. Provencher. "Introducing *CFC Intersections*." *CFC Intersections*, vol, 1, 2022, pp. 1–12.
Çalışkan, Dilara. "Queer postmemory." *European Journal of Women's Studies*, vol. 26, no. 3, 2019, pp. 261–73.
Caron, David. *My Father and I: The Marais and Queerness of Community.* Cornell UP, 2009.
Cvetkovich, Ann. *An Archive of Feelings: Trauma, Sexuality, and Lesbian Public Cultures.* Duke UP, 2003.
Duggan, Lisa. "The new heteronormativity: The sexual politics of neoliberalism." *Materializing Democracy: Toward a Revitalized Cultural Politics*, edited by Russ Castronovo and Dana D. Nelson. Duke UP, 2002, pp. 175–94.
Edelman, Lee. *No Future: Queer Theory and the Death Drive.* Duke UP, 2004.
Fassin, Éric. "L'Illusion anthropologique: homosexualité et filiation." *Témoin*, vol. 12, 1998, pp. 43–56.
———. "Same-sex marriage, nation, and race: French political logics and rhetorics." *Contemporary French Civilization*, vol. 39, no. 3, 2014, pp. 281–301.
Flandrin, Antoine. "Joséphine Baker au Panthéon, un puissant message d'ouverture sur le monde." *Le Monde.fr.* November 26, 2021. Web.
Foerster, Maxime. *La différence des sexes à l'épreuve de la République.* L'Harmattan, 2003.
"France's Assemblée Nationale approves bill to rehabilitate people convicted of homosexuality." *Le Monde.* March 7, 2024. Web.
Gaspar, Romain. "Noms de rues: 'rééquilibrer l'histoire grâce à 318 personnalités issues de la diversité.'" *La Gazette.* March 24, 2021. Web.

Gey, Pierre. "Marche des fiertés: La Ville de Paris veut-elle vraiment d'un centre d'archives LGBT +?" *Télérama.fr*. June 25, 2022. Web.
Gröning, Sarah. "Les 'lieux de traumatisme' dans la littérature antillaise contemporaine." *Revue des sciences humaines*, vol. 321, January–March 2016, pp. 193–209.
Halberstam, Jack. *The Queer Art of Failure*. Duke UP, 2011.
———. *In a Queer Time and Place: Transgender Bodies, Subcultural Lives*. New York UP, 2005.
Hayes, Jarrod. *Queer Nations: Marginal Sexualities in the Maghreb*. U of Chicago P, 2000.
Hirsch, Marianne. *The Generation of Postmemory: Writing and Visual Culture after the Holocaust*. Columbia UP, 2012.
Khadraoui-Fortune, Sophia. "The abolition of slavery." *Postcolonial Realms of Memory: Sites and Symbols in Modern France*, edited by Étienne Achille, Charles Forsdick, and Lydie Moudileno. Liverpool UP, 2020, pp. 195–203.
Landsberg, Alison. *Prosthetic Memory: The Transformation of American Remembrance in the Age of Mass Culture*. Columbia UP, 2004.
Lavau, Géraldine Cornet. "Bernard Bousset, l'un des derniers condamnés pour homosexualité en France." *L'INA éclaire l'actu*. April 3, 2024. Web.
Morris, Charles E. "Archival queer." *Rhetoric and Public Affairs*, vol. 9, no. 1, 2006, pp. 145–51.
Muñoz, José Esteban. *Cruising Utopia: The Then and There of Queer Futurity*. New York UP, 2009.
———. *Disidentifications: Queers of Color and the Performance of Politics*. U of Minnesota P, 1999.
Nayeri, Farah. "In a palace of colonialism, a quiet 'revolutionary' takes charge." *NYTimes.com*. March 17 2021. Web.
Nora, Pierre, ed. *Les Lieux de mémoire*, 3 vols. Gallimard, 1984–92.
Ozouf, Mona. "Le Panthéon: l'école normale des morts." *Les Lieux de mémoire*, vol. 1, *La République*, edited by Pierre Nora. Gallimard, 1984, pp. 130–96.
Panaïté, Oana. "Archives." *Postcolonial Realms of Memory: Sites and Symbols in Modern France*, edited by Étienne Achille, Charles Forsdick, and Lydie Moudileno. Liverpool UP, 2020, pp. 23–33.
Perreau, Bruno. *Queer Theory: The French Response*. Stanford UP, 2016.
Provencher, Denis M. "Abdellah Taïa's *transfilial* myth making and unfaithful realms of memory." *Abdellah Taïa's Queer Migrations: Non-Places, Affect, and Temporalities*, edited by Denis M. Provencher and Siham Bouamer. Lexington Books, 2021, pp. 219–55.
———. *Queer French: Globalization, Language, and Sexual Citizenship in France*. Ashgate, 2007.

———. *Queer Maghrebi French: Languages, Temporalities, Transfiliations.* Liverpool UP, 2017.
Puar, Jasbir K. *Terrorist Assemblages: Homonationalism in Queer Times.* Duke UP, 2007.
Robcis, Camille. *The Law of Kinship: Anthropology, Psychoanalysis, and the Family in France.* Cornell UP, 2013.
Rosello, Mireille. "Jeanne Duval." *Postcolonial Realms of Memory: Sites and Symbols in Modern France,* edited by Étienne Achille, Charles Forsdick, and Lydie Moudileno. Liverpool UP, 2020, pp. 307–13.
Rothberg, Michael. "Introduction: Between memory and memory. From *Lieux de mémoire* to *Nœuds de mémoire*." *Yale French Studies,* vol. 118/19, 2010, pp. 3–12.
Rothberg, Michael, Debrati Sanyal, and Maxim Silverman. "Editors' note. *Nœuds de mémoire*: Multidirectional memory in postwar French and francophone culture." *Yale French Studies,* vol. 118/19, 2010, pp. 1–2.
Shepard, Todd. *Sex, France, and Arab Men, 1962–1979.* U of Chicago P, 2017.
Sibalis, Michael. "Paris." *Queer Sites: Gay Urban Histories since 1600,* edited by David Higgs. Routledge, 1999, pp. 10–37.
Strong, Lester Q. "Josephine Baker's Hungry Heart." *G&LR: Gay and Lesbian Review,* vol. September–October 2006. Web.
Suaudeau, Julien, and Mame-Fatou Niang. *Universalisme.* Anamosa, 2022.
Têtu. vol. 1, inaugural issue, July–August 1995. Cover page.
Viala, Fabienne. "The Memorial ACTe." *Postcolonial Realms of Memory: Sites and Symbols in Modern France,* edited by Étienne Achille, Charles Forsdick, and Lydie Moudileno. Liverpool UP, 2020, pp. 186–93.
Viollet, Roger. "La diversité, une richesse." *Roget-Viollet.fr.* Web.
Wood, Nancy. *Vectors of Memory: Legacies of Trauma in Postwar Europe.* Berg, 1999.

I

Institutions and Monuments

CHAPTER ONE

Presenting the present
Queer memories beyond same-sex marriage

Bruno Perreau
Translated by Patsy Baudoin

The law that made it possible for same-sex couples in France to get married is known as the "marriage-for-all" law or the "Taubira law," named for the Minister of Justice, Christiane Taubira, who backed it. The National Assembly passed it on April 23, 2013, and it was officially enacted on May 17, 2013, by President François Hollande about a year after his election. This followed upon months of bitter parliamentary debates and the significant mobilization of its opponents both in the streets and in the media (Perreau, *Queer Theory* 17–74). Ten years later, the French seem to have mostly accepted the Taubira law: the press widely reported on a 2022 study from the polling institute Ipsos, showing that 59 percent of the population say they are in favor of the policy (15 percent are against it but admit that other types of union are needed; 7 percent reject any legal recognition; and the remainder offer no comment). Most of the politicians who opposed the law even ended up backing it. Marriage-for-all has now become a part of France's heritage of great republican laws to the point where being against it would likely amount to political marginalization. President Hollande, strongly criticized for giving up on his campaign promises in economic matters, himself regularly pointed to marriage-for-all as the flagship project of his five-year term (Petit-Felici). Still, there is a downside to such celebration: it dilutes the complexity of history. Not only is 2013 not year zero of LGBT+ struggles, but the sanctuarization of marriage-for-all makes invisible the critical, activist contributions that often have not been in the spotlight despite being essential. Creating a history of the present is to create both a history of presence and a history of absence. Erasure and obscurity do not belong to the distant past: they are at the heart of the fabric of all memory.

For lesbian and gay organizations, demanding marriage rights was not a choice but a necessity. In the 1970s and 1980s, most of them saw marriage as an institution that was antithetical to homosexual lifestyles (Gunther). The AIDS epidemic, which decimated the gay population starting in the early 1980s, changed things, since ensuring the surviving partner's material security became paramount. In 1989, the *Cour de cassation* [France's highest Court of Appeal] refused to recognize homosexual cohabitation; several civil union proposals were formulated by the *Aides* organization (the first HIV activist and support group in France, established by Daniel Defert in 1984 after his partner, the philosopher Michel Foucault, died) and a few left-wing elected officials. Added to the socialist government's agenda after the surprise dissolution of the National Assembly in 1998, these civil union contracts ended up as a single bill named the *Pacte civil de solidarité (PaCS)* [civil solidarity pact]. It was vehemently attacked by the right; part of the left (many socialist *députés* [Members of the National Assembly] did not show up to vote, leading to the bill's first-draft failure); and by certain left-leaning academics such as anthropologist Françoise Héritier, sociologist Irène Théry, philosopher Guy Coq, and psychoanalyst Caroline Eliacheff. Relying on this "expertise," Prime Minister Lionel Jospin emptied the *PaCS* of part of its substance by rejecting the contract's slightest impact on parenting or acquiring citizenship and by being against granting contracts in city halls. Thus, quite paradoxically, the law's enactment on November 15, 1999, made marriage necessary.

Five years later, during a session of the *Sociologie des homosexualités* seminar led by Françoise Gaspard and Didier Eribon at the École des hautes études en sciences sociales, law professor Daniel Borrillo, who already was a promoter of civil unions within *Aides*, called for mayors to generate case law by performing marriages, as modeled by then Mayor Gavin Newsom of San Francisco (Eribon 84–88). A petition followed – "the Manifesto for equal rights" – and then, on June 5, 2004, Noël Mamère, the Green Party mayor of Bègles, near Bordeaux, performed the first same-sex marriage in France. The Socialist Party changed its program as discussions stirred public opinion for months: at first hostile to marriage, the Party ended up backing same-sex marriage, first without including filiation, before agreeing to joint adoption and then medically assisted reproduction (which the socialist government eventually left out of the Taubira law). This very troubled history, also inflected by significant European collective activism across borders (Paternotte), resists political discourses, which tend to make marriage-for-all a point of convergence or agreement. A few weeks before the Bègles marriage ceremony, public support for same-sex marriages was already at 57 percent, again according to Ipsos. It is therefore legitimate to ask whether including marriage-for-all in the heritage of France ten years after its enactment attests to a real normative change beyond the much-needed extension of fundamental civil rights to same-sex couples.

Making marriage-for-all French heritage

All the rainbow flags, ceremonies with the same-sex couples who were married in 2013, and festivities in public places, in many towns and notably at City Hall in Paris, turned marriage-for-all into a visibility issue ("Le mariage"). Television news, the press, and online media stressed the extent to which marriage-for-all seeped into the cultural fabric and is now part of France's national heritage. The front cover of *Causette* magazine featured a photograph of François Hollande wearing a rainbow sash and marrying two women ("Le mariage"). Like rainbow pedestrian crossings, the colors of LGBT+ movements, which until 2013 only took place in activist and commercial spaces (Blidon), had become a thing to officially display. Behind these stereotypical images, however, hide more complex uses of marriage-for-all. In the ten years since the law was passed, nearly 70,000 same-sex couples have been married; the figures are higher in 2013 and 2014 as an effect of "catching up." About 3 percent of marriages each year are same-sex marriages (INSEE). On the one hand, from a legal perspective, marriage provides security for the couple; on the other hand, it confirms the "gay friendliness" of the couple's entourage. Straight people attending a gay or lesbian wedding don't just assent to this sole gay marriage; they are also cementing their own gay-friendly identity, as most neighbors do in gay neighborhoods (Tissot). Marriage is therefore, literally, for all.

Turning to marriage, though, is an answer to a variety of different needs: in France, heterosexual couples marry on average at 36.5 years of age, lesbian couples at just under 41, and gay couples at almost 46 (and gay couples are also more urban and reside more frequently in greater metropolitan Paris). For lesbians, marriage is often a step towards parenthood; social homogamy (similar age, level of education, profession, place of residence, nationality) is much more pronounced between lesbian spouses, since meeting other lesbians is a more often privatized affair (mutual friends, workplace, etc.) than are the methods gay men use to meet each other (cruising spots, bars, apps, etc.) (Meslay). Conversely, people who opt for a *PaCS* contract are more frequently non-religious, left-leaning, and have had more sexual partners before the contract than people bound by marriage (Rault).

As central as it was to the political agenda of the early 2010s, the marriage-for-all law struggled to relate to other issues. It deliberately set aside certain fundamental rights (medically assisted reproduction for all women, surrogacy, adoption by unmarried couples, recognition of step-parents, and multiparenting). It did not lead to other major reforms regarding the rights of transgender people and large-scale policies to fight against homophobic and transphobic violence. It did not facilitate asylum access for LGBT+ people, nor did it promote more inclusive health policies and policies towards the LGBT+ elderly. New laws and departmental circulars addressed some of these issues, on a case-by-case basis, without any overall policy. The law of November 18, 2016, for example, authorized changes in the civil status of transgender people without imposing any medical conditions (such as an operation or hormonal treatment), but this change must be granted by the *Tribunal judiciaire* [Civil High court]. Other reforms were initiated by other political majorities: under Emmanuel Macron's presidency, the bioethics law of August 2, 2021, made medically assisted reproduction available to all women, and the law of February 22, 2022, extended adoption to unmarried couples.

Furthermore, the question arises of the effectiveness of the 2013 law at a practical level: for lack of a global reconfiguration of France's adoption system, the small number of adoptable children poses significant challenges for lesbians and gay men seeking to become parents (Delbecque). Finally, while marriage-for-all has brought more visibility to lesbians and gay men, especially in the media, a greater, general tolerance regarding gender and sexuality is largely due to other factors (Bénit). Among them are a generational shift, the widespread use of social media, mobilizing against sexual and gender-based violence, and reconceptualizing gender categories. Thus, for Generation Z, the fact that same-sex marriage is taken for granted can lead to more complex practices – of distance and proximity to the institution of marriage (Valdayron).

Homophobia-for-all

While research reports point to very widespread acceptance of homosexuality in France ("L'homosexualité"), there are three significant limits: such reports emphasize averages, do not consider international contexts – gay men and lesbians, and, even more, transgender people are subjected to remarkable rejection in a large number of countries in the world (OCDE) – and rely simply on statements. Greater visibility of gay and lesbian issues in the public sphere can lead to insincere responses when asked about homosexuality, regardless of actual beliefs. While it is, moreover, difficult to measure the exact extent of homophobic acts (social condemnation of homophobia necessarily leads to an increase in complaints regarding homophobic acts since they are more perceived and referred to as such), the possibility of homophobia remains a constituent element of all gay and lesbian lives, including the most privileged.

As a result, the 2013 law may have given the impression that the problem of homophobia was largely settled or, at the very least, on its way to being so. But the workings of homophobia run so deep and are so complex that a law cannot, on its own, neutralize them. Several literary accounts have highlighted this very phenomenon for a decade now. Edouard Louis's *En finir avec Eddy Bellegueule* [The End of Eddy], for example, has been the subject of significant controversy. The author describes the life of a young boy in a small village in northern France who is plagued by his family's, his school friends', and, more broadly, the entire village community's homophobia. Many journalists questioned the reality of violence and accused Louis of exaggerating and even exploiting his experience of homophobia to careerist ends (Sire). All as if the reality of homophobia in France, after the passage of the Taubira law, were no longer believable and could only be a fantasy, and as if gay men and lesbians themselves invented their destiny as victims. The vast number of assaults on lesbians and gays and the fact of being accustomed to violence from an early age get very little attention from the media and in the political sphere. In the context of the ten-year anniversary of marriage-for-all, there were reports and articles about the ambushes that gays face online and in cruising areas (Brethes). But in most cases homophobia is condemned as an abstract phenomenon and isolated occurrences.

On March 27, 2023, the *Manif pour tous* (the main movement against the bill in 2012–13) attempted a media stunt: its president, Ludovine de la Rochère, announced that the *Manif pour tous* was changing its name.

In the context of massive strikes against the pension reform in France, the association became the *Syndicat de la famille* [Union for Families]. On April 5, 2023, pressure from reactionary right groups close to the *Manif pour tous* caused the cancellation of Bilal Hassani's concert, a genderqueer singer known for representing France at the 2019 Eurovision Competition and his role on *Dancing with the Stars*, where he got to dance with a man. The first performance of his 2023 tour was scheduled to take place in Metz in a former basilica deconsecrated almost five hundred years ago and now a concert hall. A "Catholic Lorraine" collective decried the desecration. Civitas, an anti-abortion group close to the Vatican and the *Manif pour tous* (the group organized street prayers against the Taubira law in 2012–13), called for a rally outside the performance space. With increasing physical threats against his fans, Hassani cancelled the event. This was not an isolated case. Resistance to full equality and freedom for sexual and gender minorities is plentiful and organized. A counter-revolutionary ideology is taking root in France and Europe (Perreau, "Reflections"). It is happening because of a set of intimidations, but also because of a majority rewriting of minority memories.

One memory can cover up another

In order to give itself legitimacy, every majority institution tends to erase the memories of its minorities. The rewriting of minority struggles by certain academics and political leaders who long objected to them accentuated the risk of being crushed by the majority. Initially hostile to *PaCS* and/or marriage, they rallied to it late and are now trying to erase the traces of their past positions. In doing so, they continue to attack early activists who confront them with the facts.

Valérie Précresse, for example, a member of the *Les Républicains* party and president of the Île de France region, who proposed converting same-sex marriages into civil unions, said she "changed her mind" and denied ever wanting to "unmarry" anyone ("Mariage pour tous"). The Minister of the Interior, Gérard Darmanin (2020–24), who as mayor maintained his opposition to celebrating same-sex marriages, simply said that he was wrong ("Je me suis trompé"). In 2022, Marine Le Pen, the leader of the *Rassemblement National*, affirmed: "je ne retirerai aucun droit aux Français" ["I will not take away any rights from the French"] ("'Je ne retirerai'"). As Denis Quinqueton, a co-director of the

LGBTI+ Observatory of the Jean-Jaurès Foundation, points out during an interview on *France Inter* on April 21, 2023, certain opponents' remorse ought only to be judged by their actions. The *mea culpa* policy costs minorities dearly: it contributes to erasing past antagonisms, as if winning new rights were as easy as a change of opinion several years later. As the author of a report on "unmarriage," Irène Théry fought against the *PaCS* in abusive terms (Théry, "Le contrat" 163). Her arguments enabled Lionel Jospin's teams to make sure that the *PaCS* would have no effect on parenting, something that would not change until a little more than 22 years later with the law of February 22, 2022. Théry (among others) therefore contributed to causing a considerable delay in equal rights, leaving many gay and lesbian families without legal protection. During the 2000s, thanks to her meetings with various members of the Association of Gay and Lesbian Parents and Future Parents, Théry realized the value of transforming family law by using the demands of lesbians and gays. She then supported the *PaCS*, marriage, assisted procreation, and surrogacy. At first, she explained that she changed her mind and then presented herself, starting in the early 2010s, as *always* having been an advocate for equality. Through her institutional footing, she became an important figure in the struggles for marriage-for-all. Her mobilization was decisive, even. But, by rewriting history and offering herself up as the figurehead of equality (this is especially true in the documentary, *La Sociologue et l'Ourson*, which her director-son devotes to her), she helped make invisible the activists from the early years, most often lesbians and gays, fighters whose contractualist conception of the family she never fails to describe as "egotistical individualism" (Théry, "Introduction") and whom she used to call the "ayatollahs of equality" (Borrillo and Lascoumes).

History as fiction

Resisting the rewriting of LGBT+ histories is essential. In France, minority memories are often accused of undermining the national narrative (Nora and Chandernagor) and are even described as a threat (Nora 1008). Such a denunciation is accompanied by diatribes against ecology, May 1968, the loss of authority, characteristic of reactionary thinking (Idier). Notwithstanding, the sites of minority memory are disparate by definition. Their universality stems precisely from their vernacular and volatile character. As faithful as memory is to the archives, it is always retrospective and can only restore the past by fictionalizing it. As minorities constantly grapple with majority narratives, they are already fictionalizing their lives. As a result, they can radicalize their relationship to memory, not as a link between several eras but as a way of existing *through* several eras.

The ten-year anniversary of marriage-for-all, therefore, raises the question of the making of history. As Georges Didi-Huberman noted, "le discours historique ne 'naît' jamais. Toujours il recommence" ["historical discourse is never 'born.' It always recommences"] (1). We are always caught in analogical relation to the past: we compare ourselves to the beings who preceded us; we project our categories of thought when we study their ways of life; we justify our collective choices by referring to older modes of organization. In other words, we establish continuities and ruptures with the past, which, in both cases, make it possible to establish a certain problematization of the present: we idealize the past in the sense that we create a certain "idea" of it, which in turn governs what and who we are. "Cela ne s'avère possible que parce que l'objet de l'imitation n'est pas un objet mais l'idéal lui-même" ["This only turns out to be possible because the object of imitation is not an object, but rather the ideal itself"], Didi-Huberman tells us again (10). It is *as* an absence that the past imposes its presence on us. How, then, to establish the truth of bygone facts, that is to say, facts that are no longer physical? (Cassirer 202). Such work is only possible by thickening the "we" of the story. Minority groups – groups that are durably and strongly constrained by unfavorable power relations (Perreau, *Spheres* 6–8) – do not, in fact, conceive of their relationship to history as do majority groups. Not only are their memories less institutionalized (they are less taught, less commemorated, less represented, etc.), but they are also interpreted under the light of majority memories. This distortion is an issue of both temporal and territorial struggle (Halberstam 6–7). Minority memories are scattered, polysemic, sensitive, and interstitial because dispersion, reinterpretation of the canon, affect, and dislocation are all forms of resistance to domination. Minority groups must always work from and against majority problematizations at once. This is particularly the case for almost all of LGBT+ people, who are raised in heterosexual and cisgender families. Such work leads them to invent parallel stories, that is to say, to make of their very lives a fiction. In doing so, minorities destabilize the majority relationship to the archive, as a place for grasping the real, because they remind us that the real is, in fact, always transfused by fiction (Le Brun).

Minorities experience the regime of majoritarian historicity as summoning them to interpret things a certain way and, in doing so, as denying the uniqueness of their experiences. Not having any children, Roland Barthes reworked his relationship to his ancestors, in this case his mother. He writes in *Camera Lucida*, "Moi qui n'avais pas procréé, j'avais, dans sa maladie même, engendré ma mère" ["I who had not procreated, I had, in her very illness, engendered my mother."] (72). This sort of transformation of generational relationships becomes camp photography in Michel Journiac's work (Crenn), ironically titled "Tribute to Freud." It displays four photographs side by side: of his father and his mother, and two of him disguised as them. The photographs are captioned as follows: "Michel Journiac cross-dressed as Renée Journiac," "Michel Journiac cross-dressed as Robert Journiac," but also and even more powerfully, "Renée Journiac cross-dressed as Renée Journiac" and "Robert Journiac cross-dressed as Robert Journiac." Journiac's very queer, corporeal art allows him to simultaneously reverse the relationship to time and identity: the copy deconstructs the very idea of origins and original (Provencher 163). This double metamorphosis violates the linear conception of genealogy that a majority archive introduces – an archive of roots, inheritance, and transmission while accepting the logic of exposure and institutional constraints. Inventiveness, then, consists in carrying minority transformations into the most standardized and ordered spaces (Reay).

As evidenced by François Noudelmann's deconstruction of origins (101), minority relationships to history are about making the social world un-real, through a more or less sudden or more or less acute awareness of the crumbling of one's presence in the world. Where Jean-Paul Sartre describes the emergence of existence in the face of an event (in his case, World War II) as a moment of incarnation (*The Roads to Freedom*), minorities experience more of an exit from oneself in relation to history; they are the point of subjectification that cuts into what Foucault describes as modern objectification (365). This way of relating to the group through a practice of distancing from oneself, especially from embodied majority norms – what I call "minority dissociation" (Perreau, *Spheres* 195) – is a type of relationship to time and space that gives life to fiction against all the deadly policies of the archive (Hartog 177). We are as much the past and the present as the future. Minority dissociation contributes to deconstructing reality all while making it more tangible (Certeau 199–203).

Still, this dissociation does not do justice to the whole of minority experience. Ann Cvetkovich studied the minority archives that are broadly circulated. That's how some accounts of homophobic crimes help support legislative change. Cvetkovich explained that such circulation is possible when archives manage to reach different audiences. But to do this, they must be purged of certain elements, "at the price of domesticating the more specifically queer issues" (Cvetkovich 277). How one ought to die to count in the eyes of history? This is the question that Judith Butler asked in *Precarious Life* (2004), using the deaths of people with AIDS as an example: they questioned the institutional mechanisms that determine which lives are worthy and which are unworthy of national mourning (Butler 34–35). Cvetkovich deems that the circulation of certain minority archives comes from the fact that they lend themselves more than others to spectacle, namely to one of the pillars of contemporary capitalism. I would like to suggest a complementary interpretation: celebrating marriage-for-all amounts to far more than capitalist spectacularization; it creates a sort of chronology of gay and lesbian cultures in which each new story is superimposed on the previous one in a logic of idealized majority democratic progression. Building this chronology impedes a critique of the norm – a critique that allows for the coexistence of multiple minority temporalities. Thus, social practices that are still alive, such as cruising spots, single-sex spaces, transgenerational friendships and loves, celibacy, etc., disappear from areas the law covers (Warner; Cobb; Martin). These practices cry out for the invention of new solidarity contracts without conditions of conjugality or marriage; for authorizing adoption between adults; for offering a possibility to de-gender civil status; for recognizing multiple partnerships; for decriminalizing sexuality outside the domestic space; etc.

In this chapter, I showed that, ten years after it was enacted, the law that enabled same-sex marriage is an integral part of French identity. Almost the entire political arena, including members of the extreme right, celebrates the law as the emblem of a modern France. Republican institutions are now the guardians of the memory of marriage-for-all, as the official ceremonies of May 2023 attest. But the memory of marriage-for-all is at once a site of pride and a site of oblivion. Indeed, for lesbians and gays, transmission from one generation to another has been a community practice for a long time, a practice of heterotopic spaces, vernacular references, friendships, and transgenerational loves. Does gay marriage depoliticize queer memory? I argue that memory is not about transforming the archives of a set of individuals into an institutional archive; it is always a matter of building community.

Changes in LGBT+ lifestyles in the wake of marriage-for-all as well as #MeToo, COVID-19, and social media, reveal more than fragmentary memories; they reveal a fragmented queer community. A queer politics of memory must therefore set itself the task of making the multitudes coexist (Hollenstein). Each era superimposes different conceptions of gender and sexuality: the *Arcadie* generation rubbed shoulders with that of the *Front homosexuel d'action révolutionnaire* (Arcadie was a "homophile" organization founded by seminarist André Baudry in 1954 with the goal to obtain recognition of homosexual respectability, while the Homosexual Front of Revolutionary Action, founded in 1971 in the wake of the Women's Liberation Movement, advocated a destruction of social and family norms), and then that of AIDS activism, which itself enabled the emergence of the *PaCS* generation and the marriage generation. It is up to the latter to ensure the presence of other issues, other people, and other ways of thinking, that is to say, to allow everyone to enjoy their own space and temporality, a space and time of their own, as it were.

Works cited

"10 ans déjà!" *Causette*, no. 144, May 2023. Web.
Barthes, Roland. *Camera Lucida: Reflections on Photography*. Translated by Richard Howard. Hill & Wang, 1981.
Bénit, Simon. "Attitudes envers l'homosexualité et l'homoparentalité en France et en Europe." MA thesis, Leiden University, 2019.
Blidon, Marianne. "Ville et homosexualité, une relation à l'épreuve de la cartographie." *Données Urbaines*, no. 5, 2007, pp. 67–76.
Borrillo, Daniel, and Pierre Lascoumes. *Amours égales? Le PaCS, les homosexuels et la gauche*. La Découverte, 2002.
Brethes, Sarah, et al. *Guet-Apens: des crimes invisibles*. Mediapart, 2023.
Butler, Judith. *Precarious Life: The Powers of Mourning and Violence*. Verso, 2004.
Cassirer, Ernst. *An Essay on Man: An Introduction to a Philosophy of Human Culture*. Yale UP, 1944.
Certeau, Michel de. *Heterologies: Discourse on the Other*. Translated by Brian Massumi. U of Minnesota P, 1986.
Chaillou, Étienne, and Mathias Théry. *La Sociologue et l'Ourson*. Quark Productions, 2016.
Cobb, Michael. *Single: Arguments for the Uncoupled*. New York UP, 2005.

Crenn, Julie. "Michel Journiac: sublimer les normes." *Julie Crenn's Website.* February 16, 2012. crennjulie.com/2012/02/16/michel-journiac-sublimer-les-normes/.
Cvetkovich, Ann. *An Archive of Feelings: Trauma, Sexuality, and Lesbian Public Cultures.* Duke UP, 2003.
Delbecque, Céline. "Mariage pour tous: dix après la loi, les discriminations subsistent." *L'Express.* November 17, 2022. Web.
Didi-Huberman, Georges. *The Surviving Image: Phantoms of Time and Time of Phantoms: Aby Warburg's History of Art.* Translated by Harvey L. Mendelsohn. Pennsylvania State UP, 2017.
Eribon, Didier. *Sur cet instant si fragile: carnets janvier–août 2004.* Fayard, 2004.
Foucault, Michel. *The Order of Things: An Archaeology of the Human Sciences.* Translated by Alan Sheridan. Routledge, 2002.
Gunther, Scott. "Building a More Stately Closet: French Gay Movements since the Early 1980s." *Journal of the History of Sexuality*, vol. 13, no. 3, July 2004, pp. 326–47.
Halberstam, Jack. *In a Queer Time and Place: Transgender Bodies, Subcultural Lives.* New York UP, 2005.
Hartog, François. *Confrontations avec l'histoire.* Gallimard, 2021.
Hollenstein, Nils. "Mémoires LGBTQI+: des archives vivantes, partout, et pour tout le monde." *Basta!* May 16, 2023. Web.
"L'homosexualité largement tolérée, mais loin d'être banalisée." *Observatoire des inégalités.* January 4, 2023. Web.
Idier, Antoine. "Mémoires." In *Catégoriser*, edited by Marlène Bouvet, Florent Chossière, Marine Duc, and Estelle Fisson. ENS Éditions, forthcoming.
INSEE. "Mariages et *PaCS*. Données annuelles de 1990 à 2022." *Insee.fr.* January 17, 2023. Web.
"'Je me suis trompé,' assure Darmanin qui annonce des mesures contre l'homophobie." *La Voix du Nord.* April 20, 2023. Web.
"'Je ne retirerai aucun droit aux Français' assure Marine Le Pen." *Valeurs Actuelles.* April 15, 2022. Web.
Le Brun, Annie. *Reality Overload: The Modern World's Assault on the Imaginal Realm.* Translated by Jon E. Graham. Inner Traditions, 2008.
Louis, Édouard. *The End of Eddy.* Translated by Michael Lucey. Farrar, Straus & Giroux, 2017.
"Mariage pour tous: ces politiques qui ont changé d'avis." *Franceinfo.* April 24, 2023. Web.
"Le mariage pour tous célèbre ses dix ans." *Paris.fr.* May 17, 2023. Web.
Martin, Marc. *Les tasses: toilettes publiques, affaires privées.* Agua, 2019.
Meslay, Gaëlle. "Five Years of Same-Sex Marriages in France: Differences between Male Couples and Female Couples." *Population*, vol. 74, no. 4, 2019, pp. 499–519.

Nora, Pierre. "L'ère de la commémoration." *Les Lieux de mémoire*, vol. 3, *Les France*, book 3, *De l'archive à l'emblème*, edited by Pierre Nora. Gallimard, 1992.

Nora, Pierre, and Françoise Chandernagor. *Liberté pour l'histoire*. Éditions du CNRS, 2008.

Noudelmann, François. *Pour en finir avec la généalogie*. Léo Scheer, 2004.

OCDE. *Panorama de la société 2019: les indicateurs sociaux de l'OCDE. Chapitre 1. Le défi LGBT*. July 29, 2019.

Paternotte, David. *Revendiquer le "mariage gay": Belgique, France, Espagne*. Éditions de l'Université Libre de Bruxelles, 2011.

Perreau, Bruno. *Queer Theory: The French Response*. Translated by Deke Dusinberre. Stanford UP, 2016.

———. "Reflections on a New Ethnonational Counterrevolution." *On the Subject of Ethnonationalism*, edited by Joshua Branciforte and Ramsey McGlazer. Fordham UP, 2023, pp. 263–96.

———. *Spheres of Injustice. The Ethical Promise of Minority Presence*. MIT P, 2025.

Petit-Felici, Lucien. "'Je suis fier': François Hollande revient sur les 10 ans de l'adoption du mariage pour tous." *Le Journal du Dimanche*. April 23, 2023. Web.

Provencher, Denis M. *Queer Maghrebi French: Language, Temporalities, Transfiliations*. Liverpool UP, 2017.

Rault, Wilfried. "Is the *PaCS* the future of marriage? The several meanings of the French Civil Union." *International Journal of Law, Policy and the Family*, vol. 33, no. 2, 2019, pp. 139–59.

Reay, Barry. *Sex in the Archives: Writing American Sexual Histories*. Manchester UP, 2018.

Sartre, Jean-Paul. *The Roads to Freedom*, 3 vols. *Age of Reason*. Translated by Eric Sutton. Vintage Books, 1947. *The Reprieve*. Translated by Eric Sutton. Vintage, 1947. *Troubled Sleep*. Translated by Gerard Hopkins. Knopf, 1951.

Sire, Benjamin. "Édouard Louis, l'homme qui en bavait trop." *Franc Tireur*, no. 8, January 5, 2022. Web.

Théry, Irène. "Le contrat d'union sociale en question." *Esprit*, no. 236, October 1997, pp. 159–211.

———. "Introduction: la grande bataille du mariage pour tous." *Mariage et filiation pour tous*. Seuil, 2016. Apple books edition.

Tissot, Sylvie. *Gay Friendly: Acceptance and Control of Homosexuality in New York and Paris*. Translated by Helen Morrison. Polity Press, 2023.

Valdayron, Floriane. "La jeunesse queer veut-elle encore du mariage?" *Têtu.com*. June 8, 2022. Web.

Warner, Michael. *The Trouble with Normal: Sex, Politics, and the Ethics of Queer Life*. Harvard UP, 1999.

CHAPTER TWO

Queer memory takes a monumental turn
Commemorating Bruno Lenoir and Jean Diot

Stephen Shapiro

Paris abounds with improvised, creatively re-appropriated queer *lieux de mémoire*: the graves of Oscar Wilde, Marcel Proust, and Gertrude Stein along with many others in the city's historic cemeteries have long been sites of pilgrimage and spontaneous tributes. More recently, the gilded replica of the Statue of Liberty's torch sitting atop the Pont de l'Alma tunnel became a makeshift commemoration of Princess Diana's AIDS advocacy work as well as her status as a gay icon. Without access to governmental memory regimes, queer memorial practices in Paris have largely adopted what Michel de Certeau has termed tactical methods, namely the impromptu transformation of existing sites in ways that often subvert their original intents and purposes (30). In October 2014, however, Parisian queer memory took an official turn with the dedication of a plaque in the rue Montorgueil commemorating the little-known case of two men arrested for sodomy and burned at the stake in 1750 (Figure 2.1). Inspired by a constituent's suggestion in an online chat, Paris city councilor Ian Brossat set the project in motion in 2011 and, three years later, Mayor Anne Hidalgo unveiled a memorial plaque on October 18, 2014:

> Le 4 janvier 1750, rue Montorgueil entre la rue Saint-Sauveur et l'ancienne rue Beaurepaire furent arrêtés Bruno Lenoir et Jean Diot. Condamnés pour homosexualité ils furent brûlés en Place de Grève le 6 juillet 1750. Ce fut la dernière exécution pour homosexualité en France.

[On January 4, 1750, in rue Montorgueil between rue Saint-Sauveur and the former rue Beaurepaire, Bruno Lenoir and Jean Diot were arrested. Convicted of homosexuality, they were burned in the Place de Grève on July 6, 1750. This was the last execution for homosexuality in France.][1]

Figure 2.1 Plaque commemorating Bruno Lenoir and Jean Diot in the rue Montorgueil (Paris), dedicated on October 18, 2014

While previous *lieux de mémoire* seized pre-existing sites and transformed them, this memorial plaque represents a new official heritage initiative that constitutes what Thomas Dunn calls "the queer monumental turn," namely, "an ongoing and evolving assortment of efforts to give [...] shared pasts a weightiness and timelessness and grandeur in order to activate collective power and effect social change" (21). In the case of the plaque honoring Bruno Lenoir and Jean Diot, this monumental turn is also a textual turn in which the inscription centralizes collective memory in order to fix and stabilize it. This chapter examines the narrative this new monument seeks to impose. What emerges

1 All translations are my own.

contradicts Nora's assertion that a "patrimonial explosion" – a growing interest in the history of groups and communities – has supplanted the national narrative and its universal, unitary values: indeed, as queer memory becomes the object of official memory practices, it tends to lose its queer specificity which is subordinated to the service of normative values, economic development, and political posturing ("Era" 630). At the same time, however, we will also consider how monuments, far from eternally fixing a dominant narrative, can become sites of continual queer tactical re-appropriation as *lieux de mémoire*.

The story of Lenoir and Diot's arrest, trial, and execution is far from clear; the archive does not provide a definitive understanding of just what happened on the night of January 4, 1750, when the sergeant of the watch arrested Bruno Lenoir and Jean Diot "en posture indécente et d'une manière répréhensible" [in an indecent position indicative of a base demeanor] (Courouve). Lenoir, a twenty-something apprentice cobbler explained that he had only just met Diot half an hour earlier when the 40-year-old unmarried domestic "a défait sa culotte et a commis sur lui des indécences" [undid his pants and performed indecent acts upon him] (Courouve). Diot denied knowing Lenoir and asserted that he was trying to help the youth who had passed out in a doorway. Subsequent interrogations revealed conflicting elements: Diot claimed that he had merely lowered his pants to urinate while Lenoir denied any recollection of events. In a curious police document archived separately from the remnants of the trial materials, Lenoir asserted that Diot had asked him to "le lui mettre par derrière" [to put it in his behind] and that he had been unable to "finir l'affaire" [finish the deed] (AB 11717 fos. 246–247). In spite of the doubts surrounding the encounter, the men were condemned to be "brûlés vifs avec leur procès, leurs cendres ensuite jetés au vent, leurs biens acquis et confisqués au roi" [burned alive along with their trial records, with their ashes thrown to the wind, and their possessions taken and confiscated by the king] (Merrick 310; modernized).

The fate of Lenoir and Diot has puzzled historians, since ample archival evidence points to the utter banality of this failed hookup. Throughout the eighteenth century, police arrested, interrogated, and most often released men cruising for sex in parks and along the *quais*. Even men surprised *in flagrante delicto* like Lenoir and Diot did not end up in the Place de Grève. Barbier, an eighteenth-century diarist, was shocked by the grisly execution, which, he concluded, took place "pour faire un exemple" [for the sake of example], and because Lenoir and Diot's humble origins meant they could be executed "sans aucune conséquence pour les suites" [without any concern for the consequences] (447). Yet Lenoir and Diot perished anonymously and never assumed a dissuasive exemplarity: "On n'a point crié le jugement pour s'épargner apparemment le nom et la qualification du crime" [the sentence was not publicly proclaimed in order to prevent spreading the name and details of the crime] (Barbier 448). In a further effort to explain this enigmatic case, some modern historians have argued that the extraordinary execution was meant to quiet public outrage provoked by an unrelated police scandal involving child abduction that took place in the spring of 1750. But even this explanation falls short, since the death penalty had already been sought in the case well before the police crimes came to light (Merrick 281).

It is also surprising that this spectacular and rare public execution did not touch collective memory. The burning at the stake of men accused of sodomy in seventeenth- and eighteenth-century Paris generally left lasting impressions in popular culture and the sodomite subculture. Chausson (executed in 1661 for the attempted rape of a noble youth) was celebrated in song in the streets and his name became synonymous with sodomy.[2] The execution of Deschauffours in 1726 for sodomy and violent child sexual abuse made him something of a criminal folk hero whose notoriety caught the attention of Voltaire and inspired popular songs and a curious satirical play.[3] The case of Lenoir and Diot, however, left no such legacy and has only been cited in legal treatises as a curiosity.

As an obscure historical event unencumbered by an enduring fixed meaning, the story of Lenoir and Diot can serve a variety of ideological and political goals. While the symbolic work and mythologizing of the *lieu de mémoire* separates it from the domain of history, in this case we have a historical event that is already a free-floating signifier ready to be pressed into action. Indeed, the Lenoir–Diot plaque shows how multiple meanings have been enfolded into a memorial that speaks to a

---

2 On the commemoration of Chausson in popular song, see Nicholas Hammond, *The Powers of Sound and Song in Early Modern Paris* (Penn State UP, 2019), pp. 95–124.

3 On the cultural legacy of Deschauffours, see Martial Poirson, "Relevons l'infâme! Deschauffours ombre (théâtrale) projetée de la (mauvaise) conscience occidentale," *Autorité et marginalité sur les scènes européennes (XVIIe–XVIIIe siècles)*, edited by Christelle Bahier-Porte and Zoé Schweitzer (Classiques Garnier, 2017), pp. 239–62. On criminal celebrity in eighteenth-century Paris, see Antoine Lilti, *The Invention of Celebrity: 1750–1850*, translated by Lynn Jeffress (Polity, 2017).

queer longing for historically grounded identities while also censoring the past in a bid for acceptability. It shows how queer memory can be instrumentalized for political and economic advantage while also defying the logic of commemoration that seeks to eternally stabilize the past and its meaning. The short history of this memorial shows that far from permanently fixing memory to confront what Nora calls "the acceleration of history" and "a general perception that anything and everything may disappear," it also demonstrates a potential to evolve and recreate itself, revealing that monuments, like memory, are both living and evolutive (Nora, "Between" 7).

First and foremost, the memorial plaque seeks to render the queer past visible and correct for the systematic suppression of queer historical presence. It is a belated form of reparative justice that undoes the sentence of *damnatio memoriae*, the eternal erasure of Lenoir and Diot from historical, judicial, or funereal remembrance through the burning of trial records and the dispersal of their ashes. By weaving the story of two ordinary men into the historical fabric, it marks a turn away from an older conception of homosexual history as a list of lofty figures such as kings, noblemen, and generals, thereby embracing a democratic notion of history. Ian Brossat, the Communist city councilor who shepherded the project through the Conseil Municipal, explained in *L'Humanité* that the plaque "témoigne [...] d'une autre histoire de l'homosexualité. Une histoire souterraine [...] celle d'hommes et de femmes engloutis par l'histoire" [bears witness [...] to an alternative history of homosexuality. An underground history [...] of men and women cast aside by history]. Finally, the plaque also attaches Lenoir and Diot to the narrative of the nation by virtue of their deaths being "la dernière exécution pour homosexualité en France" [the last execution for homosexuality in France].

Set into the ground at street level, the memorial plaque resembles a tombstone with sparse wording that highlights places, dates, and names. The conservative design creates a solemn tone that evokes traditional, funereal memory practices' genealogical orientation. In short, the plaque may signify queerness but it does not signify queerly. It further develops a continuous filiation between past and present through the repeated use of the term *homosexualité*, a fraught term whose meanings can vacillate between sexual acts between same-sex partners and a sexual identity. Ever since Foucault drew a distinction between the early–modern sodomite who "indulged in a category of forbidden acts" and the homosexual, a nineteenth-century invention who was "a personage, a past, a case history, and a childhood [...] a type of life, a life form, and a morphology," scholars of pre-modern sexuality have interrogated Foucault's timeline, highlighting the complexity of historicizing sexuality (43). So, while the plaque's wording does allow for a reading that emphasizes the men's conviction for an act, sodomy, it also evokes an anachronistic, modern, identitarian meaning. Rather than representing the complexity of understanding sexuality historically or questioning the binary categories of heterosexual and homosexual, the plaque instead suggests that Lenoir and Diot were persecuted for an identity, thus rendering them recognizable to a modern public.

While we might be tempted to decry the language of the plaque as a historical error or misrepresentation, it is ultimately more useful to examine it as an example of collective memory's fashioning a usable past out of a limited historical corpus in order to access the authority of historical precedent. Making Lenoir and Diot's story an example of homophobic identity policing ultimately testifies to a modern desire for "being long," which Elizabeth Freeman sees as the fundamental quest of queer kinship, namely "to long to be bigger not only spatially, but also temporally, to 'hold out' a hand across time and touch the dead or those not born yet, to offer oneself beyond one's own time" (299). The plaque's resolutely modern wording erases historical differences in order to foster a trans-historical solidarity. By treating homosexual identity as a timeless universal, the plaque transforms a historical event into a *lieu de mémoire* that bolsters a contemporary collective identity.

Attaching Lenoir and Diot's story to a unitary metanarrative of *homosexualité* makes the plaque more inclusive by allowing women to see themselves reflected in it, thereby confronting lesbian invisibility and what Louis Crompton has called "the myth of lesbian impunity," the belief that lesbian behavior escaped policing and persecution. At the same time, however, the imposition of the homosexual identity category shuts off consideration of Lenoir and Diot as uncategorizably queer and representative of the great diversity of same-sex erotic experiences in early–modern France. Moreover, by focusing uniquely on the question of sexuality, the plaque excludes the intersectional, in particular, the discourse on class that the eighteenth-century sources evoke and that Brossat emphasized in *L'Humanité*, where he described Lenoir and Diot as "hommes du peuple" [commoners] who had the misfortune of being "mal nés" [of low birth]. The plaque confirms Robert Mills's observation that in the work of institutions of queer memory, "[i]ntersections of race and class with gender and sexuality risk being articulated poorly when viewed through the lens of sexual orientation" (259). In short, the plaque seems to strike a single, essentialist, identitarian note that narrows its message, audience, and influence.

The plaque's language also points towards how this *lieu de mémoire* is built upon what Nancy Wood has termed the *lieu d'oubli* since its representation of the past suppresses inconvenient, unsavory details. The term *homosexualité* functions euphemistically, sanitizing the explicit language of the historical documents and the men's conviction for sodomy. The plaque erases the messiness of fleeting, anonymous, public sex that queerly contests norms. The "specter of public sex" described by José Muñoz here holds a ghostly presence in queer memory where it has been "ostracized by many 'legitimate' factions within the queer community" (46). In addition to this erasure, the memorial to Lenoir and Diot allows for the creation of a counter memory of queer coupledom and even marriage, simply by virtue of its dedication to both men. In a statement published on Facebook for the 2014 dedication of the plaque, Mayor Anne Hidalgo spoke of the men as a loving, committed couple:

> J'inaugure aujourd'hui la plaque honorant la mémoire du dernier couple exécuté parce qu'homosexuel [...]. Il est de notre devoir de nous souvenir de l'horreur qu'eurent à affronter les couples homosexuels pendant des siècles. Nous ne pouvons pas oublier la souffrance que subirent ceux qui n'avaient pas commis d'autre crime que celui d'aimer, ni nier les persécutions dont ils furent la cible.
>
> [Today I inaugurate a plaque honoring the memory of the last couple executed for being homosexual [...]. It is our duty to remember the horrors faced by homosexual couples over the centuries. We cannot forget the suffering of those whose only crime was love nor can we deny the persecution that targeted them.]

Numerous media outlets echoed Hidalgo's vision by referring to Lenoir and Diot as "amants" [lovers]. The contemporary imagination transformed the unpalatable story of a drunken hookup into a less-threatening, normative love story that nodded toward the current debate over same-sex marriage which was unfolding on the political and cultural stage at the same time. Commemoration is not a historical process that fixes in place "the past as it really was," but rather a technology of memory that shows us that, as Nora explains, "[w]hat matters is not what the past imposes on us but what we bring to it [...] history proposes but the present disposes" ("Era" 618).

The plaque's orientation toward the present also emerges from its explicit commemoration of "the last execution for homosexuality in France," which invites us to celebrate progress and the triumph of modernity over the barbarity of the past. It promotes a linear, teleological vision of history that evokes Foucault's "repressive hypothesis" of a progressive movement from oppression to liberation and strikes a self-congratulatory tone of modern superiority. In this respect, it commemorates its own commemoration of the past, seeing its own existence as a milestone in the movement from the darkness of the past into the light of the present. Moreover, it shows how queer collective memory gravitates towards "queer agony" by persistently focusing on the history of policing, homophobia, and queer victims. In the years following the Lenoir–Diot plaque, the city of Paris has continued to privilege queer martyrdom as it has renamed streets for LGBTIQ historical personalities who died largely by homophobic violence or AIDS, such as Harvey Milk, Pierre Seel, and Cleews Vellay. While homophobia is essential for understanding queer history and experience, it is not and should not be the only narrative. A very particular vision of the queer past as a parade of martyrs emerges from these heritage initiatives that privilege death over life, obfuscating the resistance, resilience, and creative ingenuity of queer lives in favor of what Jasbir Puar has termed "queer necropolitics" in which the queer is "predominantly understood as implicitly or explicitly targeted for death" (35–36).

While the plaque appears to fix state homophobia firmly in the realm of the past, it also invites us to consider that "l'homophobie demeure très présente à Paris et qu'il est nécessaire de la combattre par tous les moyens dont nous disposons" [homophobia remains very prevalent in Paris and it is necessary to combat it by all the means at our disposition] (Brossat, "Vœu présenté"). Indeed, the memorial goes beyond being a simple didactic reminder with symbolic value because it has also become a dynamic platform for public debate about gender and sexual minority rights. As Orangias, Simms, and French have shown in their work on queer monuments, "monuments are cultural agents" that "foster […] change" (705). As a backdrop for marches and rituals and even as a site of symbolic violence and vandalism, the plaque focuses society's attention on queer lives and rights and can function as a political actor in domains far removed from the experience of the two men it commemorates. Actions by Act Up-Paris and the Pride de Nuit movement as well as vigils marking homophobic violence have all used the plaque as a stage and have rewritten its meaning, allowing it to exceed the narrow limits of its sparse inscription. As an expression of memory with a physical presence in the urban landscape, the plaque can be transformed and evolve along with the different community events it is called to witness. It has already become the site of tactical re-appropriation, imbued with new meanings that exceed those envisioned by its creators.

Moreover, as Orangias, Simms, and French have noted, sites such as the Lenoir–Diot plaque "expand and strengthen advocacy" (718). The numerous incidents of vandalism that have plagued the plaque have each time garnered significant media attention, pushing public figures to respond with declarations of outrage and support and serving as a call to action. The re-dedication of the plaque on May 17, 2021, following a vandal's attack, also marked the International Day against Homophobia, Transphobia, and Biphobia and provided the City of Paris the occasion to declare itself a "Zone de Liberté LGBTQ+" in response to right-wing "LGBT-free zones" created in parts of Eastern Europe. Showing again how memory can be continually re-instrumentalized to serve in a variety of contexts, this event used the plaque to position the city of Paris as an actor in international queer advocacy, replacing state leadership on the question. Such uses of queer monuments make them dynamic actors in the public domain where they perform political work.

As an initiative of local government, the Lenoir–Diot plaque shows how queer memory has been decentralized: while the state continues to trumpet an official discourse of universal values as opposed to communitarianism, queer memory projects devolve to local jurisdictions, which have greater freedom from the constraints of the state memory regime. Indeed, Paris occupies a unique place: as the national capital, its local history often is the national narrative and the Lenoir–Diot plaque's evocation of "la dernière exécution pour homosexualité en France" speaks in national terms from the local level thereby bypassing the official state memory machine. At the same time, however, the plaque respects tacit limits: it shies away from assigning blame, couching the fate of Lenoir and Diot in the passive voice (they "were arrested" and "were burned"), hiding the agents of the atrocity, and stopping short of any sort of national apology or admission of guilt. Indeed, official queer *lieux de mémoire* will most likely follow the gradual unfolding of memory seen with the commemoration of state complicity in the deportation of Jews or the 1961 police massacre of Algerians in Paris: "Plaques," explains Michel Laronde in *Postcolonial Realms of Memory* (2020), "are one of the steps that states are expected to take along the transitional process toward 'more' truth. Memorials, commemorations and public acts of remembrance [...] have progressively become part of the state obligation to [...] mend the grand national narrative" (114).

The commemoration of Lenoir and Diot is also an element of the City of Paris's instrumentalization of queer memory for commercial and political ends. Queer memory has become one of the necessary features that cities that aspire to global stature must cultivate to drive economic development. A 2017 study, "*Paris, ville phare de l'inclusion et de la diversité*" [Paris, a beacon of inclusion and diversity], edited by Jean-Luc Roméro, a prominent gay political figure in city and regional government, was centered around Mayor Anne Hidalgo's request to "valoriser le tourisme lié à la culture LGBT [...] qui est une composante de l'identité et de l'attractivité de Paris et un symbole d'ouverture et de tolérance qu'il convient de valoriser auprès des habitants et des visiteurs" [valorize tourism linked to LGBT culture [...] which is an element of the identity and attractiveness of Paris as well as a symbol of openness and tolerance which we should highlight to both residents and visitors] (Mairie de Paris 5). Commenting on the plaque's placement in the rue Montorgueil, on the periphery of the Marais, a member of Hidalgo's entourage remarked to *Le Point*, "C'est un lieu à la fois populaire, bobo et commerçant, donc c'est bien de le faire ici" [This area is part working-class, part bourgeois bohemian, and part shopping district, so it's a good idea to have it here], linking the commemorative plaque with a geography of urban hipsterism, gentrification, and consumerism ("Il y a plus de 250 ans"). As a symbol of an open-minded, cosmopolitan city, the monument enhances the centuries-old mythology of Paris as a city of sexual freedom and tolerance that today drives economic activity such as tourism.

The plaque also allows Paris to participate more effectively in the globalized economy where cities must adopt an entrepreneurial approach to fostering queer culture and commerce in order to attract the new global creative class that cultivates wealth. Roméro's plan included recommendations for commemorative policy such as naming streets and public spaces after LGBTIQ individuals, creating a historical archive, and building monuments, particularly to commemorate the LGBTIQ deportation during World War II. The report cites similar monuments in "Amsterdam, Berlin, Bologne, Montevideo, Nancy, San Francisco, Sydney ou Tel Aviv..." trailing off in an ellipsis that implied what Bell and Binnie term a "me-too-ism" that pushes cities to cultivate queer memory as part of an urban identity for courting capital, since "cities have to respond positively to gay culture in order to maintain their competitive edge" (1814). This commodification of queer *lieux de mémoire* recalls Aaron Betsky's observation that queer spaces have been consistently undercut "as their very power became useful for advertising, lifestyles, and the occupation of real estate" (17).

This instrumentalization of queer memory for commercial and political ends as well as the Lenoir–Diot plaque's multivocality and repositioning show that the monumental turn of queer *lieux de mémoire* does not necessarily participate in monumentality's "incessant, mindless drive to unification, sameness, and moralism" (Dunn 31). Future queer heritage initiatives will have to wrestle with these tendencies, and the Lenoir–Diot plaque usefully points to the complexity of representing sexuality and its multiple intersections in monumental form. Indeed, the plaque should push us to reconsider the notion of collective memory at the heart of Nora's *lieu de mémoire* not only as a question of the inclusion of the queer in the collective memory but also as a question of what a queer collective memory might be and who might be its guardian. In future commemorative projects, community involvement will become more important; inclusivity and diversity of representation will have to be addressed along with questions of sexual citizenship. Will "good" (coupledom and bourgeois values) or "bad" (anonymous sex and queer transgression) sexual citizenship be commemorated? How can commemoration go beyond a focus on queer necropolitics to focus on living citizenship? Whatever the shape of future monuments, the most successful will offer multiple points of access, room for continually re-shaping the past, calls for public action, and inspiration for living authentic, historically informed queer lives in the present.

Works Cited

Archives de la Bastille 11717.
Barbier, Edmond Jean François. *Chronique de la régence et du règne de Louis XV*, vol. 4. Paris, 1858.
Bell, David, and Jon Binnie. "Authenticating queer space: Citizenship, urbanism and governance." *Urban Studies*, vol. 41, no. 9, 2004, pp. 1807–20.
Betsky, Aaron. *Queer Space: Architecture and Same-Sex Desire*. William Morrow, 1997.
Brossat, Ian. "Affaire Diot-Lenoir: briser le silence, 250 ans plus tard." *L'Humanité*. January 10, 2014. Web.

———. "Vœu présenté par Ian Brossat, le Groupe Communiste et élus du Parti de Gauche relatif à un hommage de la Ville de Paris à Bruno Lenoir et Jean Diot." Conseil de Paris. 2011.

Certeau, Michel de. *The Practice of Everyday Life*. Translated by Steven Rendall. U of California P, 1984.

Courouve, Claude. "L'Affaire de Lenoir et Diot." *Connaissance Ouverte*. August 27, 2014. https://laconnaissanceouverteetsesennemis.blogspot.com/2014/08/laffaire-de-lenoir-et-diot-paris-1750.html.

Crompton, Louis. "The myth of lesbian impunity: Capital laws from 1270 to 1791." *Journal of Homosexuality*, vol. 6, no. 1–2, 1981, pp. 11–25.

Dunn, Thomas R. *Queerly Remembered: Rhetorics for Representing the GLBTQ Past*. U of South Carolina P, 2016.

Foucault, Michel. *The History of Sexuality*, vol. 1, *An Introduction*. Translated by Robert Hurley. Pantheon, 1978.

Freeman, Elizabeth. "Queer belongings: Kinship theory and queer theory." *A Companion to Lesbian, Gay, Bisexual, Transgender, and Queer Studies*, edited by George E. Haggerty and Molly McGarry. Blackwell, 2007, pp. 295–314.

Hammond, Nicholas. *The Powers of Sound and Song in Early Modern Paris*. Penn State UP, 2019.

Hidalgo, Anne. Inauguration of plaque honoring Bruno Lenoir et Jean Diot. *Facebook*. October 18, 2014. www.facebook.com/HidalgoAnne/photos/jinaugure-aujourdhui-la-plaque-honorant-la-mémoire-du-dernier-couple-exécuté-par/10152601302984597/.

"Il y a plus de 250 ans la dernière exécution d'un couple homosexuel à Paris." *Le Point*. October 18, 2014. Web.

Laronde, Michel. "17 October 1961." *Postcolonial Realms of Memory: Sites and Symbols in Modern France*, edited by Étienne Achille, Charles Forsdick, and Lydie Moudileno. Liverpool UP, 2020, pp. 109–18.

Mairie de Paris. Direction de l'Attractivité et de l'Emploi/Mission Partenariats et Tourisme. *Paris, ville phare de l'inclusion et de la diversité*. 2017.

Merrick, Jeffrey. *Sodomy in Eighteenth-Century France*. Cambridge Scholars Publishing, 2020.

Mills, Robert. "Queer is here? Lesbian, gay, bisexual and transgender histories and public culture." *History Workshop Journal*, vol. 62, no. 1, 2006, pp. 253–56.

Muñoz, José Esteban. *Cruising Utopia: The Then and There of Queer Futurity*. New York UP, 2009.

Nora, Pierre. "Between memory and history: *Les Lieux de mémoire*." Translated by Marc Roudebush. *Representations*, vol. 26, 1989, pp. 7–24.

———. "The era of commemoration." *Realms of Memory: The Construction of the French Past*, vol. 3, *Symbols*, edited by Pierre Nora and Lawrence D. Kritzman. Translated by Arthur Goldhammer. Columbia UP, 1998, pp. 609–37.

Orangias, Joseph, Jeannie Simms, and Sloane French. "The cultural functions and social potential of queer monuments: A preliminary inventory and analysis." *Journal of Homosexuality*, vol. 65, no. 5, 2018, pp. 705–26.

Puar, Jasbir K. *Terrorist Assemblages: Homonationalism in Queer Times.* Duke UP, 2007.

Wood, Nancy. *Vectors of Memory: Legacies of Trauma in Postwar Europe.* Berg, 1999.

CHAPTER THREE

The monument and the anti-monument
Aesthetic strategies for remembering two crises from French LGBTQ history

Scott Gunther

This chapter examines the aesthetic strategies behind the design of two new memorials in Paris: the first, from a group called *Les Oublié·e·s de la Mémoire*, will be dedicated to the remembrance of French homosexual deportees during World War II, and the second, *L'Artère, le jardin des dessins*, is a memorial designed by the artist Fabrice Hyber that commemorates the AIDS crisis in France from the early 1980s to the present. I have chosen to look at these projects specifically, because they provide two contrasting examples of how a marginalized group, in this case LGBTQ people, might attempt to shape historical memory: either through associating themselves with *lieux de mémoire* from which they have historically been dissociated (monuments commemorating deportations) or by dissociating themselves from *lieux de mémoire* from which they have been inextricably associated (monuments commemorating the AIDS crisis). The first memorial is still in the planning stages, and the second, which was inaugurated in 2006, remains a work in progress, with Hyber beginning a significant update of the memorial in spring 2021. Rather than analyzing the effects of *established* LGBTQ *lieux de mémoire*, this chapter focuses on the various considerations and strategies that have preceded the construction of two *new* and quite different LGBTQ *lieux de mémoire*. Looking at works in progress like these as opposed to more established monuments provides insight into the extent to which the designers see their mission of memorializing the past primarily as a means of engaging with the present. Analysis of interviews with the organizers and designers of these two projects and of written materials produced in the planning stages show how fundamental differences between the two crises they commemorate have translated into differences in design and aesthetic choices.[1]

What these two queer memorials share is an incongruence with Pierre Nora's conceptualization of *lieux de mémoire*. In recent years, Nora's work has been criticized primarily in two ways: first, for excluding the memories of marginalized individuals, particularly those memories linked to France's colonial past (Achille and Moudileno); and second, for presenting memory-making as a process that contributes to a single, homogenized identity within a community (Rotherberg). With regard to the first criticism, the project from *Les Oublié·e·s de la Mémoire* starts to rectify one of the gaps in the *lieux de mémoire* analyzed in Nora's work by bringing to light the largely unknown memory of a marginalized group. As for the second criticism, to the extent that it lends itself to multiple interpretations, Hyber's *L'Artère* defies the homogenizing effect that Nora's *lieux de mémoire* might have.

The long road from commemorating political deportees to commemorating homosexual deportees

French commemoration of the Deportation has been evolving from the end of World War II to the present, with the specificity of the experiences of different categories of deportees coming increasingly into focus, going from all deportees lumped into a single category of "political deportees," to the creation of a separate category of "martyrs," to the recognition of the particular situation of Jewish "victims," and, most recently, to the inclusion of "homosexual" deportees as a distinct category (Schlagdenhauffen 41). The first discussion of commemorations began even before the official end of World War II. As early as 1944, the *Fédération nationale des déportés et internés résistants et patriotes* (National Federation of Deported and Imprisoned Resistance Fighters and Patriots)[2] had begun making plans to preserve the memory of the deportation. The first memorials commemorated political deportees and

---

1   Except where noted otherwise, all translations are my own.
2   Its name was *Fédération nationale des centres d'entraide des déportés et internés politiques* from 1944 to 1945.

aimed to inscribe the remembrance of the deportation within a memory of patriotic combat and resistance (Schlagdenhauffen 39). The historian Annette Wieviorka explains that "the first ephemeral awareness of what happened to the deportees in Nazi concentration camps appeared in the form of a shock in April 1945 with the return of the deportees" (433), yet in the early postwar period, the fate of deported Jews was not understood in its specificity. Instead, the small number of Jewish survivors returning from Auschwitz were merely included within the category of "political deportees" (433). It was not until many years later that sites specifically dedicated to the memory of Jewish deportation were established, such as the Tomb of the Unknown Jewish Martyr in 1957 and annual remembrances of the deportation of Jews at the *Synagogue de la Victoire*, which began the same year. This reflected a shift in the conceptualization of some deportees from "patriotic *résistants*" to "martyrs," but intentionally steered clear of labelling deportees "victims" (Schlagdenhauffen 41). In 1964, the *Mémorial des martyrs de la Déportation*, constructed near Notre-Dame Cathedral on the Ile de la Cité and dedicated to the memory of French deportees, opted for the label "martyr" as well. It was to become the main site dedicated to the memory of French deportations, and although it made no distinction between political and Jewish deportees, presenting itself simply as a memorial for all French deportees, it would eventually become clear the inclusion of homosexual deportees was not part of what the memorial's creators had in mind.

One reason for the reluctance to include specific mention of the homosexual deportees is that there was an association between homosexuality and collaborators or Nazi sympathizers – in particular, insinuations that collaborators, including Robert Brasillach, Henry de Montherlant, and Drieu La Rochelle, were homosexual (Bertrand 168). Jean-Paul Sartre contributed to this association of collaboration with homosexuality in an article titled "Qu'est-ce qu'un collaborateur?" where he wrote that

> Insofar as one can imagine the collaborator's state of mind, one senses something like a climate of femininity. The collaborator speaks in terms of force, but he does not possess force ... It seems to me there is a strange mixture of masochism and homosexuality here. And Parisian homosexual circles provided many a brilliant recruit. (Sartre 60)

Sartre suggested that homosexuals were easily seduced by the virility of the military occupiers and their fascist ideology, with some even displaying their anti-Semitic hatred in newspapers controlled by Nazi propaganda (Le Bitoux 168). The notion that homosexuals were likely collaborators did not go away with the end of the war. Indeed, as Julian Jackson has pointed out, the association of homosexuality with fascism continued to resonate in Europe until at least the 1970s (56).

The first act of remembrance of the deportation of French homosexuals did not happen until April 1975, when the *Groupe de libération homosexuelle* brought flowers to the annual ceremony commemorating deportation that was held at the *Mémorial des martyrs de la déportation*. At the time, few people, including homosexuals, even knew that French homosexuals were among the deportees, and these first acts of remembrance met fierce resistance.[3] Following this first act of remembrance, the official association of French deportees asserted that their "bouquet tarnish[ed] the memory of millions of martyrs" (Grosjean). In following years, gay activists were regularly met with hostility. In 1985, about ten former deportees attacked six homosexuals in Besançon while shouting, "we should reopen the ovens for them" (Grosjean). In 1998, the mayor of Reims barricaded access to the memorial ceremony, and in Caen, Lille, and Lyon, activists wearing the pink triangle were denied entry (Grosjean).

The next key moment was in 1994, when Pierre Seel was at last able to publish his book with the assistance of gay activist and founder of the gay magazine *Gai Pied*, Jean Le Bitoux. Seel's memoire, *Moi, Pierre Seel, déporté homosexuel*, is an account of his own deportation as a French homosexual. Its publication did not lead to any immediate change in attitudes, however. That same year, gay activists planned to gather once again at the *Mémorial* to seek recognition. Pierre Eudes, the spokesperson for the official deportee associations, learned of their plans and responded, "we cannot tolerate any demonstration on your part or that of your peers at our patriotic events. Our security will oppose your intrusion with all its authority" (Schlagdenhauffen 41). Indeed, when the activists arrived, they were met by a line of police who blocked their way, and so beginning in 1995, each April there were two separate ceremonies: first, the official one, followed by an unofficial event to recognize the homosexual deportees. This hostility toward

---

3   One reason for the refusal to recognize the deportation of homosexuals is that all the French deportees were arrested while in the region of Alsace or the *département* of Moselle in the region of Lorraine, which had been annexed by Germany.

a recognition of homosexual deportees continued until April 2001, when prime minister Lionel Jospin, while presenting an homage to the French deportee and *résistant* Georges Morin, became the first French president to mention homosexuals as a category of deportees, opening the possibility for them at last to be recognized in the annual ceremony (Grosjean).

It is in this context of the first official recognition of French homosexual deportees that the idea for an association devoted to the memory of their deportation, *Les Oublié·e·s de la Mémoire* [the ones forgotten from memory], was conceived. Established in 2003, the primary purpose of the association was to raise awareness of the deportation of homosexuals and ensure that this history would never be forgotten. As indicated by the association's name, awareness remained quite limited in 2003 despite Jospin's official recognition two years prior. One of their first actions was to ask the city of Toulouse to recognize the memory of Pierre Seel, which the city did in 2008 by naming a street after him. Then, in 2010, they were successful in having Mulhouse, the city where Pierre Seel was arrested, create a memorial plaque for him (Figures 3.1 and 3.2). That

Figure 3.1 Toulouse plaque

Figure 3.2 Mulhouse plaque

same year, Olivier Ducastel and Jacques Martineau's film, *L'arbre et la forêt*, inspired by the life of Pierre Seel, came out in cinemas.

Finally, in 2014, as awareness of the deportation of homosexuals gradually increased, the association decided to begin plans for a more substantial monument dedicated to the memory of all French homosexual deportees (*Les Oublié·e·s de la Mémoire*). As David Kupina, president of *Les Oublié·e·s de la Mémoire* explained, they decided that the monument's message would be threefold:

> First, with respect to the past, as a reminder of the deportation and persecution of homosexuals after the war, because it continued afterwards; with respect to the present, as a recognition of the suffering that members of the LGBT community continue to endure; and, with respect to the future, as a pedagogical vision, teaching a new generation in respect and tolerance, it will also be a monument of hope. (Kupina)

It has taken more than 50 years for the history of the deportation of French homosexuals to be commemorated. This delay has had an influence on the kind of monument that the members of *Les Oublié·e·s de la Mémoire* envision, where the emphasis is on the monument's permanence. Several differences exist when comparing the commemoration of *Les Oublié·e·s de la Mémoire* and the commemoration of those who disappeared during the AIDS crisis. For one thing, the commemoration of the AIDS crisis has been happening for a much longer time, starting just a few years after the first cases of the disease were identified. Another difference for the two specific monuments discussed here is that a large number of individuals have been consulted for the deportation memorial, while the decision-making for the AIDS monument was almost entirely in the hands of a single artist. Although exploratory committees for both memorials began discussions in the early 2000s (2001 for the AIDS memorial, 2004 for the deportation memorial), it took just five years for the AIDS project to become a physical reality, while the discussions of the deportation memorial are ongoing and the public call for artistic proposals is yet to be made, so organizers estimate that it will be at least five years before the project is completed (Chaimbault). As we will see in the sections below, these two differences – the fact that the history of commemorating AIDS is longer than the history of commemorating the homosexual deportation, and that the artist in charge of the AIDS project basically had full control over what it would look like – led to imagining a very different style of monument in Fabrice Hyber's *L'Artère, le jardin des dessins*.

From the AIDS Memorial Quilt to *L'Artère, le jardin des dessins*

The first large-scale public commemoration of AIDS came in 1987 in the form of the Names Project AIDS Memorial Quilt in the United States, which recorded the names of those who had died from the disease. Similar projects in other countries followed, including in France, where the HIV/AIDS activist Jacques Hébert created, *le patchwork des noms*, in 1989. Then, in 1991, the National AIDS Memorial Grove, which also listed the names of the individuals who had died of AIDS, was established in San Francisco's Golden Gate Park (Brito). The character of more recent commemorations has been different, however. In their analysis of recent AIDS memorials, the queer writer Daniella Brito explains that:

> The most recent wave of AIDS memorials are diverging from these earlier attempts to tabulate and catalogue the deceased. Instead, they embody uncertainty and resistance within the pandemic's calamitous history and yet-to-be-determined future [...]. Decades later, still reeling from incomprehensible loss, our approach to commemoration today not only sets out to report our collective loss, but also leans into the unknown. (Brito)

One example of this new approach is the New York City's AIDS Memorial Park at St. Vincent's Triangle, created in 2016. The monument is inscribed with a text from the conceptual artist, Jenny Holzer, who explains that "the illness isn't beaten although treatment options are so much better. The disease persists as a threat to many, especially the most vulnerable. However, there is great joy in that much shame is gone and openness is relatively possible" ("Jenny Holzer Talks"). Its abstract form represents a departure from earlier, more explicit recognition of specific individuals who died from AIDS. A similar shift in the representation of HIV/AIDS has occurred in France, particularly in literature and cinema. This shift has coincided with medical advances both with drugs that mean that an HIV positive status is no longer a death sentence and with the availability of the pre-exposure prophylaxis PrEP that prevents infection in the first place.[4]

---

4 Daniel Maroun situates this shift historically as the period since 2005, when a new tendency in French literary representations of HIV/AIDS "positively reframes the disease, [as] still a chronic ailment but one that slowly distances itself from the macabre affliction it once represented" (183).

It is in this context of shifting representations of the virus that Hyber's project was inaugurated in 2006. The idea for a French monument to commemorate the history of AIDS began several years earlier, in 2001, when the president of *Sidaction*, Pierre Bergé, formed a committee comprised of himself, Line Renaud (vice president of *Sidaction*), and Jean-Jacques Aillagon (*L'Artère, le jardin des dessins: une œuvre de Fabrice Hyber* 16). They began by drawing up a call for artistic proposals for a project that would bear witness to the history of AIDS. The committee would evaluate proposals based not only on aesthetic grounds but also based on the memorial's ability to provide access to a large number of people in a frequently visited public space (*L'Artère, le jardin des dessins: une œuvre de Fabrice Hyber* 6). Four artists were selected as finalists, and, of those, Fabrice Hyber's project was the one that was ultimately selected (*L'Artère, le jardin des dessins: une œuvre de Fabrice Hyber* 6). His project involved the production and installation of tiles covering an outdoor space of 1,001 square meters in the Parc de la Villette in northeastern Paris. It took a total of four

Figure 3.3 *L'Artère, le jardin des dessins*: People dancing the tango on *L'Artère, le jardin des dessins*, Parc de la Villette, Paris, 2023 Photograph: author

years of work including one year of design, eight months of making the tiles, one year of landscaping, and finally one year of installing the tiles (*VIH – L'Artère*). In his proposal, Hyber emphasized the importance of not creating a monument to the dead, but instead, an open, informative, and even playful space. He explains that "from the beginning, it was clear to me that this was to be a place for people to gather. It's a place for walking for getting together. It's the very idea of an artwork that continues to reinvent itself in the present" (Hyber 35).

L'Artère is comprised of thousands of original drawings across 10,000 white tiles arranged in the shape of the red AIDS ribbon, with its knot untied to represent a future gradually freed from the past (Figure 3.3). Like much of Hyber's earlier work, many of the drawings in *L'Artère* present the human body as colorful masses of cells absorbing and processing information. Other slabs feature symbols, words, numbers, and shapes representing significant landmarks of the fight against AIDS.

As mentioned earlier, a single artist was essentially given *carte blanche* to design an AIDS monument while decisions for the deportation memorial have involved discussions among a large number of advisors. Limiting the number of decision-makers for *L'Artère* has been efficient, but is also likely responsible for some of the recent controversy surrounding the monument. Critics have highlighted several issues, including the memorial's lack of permanence, its location far from the center of Paris and the gay neighborhood of the Marais, and its lack of political messaging (Scheffer). However, not everyone agrees that a monument to the dead is what is called for, mostly since the fight against HIV is not over. "If we compare the monuments to the dead from the world wars, they were built only after the wars had ended," explains Florence Thune, general director of *Sidaction*.[5] For her, a memorial is something that settles the historical record for the long term, and that a memorial to AIDS victims would obscure the fact that people continue to die from it today. The primary disadvantage would be that it would contribute to putting the fight against HIV/AIDS into the history books once and for all, even though the struggle remains urgently current (Scheffer).

---

5 It would be overly simplistic to say that the war ended for deportees when they returned home. For example, for Pierre Seel, his children, and grandchildren, the effects of his deportation remain a part of the present. His wife divorced him when he was in his 50s and he found out shortly before his death in 2005 that his estranged family had removed his name from the family tomb (Nivelle).

Two very different kinds of commemoration

The differences in the styles of the two monuments outlined above stem from a few fundamental differences between the two crises they commemorate. The first difference is that the deportation is an event from the past, while HIV/AIDS is ongoing. For the historical event of the deportation, the primary goals have been both to keep memory of the event alive but also to keep it relevant by connecting it to current events, a recognition of Nora's claim that "memory is a perpetually actual phenomenon" ("Between Memory" 8). The goal for the commemoration of an ongoing event like HIV/AIDS, however, has had less to do with remembering the past than with offering hope for a post-HIV/AIDS future. It would be a mistake to interpret this as an attempt to erase history, or as a "site of oblivion," to use a term coined by the historian Guy Beiner. As a complement to Nora's *lieux de mémoire*, Beiner's *Forgetful Remembrance: Social Forgetting and Vernacular Historiography of a Rebellion in Ulster* offered a study of "sites of oblivion," that is, sites whose aim is to encourage collective forgetting of shameful events from the past (Beiner). It seems inappropriate to label *L'Artère* a site of oblivion, however, since Hyber's aim is not to obscure the past, but rather to begin to imagine and to celebrate what he believes will someday be our post-HIV future. In this way, his project is more in alignment with the theorists of queer futurity. Although Hyber does not explicitly draw this connection, his vision of a post-HIV world reflects the aesthetic of queer utopianism as articulated by queer futurists such as José Esteban Muñoz:

> The here and now is a prison house. We must [...] dream and enact new and better pleasures, other ways of being in the world, and ultimately new worlds. [...] Queerness is that thing that lets us feel that this world is not enough, that indeed something is missing. Often we can glimpse the worlds proposed and promised by queerness in the realm of the aesthetic. The aesthetic, especially the queer aesthetic, frequently contains blueprints and schemata of a forward-dawning futurity. (Muñoz 1)

A second difference is that the deportation was conducted by human beings, while HIV/AIDS came from nature. We know this to be true, even though many outside the scientific community have portrayed the transmission of the HIV more as a social plague and "as a calamity one brings on oneself" (Sontag 26). There are lessons to be learned from calamities brought about both by humans and by nature, though it is perhaps easier to be hopeful that a dangerous natural force in the form of a virus may one day be contained than it is to imagine the containment of dangerous forces lurking in our human nature. While it is possible to imagine an end to the spread of the stigma of being HIV positive in a post-AIDS world, the potential for social contagion of fascist thinking will always remain a threat, requiring constant vigilance through permanent commemoration in the present of the victims of Nazism.

The third difference is that *L'Artère* is about diminishing the association of a virus with being homosexual, while the other memorial is about bringing LGBTQ people into a history from which they have frequently been excluded. The deportation of other groups has eclipsed the memory of the deportation of homosexuals; while for HIV/AIDS, it is the opposite. Frequently thought of as a "gay disease," its non-gay victims are the ones who are often overlooked. Susan Sontag pointed this out in her 1989 book, *AIDS and Its Metaphors*, where she explained that despite the fact that HIV transmission may occur without homosexual sexual activity, most people – outside of sub-Saharan Africa – understand AIDS as a "disease not only of sexual excess but of [homosexual] perversity [and] that heterosexual transmission is extremely rare, and unlikely" (26).

These three differences have translated into several different responses to aesthetic choices. The first is the choice between permanence and ephemerality. While the memorial for deportees is about making sure that a frequently overlooked history is told and never forgotten, *L'Artère* expresses the hope that someday we will be in a post-AIDS era when the memorial will no longer be needed. In speaking of the deportation moment, Matthieu Chaimbault emphasized the need for permanence, explaining that "in terms of its form, what we can say now is that the monument's solidity and its durability are essential. We need something solid" (Chaimbault). Meanwhile, Hyber expects that over time *L'Artère*, whose painted tiles visitors can walk on, will gradually disappear due to the steady pedestrian traffic, one reason he labels it an "anti-monument." Hyber explains that "there is the idea that it can self-destruct. The more people walk on it, the more it will disappear, just as the virus will also wear itself out" (Hyber 29). The decision to commemorate HIV/AIDS with a monument that will eventually fade away has not been beyond reproach. The monument has been criticized for several reasons, with groups like *AIDES* and *Act Up-Paris* calling for the construction of a "real," that is, permanent, AIDS memorial. It is hardly surprising that these two groups, whose political militancy focused on increasing the visibility of HIV/AIDS, would oppose a monument designed to disappear. The LGTBQ magazine *Têtu* was also critical of the project, asking shortly after its construction, "Why does Paris still not have a veritable memorial for the victims of HIV/AIDS?" (Scheffer). The LGTBQ activist and *Têtu*'s first editor in chief, Didier Lestrade, commented that,

> In Paris, the worst possible option was achieved with *L'Artère, le jardin des dessin*s, the tiled court created by the artist Fabrice Hyber, which cost 1.75 million euros. After many months of delays, and costs that went far beyond the budget [...] when you go to the *Parc de la Villette* where it's located, you don't even realize that you're walking on [an AIDS monument]. (Lestrade)

Têtu's critical views of the monument are perhaps to be expected, given that Pierre Bergé, who provided financial backing for the magazine's creation, was also an active supporter of *Act Up-Paris*.

A second choice in the design of each monument has had to do with the extent to which the monument would present the crisis it commemorates as something that specifically affected gay men. In speaking about the deportation monument, David Kupina from *Les Oublié·e·s de la Mémoire* made it clear that the monument would serve to educate people about the deportation of French homosexuals specifically and the continued menace of homophobia today. However, for Hyber, after decades of commemorating the deaths of primarily gay men with projects such as the AIDS Memorial Quilt that often made a point of remembering individual victims, it was time for something different; something that made some reference to the past, yes, but that was primarily about our collective present and our future. This again echoes the aesthetics of queer futurists who view "queerness as a temporal arrangement in which the past is a field of possibility in which subjects can act in the present in the service of a new futurity" (Muñoz 16). Above all, Hyber aimed to create something aesthetically pleasing for everyone who visits. In his words, as opposed to a place for gays to connect with their history, it should be a place where "anyone can find something to identify with" (19).

The final aesthetic choice has to do with the general emotional atmosphere the monument is intended to evoke. Should it serve as a somber reminder of the lives lost or a message of hope for a brighter future? For David Kupina, the monument for the deportation should

The monument and the anti-monument 67

serve a pedagogical function, educating the public about a dark period in the history of French gay men, and be a solemn reminder of the struggles LGBTQ people continue to face today. Hyber's vision has been quite different. For Hyber, *L'Artère* is not a "monument in memory of AIDS victims," but rather a site that celebrates life. Not everyone has agreed with the idea of creating such a cheerful space, however. Jérôme Martin, president of *Act Up-Paris* from 2003 to 2005, argued that "A monument must have a political vision [...] we have always fought to increase the visibility of AIDS deaths. We made this the basis for our struggle; we wanted a monument that insists upon the State's responsibility for this epidemic. It needed to show that these deaths could have been avoided with a genuine health policy" (Scheffer). Although *L'Artère* is not entirely apolitical – indeed some drawings clearly commemorate the struggles and political engagement of the last four decades – Hyber has explained that a commemoration of political struggle was not his primary aim. He hoped to create a pleasant meeting place that would bring people together. To that end, the project includes a bench 40 feet long where people can "rest, reflect, converse, and [even] flirt" (Ministère de la Culture). He explains that he wanted it to be "a festive place" and is delighted to see that it has become a popular place for Parisians to have picnics (36). More than anything, he wanted it to be an attractive place, since, in his words, most "monuments related to AIDS are generally lacking aesthetically. Here, it's a giant ribbon, over there it's an inferior version of a Richard Serra sculpture on which we couldn't help ourselves from engraving a list of names [...]. The aesthetics of these monuments is hardly ever ambitious" (31).[6]

This chapter began by saying that it would consist of an analysis of two very different *lieux de mémoire*, but in the end that label is problematic for both projects. Pierre Nora defined a *lieu de mémoire* as "any significant entity, whether material or non-material in nature, which by dint of human will or the work of time has become a symbolic element of the memorial heritage of any community" (Nora, Preface xvii). For the commemoration of the deportation, a yet-to-be built monument cannot be qualified as having "become a symbolic element." Consequently, it would be more appropriate to see it as a *lieu de mémoire* to come (or at least that is what the organizers of the project are hoping for). Meanwhile, *L'Artère* intentionally eschews the

---

6   Richard Serra is a contemporary artist known for his monumental and extremely minimalist steel sculptures.

permanence that a "memorial heritage" would require and does not seek to address a single "community" but to be something for everyone; a more suitable label could come from Hyber's own qualification of it as an "anti-monument." In this way, it is not just a *lieu de mémoire*. In fact, it is quite intentionally an anti-*lieu de mémoire*.

Works cited

Achille, Étienne, and Lydie Moudileno. *Mythologies postcoloniales: pour une décolonisation du quotidien*. Honoré Champion, 2018.

Beiner, Guy. *Forgetful Remembrance: Social Forgetting and Vernacular Historiography of a Rebellion in Ulster*. Oxford UP, 2018.

Bertrand, Mickaël. "Mickaël Bertrand, 'Homocauste: un passé qui ne passe plus' in Boulligny." *Les homosexuel·le·s en France. Du bûcher aux camps de la mort: histoire et mémoire d'une répression*, edited by Arnaud Boulligny. Éditions Tirésias – Michel Reynaud, 2018, pp. 159–70.

Brito, Daniella. "How a new generation of AIDS memorials is shedding light on the epidemic." *Them*. October 15, 2021. Web.

Chaimbault, Matthieu. Interview with author. February 11, 2022.

Ducastel, Olivier, and Jacques Martineau. *L'arbre et la forêt*. Feature Film. Les Films du Lendemain and Maïa Cinéma, 2010.

Grosjean, Blandine. "Les homosexuels déportés reconnus." *Libération.fr*. April 27, 2001. Web.

Hyber, Fabrice. *L'Artère, le jardin des dessins*. Cécile Defaut, 2009.

Jackson, Julian. "Homosexuality, collaboration, and resistance in occupied France." *Contemporary French Civilization*, vol. 31, no. 2, 2007, pp. 53–81.

"Jenny Holzer talks about her NYC AIDS." *Phaidon.com*. November 21, 2017. Web.

Kupina, David. Interview with author. February 11, 2022.

L'Artère, le jardin des dessins: une œuvre de Fabrice Hyber. Parc de la Villette, December 1, 2006. www.cite-sciences.fr/fileadmin/fileadmin_CSI/fichiers/au-programme/lieux-ressources/cite-de-la-sante/_documents/Au_programme/Artere_Sida_Fabrice_Hyber.pdf.

Le Bitoux, Jean. *Les Oubliés de la mémoire*. Hachette, 2002.

Les oublié-e-s de la mémoire. *Projet pour l'édification d'un monument LGBT en France*. December 2014.

Lestrade, Didier. "Nommer des rues en hommage à des personnalités LGBT+, un petit geste qui veut dire beaucoup." *Slate.fr*. June 25, 2019. Web.

Maroun, Daniel. "Forty years of HIV/AIDS narratives: What's next?" *Contemporary French Civilization*, vol. 46, no 2, 2021, pp. 179–96.

Ministère de la Culture. *Fabrice Hyber, L'Artère 2021 – Le jardin des dessins à la Villette*. May 19, 2021. www.culture.gouv.fr/Regions/Drac-Ile-de-France/DRAC-INFOS/Fabrice-Hyber-L-Artere-2021-Le-jardin-des-dessins-a-La-Villette.
"Mulhouse plaque" (image). *Wikipedia.org*. Web.
Muñoz, José Esteban. *Cruising Utopia: The Then and There of Queer Futurity*. New York UP, 2009.
Nivelle, Pascale. "Pierre Seel, 78 ans. Sa gay pride." *Libération.fr*. December 8, 2001. Web.
Nora, Pierre. "Between memory and history: *Les Lieux de mémoire*." Translated by Marc Roudebush. *Representations*, vol. 26, 1989, pp. 7–24.
———. "Preface to the English Language Edition." *Realms of Memory: Rethinking the French Past*, vol. 1, *Conflicts and Divisions*, edited by Pierre Nora and Lawrence D. Kritzman. Translated by Arthur Goldhammer. Columbia UP, 1996, pp. xv–xxiv.
Rothberg, Michael. "Introduction: Between memory and memory. From *Lieux de mémoire* to *Nœuds de mémoire*." *Yale French Studies*, vol. 118/19, 2010, pp. 3–12.
Sartre, Jean-Paul. *The Aftermath of War (Situations III)*. Translated by Chris Turner. Seagull Books, 2008.
Scheffer, Nicolas. "Pourquoi Paris n'a toujours pas de véritable mémorial pour les victimes du VIH/sida?" *Têtu.com*. April 21, 2021. Web.
Schlagdenhauffen, Régis. "De l'oubli à la commémoration des victimes homosexuelles de la Déportation en France." *Revue des sciences sociales*, vol. 44, 2010, pp. 38–45. https://halshs.archives-ouvertes.fr/hal-01290446/.
Seel, Pierre. *Moi, Pierre Seel, déporté homosexuel*. Calmann-Lévy, 1994.
Sontag, Susan. *AIDS and Its Metaphors*. Farrar, Straus, and Giroux, 1989.
"Toulouse plaque" (image). *Wikipedia.org*. Web.
VIH – L'Artère, le jardin des dessins, dénouer le nœud du sida | Transversa: VIH & sida aujourd'hui. Transversalmag.fr. Web.
Wieviorka, Annette. *Déportation et génocide: entre la mémoire et l'oubli*. Plon, 1992.

CHAPTER FOUR

Queer experiences in Parisian *collèges* between 1869 and 1873

Michael Rosenfeld and Clive Thomson

Introduction

Pierre Nora's *Lieux de mémoire* (1986) contains several studies that focus on topics related to French educational institutions, such as Daniel Milo's chapter on *"Les classiques scolaires."* In his valuable analysis of the academic curricula followed by students in the *lycée* and *collège* systems from the seventeenth to the twentieth centuries, Milo shows how and why the canon of literary texts underwent significant shifts. He also points out in passing that many other aspects of the French school system remain to be studied, such as what he refers to as *"les coulisses du système scolaire"* [behind the scenes in the school system] (521). Denis Provencher and Luke Eilderts take a step in the direction suggested by Milo with their more recent article on representations of masculinity and male citizenship in Ernest Lavisse's *Histoire de France* (1884). Their article uncovers the implicit heteronormative (i.e., canonical) narrative strategies in the Lavisse text that were directed at schoolboys and a wider male readership. In our chapter, we propose to venture into uncharted territory by studying a site of queer remembering from the nineteenth century – the *"collège"* – that was neglected by Pierre Nora and his colleagues and one that has received little consideration from other researchers.

In their introduction to this current volume, Bouamer, Provencher, and

Schroth point out that little attention has been given to the "affective" elements in the queer archive and that, in general, much more archival research needs to be done in order to make this kind of queer experience visible. One of our aims is to give visibility to the young queer men whose letters we examine and who write extensively about their fears, disappointments, and frustrations, but also about happy and playful aspects of their romantic involvements. We hope, therefore, to offset a certain popular image of the "unhappy queer archive" (to quote Sara Ahmed, referenced in the editors' introduction) and to show that such is "not the only queer archive."

Our focus is on a corpus of letters exchanged by a group of queer schoolboys – Paul Bourget, Adrien Juvigny, Georges Hérelle, Maurice Bouchor, and Félix Bourget – who attended the *Collège Sainte-Barbe*, the *Lycée Louis-le-Grand*, and the *École des Carmes* in Paris at the end of the Second Empire and during the first years of the Third Republic.[1] We use the term "queer" in our chapter to cover the non-heteronormative sexual and amorous activities that the correspondents in our corpus of letters describe. During the four years between 1869 and 1873, Hérelle, Bouchor, Juvigny, and the Bourget brothers exchanged a total of nearly 300 letters in which they discussed literary, philosophical, and political topics, as well as their intense feelings about each other and their schoolmates.[2] In 1873, several events alter the dynamics of this group of friends. Adrien Juvigny dies in early September 1873 and Georges Hérelle moves back to Paris at the end of September 1873 for two years (Thomson 59). As of 1874, there is a significant decrease in exchanges of letters between Hérelle and the Bourget brothers. The letters are held in the *Fonds Georges Hérelle* at the *Médiathèque Jacques Chirac*

---

1 All three institutions can be considered important *"lieux de mémoire,"* each with its own illustrious and fabled history. Note on terminology: we use the untranslated French terms *"collège"* and *"lycée"* throughout our chapter in reference to the pre-university educational institutions attended by French students aged 12 to 18 years. *"Collège"* and *"lycée"* are thus approximately equivalent to "middle school" and "high school" as used in the Anglo-American system.

2 The corpus of texts studied in our chapter is constituted by letters exchanged by novelist Paul Bourget (1852–1935), his brother Félix (1856–95), historian and translator Georges Hérelle (1848–1935), poet Adrien Juvigny (1849–73), and poet Maurice Bouchor (1855–1929). The page numbers refer to our edition of these letters (Bouchor et al.). Our transcriptions are an exact copy of what appears in the original manuscripts (except for the use of italics for French in this chapter) and all translations are our own.

Troyes Champagne Métropole, the *Fonds Robert de Montesquiou* at the *Bibliothèque Nationale de France*, and the *Fonds Paul Bourget – Le Plantier de Costebelle*.

In the 1870s, the French educational system was undergoing a period of fundamental renewal. Leon Sachs has described the decline in the Church's control over education and the emergence of the "école républicaine," with its ideology of "republican universalism" (37). Although there were important differences between the old and the new educational regimes, they shared one important feature – a visceral intolerance and hostility regarding sexual relations among boys attending the *collèges* and a belief that those in charge had a responsibility to detect, punish, and root out all such activities.

The letters in our corpus provide a rare glimpse into the struggles experienced by young queer students at a time when the ambient discourses in medical treatises and in publications by representatives of the Church were entering a new more aggressive phase with efforts to alert parents and their children to the dangers of daily life in schools. For example, the article on "Masturbation" in Pierre Larousse's *Grand dictionnaire universel du XIXe siècle* (1873) contains the following warning about how students can become "corrupted" while attending school:

> We have to admit, moral corruption is common, notwithstanding supervision, and children do not even blush at the excesses they admit without shame to one another and to which they encourage one another. It is no doubt one of the major disadvantages of public education, which is however mitigated by some very important advantages. (1320)

By mid-nineteenth century, representatives of the Church were already mounting an opposition to the creation of public *collèges*. Félix Dupanloup, who studied at *Sainte-Barbe* and was appointed bishop of Orléans in 1849, was a leader of the campaign to maintain the Church's dominant position in schools. Dupanloup's fervent ally, the *abbé* Adolphe Masson, rings the alarm bells in his moral guide for Catholic education, *Le Miroir des collèges ou les vices effrayants de l'éducation universitaire* (1847), with the following statement: "*il arrive dans les collèges des enfants qui n'ont pas la moindre idée du vice, et qui, mêlés et confondus avec des élèves plus âgés et souvent corrompus, finissent par perdre leur vertu*" [children arrive in the collèges without having the slightest understanding of what vice is and when they come into contact with older students who are often corrupt they end up losing their virtue] (360–61). As we will see below, echoes of several terms in the Church's moralizing discourse on the risks of life in the *collèges* can be heard in the letters of our corpus.

The schoolboys' stories of love, seduction, suffering, and trauma

In their letters, the adolescents use a variety of discursive strategies to discuss sexuality that include positive expressions of queer desire and of resistance to contemporary society's condemnation of same-sex love. These strategies reveal that such sexual activity was not just a literary or scientific trope, used to signal the dangers of close friendships between schoolboys, but also that it was a common occurrence. The letters examined here show how such love brought joy to some, but also the very real suffering and trauma inflicted on young queer students: some of the young men mentioned are brutally shamed by fellow students or teachers, others are expelled from school after being caught engaging in sexual acts, and one of them is arrested when his search for lovers leads him to frequent a group of criminals that he meets at the *Galerie d'Orléans*.[3]

Paul Bourget and Adrien Juvigny exchange ideas in their letters about *"amitiés de collège"* (their code expression for amorous relations among schoolboys) and discuss in detail plans to write poetry and prose works that include references to such relations. They tell each other anecdotes about sexual activity in *collèges*, some of which they claim to have witnessed. Even though they sometimes condemn these *"débauches"* (295), they are fascinated by and jealous of the sexual freedom their classmates exhibit. Paul Bourget states that handsome boys are the ones most likely to be debauched and declares that they swiftly go from "handshaking" to "caresses" and "kisses," which then leads to "delights of the flesh." In a letter of July 6, 1872, he gives Juvigny examples of boys he knew at *Sainte-Barbe* who "fell into vice" and "sold themselves for 20 or 100 francs, for a cake or for a ring," and reports the use among some boys of feminine names such as "Lolette, Virginie, Maria, Madeleine" (295–96). Juvigny confirms in his reply, dated around July 10, 1870, his awareness that *Sainte-Barbe*'s "moral" reputation is terrible and he gives the example of a friend who fell gravely ill because of such

---

3 The *Galerie d'Orléans* is near the *Palais-Royal* in Paris and was a well-known queer cruising site during the nineteenth century (Sibalis 19).

depravity (297–301). He also assures Bourget that such behavior is less common at the *Lycée Louis-le-Grand* where he studied before joining the *École des Carmes*. According to Juvigny, "ardent love" between boys is common at the seminary, but it rarely leads to "delights of the flesh." He ends this letter by claiming that at the *École des Carmes*, where he has been studying for the previous two years, boys who love one another are mercilessly mocked and persecuted by other students. Bourget's reaction in his letter of July 11–13, 1870, is to provide even more details on how *Sainte-Barbe* has become a *"lupanar"* [brothel] (302). He cites an example of a 12-year-old who died of *"débauches"* the year before, an event that leads the school to expel ten of the boy's *"accomplices."*[4] Nearly a year later, on March 17, 1871, Bourget relates another incident, which he claims to have witnessed: "the *Sainte-Barbe* infirmary is a real brothel, young and older students are in the same dormitory and, I regret to say, even the same bed. Manuel D. *literally* slept with a sophomore for eight nights, I saw it myself" (497). In a subsequent letter to Juvigny, from August 1871, Bourget reveals that his friend Gaston Créhange used to go to the baths in the summer to observe the "nude supple and young body of Carlos" [de Quadra] (a fellow student from *Sainte-Barbe*) (604). In the same letter, Bourget emphasizes Créhange's queerness by citing, following his telling of the anecdote about the baths, the names of two Classical philosophers well known for their contributions on Greek love: "O Plato, O Socrates."

While recounting these episodes of queer love, Bourget and Juvigny express in sensual and erotic terms their intense physical attraction for their schoolmates. They write frequently about their yearnings for the pleasures of physical intimacy while at the same time claiming to adhere to the ideal of a pure and chaste love. Paul Bourget's conflicted homoerotic desires and rather unsuccessful efforts to self-censor can be seen when he writes a sonnet using expressions such as "feverish love," "sucking rose lips," "unsatisfied voluptuousness," and "perfumed kisses" that are exchanged by two male characters (286). Fragments of this poem have survived because Juvigny translated into Latin those verses that resonated with him and sent them to Bourget on July 2, 1870. He provides more context about the sonnet and emphasizes it was written by one man for another. Juvigny also refers to queer love in his writings, as evidenced by Bourget's comment on March 17, 1871, that his

---

4   We were unable to find any mention of the death of a student at *Sainte-Barbe* in the press of 1868 and 1869 and are therefore unable to confirm Bourget's story.

use of the word "*pédéraste*" (497) is well chosen in a chapter of Juvigny's lost poetic novel *Paulin Braconnier*. In addition, the models they identify in their letters as inspiration for their writings refer to relationships between famous queer figures from Antiquity or from other historical periods: for example, Antinoüs and Hadrian, Leonardo da Vinci and his lover Salaï, Lord Byron and his lovers, John Eddlestone, Robert Peel, and Nicolo Giraud.

Juvigny uses eroticizing language to describe the bodies of teenage boys he admires. For example, in a letter from November 22, 1870, he describes a moment when he stands in line behind Albert Frézard (another *Carmes* student), so that he can "*m'enivrer des divines blancheurs de son cou*" [inebriate myself with the sublime whiteness of his neck] (408). Bourget goes even further: in a love-poem dedicated to Maurice Bouchor, he writes that he did not dare to reveal his desire for him.[5] He admits wanting to kiss him, but he feared ruining their "*chaste amour*" with such an act. It is also revealing that when Paul Bourget eventually falls out of love with Maurice Bouchor, the latter then reacts by trying to convince him of his undying love in several letters dated April 7–11, 1870: "How I love you, my dear friend, how I love you. [...] love me as much as I love you, and perhaps you will be happy" (239–42). In the second letter of this series, Bouchor confesses to having masturbated, which could be interpreted as the sublimation of his sexual desire for Bourget (241). In a final but ultimately futile attempt to reignite his lover's affection, Maurice Bouchor writes to Bourget on May 18, 1870: "I offer everything I have, heart and intelligence, my entire being, without any restriction, you can do with me whatever you wish, I love you with all of my being" (268). This letter could be read as an expression of Bouchor's desire to enter into a sexual relation with Bourget. We do not know if any sexual activity took place between Bouchor and Bourget; it is, however, interesting to note that when Bourget speaks later on of his love for 14-year-old Thérèse Maquet – the sister of the schoolboy Paul tutors at that time in Trouville – in a letter to Georges Hérelle on October 7–8, 1872, he compares this relationship to his love for Maurice Bouchor in 1869 and 1870, which he claims was a "true passion" (695–96). In a subsequent letter to Hérelle on January 4–8, 1873, Bourget describes in sensual terms his desire for Thérèse, stating that she is a virgin and that he has had the "experience of nearly all kinds of debauchery" (748). He

---

5 Paul Bourget sends this poem to Maurice Bouchor on January 10, 1870 (206) and copies it to Georges Hérelle on March 16, 1870 (222–23).

also regrets, in a letter from July 5–12, 1873, that when he "*could have embraced Maurice, he did not love him anymore*" and that when he will be able to "embrace and possess" Thérèse, he fears he might no longer love her (785–86). Our analysis of the letters exchanged by Bourget and Bouchor allows us to conclude that their feelings for one another were intensely passionate, erotic, and queer.

In discussing queer love in their letters, Paul Bourget and Georges Hérelle use a different set of narratives, no doubt because Hérelle had already admitted his queerness to his closest friend during the summer of 1869. It is not clear whether he revealed at the time to Bourget that he had been totally infatuated with him, but he does discuss these feelings openly in a letter of October 29, 1872 (719–21). What is clear is that Bourget was fully aware of Hérelle's queerness because he tries to convince him in a series of letters, written at the end of 1869 and the beginning of 1870, to abandon these feelings. On March 21, 1870, Bourget argues that they can lead to "*sodomie*," of which he adamantly disapproves (225). After several heated exchanges of opinion, Bourget admits, however, that such love is legitimate and he then candidly discusses Hérelle's queerness and that of some of their friends. When Hérelle writes to Bourget in a letter of April 15–26, 1870, that he is in love with Emmanuel Gasquet (254–55), Bourget encourages him, in his reply on April 27, 1870, to "love him like you never loved anyone else, live a soft life of tenderness and intimate confidences" (256).

A revealing moment related to Bourget's recognition of Hérelle's queerness is documented in another letter of 1872. During the summer vacations of 1870 and 1871, and perhaps in 1872 as well, Hérelle tutors Charles Henry des Tureaux (1857–1932). When Charles's mother writes to Hérelle in March or April of 1872 to inform him that her son had been expelled from *Sainte-Barbe*, Hérelle writes frantic letters to Paul and Félix Bourget to ask for more information. The letter that Paul Bourget sends him with the details of the expulsion has been lost, but Hérelle's reply in May or June 1872 reveals that Charles and a fellow student had been caught together. Hérélle adds that he feels responsible for not having stepped in to warn and protect his young charge because on an earlier occasion he had known Charles was in love with one of his schoolmates (669–73). He asks Bourget to tell him the name and age of Charles's boyfriend and to send him as many details as he can about the affair. On June 29, 1872, Bourget replies with crucial information about the incident received from a classmate of Charles Henry des Tureaux: Charles spent a night in bed with another boy and a few days later this affair is discovered when their teacher confiscates a note that Charles was attempting secretly to pass during class to his boyfriend and in which Charles mentions their night together (678). The teacher first promises not to reveal the boys' secret, on condition that Charles invent a pretext that would allow him to leave the school honorably, but the teacher breaks his promise and informs the school director, who immediately expels the young man.

Hérelle's reaction to this new information in a letter of July 4–14, 1872, is revealing: he does not pass judgment on Charles's queerness and even expresses his opinion that such a relationship could be beneficial to his young friend, adding his doubts that Charles would ever admit to his parents that he had slept with another boy (681–82). He shares with Bourget his surprise at the parents' decision following Charles's banishment from *Sainte-Barbe*: they enroll their son in another Parisian boarding school where he will risk getting into the same trouble again. On Hérelle's part, this is not just an altruistic concern for the young man's well-being; he admits to Bourget that he had fallen in love with Charles, a situation which he and Bourget discuss in subsequent letters. It is particularly noteworthy that Bourget approves Hérelle's love for Charles in a letter from October 7–8, 1872, and even encourages him to write a psychological novel about the whole affair (694–95).[6] There is, however, still a disagreement between them: Bourget expresses the opinion that Charles had been corrupted much earlier because of his masturbatory practices and he questions Hérelle's reasoning that Charles was "innocent" before being tainted at *Sainte-Barbe*. When Hérelle reveals that Charles had "normal genital organs" as proof that he had not masturbated earlier, Bourget is still not convinced.[7] Bourget then tries to console Hérelle (who feels betrayed by Charles) by suggesting that he find someone else to love. He goes on to confess that he is in love with Thérèse Maquet.

Paul Bourget's opinion of Hérelle's amorous feelings for Emmanuel Gasquet and Henry des Tureaux is complex. On one hand, we have seen that he occasionally approves of such feelings explicitly and he appears

---

6   Although Hérelle and Bourget continue to discuss plans for this book project until February 1873, we did not find a manuscript or any detailed notes in the *Fonds Hérelle*.

7   The letters from Hérelle in which these details were provided have been lost; it is our hypothesis that Hérelle is at the Henry des Tureaux family castle in the summer of 1872 to tutor Charles.

to consider – in a theoretical way – that Hérelle's queer relationships are analogous to his relationship with Thérèse Maquet. He also appears to consider that his feelings for Thérèse Maquet are similar to those he had felt previously for Maurice Bouchor over a six-month period in 1869 and 1870. On the other hand, Bourget does condemn some queer behaviors that he considers to be excessive, promiscuous, and harmful. In a letter to Hérelle from June 29, 1872, he criticizes Amédée Gasquet, whose masturbatory habits have left an "indelible mark" on him and which might be the cause leading to his "adventures" with the chaplain of Clermont-Ferrand and with older boys in school (679). He also harshly disparages their friend Auguste Gérard, whose physical traits changed because of his sexual activity. According to Bourget in a letter from the end of March 1873, Auguste slept with one of his pupils during the school vacation: "*cet élève était Permage, la putain de tout Sainte-Barbe*" [this student was Permage, the whore of all *Sainte-Barbe*] (772).

The discursive strategies used by Paul Bourget and Adrien Juvigny to describe their queer desires are diverse; using their fictional writings as a pretext, they gossip about queerness in their respective *collèges* and express their own feelings for some of their classmates. When he is in love with Maurice Bouchor, Paul Bourget expresses his desire for him in physical terms and compares his amorous feelings for the young man to love for girls. In addition, Bourget comes to accept Georges Hérelle's queerness and encourages him to love as he wishes. The various discussions of love between schoolboys by the different correspondents indicate how common queer relations were in *collèges* at the time.

The "*Affaire Touzard*"

Our final topic is the Touzard affair, which starts in February 1873: Alfred-Auguste Touzard finished *collège* in 1866 at the age of 16, obtained his "*licence*" when he was 21, was named a "*professeur de rhétorique*" in a *collège* at the age of 22, and was clearly destined for a brilliant teaching career.[8] He was also Hérelle's former classmate at

---

8 Georges Hérelle kept a file with the title "*L'Affaire Gélinier-Touzard: 1873*," which contains numerous newspaper clippings about the affair (*Fonds Hérelle*, MS 3404). He also included a detailed description of the scandal in his (unpublished) manuscript of *Nouvelles études sur l'amour grec* (*Fonds Hérelle*, MS 3188, t. III, fos. 439–440).

Sainte-Barbe and his colleague at the *collège* in Dijon from December 1869 to June 1870. Hérelle mentions him in letters to his mother, but we do not know how well acquainted they were.[9] Touzard's queerness and his involvement with students at the *collèges* where he taught resulted in his being dismissed from one school after another, until he ends up in Paris as a low-level clerk at the Ministry of Finance. He becomes romantically involved with 17-year-old apprentice jeweler, Eugène Renault, whom he met at the *Galerie d'Orléans*. Renault is a member of the "black cap knights," a gang of young queer criminals, and Touzard is arrested with them around mid-February 1873. Although a fuller account of this fascinating tale of queer life is warranted, we limit our analysis to the moment when Touzard is arrested, as it is discussed by Hérelle and the Bourget brothers.[10]

Paul Bourget first informs Hérelle that Touzard has been arrested on February 15, 1873, and hints at the queer nature of the relationship between him and one of the gang members (759–60). Hérelle's reply to Paul has been lost but he does mention Touzard in two letters to Félix Bourget, who is 17 years old at the time and in the process of discovering his own queerness.[11] In the first letter, from March 17, 1873, Hérelle gives his opinion of the various classmates in whom Félix expresses an interest, some of whom he remembers from his own time at *Sainte-Barbe* (768–69). Hérelle legitimizes his positive opinion of queer love by mentioning several texts from Antiquity: a homoerotic poem by Anacreon about Bathyllus and Plato's *Banquet* in which the story of the love between Socrates and Alcibiades is told. He also compares one of Félix's schoolmates to Antinoüs. He then explains that contemporary society is less tolerant of such love than in ancient times and cites as

---

9 We did not find any letters or other documents related to the Touzard affair in the *Fonds Hérelle*.

10 Even though his involvement with the gang's crimes of robbery, break-ins, and blackmail was minor – Touzard fenced a few of the stolen items – he is harshly criticized during his trial by the judge who denounces him as a danger to schoolboys and condemns him to 15 years of forced labor in a penal colony (*La Presse*, August 27, 1873, 2–3). Our recent archival discoveries reveal that this sentence was commuted in January 1874 to ten years in prison, and then further reduced in 1879. Touzard lived in Paris after his release from prison in 1880, he married in 1882 and died on April 12, 1893. We analyze this affair in the introduction to the correspondence (Bouchor et al. 49–58).

11 Félix's letters to Hérelle from this period have been lost, as well as one of Hérelle's letters to Félix, a draft of which is in the *Fonds Hérelle*.

examples two men marginalized by their queerness: Vautrin in Balzac's novels and Auguste Touzard. His advice to Félix is to love as freely as possible *"au collège,"* and he urges his young friend to hide his queerness as an adult.

Hérelle discusses queer love in a very direct manner in his next letter to Félix from April 1–6, 1873, of which only a draft has been preserved.[12] He requests that Félix destroy the letter after reading it (775–79), thus emphasizing his desire that the letter remain strictly confidential (this also explains why the final version of the letter is not in the archives). Hérelle starts by admitting to his young friend that he was in love with several of his classmates when he studied at *Sainte-Barbe*, including Paul Bourget, and he also expresses his approval of some of Félix's love interests. He then discusses Touzard's lover "L. B." (whom we have been unable to identify), using this story as a cautionary tale. According to Hérelle, L. B. was "debauched" early on by Touzard, whom he described as currently "imprisoned at *Mazas* prison for theft and murder, but actually because of his peder."[13] Hérelle goes on to give an account of their relationship: Touzard was fired as a teacher at *Sainte-Barbe* after he was caught in a sexual act with L. B., but they continued seeing each other and L. B. became Touzard's *"enculé"* [passive sexual partner]. The use of this word is significant because it is the only occurrence in the correspondence of a slang term referring to queer sexuality. According to Hérelle, Touzard became involved with the band of criminals after he started drinking and searching for lovers in the *Galerie d'Orléans* (yet another mention of this well-known site of queer memory in Paris where men from the margins of society congregated). Hérelle's appraisal of the challenges facing queer adult men is clear, as he advises Félix to be discreet and to be prepared to make compromises. This explains why he concludes his letter by urging Félix to enjoy the relative freedom of *"amours de collège"* for as long as they last.

Conclusion

The aim of our chapter has been to provide a glimpse of how a particular group of queer schoolboys lived, loved, and survived at a pivotal moment

---

12 This draft letter is very elaborate and contains few crossed-out words; it is thus probably a second draft of the letter.
13 Hérelle does not write the word *"pédérastie"* [pederasty] in full.

in the history of the French educational system. The stories they tell in their letters are consistent with those that appear, albeit rarely, in other texts of the same period. It is not at all surprising that the letters exchanged by Georges Hérelle, Maurice Bouchor, the Bourget brothers, and Adrien Juvigny express, as we have shown, conflicting opinions, doubts, and anxieties related to the topic of what they euphemistically called "*amours de collège.*" Daily life in the *collèges* was indeed characterized by immense suffering for the young men because of the suffocatingly repressive atmosphere created by teachers and administrators. What is perhaps surprising is the way in which the students' creativity and resistance flourished: we see their resistance on those occasions when they condemned the injustices inflicted on their fellow queer students. We witness, in more joyful moments, a considerable resilience when they recounted their experiences of falling in love or when they expressed, in tender and affectionate terms, appreciation for support from their friends. A more complete study of the letters in our corpus would focus on the correspondents' inventiveness as they search for new ways to name and express their feelings of attraction for each other at a time when terms like homosexual, invert, and queer had not yet been invented. Other projects for future researchers interested in schools as queer "*lieux de mémoire*" in the nineteenth century are possible. One such project would be to search, in public and private archives both in France and its former colonies, for new correspondences and other types of first-person narratives written by queer men and women during their "*collège*" years. Uncovering the history of same-sex desire during the formative years of these persons will undoubtedly deepen our understanding of their queerness at later stages in their lives and of the societies in which they lived.

Works cited

Achille, Étienne, Charles Forsdick, and Lydie Moudileno. "Introduction." *Postcolonial Realms of Memory: Sites and Symbols in Modern France*, edited by Étienne Achille, Charles Forsdick, and Lydie Moudileno. Liverpool UP, 2020, pp. 1–19.

Bouchor, Maurice, Félix Bourget, Paul Bourget, Georges Hérelle, and Adrien Juvigny. *Correspondance croisée 1869–1873*, edited by Michael Rosenfeld and Clive Thomson. Classiques Garnier, 2024.

"Le Monde judiciaire. Cour d'assises de la Seine." *La Presse*. August 27, 1873, pp. 2–3.

Masson, Adolphe. *Le Miroir des collèges ou les vices effrayants de l'éducation universitaire, sous le triple rapport du physique, de l'intelligence et du moral*. Jacques Lecoffre et Compagnie, 1847.

"Masturbation." *Grand dictionnaire universel du XIXe siècle*, edited by Pierre Larousse, vol. X, 1873, pp. 1320–22.

Milo, Daniel. "Les classiques scolaires." *Les Lieux de mémoire*, edited by Pierre Nora, vol. 2, *La Nation*, book 3, *Les Lieux*. Gallimard, 1986, pp. 517–62.

Nora, Pierre. "Between memory and history: *Les Lieux de mémoire*." Translated by Marc Roudebush. *Representations*, vol. 26, 1989, pp. 7–24.

Provencher, Denis M., and Luke L. Eilderts. "The nation according to Lavisse: Teaching masculinity and male citizenship in Third-Republic France." *French Cultural Studies*, no. 18, vol. 1, 2007, pp. 31–57.

Sachs, Leon. "L'École républicaine." *Postcolonial Realms of Memory: Sites and Symbols in Modern France*, edited by Étienne Achille, Charles Forsdick, and Lydie Moudileno. Liverpool UP, 2020, pp. 34–43.

Sibalis, Michael. "Paris." *Queer Sites: Gay Urban Histories since 1600*, edited by David Higgs. Routledge, 1999, pp. 10–37.

Thomson, Clive. *Georges Hérelle. Archéologue de l'inversion sexuelle "fin de siècle."* Éditions du Félin, 2014.

CHAPTER FIVE

Archiving queer France
Constructing a community at the intersection of history and memory

Andrew Israel Ross[1]

The exclusion of LGBTQI existence from "the archive" – in both its literal and metaphorical guises – is now a longstanding area of concern amongst theorists, activists, and historians interested in understanding and documenting the queer past (Cvetkovich; Danbolt; Rawson, "Archive This!"; Edenheim). Skepticism regarding the ability of "traditional," "scholarly," or "public" archives, as they are variously called, to reveal the past of groups that state forces have oppressed is well founded. As Sam Bourcier, one of the leaders of the Collectif archives LGBTQI (henceforth the Collective), a group founded in 2017 that is trying to establish an LGBTQI community archive in Paris, argued in an interview with *Le Monde*: "Les Archives nationales nous disent, 'Pourquoi vous voulez votre centre d'archives? Elles sont chez nous!' Oui, ils ont la police, psychiatrie" [The national archives tell us 'Why do you want your own archival center? They are here!' Yes, they have the police, psychiatry] (V. Faure).[2] The provenance of state archives – whether national, municipal, or institutional – can never lead to a

---

[1] I would like to thank Tamara Chaplin, Hannah Frydman, as well as the editors of *Queer Realms of Memory*, for their insightful comments as I developed this chapter.

[2] Unless otherwise noted in the bibliography, all translations are my own.

complete understanding of the queer past because the documents and records they contain are the remnants of oppressive institutions.

In response, community archives dedicated to the preservation of the queer past have opened around the world. Reacting to a "désir d'archives" [archival desire], as Bourcier put it, archives such as the ONE National Gay and Lesbian Archives in California and the ArQuives in Toronto engage more directly with the desires and needs of the communities they seek to document than traditional archives dedicated to a fictive objectivity (Cook 97; on these archives specifically, see Sheffield). Complementing these institutions, a range of scholars have theorized new ways for archives to capture and preserve queer life (Marshall, Murphy, and Tortorici; Gérardin-Laverge, Guaresi, and Abbou). These activists, archivists, and scholars have asked how one might construct an archive that, in the words of Joan Nestle describing the origins of the Lesbian Herstory Archive in New York City, showcases an "appreciation for the shamed and the derided, for the defiant and the lustful" (236). An archive, in other words, not focused on or from the viewpoint of the powerful forces that, among other acts, enforced this shaming, but on those people who resisted them. Such archives put into practice Ann Cvetkovich's influential call to create "a radical archive of emotion in order to document intimacy, sexuality, love, and activism – all areas of experience that are difficult to chronicle through the materials of the traditional archive" (241).

The quest to link archival inclusion to historical existence and hence to present-day memory would be familiar to readers of Pierre Nora's *Les Lieux de mémoire*. "Modern memory," Nora declares, "is first of all archival. It relies entirely on the specificity of the trace, the materiality of the vestige, the concreteness of the recording, the visibility of the image" (8). Nora argues that because modern society has lost the ability to remember organically, we require evidence in order to constantly remind us of our past and heritage. The importance of the archive in this process has, according to Nora, made it inevitable for oppressed groups to seek their own historical traces there: "Those who used to be left out of the official histories are not the only ones obsessed with recovering their buried pasts. Practically every organized social group [...] has followed the lead of the ethnic minorities in seeking their own roots and identities" (10). The archive thus becomes a key institution of modern identity, the repository of an effort not simply to remember for the sake of remembering, but to remember for the sake of ensuring one's (or one's group's) very existence, especially vis-à-vis the national patrimony.

Such might be considered the goal of activists in Paris calling for opening an LGBTQI archive in the French capital. Building on a decades-long effort, this demand reached a new audience with the January 8, 2021 publication in the newspaper *Libération* of an open letter from the Collective and signed by 45 museums, centers, and archives in France and from around the world. In the letter, the Collective called for the creation of an independent archive in Paris for LGBTQI cultures. This goal was necessary, first, to ensure the creation of a center dedicated to countering the "exclusion" of LGBTQI life from "les institutions traditionnelles" [traditional institutions] and second, to ensure that this archive serves the interest of the LGBTQI community itself, which knows best how to "identifier les qualités indispensables à leur succès" [identify the qualities necessary to their success] (Collectif archives, "Comment Paris"). In February 2021, the Collective achieved an important milestone, with the Conseil de Paris unanimously approving the creation of an independent LGBTQI archive, managed by the Collective. However, the Collective continued to face obstacles from the city government (Collectif archives, "Comment Jean-Luc Roméro-Michel"). It is currently seeking additional monies through crowdfunding, fundraising events, and the support of governmental and other agencies to support the creation of a permanent archive in the 19th *arrondissement* of Paris (Collectif archives, "Rapport d'activité 2022" 32–33). At the time of this writing, at the end of 2023, the Collective had signed a lease for their space at 149 rue de l'Ourcq and hopes to open in 2025 (Collectif archives, "Rapport d'activité 2023" 5–8).

The open letter can be figured as one instantiation of the queer archive as *lieu de mémoire* in modern France. As such, it reflects the project dismissively described by Nora when he claimed that "certain minorities create protected enclaves as preserves of memory to be jealously safeguarded" against the "sweep" of an all-encompassing history (7). Nora recognizes the link between archiving and identity construction, but his is a notably static interpretation. "Certain minorities" seek out history in the archive in order to ensure their survival, but the process of becoming an identity or community in the first place remains absent. Seeking as it does to "créer une mémoire publique LGBTQI" [create a public LGBTQ memory], the Collective tries not only to preserve a common heritage, but to create one (Collectif archives, "Comment Paris"). It thus presents a much more nuanced vision than that of Nora. While same-sex sexual desire and gender identities outside the binary have always existed, LGBTQI identities themselves are of relatively recent provenance. The process of archiving brings LGBTQI people together to make their own past, present, and future. As the Collective declares in a 2023 call to action,

> [I]l est nécessaire de former et partager nos savoirs pour ne plus nous contenter des traditionnelles archives de la Police, de la Justice et de la Médecine: ne plus être objets d'études et de recherches, mais sujets de notre histoire et de nos mémoires. (Collectif archives, "Tou-te-s à l'assemblée générale des archives LGBTQI+!")

> [It is necessary to give shape to and share our knowledge so that we no longer content ourselves with traditional archives of the Police, of the Judiciary, and of Medicine: to no longer be the objects of study and research, but the subjects of our [own] history and memory.]

These activists and scholars like Nora do share one assumption: the history to be found in traditional archives will not necessarily serve queer purposes today. Such a history will instead be created in new institutions. State archives, however, do contain queer history. They contain records that reveal intense same-sex relationships, gender identities outside the binary, and efforts to create queer communities. Often, these ephemera were shaped by institutions that sought to repress them. And yet, they remain. Their relationship to these institutions, alongside their unfamiliarity or difference from the present, may mean that they cannot serve as a queer realm of memory for present LGBTQI people. But they may, nevertheless, serve to construct a queer realm of history. One way the archive might make "queer experiences more visible," as this volume seeks to do, may indeed be by recognizing that the limitations of the traditional archive remain part of our history too. Rather than reject the traditional archive, we might lean into it in dialog with emerging queer community archives in order to more fully engage with the way it might reveal something queer about the past.

The relationship between queer history and memory might be best understood through the three approaches to the history of sexuality laid out in Laura Doan's *Disturbing Practices* (2013). The first, "ancestral genealogy," seeks to recover the existence of LGBTQI people in the past. The second, "queer genealogy," looks to history in order to understand the construction of those identities. The third, "queer critical history [...] construct[s] the historical meanings of sex and sexuality [...] not by tracing back modern sexual identities with a knowingness of what these identities mean to us now but by acknowledging at the outset the unknowability and indeterminacy of the sexual past" (61). While the traditional archive often fails to fulfill the first goal and only helps accomplish the second through the lens of the powerful, it might illuminate a great deal about queer critical history. Insofar as the ephemera of queer life that remains in those institutions is always, in some sense, accidental, they provide us with a window into an otherwise unknowable past.

Without referring to Doan, Ruby Faure has encapsulated how these three approaches might relate to archival work: if the ancestral approach seeks to recover LGBT life out of silence, the queer genealogical approach reads the archive "à rebours *(against the grain)*" (5) in order to reckon with the ways the archives were shaped by the operations of power. A critical method, on the other hand, reads the archive "suivant le grain *(along the grain)*" (8), allowing the researcher to attempt to reckon with the past's fundamental difference from the present. Queer archives respond to the difficulties in accomplishing the first two tasks by seeking to serve queer memory as they collect, catalogue, and ensure the preservation of queer life in both the past and the present. Traditional archives complement this work by revealing a queer history that we cannot know in advance.

The archive is most fully addressed by Krzysztof Pomian, who traces the development of French state archives since the French Revolution in the final volume of *Les Lieux de mémoire* (published in English in the fourth volume of *Rethinking France* [2010]). According to Pomian, throughout their existence, these institutions have served both history and memory, a tension that has become more important as they increasingly collect private archives as well as official documents (80–81). The distinction between history and memory is reinscribed by the research process itself. Pomian asserts that the documents contained in the archive serve history when the researcher "distanc[es themselves] from their authors, by regarding them from the outside, by integrating them in a larger ensemble of which they are a part" (36). This material serves memory when its reader "identifies him or herself with the individual who secreted the archives, when he or she appropriates the latter's point of view, interests, judgments, or even emotions" (36). Through these two axes – the collection of documents and the reading of documents – Pomian constructs a dichotomy that equates public history with objectivity and private memory with subjectivity.

The ways historians and other scholars use archives belies such a dichotomy (see, for instance, Farge 15; Burton 9; Steedman, esp. chap. 4), but this conception of the archives poses challenges for community archives dedicated to the preservation of memory, especially those of marginalized groups in France. Indeed, this dichotomy parallels recent debates over first the *Pacte civil de solidarité* (*PaCS*) and then marriage equality, as opponents of LGBTQI inclusion warned that such demands reflected American-style "communitarianism" and were therefore contrary to French Republican "universalism" (Johnston; Robcis 451–53; Perreau 145; Gunther 141–42). Indeed, according to Bourcier, one reason Paris did not open an LGBTQ history center earlier was due to then mayor Bertrand Delanoë's "fear [...] of communitarianism" (Cassell). The creation of an LGBTQI archive controlled by the community itself is suspicious to these critics – even gay critics like Delanoë – because it could never serve history, only memory.

This difficulty has not been the only challenge to the project of creating a queer archive in Paris, of course. Another is the very definition of the community such a project might serve. The precise relationship between the Collective and already existing archives and historical centers remains contentious. In 1983, a collective of lesbian feminists founded the Archives, Recherches, Cultures Lesbiennes (ARCL) ("Histoire de l'association"). Beginning in the late 1980s, Hoàng Phan Bigotte and his partner Thomas Leduc began collecting materials related to LGBT history; they now hold one of the largest collections in the country under the banner of the Académie Gaie et Lesbienne (V. Faure). In the first decade of the 2000s, Jean le Bitoux, one of the founders of the important magazine *Gai Pied*, and Louis-Georges Tin, one of the most significance gay rights and anti-racist activists in French academia, each tried to found a center as well (Collectif archives, "Historique"). Conflict between the Académie, the ARCL, and the Collective is one reason the Paris Municipal Council has failed to release the promised funds for the new archive in 2022 (Collectif archives, "Comment Jean-Luc Roméro-Michel"; V. Faure). As of August 2023, neither the Académie nor the ARCL is participating in the Collective's project (Lorriaux).

These tensions within the community speak to the seriousness with which we should take the Collective's declared desire to "create a public memory." The constitution of a LGBTQI archive does as much to create the community being documented as it does to recover and memorialize that group (Rawson, "The Rhetorical Power" 332; Caswell 6). Indeed, while the Collective seeks to bring together those archives already collected by the ARCL and the Académie into a single physical space if not into a single archive, it is precisely that project that might most concern those two organizations. The ARCL for instance, was founded in response to the exclusion of lesbians from both feminist and homosexual spaces ("Histoire de l'association"). Whose memory, exactly, will be served by a community that is always in the process of forming and re-forming? What choices will be made as the community archive seeks new material? Does the constitution of a lesbian, gay, bisexual, transgender, queer, and intersex archive risk diluting the specificity of each category as it constructs a community memory?

The traditional archive may not hold answers to these questions, but it does provide one more avenue toward locating a capacious history of these sexual communities. All archives, after all, are "constituted by exclusion" (Danbolt 93) and it is as much how we use archives as what those archives contain that will enable us to create a queer past (Idier 11). As Anjali Arondekar encourages, we might "break[] with such moribund conventions" as lost archives and instead "summon[] more abundant and joyful lineages of possibility and freedom" (22) in what remains. Indeed, the queer potential of state archives has recently received newfound appreciation. Researchers have published material drawn from police and other judicial archives in both French and English, directed at both scholarly and general audiences (Houbre; Willemin; Féray; Merrick, *Sodomites, Pederasts, and Tribades*). Others have recovered new understandings of queer life through the discovery of documents once thought lost (*The Italian Invert*; R. Faure). This is not to discount the ways these archives shape historical understanding through exclusion. My own research in police archives, as well as the French National Archives and the Archives de Paris, for instance, came up with little (though not nothing) on nineteenth-century lesbian history. And yet, such exclusions might owe as much to the researcher as it does the archive itself. Tamara Chaplin's recent book on the history of lesbianism in twentieth-century France (*Becoming Lesbian*) relies, in part, on archives we thought were not there. And Hannah Frydman has shown how lesbians used the mass press to make themselves known to others. Their absence in state archives is not only an effect of archival policing (Maynard) but is also an effect of strategic modes of visibility and invisibility used by lesbians themselves (Frydman 35–36). Just as recent work on the relationship between the police and men who sought sex with other men has emphasized a more subtle relationship between the two groups than one of simple repression and exclusion (Jaouen; Ross, "The Queer Gaze"), so too might we need a more nuanced understanding of how state and traditional archives construct the queer past.

The histories recovered and recoverable in traditional archives may not serve either the purpose of memory as defined by queer activists in the present nor of history as defined by Nora and Pomian, but they do serve queer history. In his *Sins against Nature*, for instance, Zeb Tortorici describes his encounters with colonial archives of New Spain. Following Antoinette Burton's notion of "the archive [...] as a contact zone 'between past and present,'" Tortorici opens his method to the unexpected (7). His first chapter engages with how a visceral response to the archive may reveal how fundamentally different our own reactions to the documents may have been from those who collected them in institutions. Attention to viscerality, Tortorici argues, may help explain why an archivist sanitized a catalog entry on necrophilia in an archival database, as well as Tortorici's own fascination with the file. In doing so, he draws our attention to the "surprising points of connection (and disjuncture) between the past and the present, between the ways that historical actors and we ourselves may (or may not) share certain responses in the face of a particular image or event" (32). The disjuncture between what we hope to find in the archives and what we do find might provide a framework for using public archives to locate a queer past, even if it may or may not serve to construct a common memory today.

Wrestling with the link between what we desire of the archives and what they might or might not do to fulfill that desire provides an entry point to new understandings of the queer past, in France and elsewhere. Fortunately, this work is ongoing. For example, ever since Michel Rey published his groundbreaking essays on male same-sex sexual activity in eighteenth-century Paris, historians of the period have debated his two interlocking central claims: that over the course of the eighteenth century, French authorities came to understand sodomy in terms of social disorder, rather than sin, and second, that men who sought sex with other men began to construct an identity for themselves that bound them together into a community (Rey, "Police et sodomie"; Rey, "Parisian Homosexuals"). These claims provide one link between contemporary queer identities and those of the past, as Rey argued that the twin forces of secularization and identification rendered men who sought sex with other men into a recognizable subculture.

Rey rested his analysis largely on records of the morals police from the Archives de la Bastille that were available to him in the 1980s. More recently, Jeffrey Merrick has begun excavating the relevant records in a more general series contained there, notably the prisoners series (from which the morals series was drawn), the records of the *commissaires*, and the Paris watch ("New Sources and Questions"). Merrick's conclusions are much more tentative than Rey's. The broader set of documents fail to provide insight into "the mindset of the men arrested by the police" even as they continue to indicate the existence of a queer male subculture in eighteenth-century Paris (Merrick, "New Sources and Questions" 24–25). Merrick, along with several collaborators, is currently leaning into the archival impulse and is in the process of producing a digital archive of these records (Ragan) and has recently published a selection of these documents, in English, as *Sodomites, Pederasts, and Tribades in Eighteenth-Century France* (2019). Merrick's reticence to precisely pinpoint the feelings and thoughts of these men – a reticence wholly appropriate to the documents we have available to us – showcases the challenges of interpreting these materials. While, in reading of the arrests of men cruising for other men, we cannot help but see connections between ourselves and these figures from the past, the documents themselves refuse to answer what is, perhaps, for some, an equally important question: would these men from the past recognize us? That we cannot know is precisely where the critical queer potential of these archives lies.

In my own research on the sexual subcultures of nineteenth-century Paris, I argue that men who sought sex with other men might have seen themselves as much as part of a prostitutional milieu as a homosexual one (Ross, "Sex in the Archives"). By reading police archives through their very structure, I witnessed the emergence of connections I had not expected between men who sought sex with other men and female sex workers who also sought sex with men in public. The traditional archive thus does indeed contain queer history, but that history might not reveal the connections we expect. In my case, I wonder about how a connection between men who sought sex with other men and female sex workers in the past might give way to a queer politics that emphasizes similar connections in the present. The history we might find in the traditional archives therefore is not the history of Pierre Nora, who declared that "history belongs to everyone and to no one and therefore has a universal vocation" (Nora 9). Rather, we might find a queer critical history that belongs to queer people, but in ways that either cut across or support the effort to construct a common history amongst LGBTQI individuals.

The current impasse facing the Collectif archives LGBTQI speaks to the continued importance of their endeavor and the ways some aspects of French politics remain mired in the same debates as they were decades ago. Even as we must continue to support institutions with the explicit goal of shoring up the political capital of the LGBTQI community, especially in a moment of rising right-wing, anti-queer politics, however, we should not neglect the rich sources contained elsewhere that might show new ways of building connections. These institutions do indeed rest on historical exclusions. But such exclusion can only ever be partial and, indeed, constitutes our heritage as well. Engaging more directly with this fact may enable activists to engage more fully with one another, across the different identities constituted by the acronym LGBTQI and beyond. Even more, we should not be afraid of a past that does not immediately serve the present. One that might not reflect the memory we seek. Or even the history we desire. Rather, that we might nonetheless find connections with unfamiliar and sometimes repressed histories speaks to the power of the queer critique. Even across time, we remain enchanted by our common difference.

Works cited

Arondekar, Anjali. *Abundance: Sexuality's History*. Duke UP, 2023.

Burton, Antoinette. "Introduction: Archive Fever, Archive Stories." *Archive Stories: Facts, Fictions, and the Writing of History*, edited by Antoinette Burton. Duke UP, 2005, pp. 1–24.

Cassell, Heather. "Out in the world: French LGBTQ preservationists push back against government." *Bay Area Reporter*. January 13, 2021.

Caswell, Michelle, Alda Allina Migoni, Noah Geraci, and Marika Cifor. "'To be able to imagine otherwise': Community archives and the importance of representation." *Archives and Records*, vol. 38, no. 1, 2017, pp. 5–26.

Chaplin, Tamara. *Becoming Lesbian: A Queer History of Modern France*. U of Chicago P, 2024.

Collectif archives LGBTQI. "Comment Jean-Luc Roméro-Michel, Alice Coffin et Anne Hidalgo bloquent le projet de centre d'archives LGBTQI+. On fact-check les mensonges?" *https://web.archive.org/web/20220814131528/ https:/archiveslgbtqi.fr/wp-content/uploads/2022/03/CP_Fact_ Checking_29_03_2022-1.pdf*. March 29, 2022. Web.

———. "Comment Paris peut soutenir la préservation de l'histoire et de la culture LGBTQI." *Libération*. January 8, 2021.

———. "Historique." *Archiveslgbtqi.fr*. Web.

———. "Rapport d'activité 2022." *https://web.archive.org/web/ 20230720193630/http://archiveslgbtqi.fr/wp-content/uploads/2023/07/ Rapport-dactivite-2022-optimise.pdf*, 2023. Web.

———. "Rapport d'activité 2023." *Archiveslgbtqi.fr* 2024. Web. [Currently unavailable online].

———. "Tou-te-s à l'assemblée générale des archives LGBTQI+!" old. *archiveslgbtqi.fr* January 21, 2023. Web.

Cook, Terry. "Evidence, memory, identity, and community: Four shifting archival paradigms." *Archival Science*, vol. 13, no. 2, 2013, pp. 95–120.

Cvetkovich, Ann. *An Archive of Feelings: Trauma, Sexuality, and Lesbian Public Cultures*. Duke UP, 2003.

Danbolt, Mathias. "We're Here! We're Queer? Activist Archives and Archival Activism." *lambda nordica*, vol. 15, nos. 3–4, 2010, pp. 90–118.

Doan, Laura. *Disturbing Practices: History, Sexuality, and Women's Experience of Modern War*. U of Chicago P, 2013.

Edenheim, Sara. "Lost and never found: The queer archive of feelings and its historical propriety." *differences*, vol. 24, no. 3, 2014, pp. 36–62.

Farge, Arlette. *The Allure of the Archives*. Translated by Thomas Scott-Railton. Yale UP, 2013.

Faure, Ruby. "Tordre les archives (*queering archives*): Oui, mais dans quel sens?" *GLAD! Revue sur le langage, le genre, les sexualités*, vol. 11, 2021. https://journals.openedition.org/glad/3255.

Faure, Valentine. "Les Gardiens de la mémoire LGBT." *Le Monde*. May 7, 2022. Web.

Féray, Jean-Claude, ed. *"Pédés": Le premier registre infamant de la préfecture de police de Paris aux XIXe siècle suivi d'un dictionnaire des noms propres et noms communs les plus significatifs du registre, et d'annexes*. Quintes-feuilles, 2012.

Frydman, Hannah. "Reading Incognito: Periodicals, Sapphic Fictions, and Lesbian Communication." *Dix-Neuf*, vol. 26, no. 1, 2022, pp. 35–55.

Gérardin-Laverge, Mona, Magali Guaresi, and Julie Abbou, eds. "Archives, genre, sexualités, discours." *GLAD! Revue sur le langage, le genre, les sexualités*, vol. 11, 2021. Web.

Gunther, Scott. "Making sense of the anti-same-sex-marriage movement in France." *French Politics, Culture & Society*, vol. 37, no. 2, 2019, pp. 131–58.

"Histoire de l'association." *Archives, Recherches, Cultures Lesbiennes*, Arcl.fr. Web.

Houbre, Gabrielle, ed. *Le Livre des courtisanes: archives secrètes de la police des mœurs (1861–1876)*. Tallandier, 2006.

Idier, Antoine. "Introduction: Absences, silences et politique de l'histoire." In *Archives des mouvements LGBT+: une histoire de luttes de 1890 à nos jours*, edited by Antoine Idier. Textuel, 2018, pp. 6–14.

The Italian Invert: A Gay Man's Intimate Confessions to Émile Zola. Translated by Nancy Erber and William A. Peniston, edited by Michael Rosenfeld with William A. Peniston. Columbia UP, 2022.

Jaouen, Romain. *L'inspecteur et "l'inverti": la police face aux sexualités masculines à Paris, 1919–1940*. Presses universitaires de Rennes, 2018.

Johnston, Cristina. "(Post-)queer citizenship in contemporary Republican France." *Contemporary French and Francophone Studies*, vol. 12, no. 1, 2008, pp. 89–97.

Lorriaux, Aude. "Paris: le future centre d'archives LGBTQI+ plombé par des querelles intestines?" *20minutes.fr*. August 2, 2023. Web.

Marshall, Daniel, Kevin P. Murphy, and Zeb Tortorici, eds. "Queering archives: Historical unravellings." *Radical History Review*, vol. 2014, no. 120, 2014.

———. eds. "Queering archives: Intimate tracings." *Radical History Review*, vol. 2015, no. 122, 2015.

Maynard, Steven. "Police/archives." *Archivaria*, no. 68, 2009, pp. 159–82.

Merrick, Jeffrey. "New sources and questions for research on sexual relations between men in eighteenth-century France." *Gender and History*, vol. 30, no. 1, 2018, pp. 9–29.

———. ed. *Sodomites, Pederasts, and Tribades in Eighteenth-Century France: A Documentary History*. Penn State Press, 2019.

Nestle, Joan. "Who were we to do such a thing? Grassroots necessities, grassroots dreaming: The LHA in its early years." *Radical History Review*, vol. 2015, no. 122, 2015, pp. 233–42.

Nora, Pierre. "General introduction: Between memory and history." *Realms of Memory: Rethinking the French Past*, vol. 1, *Conflicts and Divisions*, edited by Pierre Nora and Lawrence D. Kritzman. Translated by Arthur Goldhammer. Columbia UP, 1996, pp. 1–20.

———. ed. *Les Lieux de mémoire*, 3 vols. Gallimard, 1984–92.

Perreau, Bruno. *Queer Theory: The French Response*. Stanford UP, 2016.

Pomian, Krzysztof. "The archives: From the *Trésor des Chartes* to the Caran." Translated by Christine Haynes. *Rethinking France: Les Lieux de mémoire*, edited by Pierre Nora and David P. Jordan, vol. 4. U of Chicago P, 2010, pp. 27–99.

Ragan, Tip, Jennifer Golightly, Jeffrey Merrick, Benjamin Bernard, Eric Albrand, and Michael Sorensen. "Policing homosexuality: 18th-century Paris." https://sites.coloradocollege.edu/dlaatcc/projects/policing-homosexuality/.

Rawson, K.J. "Archive this! Queering the archive." *Practicing Research in Writing Studies: Reflexive and Ethically Responsible Research*, edited by Katrina M. Powell and Pamela Takayoshi. Hampton Press, 2012, pp. 237–50.

———. "The rhetorical power of archival description: Classifying images of gender transgression." *Rhetoric Society Quarterly*, vol. 48, no. 4, 2018, pp. 327–51.

Rey, Michel. "Parisian homosexuals create a lifestyle, 1700–1750: The police archives." *Eighteenth-Century Life*, vol. 9, no. 3, 1985, pp. 179–91.

———. "Police et sodomie à Paris au XVIIIe siècle: du péché au désordre." *Revue d'histoire moderne et contemporaine*, vol. 29, no. 1, 1982, pp. 113–24.

Robcis, Camille. "Liberté, égalité, hétérosexualité: Race and reproduction in the French gay marriage debates." *Constellations*, vol. 22, no. 3, 2015, pp. 447–61.

Ross, Andrew Israel. "The queer gaze in Haussmann's Paris, 1850–1900." *Histories of French Sexuality: From the Enlightenment to the Present*, edited by Nina Kushner and Andrew Israel Ross. Nebraska UP, 2023, pp. 133–59.

———. "Sex in the archives: Homosexuality, prostitution, and the Archives de la préfecture de police de Paris." *French Historical Studies*, vol. 40, no. 2, 2017, pp. 267–90.

Sheffield, Rebecka Taves. *Documenting Rebellions: A Study of Four Lesbian and Gay Archives in Queer Times*. Litwin Books, 2020.

Steedman, Carolyn. *Dust: The Archive and Cultural History*. Rutgers UP, 2002.

Tortorici, Zeb. *Sins against Nature: Sex and Archives in Colonial New Spain*. Duke UP, 2018.

Willemin, Véronique. *La mondaine: histoire et archives de la police des mœurs*. Éditions Hoëbeke, 2009.

II

Centers and Peripheries

CHAPTER SIX

Paris, erotic capital of the nineteenth century

The *tournée des grands-ducs* and the emergence of queer *lieux de mémoire* during the Third Republic

Leslie Choquette

During the Third Republic, queer urban spaces gained prominence in journalism, literature, and art, as Paris became not just the cultural but the erotic center of the Western world (Kalifa, *Paris*).[1] Depictions of this queer Paris are often sensational and distorted by outrage, but, without them, the scattered traces of queer life in fiscal, judicial, and even police archives would be hard if not impossible to find. While presented as contemporary knowledge, descriptions of queer sites had a long afterlife, as authors continued to reminisce about past establishments, even ephemeral ones, transforming them into veritable *lieux de mémoire*.

1 We take for granted that Paris is the "city of love," but the late historian Dominique Kalifa showed in his erotic history of Paris that this representation has a history. Exploring the city's reputation as the capital of sexual pleasure, Kalifa focused on the century from 1860 to 1960, with the *Belle Époque* as its epicenter. Patrice Higonnet likewise traced the origin of this myth of Paris to the 1860s, pointing to Alfred Delvau's *Les plaisirs de Paris*, a guidebook commissioned for the 1867 World's Fair (Higonnet 291). The even more extravagant World's Fairs of 1889 and 1900, quintessential celebrations of the Third Republic, further cemented the association of Paris with love and lust.

Yet their remembrance was transient, as the French national narrative has largely excluded queerness.[2] Building upon several decades of new scholarship (Choquette; "Écrire l'histoire des homosexualités"; Hahn; Higgs; Merrick and Ragan; Merrick and Sibalis; Peniston; Revenin; Tamagne), this essay aims to counter queer erasure by placing period representations, including a few by queer authors, into conversation with archival production, allowing us to excavate and reclaim what are now forgotten realms of queer Parisian memory.

What enabled queer seeing and remembering during the Third Republic was a peculiar conception of what constituted erotic fun in bourgeois society. Exemplified in what became known in the 1890s as *la tournée des grands-ducs*, it was a voyeuristic spree whose primary ingredients were social and sexual otherness and transgression, preferably in combination. The *tournée* owed its name to the visit of Tsar Nicholas II and his entourage to Paris in September 1896, but it first took shape in the years after the Commune when the *flâneur*, often a policeman, put his specialized knowledge of the Parisian lower depths to commercial use. As a literal or literary tour guide, he escorted the *badaud*, the wide-eyed bourgeois or upper-class onlooker, through scenes of class and sexual danger designed both to shock and titillate.

Why did bourgeois and aristocrats take pleasure in visiting ill-reputed establishments frequented by working-class marginals, especially criminals, sex workers, and queers? Journalist and man of letters Hugues Le Roux explained part of the attraction thus in 1889:

> These joys ... make them dream despite themselves of civil war and barricades, and strike into their bone marrow that thrill you feel before the cages of wild beasts, when you think that the gate could open and the lion, claws outstretched, could hurl himself upon the spectators ... But this obscure, indefinable anguish is itself sweet, and certainly this apprehension is half the pleasure that many pretty women feel in coming

---

2 Pierre Nora's inclusion of Antoine Compagnon's brilliant essay, "Marcel Proust's Remembrance of Things Past," in the second volume of *Realms of Memory* is the exception that proves the rule. Asking "How in the world did a Jewish homosexual and snob become the uncontested paradigm of the great French writer?" (234), Compagnon shows that the novel became "the quintessential *lieu de mémoire* of French literature" (214), largely despite Sodom and Gomorrah, although growing interest in various forms of marginality has enhanced Proust's reputation and appeal (234).

amidst the crowd to rub against the rather rough elbows of the common people. (Le Roux, *Les jeux du cirque* 28)[3]

Additionally, an omnipresent feature of the *tournée des grands-ducs* was the incessant slippage between class and sexual transgression. As Adrien Rifkin observed, "So each sex is classed as classes are sexed, and class and sex often stand in for each other in relations of power and desire" (118). This game of substitution helps explain the role of homosexuality, male and female, as a leitmotiv of the *tournée* (Choquette, "Degenerate or degendered?"), which therefore offered queer people an opportunity to articulate and memorialize their own urban experience.

By 1900, the slumming industry had spawned an actual service of tour guides and interpreters (neither bourgeois Frenchmen nor grand dukes could be expected to speak *argot*), the *Cicérones parisiens* on *rue Laferrière*.[4] Catering exclusively to out-of-towners, the city's grand hotels provided similar guide services. This essay uses the tourist itinerary of the literal and literary *tournée* as a guide to entertainment venues that became queer *lieux de mémoire* in Paris during the Third Republic. Focusing on but not confined to Montmartre, it reveals a rich panorama of queer spaces within the commercialized mass culture juggernaut that was Gay Paree.

A typical *tournée* would begin with an early dinner at a lesbian restaurant in Montmartre (there were several to choose from), would continue with entertainment in a Montmartre cabaret, music hall, or dance hall, then conclude, after a marathon visit of ill-famed bars on both riverbanks, with a wee-hours supper in an all-night restaurant such as *L'Ange Gabriel* in *Les Halles*, with murals depicting the eponymous angel's own *tournée* through the Parisian underworld (*Guide des plaisirs à Paris* 125–26).[5] Our imaginary version of the *tournée* will proceed

---

[3] Author's ellipses. Translations are mine. The citation refers specifically to the *Foire du Trône*, an iconic popular fair in eastern Paris. The *tournée*'s emphasis on the disreputable poor reflects the confusion of laboring and dangerous classes, which originated with Paris's transformation into a modern, socially segregated metropolis in the first half of the nineteenth century (Chevalier; Kalifa, *Les bas-fonds*).

[4] They also published guidebooks for those too cheap to book their personalized tours, although they included strong disclaimers about unaccompanied visits (*Guide complet des plaisirs*). The identity of the professional tour guides is unknown, but tour afficionados such as Jean Lorrain described them as fellow members of the laboring and dangerous classes (Lorrain, *La maison Philibert* 110, 144).

[5] *L'Ange Gabriel* was located at 9 *rue Pirouette*.

chronologically rather than geographically, visiting both obscure and well-known places, to uncover their role in queer history and memory. While there were many more such sites than we have space to describe here, our selection reflects the variety of establishments included on typical itineraries. From the *Château Rouge* near *place Maubert*, a low-class dive bar frequented by gay men, to Montmartre's first notorious lesbian restaurant and its short-lived but even more scandalous gay counterpart, to the *Moulin Rouge*, whose neon blades anchored its Montmartre neighborhood, to a male brothel masquerading as a hotel, a whole constellation of businesses, many owned by lesbian or gay entrepreneurs, contributed to the construction of Paris as the erotic capital of the Western world while also helping create, sustain, and memorialize the city's queer community.

The *Château Rouge*, 57 *rue Galande*

In this bourgeois republic born of bloodshed, the earliest iterations of what would become the *tournée des grands-ducs* emphasized social alterity by highlighting the poverty on display in the narrow and sordid streets around *place Maubert*, remnants of medieval Paris that had temporarily escaped Haussmannization. Following in the footsteps of savvy policemen and their well-heeled clients, we begin our *tournée* by visiting one of the neighborhood's several notorious taverns, the *Château Rouge*, an establishment catering to homosexuals as well as pimps, prostitutes, thieves, and vagabonds. Also known as the Guillotine for its blood-red façade and interior mural featuring "the horrible instrument erected over a pile of cadavers and surrounded by a flock of ravens" ("Vieux coins de Paris"), the *Château Rouge* was founded in 1845 as an elegant dance hall (Lenôtre). Losing its luster after the Revolution of 1848, it survived as a *bal populaire* until the Commune, after which, shorn of its gardens, it was reborn as a low tavern frequented by denizens of the Parisian underworld ("*la pègre des bas-fonds parisiens*") (Huart 2). Decades later, cabaret performer Yvette Guilbert, she of the wasp waist and elbow-length black gloves immortalized by Toulouse-Lautrec, recalled her curiosity-fueled foray into this den of poverty and prostitution, which took place five years before the grand dukes' arrival, in the winter of 1891:

> And one evening, off we go with Hugues Le Roux to the famous *Château-Rouge, rue Galand*, [...] escorted by Jaume, the famous

policeman. Ah, unforgettable evening! [...] The owner of the den, pistol in belt, is ensconced behind a high counter and serves wine and spirits to women and men come there to warm up and sleep. [...] They look at me with hostility. [...] Finally, we climb to the second floor. Ah, there I saw Hell! Old men, young men pall mall, sleeping on the floor, sordid rags, [...] lighted by a miniscule gaslight in case of fights, and an odor, a terrible odor! (Guilbert 135–37)[6]

Although Guilbert was likely queer herself (Choquette, "Toulouse-Lautrec's lesbian Paris" 128), she did not mention the bar's homosexual clientele, but others were less circumspect. In "Love and death in gay Paris," William Peniston describes a sensational murder that occurred after two regulars, a gay couple in a tempestuous relationship, quarreled there on October 1, 1877 (Peniston). Although his account is based entirely on judicial and police records, the affair also received extensive coverage in the press, which reported explicitly on the men's homosexual proclivities and their patronage of the *Château Rouge* (for example, *Le Droit*).

The tavern's status as a queer *lieu de mémoire* was clinched in the following decade by writer policeman Oscar Méténier, a gay man himself, who used it as the setting of a short story featuring a character based on his flamboyantly queer friend, author Jean Lorrain. In "L'aventure de Marius Dauriat," a male sex worker named Nicolas the Butcher aka Pacha aka Adonis wreaks revenge on Marius, the wealthy *copaille* (faggot) who has tired of him. The first words of the story are "*Rue Galande*, at the *Château Rouge*. Midnight." (Méténier 329).[7]

The tavern closed in 1899, when the building was slated for demolition, generating a wave of nostalgia in the press. Although today an informational plaque placed at number 56 informs passersby interested in Paris history that *rue Galande* harbored "suspect dens" like the *Château Rouge*, "lairs of beggars and alcoholics," its role in queer history is unacknowledged ("*Château Rouge* plaque").

---

6 Le Roux's own romanticized account of the evening features an artistic exchange between the regulars, singing of knives and guillotines, and Yvette, bringing tears to the outcasts' eyes with her love songs (Le Roux, "Trois femmes").

7 The story first appeared in the version of *La chair* that Méténier published in Brussels in 1885 or 1886. Omitted from the shorter French version of 1889, it was republished as Chapter 14 of *La lutte pour l'amour. Études d'argot*, in 1891.

106 *Queer Realms of Memory*

The *table d'hôte* of Louise Taillandier, 17 *rue des Martyrs*, Asnières, and Monaco

"We are all going to dine this evening in Montmartre, [...] we have to dine in Lesbos to see" (Lorrain, *Madame Baringhel* 269). The second stop of our *tournée* takes us to Montmartre, on the cusp of its *Belle Époque* transformation from dormitory for downtown prostitutes into the epicenter of "Gay Paree." Central to this transition were the city's first lesbian restaurants, serving a mixed clientele of local sex workers and wealthy voyeurs.

The lesbian restaurant originated in the *table d'hôte*, a meal service provided by a hostess for a regular clientele. Montmartre's *tables d'hôte* flourished from the mid-nineteenth century, catering to prostitutes living in the neighborhood, then the primary residential area for boulevard streetwalkers. Hostesses tended to be older women, retired from active prostitution, but still involved in the industry: lodging, feeding, even finding customers for younger recruits. When a hostess identified as lesbian, as was often the case, her *table d'hôte* became a locus of lesbian sociability (Choquette, "Gay Paree").

The *table d'hôte* became a restaurant when its hostess opened it to the general public, and the first woman to do so was Louise Taillandier, an enigmatic figure described by contemporaries as a fat, aging former courtesan and madam. Effective January 1, 1867, she signed a six-year lease for a spacious apartment above the ground floor at 17 *rue des Martyrs* (*Archives de Paris*, D1P4 705–706). Her annual rent was 1,800 francs, a solid bourgeois rate at a time when inexpensive lodgings cost between 120 and 500 francs, and luxury apartments over 3,000. No sooner had it opened than Madame Taillandier's restaurant was listed in *Les plaisirs de Paris*, the specialized guidebook written for the 1867 World's Fair by man-about-town Alfred Delvau (143). Despite the *patronne*'s unsuccessful defamation suit against a snide journalist in 1874,[8] her establishment was still thriving in 1878, when Émile Zola showed up, notebook in hand, to do research for his novel *Nana*. Zola's laconic scribbles, which inspired his over-the-top fictional description of the lesbian restaurant, provide a fascinating picture:

> 3 dining rooms, Friday busy day, sometimes 150 women and 10 men. In couples the women. All of them kiss Louise on the mouth. Mistresses

---

8 Taillandier sued over an article by Alfred Delilia in the satirical weekly *Le Tintamarre*. For the judgment, see D1U6 49 (December 3, 1874) and d'Orcières.

of grave bourgeois who come to have fun. The girl [*la petite*] dressed as a man. 3 fr. for the dinner, lots of dishes, chicken with rice that they stuff themselves with, leg of lamb with beans, old-fashioned chic: *vol au vent*. Not great. Wine undrinkable. Maternity of the Taillandier, this fat monster. The maid skinny infirm dyke [*invalide gougnotte*]. Second-rate actresses. Fortunes earned dyking it up in town. An old slut [*garce*], as soon as she finds a pretty novice, brings her there, and all the fat women woo her. Horrible fat women. (*Bibliothèque nationale de France, Nouvelles acquisitions françaises* 10.313, 76–77)

Madame Taillandier closed her Paris business in 1879, one year before Zola immortalized it in the central scene of *Nana* as the epitome of a world upside down;[9] however, she continued to operate a restaurant called Villa Taillandier (Virmaître 63–68; "Asnières décentralisateur"; *Annuaire-almanach du commerce* 2527) in the suburb of Asnières, "this branch of *Montmartre-sur-Lesbos*" (Lorrain, *Dans l'oratoire* 49), and another one in Monaco during the winter season (*Gil Blas*, December 27, 1881).

Zola's *succès de scandale* instantly transformed Madame Taillandier's former restaurant into a lesbian *lieu de mémoire*, with the words "*table d'hôte de la rue des Martyrs*" becoming a shorthand for lesbian sociability. A decade later, his infamous description even inspired a lesbian rewrite in À Lesbos, by "Jehan de Kellec" (the Breton word for testicles), a lesbian *Bildungsroman* whose artist heroine, Andrée, finds professional success and lesbian love.[10] As in *Nana*, the restaurant occupies the center of the novel (129–39) and plays a key role in the heroine's psychosexual development, but instead of plumbing the depths of degeneracy, Andrée awakens to desire. While Zola describes the *patronne* as a "monster," Kellec's portrayal is comedic, and she expresses sympathy for the plight of sex workers through her portrait of Andrée's desperately poor, tubercular dinner companion.

Despite the ubiquitous references to Mme Taillandier's *table d'hôte* during the *Belle Époque*, its memory faded as the twentieth century progressed. There are currently no historical plaques in the rue des Martyrs.

9 For the description of the restaurant in *Nana* (which inspired my own decades-long search for the *lieux de mémoire* of Gay Paree), see pp. 1300–1303.

10 I have made a preliminary identification of the author, along with that of an 1887 novel about lesbians signed "Maurice de Souillac," to be discussed in a forthcoming article.

The *Moulin Rouge*, 82 *boulevard de Clichy*

No *tournée des grands-ducs* would be complete without a visit to the legendary *Moulin Rouge*, the giant dance hall opened by impresario Joseph Oller in 1889 to profit from the tourist boom generated by the World's Fair. The establishment quickly came to epitomize the Parisian entertainment industry and even Montmartre itself as the neighborhood evolved into the primary center of Parisian prostitution, nightlife, and rackets. Like Louise Taillandier's *table d'hôte*, the *Moulin Rouge* catered to a mixed clientele consisting of lower-class neighbors, bohemian artists, wealthy slummers, and a full spectrum of prostitutes from lowly streetwalkers to grand courtesans. The stars were the house dancers, from *La Goulue* (glutton) and *Grille d'Égout* (sewer grate) to *La Môme Fromage* (cheese kid), Jane Avril, May Milton, May Belfort, and Cha-u-Kao (an Orientalized version of *chahut-chaos*, the popular ancestor of the French cancan). All were working-class entertainers, and most were queer. Henri de Toulouse-Lautrec, an assiduous client whose studio on *rue Tourlaque* was just to the north, took pleasure in depicting them in commercial posters and paintings, becoming in the process the chronicler *par excellence* of Montmartre's lesbian showgirls.

Toulouse-Lautrec's art transformed the *Moulin Rouge* into a lesbian and even gay (through his inclusion of Oscar Wilde in a painting of the establishment's belly dancers) *lieu de mémoire*, although a relentlessly formalist reading of his work long prevented us from seeing that obvious fact (Choquette, "Toulouse-Lautrec's lesbian Paris").[11] In contrast, none could ignore the scandal of *Rêve d'Égypte*, a 1907 pantomime featuring Colette as a sexy Egyptian mummy who sheds her strips in an erotic dance, only to be revived by a kiss from the archaeologist who finds her, played by Colette's lesbian lover, Mathilde de Morny (niece of the former emperor), in drag. Alas, summoned by the Morny family, the police intervened, and the show was banned, but it remains one of the fabled moments in *Moulin Rouge* history.

In 1914, with the publication of Francis Carco's novel about Montmartre's male prostitutes, *Jésus la Caille*, the *Moulin Rouge* blossomed into the gay *lieu de mémoire* that Toulouse-Lautrec had only hinted at. Besides *Jésus la Caille*, who visits often, Carco's characters

---

11 Lautrec portrayed Wilde as a member of the *Moulin Rouge* audience in a panel depicting *La Goulue* as a belly dancer, painted in 1895 for her booth at the *Foire du Trône*.

include Olga, Titine, and *Gueule d'Amour*, a trio of male hustlers whose daily presence at the bar, commenting on the action, conveys upon them the role of the three Fates.

Today, the *Moulin Rouge* merits its own interpretive plaque, the text of which is carefully crafted to suppress the establishment's queer history. Even though it mentions the *Rêve d'Égypte* incident, the uninformed reader will wonder why Colette and her "*amie*" provoked such a "resounding scandal," perhaps assuming it had something to do with her costume of "lightweight veils" ("*Moulin Rouge* plaque").

The *Scarabée*, 84 *rue de Dunkerque*

There may have been gay bars in Paris before 1900, but perhaps none like the *Scarabée*, the penultimate stop on our *tournée* and a Montmartre icon at the turn of the century. In the late 1800s, gay men congregated mostly in elegant boulevard cafés or, as we saw at the *Château Rouge*, in rundown taverns catering to the urban underclass. In neither case were they anywhere close to a majority of the clientele. This would change with the *Scarabée*, a Montmartre brasserie, or modest restaurant offering alcoholic beverages (especially but not exclusively beer) and a limited repertoire of meals. The *Scarabée*'s owners were a lesbian couple, popular singer Andrée Philip and her partner Marie-Augustine Dubois (Avril 71). Philip, whose real name was Suzanne Beaugé (*Archives de Paris, État civil*), was the daughter of a well-known theater director who put her on stage at age four. As a child star in the 1870s, she specialized in trouser roles and expressed great regret at not being a boy (*Les soirées parisiennes* 56). As an adult, she became a "*chanteuse typiquement réaliste*" (*L'Art lyrique* 8). Her brasserie at 84 *rue de Dunkerque*, opened around the turn of the century for 1,400 francs in rent (*Archives de Paris*, D9P2 219), quickly became a Montmartre destination. In December 1900, when police raided the establishment at the urging of neighbors, a long line of carriages was stationed in front. Inside, as in nearby *cabarets artistiques* like the *Chat Noir*, a chic clientele of artists, writers, courtesans, and men-about-town consumed overpriced fare in spartan surroundings. But, rather than poetry and song, the primary attraction of the *Scarabée* consisted of young men sporting female sobriquets, wearing make-up, even dressing as women – the common face of male prostitution since at least the mid-nineteenth century (Legludic; Hahn).

Although police witnessed no indecent acts at the *Scarabée*, they checked everyone's identification and arrested nine people, including the two bar owners. Both women and four of the men were exonerated for having a fixed domicile and legitimate means of support. The remaining three, including Jean-Pierre Apestéguy, alias Jeannette, were indicted for vagabondage. At the trial, Apestéguy, a 24-year-old "lyric artist," got off because his protector rented him an apartment in his own name. His fellow defendants, both minors with no permanent address, were convicted and sentenced to six months in prison (*Archives de Paris*, D1U6 738).[12]

The "*Scarabée* Affair" received extensive press coverage, probably because some notable, if unnamed, personalities were present in the bar during the bust (*Gil Blas*, December 7, 1900). Within weeks, the word "*scarabée*" (beetle) had become a new slang term for male homosexual (*Gil Blas*, January 1, 1901 and March 8, 1902), and arrests of gay men a matter of considerable public interest. Police raids on lowly dives suddenly appeared in the news under the rubric of "Another *Scarabée*" or "A new *Scarabée*" (*Gil Blas*, February 13, 1901), though reporters noted they belonged to a "thoroughly inferior genre" (*L'Aurore*). The original *Scarabée*, now closed, lived on in urban myth for years, contributing even in its afterlife to Montmartre's mystique as a delinquent destination;[13] however, today, the *rue de Dunkerque*, like the *rue des* Martyrs, has no historical markers to remind us.

The *Hôtel Marigny*, 11 *rue de l'Arcade*

For the final stop on our *tournée des grands-ducs*, we descend from Montmartre to the grand boulevards, where, just north of the Madeleine, we visit the *Hôtel Marigny* at 11 *rue de l'Arcade*. This hotel, in reality a male brothel, was the second of several gay-themed businesses owned by Albert Le Cuziat, the Breton valet to princes turned homosexual entrepreneur (perhaps with financial assistance from his friend Marcel Proust, who donated some of his late parents' furniture for use in the

---

12 Both appealed their convictions but lost, receiving five years of exile from Paris in addition to their prison sentences (*Archives de Paris*, D3U9 182).

13 For example, newspapers and guidebooks were still referring to the *Scarabée* in 1904 ("Fin de race"; Leca 167) and 1909 ("L'Hérésie sentimentale"). Jane Avril's reminiscences about the bar date from 1933.

brothel) (White 135–36).¹⁴ A police report by officer Tanguay recounts the raid he carried out there in January 1918, after receiving a letter from an anonymous tipster:

> I visited during the night of the 11th to 12th of this month, at midnight, the *Hôtel Marigny*, 11 *rue de l'Arcade*, run by a Mr. Le Cuziat [...]. This hotel had been reported to me as a rendezvous for pederasts, adult and minor. The owner of the hotel, homosexual himself, was facilitating the meeting of adepts of unnatural [*anti-physique*] debauchery [...]. Upon my arrival, I found Mr. Le Cuziat in a parlor on the ground floor, drinking champagne with three individuals who looked like pederasts. In each of the rooms [...] I found a male couple. Each couple was composed of an adult and a minor and their attitude left no doubt about the motive for their presence in these rooms. (*Archives de la Préfecture de Police*, Paris, BM2 43/JC 52)

Tanguay identified Le Cuziat's drinking companions as two infantry soldiers on medical leave and "PROUST, Marcel, 46 years old, private income [*rentier*], 102 *boulevard Haussmann*" (*Archives de la Préfecture de Police*, Paris, BM2 43/JC 52). The *Hôtel Marigny* became a queer *lieu de mémoire* when the writer included it in a central scene of his novel *Le temps retrouvé*, published posthumously in 1927. In describing "Jupien's" brothel, Proust emphasized the two intersecting themes of the *tournée des grands-ducs*: social and sexual transgression.¹⁵ Not only does Monsieur de Charlus come to the brothel for gay sado-masochism; he needs it to be administered by "one of the most dangerous *apaches* of Belleville" if not a "butcher of beef cattle" (*tueur de bœufs*) from the

---

14 According to police reports, Le Cuziat's first business was a bath house on *rue Godot-de-Mauroy*, in the same neighborhood as the *Hôtel Marigny*. He operated the "hotel" from 1917 to 1922, when he sold it to purchase a grander one for the same purpose at 15 *rue Saint-Augustin*, open from 1922 to 1933 (*Archives de la Préfecture de Police*, Paris, BM2 43/JC 52, BM2 60/JC 38). In the 1920s and 1930s, Le Cuziat also co-owned a dance hall in the infamous *rue de Lappe*, *Les Trois Colonnes*, nicknamed "*le musette des tapas*" (the fairies' dance hall) (Wise; *Archives de Paris*, D31U3 2433).

15 Indeed, Proust's description also reflects a third theme of racial transgression, which increased in importance with the service of more than 800,000 French colonial troops and workers in World War I, followed by the immigration of African Americans to Paris in the 1920s. Jupien's brothel also caters to customer demands for "a Negro chauffeur" (Proust 402). In André Warnod's 1930 description of the *tournée des grands-ducs*, "*les nègres de la rue Blomet*" (the *Bal nègre*, frequented by West Indian immigrants) precede "*les apaches de la rue de Lappe*" (Warnod 360).

city slaughterhouse. (While these two sex workers turn out to have less fearsome second jobs – jewelry worker and hotel employee – they are nonetheless members of the working class [Proust 396–97].)

The *Hôtel Marigny* remains in business today as an ordinary tourist hotel. Although its art deco sign evokes its appearance during World War I,[16] only a knowledgeable *flâneur* will be able to identify it as a queer *lieu de mémoire*.

Time Regained and Time Lost

At the end of our imaginary tour of Gay Paree during the early Third Republic, two points seem clear. First, the city witnessed a flourishing of queer commercial culture as part of the bourgeoning mass entertainment industry, with establishments owned and/or patronized by gays and lesbians marking the contemporary imagination to the point of transforming them into queer *lieux de mémoire*. Second, queer *lieux de mémoire* that were vividly recalled by many Parisians into the interwar period gradually disappeared from memory thereafter. What explains the subsequent erasure of the *Belle Époque*'s queer landmarks, when the image of characters who had frequented them (the *apache* and the prostitute, for example) lived on, capable of evoking nostalgic Frenchness with the simple squeeze of an accordion?

The first devastating world war marked the start of a profound cultural shift: *le titi parisien* and the good-hearted whore (nostalgic roles played by Jean Gabin and Arletty in films of the 1930s) came increasingly to embody Frenchness, but at the price of evacuating the frisson of danger and transgression. The kernel of this change could already be found in some cultural productions of the *Belle Époque*. Works in the spirit of the *tournée des grands-ducs* that celebrated prostitutes, pimps, and felons, the hungry, homeless, poor, and outcast – Aristide Bruant's songs come to mind – at once mythified and sentimentalized criminals as the ultimate avatars of working-class Paris. By the interwar period, after the sacrifice of countless *poilus* on the battlefield, they had become veritable icons of Frenchness.[17] But the nature of these working-class heroes had

---

16 For a period photograph of the hotel, see Canet 48.

17 Symbolizing the shift from danger to nostalgia, the *Caveau Rouge*, a wax museum devoted to the turn-of-the-century Paris underworld, shared space at the *Moulin Rouge* from 1930 to 1938 (Barnicaud).

changed (Rearick). Normative sexualities and gender hierarchies were reimposed in the interwar *"chansons réalistes"* of queer entertainers like Mistinguett, Damia, Fréhel, and Piaf, in contrast to Yvette Guibert, whose *fin-de-siècle* repertoire included her signature song extolling sapphism, Éros vanné, with sheet music featuring a lesbian couple drawn by Toulouse-Lautrec.[18] By the end of the Third Republic, the discursive regime of *Belle Époque* eroticism was drawing to a close, making way for a less transgressive if equally voyeuristic celebration of the lower depths.[19] Voyeurism, as Adrian Rifkin reminds us, "is an act of knowing, of bravado, or power, exercised by the seeing, bourgeois man" (or woman) (103). The balance of power in the system of class differences that was Paris in the Third Republic was never in question, but with the unintended consequence that, for a time, it rendered queerness visible and gave queer artists and entrepreneurs opportunities to create spaces of community and memory.

Archival sources consulted

Archives de Paris
Calepins des propriétés bâties. D1P4 705–706 (17 *rue des Martyrs*).
Cour d'appel de Paris. Registre des arrêts. D3U9 182 (February 1901).
État civil. *17ᵉ arrondissement.* January 14, 1866 (*Acte de naissance de* Beaugé/ Baugé, Suzanne Renée).
Registre des patentes. D9P2 219 (84 *rue de Dunkerque*).

18 Queer expression did not, however, disappear completely from the interwar song repertoire (Pénet).

19 Although significant change was underway, scandalous descriptions of queer venues, present and past, continued to be produced during the interwar period, as we have seen. Likewise, wealthy slummers carried on with their *tournées*. To give one example, Elisabeth de Gramont, Duchess of Clermont-Tonnerre, wrote in her memoirs of receiving a well-born British lady whose tourist agenda, duly noted in her appointment book, was to "See the *Faubourg Saint-Germain* and the *Petite Chaumière*" (Gramont 345). Although largely unknown today, the *Petite Chaumière*, a jerry-built, run-down Montmartre bar featuring a transvestite chorus line and servers, was on the agenda of every savvy tourist in the interwar years, alongside the Eiffel Tower and the *Sacré-Cœur* (Barféty). It owes its consecration as a queer *lieu de mémoire* to its passage into literature in works as different as the duchess's memoirs (1928–35) and Jean Genet's *Notre-Dame-des-Fleurs* (1948), where it became *Le Tavernacle*. Genet's wild popularity in 1950s Paris, I would argue, was the last gasp of the old mentality.

Tribunal correctionnel de la Seine. Registre des jugements. D1U6 49 (December 3, 1874), D1U6 738 (January 5, 1901).

Archives de la Préfecture de Police, Paris
Rapports de la Police (1870–1940). BM2 43/JC 52 (11 *rue de l'Arcade*), BM2 60/JC 38 (15 *rue Saint-Augustin*). Series BM2 has been reorganized into series JC. I provide both old and new reference numbers.

Bibliothèque nationale de France
Département des manuscrits. *Nouvelles acquisitions françaises* (NAF) 10.313. Zola, Émile. *Nana. Dossiers préparatoires* 1878.

Works cited

Annuaire-almanach du commerce... Didot et Bottin. Paris, 1885.
L'Art lyrique et le music hall, journal hebdomadaire indépendant, 1896–97.
"Asnières décentralisateur." *Le Voltaire.* July 7, 1883, p. 3.
L'Aurore. December 20, 1900, p. 3.
Avril, Jane. *Mes mémoires* (1933). Phébus, 2005.
Barféty, Jean-Marc. "Histoire de *La Petite Chaumière* (1921–1939)." Maurice Duplay, *Adonis-Bar*. Bibliothèque GayKitschCamp, 2023, pp. 185–410.
Barnicaud, Jeanne. "Le Caveau rouge, musée de cire du Paris apache." *Retronews.fr.* August 21, 2022. Web.
Bruant, Aristide. *Dans la rue. Chansons et monologues.* Paris, [1888].
Canet, Nicole. *Hôtels garnis. Garçons de joie. Prostitution masculine. Lieux et fantasmes à Paris de 1860 à 1960.* Galerie Au Bonheur du Jour, 2012.
Carco, Francis. *Jésus la Caille.* Mercure de France, 1914.
"Château Rouge plaque." *Panneau Histoire de Paris.* Fr.wikipedia.org. Web.
Chevalier, Louis. *Classes laborieuses et classes dangereuses à Paris pendant la première moitié du XIXe siècle.* Plon, 1958.
Choquette, Leslie. "Beyond the myth of lesbian Montmartre: The case of chez Palmyre." *Historical Reflections/Réflexions historiques*, vol. 42, no. 2, 2016, pp. 75–96.
———. Degenerate or degendered? Images of prostitution and homosexuality in the French Third Republic." *Historical Reflections/Réflexions historiques*, vol. 23, no. 2, 1997, pp. 205–28.
———. "Gay Paree: The origins of lesbian and gay commercial culture in the French Third Republic." *Contemporary French Civilization*, vol. 41, no. 1, 2016, pp. 1–24.
———. "Paris-Lesbos: Lesbian social space in the modern city, 1870–1940." *Proceedings of the Western Society for French History*, vol. 26, 2000, pp. 122–32.

---. "Toulouse-Lautrec's lesbian Paris." *Toulouse-Lautrec em Vermelho* [in Red], edited by Adriano Pedrosa. *MASP Museo de Arte de São Paulo Assis Chateaubriand*, 2017, pp. 111–32.

Compagnon, Antoine. "Marcel Proust's *Remembrance of Things Past*." *Realms of Memory: Rethinking the French Past*, vol. 2, *Traditions*, edited by Pierre Nora and Lawrence D. Kritzman. Translated by Arthur Goldhammer. Columbia UP, 1997, pp. 210–46.

Delilia, Alfred. "Amour et pharmacie." *Le Tintamarre*. October 18, 1874, pp. 2–3.

Delvau, Alfred. *Les plaisirs de Paris*. Paris, 1867.

Le Droit. February 11, 1878, pp. 1–2.

"Écrire l'histoire des homosexualités en Europe, XIXe–XXe siècles." Dossier edited by Florence Tamagne. *Revue d'histoire moderne et contemporaine*, vol. 53/54, no. 4, 2006.

"Fin de race." *Le Frou-Frou*. December 31, 1904.

Genet, Jean. *Notre-Dame-des-Fleurs*. L'Arbalète, 1948.

Gil Blas. December 27, 1881, p. 1; December 7, 1900, pp. 1, 3; January 1, 1901, p. 1; February 13, 1901, p. 3; March 8, 1902, p. 1.

Gramont, Élisabeth de. *Souvenirs du monde, 1890–1940*. Grasset, 1966.

Guide complet des plaisirs mondains et des plaisirs secrets de Paris (Paris intime et mystérieux). André Hall, undated.

Guide des plaisirs à Paris. [Paris], 1899.

Guilbert, Yvette. *La chanson de ma vie (mes mémoires)*. Grasset, 1927.

Hahn, Pierre. *Nos ancêtres les pervers: la vie des homosexuels sous le Second Empire*. Olivier Orban, 1979.

"L'Hérésie sentimentale." *Fantasio*, vol. 67, no. 1, May 1909, p. 647.

Higgs, David, ed. *Queer Sites: Gay Urban Histories since 1600*. Routledge, 1999.

Higonnet, Patrice. *Paris: Capital of the World*. Translated by Arthur Goldhammer. Harvard UP, 2002.

Huart, Marcel. "Le Château Rouge." *L'Événement*. January 21, 1899, pp. 1–2.

Kalifa, Dominique. *Les bas-fonds. Histoire d'un imaginaire*. Seuil, 2013.

---. *Paris. Une histoire érotique, d'Offenbach aux Sixties*. Payot, 2018.

Kellec, Jehan de. *À Lesbos*. Paris, 1891.

Leca, Victor. *Pour s'amuser. Guide du viveur à Paris*. P. Fort, [1904].

Legludic, H. *Notes et observations de médecine légale: attentats aux mœurs*. Paris, 1896.

Lenôtre, G. "Variétés. Au pays du 'Bigorne.'" *Le Monde illustré*. March 2, 1889, p. 131.

Le Roux, Hugues. *Les jeux du cirque et la vie foraine*. Paris, 1889.

---. "Trois femmes au Château-Rouge." *Gil Blas*. December 28, 1891, p. 1.

Lorrain, Jean. *Dans l'oratoire*. Paris, 1889.

---. *Madame Baringhel*. Paris, 1899.

———. *La maison Philibert* (1904). Christian Pirot, 1992.
Merrick, Jeffrey, and Bryant Ragan, eds. *Homosexuality in Modern France.* Oxford UP, 1996.
Merrick, Jeffrey, and Michael Sibalis, eds. *Homosexuality in French History and Culture.* Harrington Park Press, 2001.
Méténier, Oscar. "L'Aventure de Marius Dauriat." Jean Lorrain, *La maison Philibert.* Christian Pirot, 1992, pp. 329–42. (Three letters of Jean Lorrain to Oscar Méténier referring to the story are reproduced on pp. 343–49.)
"Moulin Rouge plaque." *Panneau Histoire de Paris.* Fr.wikipedia.org. Web.
Orcières, Paul d'. "Chronique des tribunaux." *L'Événement.* December 8, 1874, p. 3.
Pénet, Martin. "L'Expression homosexuelle dans les chansons françaises de l'entre-deux- guerres: Entre dérision et ambiguïté." *Revue d'histoire moderne et contemporaine*, vol. 53–54, no. 4, 2006, pp. 106–27.
Peniston, William. *Pederasts and Others: Urban Culture and Sexual Identity in Nineteenth- Century Paris.* Haworth Press, 2004, pp. 177–91.
Proust, Marcel. À la recherche du temps perdu, vol. 4. Bibliothèque de la Pléiade, 1989.
Rearick, Charles. *The French in Love and War: Popular Culture in the Era of the World Wars.* Yale UP, 1997.
Revenin, Régis. *Homosexualité et prostitution masculines à Paris, 1870–1918.* L'Harmattan, 2005.
Rifkin, Adrian. *Street Noises: Parisian Pleasure, 1900–1940.* Manchester UP, 1993.
Les soirées parisiennes de 1875 par un monsieur de l'orchestre (Arnold Mortier). Paris, 1875.
Tamagne, Florence. *Histoire de l'homosexualité en Europe. Berlin, Londres, Paris, 1919–1930.* Seuil, 2000.
"Vieux coins de Paris." *L'Intransigeant.* April 30, 1899, p. 2.
Virmaître, Charles. *Mlles Saturne.* Paris, [1898].
Warnod, André. *Visages de Paris.* Firmin-Didot, 1930.
White, Edmund. *Marcel Proust.* Viking Penguin, 1999.
Wise, Pyra. "Proust à l'hôtel, d'Albert Le Cuziat au commissaire Tanguay." *Bulletin d'informations proustiennes*, vol. 46, 2016, pp. 41–56.
Zola, Émile. *Les Rougon-Macquart: histoire naturelle et sociale d'une famille sous le Second Empire*, vol. 2. Bibliothèque de la Pléiade, 1961.

CHAPTER SEVEN

From the Marais to collective memory
How to map queer France

Kory Olson

Maps document knowledge and control over space and help their readers visualize a territory. Even as France became a fully mapped nation in the decades following the 1789 Revolution, the average French person failed to access governmental cartography or use it in any meaningful capacity. Under the Third Republic (1870–1940), however, French citizens increasingly encountered visual representations of their national territory, reflecting a broader shift from *"la fin des paysans"* [the end of peasant culture] to *"l'apogée de la croissance industrielle"* [the height of industrial growth]. This transition helped shape a national collective memory, exemplified by Pierre Nora's concept of *lieux de mémoire* (23). In "Entre mémoire et histoire: la problématique des lieux," Nora encouraged his readers to turn from history as a "une représentation du passé" [a representation of the past] towards memory, "en évolution permanente, ouverte à la didactique du souvenir et de l'amnésie [...] vulnérable à toutes les utilisations et manipulations" [in permanent evolution, open to the dialectic of remembering and forgetting, [...] vulnerable to manipulation and appropriation] (24–25). Nora's *Lieux* possesses one simple but decisive trait that sets it apart from previous historical or scientific approaches to memory, whether national or social: traditionally, history has employed *realia*, with momentous or physical manifestations (42). However, Nora argues, a dependence on tangible objects fails to incorporate the potential of shared memory, which, with regards to France, expresses itself through maps in textbooks, historical monuments, and even geographic locations that all French citizens were expected to know, encounter, or experience. Therefore, *lieux de mémoire* transform "historical criticism into critical history – and not only through its methods; it allows history a secondary, purely transferential existence, even a kind of reawakening" (24). Nora's project includes several territorial and spatial entries that helped form France's common identity, such as *Le département*; *Le "Tableau de la géographie de la France" de Vidal de la Blache*; *Paris*; *Le Centre et la périphérie*; and, *L'Hexagone*. At the same time, Nora rarely highlights minority-associated sites throughout *Lieux*, and fails to engage, or even acknowledge, queer sites.[1] In spite of this failure, Bouamer, Provencher, and Schroth argue that "queerness has always been part and parcel of the French landscape as well as a constitutive element of French imperialism" (Introduction). My chapter identifies the challenges of defining and mapping "queer France," while also exploring alternative methods that allow for its representation.[2] In addition to its geographic dimensions, queer space can be defined in both economic and physical terms. Most importantly, queer citizens actively create, assign, and negotiate their own spatial boundaries. During the Third Republic, maps helped construct a sense of national identity – of what it meant to be French. Might the act of defining and mapping space similarly help queer communities locate and cultivate a shared collective identity?

Over the last decades, scholars working on sexuality and space in a variety of disciplines, including geography, urban studies, anthropology, and linguistics, have created their own means to demarcate spaces that gay men and lesbians occupy in order to map it. To locate queer space in France, one might immediately turn to where most gay people congregate: Paris. Critical geographers argue that "spaces do not possess sexual identities, but that queer bodies [occupy] spaces as their own" (Oswin 89–93). Following that assertion, scholars may contend that Paris exemplifies the ultimate "center" of queer France, solidifying

---

1 Chapters on the *Port Royal* (Jansenists), *Le musée du Désert* (Protestants), and *Grégoire, Dreyfus, Drancy et Copernic* (Jews) address religious minoritized peoples, mostly as a point of opposition to French authority.

2 Terms such as "gay," "lesbian," and "queer" dominate the chapter although they represent only a portion of the inclusive LGBTQI+ community. Provencher perhaps best establishes a model to follow. His work relies on the term "gay" in part due to its "widespread recognition and use both among French homosexuals and in the current scholarship on sexual citizenship" (11). The use of a common term for this diverse population is practical, if imperfect.

the city's political and cultural position throughout much of the nation's history. For that reason, this chapter focuses heavily on mapping Paris but also includes Toulouse, a regional capital, in order to show how users of social media employ it to define their queer space. Throughout the nineteenth and twentieth centuries, the *Dépôt de la Guerre* and subsequent *Service géographique de l'armée* and *Institut de géographie national* (*IGN*) documented and mapped French domestic and, later, colonial spaces.³ Consequently, citizens today have easy access to maps of communities, departments, former colonies, neighboring nations, and continents. However, options such as these fall short when one wishes to delineate and map queer spaces. This chapter will provide an overview of the scholarship pertaining to queer France but also identify the challenges one may encounter when attempting to understand and visualize it.

Defining queer space

For this chapter, I focus primarily on geographic, social, and commercial means to define, and map, queer France. Yet, even with these broad parameters, numerous challenges remain. To start, how can one define "queer space?" Does it even exist? For David Bell, Jon Binnie, and Gill Valentine, space is not naturally, authentically, straight or queer, but rather "actively produced and (hetero)sexualized" (qtd. Binnie 223). Scholars argue that such space exists and have crafted their own definitions. For France, Michael Sibalis, one prominent example, goes as far as to employ the term "gay ghetto" to describe Paris's Marais neighborhood, maybe even considered its own "*lieu de mémoire*" within the boundary of certain specific streets (1741–42). Stéphane Leroy's definition for a "géographie de l'homosexualité parisienne" [geography of Parisian homosexuality] affirms the district's influence economically by counting the number of gay and lesbian businesses "entre l'Hôtel de Ville et la Place de la Bastille" [between the Mayor's Office and Place de la Bastille] versus peripheral neighborhoods or *arrondissements* [districts] (588). These two examples show how the authors' reference points rely on geography to demarcate a space. But the mapping process can take other forms as well. Denis Provencher asks self-identified

---

3 Olson examines the role of state cartography and the mapping of the national terrain.

LGBTQ citizens to map their own spaces (159), while Dominique Batiste investigates gay social media to map queer Toulouse (114).[4]

Unlike a French region or department that can be outlined by precise physical borders, identifying queer space geographically remains problematic when relying on official administrative divisions, as no established material boundaries exist. This contrasts with the static nature of existing cities, departments, and regions that often fail to adapt to the elastic nature of queer space. Instead, these "static" boundaries serve as reference points for delineating and mapping queer space. Critical geographers often depict them as zones where gays and lesbians or queers exist in opposition to and as transgressions of heterosexual space (Oswin 89). Of course, this method is not new. De Certeau showed how individuals react to what city leaders plan and build when the practices of moving about urban space conflicts with a constructed environment (151). For example, pedestrians employ "tactics" of resistance towards urban planners when they stray from city-built sidewalks or pathways to seek a more convenient or direct route (152). This "opposition" can scale up to neighborhoods where LGBTQ+ individuals congregate as queer-friendly businesses spring up to cater to them. Many of the scholars referenced in this chapter map queer space via the grouping or clustering of queer individuals, which is a method of designating queer space that may stand in opposition to more "mainstream," "official," or non-queer attempts at mapping it.

Any segregation, sexual or other, hinders the formation of a shared national identity even if it creates a more specialized one. The less memory is experienced collectively, the more it requires "people to undertake to become themselves memory individuals." Nora proposes that we think of it as if "an inner voice tells each Corsican, 'You must be Corsican' and each Breton 'You must be Breton'" (34). To understand the appeal of this sense of obligation, Nora suggests that we should think of Jewish memory, which had recently been revived among non-practicing

---

4 Scholars beyond the Hexagon also rely on both traditional and non-traditional means to identify and "map" queer space. Canham analyzes stories of Black lesbian women to map queer social spaces in Johannesburg (84). Gieseking interviews lesbians in New York City to identify queer neighborhoods there in opposition to cis-heteropatriarchal spaces (941), and Lee maps queer space in Taiwanese novels (194). With these disparate means of mapping and defining queer space, any mapping of it relies on shifting classifications and limits, where each individual employs their own criteria.

Jews. We can imagine, despite Nora's stance, a similar proclamation for queer individuals, with Nora telling them, "you must be queer," then tasking them with creating their own collective memory, no doubt based on the gathering of queer people in a shared space. The post-1980 establishment of bars and the gay bookstore Les Mots à la bouche on the rue Sainte-Croix-de-la-Bretonnerie brought many queer people to the Marais and, for the first time, a Parisian neighborhood was publicly associated with gay life and culture (Caron 63). The area's recent gentrification, however, has changed its character. The notable bookstore has been priced out and pedestrians will now see a Dr. Martens shoe store in its place. To find fellow queer book patrons, customers must now travel to the 11th *arrondissement*. No doubt an easy enough detour, but an additional obstacle that takes queer readers away from the iconic neighborhood.

A geographic definition

Perhaps the most traditional, relatable way to represent a spatial entity is geographically: situating it within established physical limits such as streets, or political or administrative boundaries. Considering the cartographic nature of the task, a geographically based definition for queer France is possibly the easiest to propose and understand. French cartographic services have been surveying, documenting, and mapping the national terrain since the eighteenth century and one can argue that it is now possible to see and know almost every square meter of the nation. While no official agency has attempted to map queer France, municipalities often include pages on official websites to acknowledge these populations. Paris's website champions the city as a "capitale des droits LGBTQI+" [capital of LGBTQI+ rights] but includes no maps. Instead, the page lists queer-friendly spaces in the city, such as the *Centre LGBT Paris* and points readers to rainbow crosswalks, for example the intersection of avenue Gambetta and rue Belgrand in the 20th *arrondissement*, to bring visitors into a neighborhood that few tourists might traverse on their own. Lyon's version directs readers to the city's various "bonnes adresses LGBT+" [good LGBT+ addresses] per Romain Vallet, a former editor of the gay magazine *Hétéroclite*.

Queer space exists wherever LGBTQI+ people congregate. However, rightfully or not, to many, "queer France" means Paris. As the largest Francophone city in France/Europe, Paris draws queer people from provincial communities and regions, but also from other Francophone countries. People have migrated to the capital for centuries in search of work, professional advancement, or a new life. However, the city has also almost certainly drawn a disproportionately high number of homosexuals, containing as much as 46 percent of France's gay men in the early 1990s (Provencher 151). Therefore, based on this congregation, scholars contend that Paris occupies the ultimate "center" of queer France, echoing the city's political and cultural dominance over the rest of the nation. Yet, Paris covers a large area, so most scholars narrow their focus to various neighborhoods and *arrondissements* as they craft their maps. For those who use a high number of gay and lesbian residents or visitors as one parameter, "queer Paris" often equals the Marais district, with the identity of the neighborhood resting on the visibility of the people who inhabit and occupy the space.

Situating queer France or queer Paris within a specific geographic or administrative division renders it more relatable to a general audience. The Marais itself represents a tangible space that one can visualize, visit, and experience. Furthermore, it is a center of gay life as defined by a network of social interactions taking place in public spaces (Caron 64). "[B]y the early 1980s, [queer communities] had come to delineate a legitimate space, one that was necessary for the formation and well-being of a distinct and cohesive gay and lesbian minority group and one that validated an ethnic minority politic" (Nash 129). Although sexual identity separates the zone from the rest of the city, it remains a "predominantly white, male, middle-class preserve" (Oswin 94). With this demographic constructing their own urban enclaves, gay men have come to "figure prominently in the urban renaissance" (Sibalis 1740) – which is to say in the redevelopment and gentrification of the inner city. Beyond its association as a gay district, the Marais came into being largely as a product of impersonal economic forces (the real estate market) and contemporary social change (the emergence of a significant urban gay population with its own distinctive subculture); reforms that, many would argue, attracted queer citizens. As opposed to public sites of memory, such as *Versailles*, the *Mur des fédérés*, or *Verdun*, queer space is a place of refuge, where "one finds the living heart of memory" (Nora 36). So, to study, observe, or map queer Paris, one must acknowledge where that shared memory occurs.

The Marais is not the first such zone to exist in the capital city. Thanks to historians, newspapers, literature, and police accounts, we know a great deal about the pre-1900 urban spaces used by Parisian homosexuals.[5] In the eighteenth and nineteenth centuries, these gathering sites, such as parks, riverbanks, and cafés, were spread across the city, but were usually situated at its margins, whether literally (on the physical periphery) or figuratively (in poorer and seamier districts) (Sibalis 1744). Starting around 1880 and up until World War II, Montmartre materialized as a queer-friendly neighborhood, and many gay and lesbian bars and restaurants operated there (Choquette 4).[6] After the brutal disruption brought about by the German occupation and Vichy, the Left Bank neighborhood of Saint-Germain-des-Prés emerged as the new Parisian center of gay and lesbian life (Caron 59). The map of queer France thus adapts and changes over time.

Mapping queer France beyond the geographic

In the present day, the geographic demarcation of the Marais works well in mapping queer France. Scholars often employ the district as a recognizable reference point, even if they fail to denote specific physical boundaries or turn to less traditional means of definitions. Stéphane Leroy's "géographie de l'homosexualité parisienne" [geography of Parisian homosexuality] relies on administrative borders as he centers the zone between the Hôtel de Ville and the Bastille. In addition to Leroy, Emmanuel Redoutey also employs a commercial definition to map his version of queer France, which focuses on Paris's Marais and its emergence as a gay business area. Redoutey draws his data from the now defunct weekly magazine *Gai pied*, the internet, and the Minitel (Reader 148). In studying the geographical distribution of gay and gay-friendly spaces across Paris, Redoutey has used the image of a cone: "The concentration of establishments in the Marais quarter – where self-identified homosexuals exert a kind of dominance over businesses and the activity of several streets, which are also valued by tourists – plays a central role" (Redoutey 60). Returning to the familiarity of the Marais, the rue Sainte-Croix-de-la-Bretonnerie is its main drag and emblem – what the rue des Rosiers is to the Jews. The street, running parallel to the rue de

---

5 For information regarding public sex and prostitution, see Ross and Choquette.
6 Choquette examines the *table d'hôte*, a meal service provided by a hostess, which developed among retired prostitutes. When a hostess identified as lesbian, as was often the case, her *table d'hôte* became a focus of lesbian sociability (3).

124 *Queer Realms of Memory*

Rivoli, meets the rue Vieille-du-Temple, where several gay bars overflow onto the sidewalks during happy hour. These three streets, along with the rue du Roi-de-Sicile, make up the heart of the Gay Marais, but the neighborhood extends well beyond them toward Beaubourg and into the 3rd *arrondissement*.

Guy Hocquenghem turns to a more structural approach to map queer France. He wrote about urban experiences in *Le Gay voyage* (1980) where he offers a guided tour of several gay urban centers and his own rendition of an imaginary (post) modern "Alexandria" (Provencher 153). For Hocquenghem's queer France, he largely avoids specific names, monuments, clubs, or restaurants when he writes "Je laisse volontairement de côté boîtes, parcs et saunas de Paris, dont on trouvera la liste dans tous les Incognito guides" [I am happy to leave out Parisian clubs, parks, and saunas found in Incognito guides] (136). He focuses instead on social and sexual encounters outside of the Marais, such as the Cinéma Paris-Louxor on the Boulevard de Magenta, near the border between the 10th and 18th *arrondissements*, an area of the city traditionally associated more with immigrants at the time of his 1980 publication than [visible] queer citizens. Hocquenghem's mapping of gay Paris and its related activities (ambiguity, anonymous, and revolutionary sexual acts, and so on) still relies on official borders, such as streets, even if he declines to privilege them.

Self-mapping

The first part of this chapter examines academically defined versions of queer France along with official government websites to define and document queer France. However, why not ask queer citizens for their interpretation/definition? Self-identification remains perhaps the most relevant and, some may argue, most accurate way to map queer France. In *Queer French* (2007), Denis Provencher demonstrates how the French capital remains an integral part of the Francophone homosexual's experience both in reality and in one's mind. More specifically, Provencher interviews gay and lesbian sexual citizens. His analysis of their responses reinforces the importance of the Marais and confirms it as a canonical gay reference or "realm of memory" for many of the nation's homosexual citizens. During semi-structured interviews with his subjects, Provencher finds that the neighborhood's prominence extends beyond Paris city limits as well. French gays and lesbians who live in the provinces reinforce the capital's importance and draw on it in the imagining of their own city's gay district. Lyon's "Le Petit Marais" [the Little Marais], situated on the city's Presque Isle, is just one example that relies, at least in name, on the canonical gay district (152). Of course, Paris remains a prime draw for queer citizens and each one defines their use and understanding of the urban space differently.

To investigate how they view and experience queer space, Provencher asked his 40 informants to draw a map of "la ville gay" [the gay city] (149) for a foreign gay or lesbian traveler who may visit. Twenty-eight of his respondents (70 percent) happily complied and enthusiastically drew their rendition of gay Paris. He then analyzed these amateur maps to illustrate how the documents visually and linguistically delineate sexual citizenship on the French urban landscape. These drawings serve as primary sources but also confirm the importance of the congregation or mingling of queer citizens. In fact, many gay and lesbian interviewees from Provencher's study spoke of the important visible nature of the gay city as represented in the Marais neighborhood.

Upon first glance, the plans produced by Provencher's interviewees mirror what academics have published about queer France, confirm the primacy of the Marais neighborhood, and define queer Paris as a space that exists almost exclusively around commercial establishments within the central *arrondissements*. Many of Provencher's interviewees crafted plans based on maps of the *métro*, or the city's subway, so they too rely on official cartography to present their own versions of queer Paris. Cartographers might argue that personalized maps, such as those gathered by Provencher, provide the "best" visualization of queer Paris as they are based on first-hand, real-life experiences. Simple in nature, the ten maps Provencher includes in his book, all authored by different people, are in many ways very similar. First, they privilege *intramuros* Paris, as nine of the ten provide a circular outline of the entire city as a stage for hosting gay life. Second, to affirm the Marais's importance to Paris allocated by scholars earlier in this chapter, his interviewees either drew a square in the city center to represent the neighborhood or focused on it exclusively to highlight the area's significance. Yet, not all his subjects embraced the Marais equally or saw themselves as part of it, nor does the Marais maintain queer exclusivity on their maps. His authors often extend their queer Paris, or queer France for that matter, beyond the district's geographical limitation into their own lived communities. As they map activity outside the central city, the interviewees incorporate borders, streets/roads, and their own experiences to map their queer space. They provide known markers, such as the Seine River, the Canal Saint Martin, or Chinatown to help situate their gay sites, such as gyms, bars, bookstores, and saunas both inside and outside of the Marais. These recognizable landmarks will help visiting queer citizens locate welcoming spaces. Some maps also include peripheral transitory zones, where one might find prostitution or cruising sites.

Even if many people acknowledge geographical markers, not everyone Provencher interviews chooses to engage in this cartographic request. He reports that some of his subjects vehemently opposed any signs of a gay neighborhood or gay city, suggesting that mapping one would help formalize an American-style ghetto as discussed by Sibalis. This anti-mapping of queer France validates a certain reluctance to segment queer France as separate from the rest of society and acknowledges the difficulty in mapping it when some queer citizens refuse to do so themselves. In sum, Provencher's examination provides specific, geographically based cartographic documents – useful tools for understanding and mapping queer France, but also reveals that not all queer people choose to identify queer space.

Dominique Batiste provides another less-traditional option that allows individuals to create maps. In his article "'0 Feet Away': The queer cartography of French gay men's geo-social media use," Batiste focuses on Toulouse, a major French regional capital that has its own draw for queer people, to investigate data concerning Grindr and Scruff, two apps that use GPS technology to show the location of nearby gay men. In contrast to Provencher's subjects, who created their own versions of gay Paris as they knew and experienced it, Batiste's subjects view "gay Toulouse" on a phone screen in real time: a template set up by another authoritative voice, a commercial smart phone application.[7]

Batiste's article focuses on one interviewee, Jorge, and readers learn about his experiences with the social media apps and his life in gay Toulouse. When Jorge opens Grindr, he finds a map of the city covered in red points, with each one representing a gay man on the app. Certain areas, near gay bars such as Le Bears, Le Grand Cirque, Le Shanghai, are always filled with red dots (125). This presentation affirms a reliance on gay landmarks to identify queer spaces but also recognizes the congregations of gays and lesbians as an additional criterion in mapping

---

7 Although no one of note in queer culture developed the application, I mention "authority" here primarily due to the fact that Grindr has become ubiquitous in queer culture.

queer space. This increased group visibility creates a sense that the city contains "gay spaces" (127). An individual can open his phone and see the gay city at any one moment.[8] Batiste's subject defines his queer space through the congregation of gay men, which remains an ever-changing dynamic in the defined urban space. Where the mental viewpoint of one's own queer space can differ from person to person, with Batiste's investigation, we can also see how queer France, or more specifically queer Toulouse, changes from day to day, hour to hour, or even minute to minute. Using technology to map queer France exposes not only the changing nature of gay space, but also shows its fleeting, yet performative, nature. Many of Nora's sites focus on static, fixed monuments rooted in the past. Queer *lieux*, on the other hand, embrace the present. Their collective nature, as demonstrated by this and similar smartphone apps, encourages both togetherness and embraces to the future.

Conclusion

This chapter has aimed to situate mapping queer France as a realm of memory. Although governments have successfully mapped French territory over the past two centuries, the definition and documentation of queer France remains outside any official narrative. Therefore, one must create and rely on informal, even performative parameters to map it. In many respects, queer France exists due to the collective memory of its individuals congregating and interacting with one another. Scholars also define queer France geographically: within established borders, landmarks, and streets. The Marais, one such example, labeled a "queer ghetto" by Sibalis, affirms a significant gay and lesbian presence in the central Parisian district and therefore serves as a perfect queer space to map. Other scholars have referred to the geographical classification to affirm the commercial power of gays and lesbians and to document locations of queer businesses there. Leroy, one example, counts such establishments between the Hôtel de Ville and the Bastille. Redoutey, on the other hand, breaks out of those geographic confines of central Paris to map a larger queer footprint as he tallies businesses throughout the entire capital. Overall, to map queer France, one must reconcile

---

8   It should be noted that this effect is lost to history. Grindr no longer shows users' exact locations due to privacy concerns.

the conflict between social (where queer people congregate, such as the *Centre LGBT Paris*) and commercial spaces (Les Mots à la bouche bookstore).

Some of the most accurate ways to map queer France originate not from academics and governmental or municipal websites, but instead from non-traditional sources: the people those academics have studied. Provencher's interviewees, one prime example, rely on their own experiences to craft maps of queer space in the capital, which represent the way they live and experience it. Their hand-drawn cartographic documents highlight both the geographic and economic factors that go into any mapping of queer peoples. Personal cartography can be complemented by a digital one. Batiste's look at social media and the real-time availability to locate gay men in Toulouse, means that we can always look for new ways to define queer space. In the *Lieux de mémoire*, Nora used sites to define a collective national French identity. This chapter presents a shared memory focused on the ever-evolving nature of the LGBTQI+ community. Mapping queer France often relies on physical boundaries and structures, such as roads or businesses, but it is also ephemeral and relies on *where* or even *when* members of the queer community gather to truly define where their space exists.

Works cited

Batiste, Dominique Pierre. "'0 Feet Away': The queer cartography of French gay men's geo-social media use." *Anthropological Journal of European Cultures*, vol. 22, no. 2, 2013, pp. 111–32.

Binnie, Jon. "Coming out of geography: Towards a queer epistemology?" *Environment and Planning D: Space and Society*, no. 15, 1997, pp. 223–37.

Bouamer, Siham, Denis M. Provencher, and Ryan K. Schroth. "Introduction: Queering *Lieux de mémoire*." *Queer Realms of Memory: Archiving LGBTQ Sites and Symbols in the French National Narrative*, edited by Siham Bouamer, Denis M. Provencher, and Ryan K. Schroth. Liverpool UP, 2025, pp. 1–23.

Canham, Hugo. "Mapping the black queer geography of Johannesburg's lesbian women through narrative." *Psychology in Society*, vol. 55, 2017, pp. 84–107.

Caron, David. *My Father and I: The Marais and the Queerness of Community*. Cornell UP, 2009.

Certeau, Michel de. *L'Invention du quotidien 1, arts de faire*. Gallimard, 1990.

Choquette, Leslie. "Gay Paree: The origins of lesbian and gay commercial culture in the French Third Republic." *Contemporary French Civilization*, 41, no. 1, 2015, pp. 1–24.
Gieseking, Jen Jack. "Mapping lesbian and queer lines of desire: Constellations of queer urban space." *Environment and Planning D: Society and Space*, vol. 38, no. 5, 2020, pp. 941–60.
Hocquenghem, Guy. *Le Gay voyage. Guide et regard homosexuels sur les grandes métropoles*. Albin Michel, 1980.
Lee, Ming-Che. "Mapping queer literature in translation: A survey of globalized queer fiction produced in Taiwan in 1990s." *Asia Pacific Translation and Intercultural Studies*, vol. 8, no. 2, 2021, pp. 194–208.
Leroy, Stéphane. "Le Paris gay. Éléments pour une géographie de l'homosexualité." *Annales de géographie*, no. 646, 2005, pp. 579–601.
Nash, Catherine Jean. "Contesting identity: Politics of gays and lesbians in Toronto in the 1970s." *Gender, Place and Culture: A Journal of Feminist Geography*, vol. 12, no. 1, 2005, pp. 113–35.
Nora, Pierre. "Entre mémoire et histoire: la problématique des lieux." *Les Lieux de mémoire*, vol. 1, *La République*, edited by Pierre Nora. Gallimard, 1997, pp. 23–43.
Olson, Kory. *The Cartographic Capital: Mapping Third-Republic Paris, 1889–1934*. Liverpool UP, 2018.
Oswin, Natalie. "Critical geographies and the uses of sexuality: Deconstructing queer space." *Progress in Human Geography*, vol. 32, no. 1, 2008, pp. 89–103.
Provencher, Denis M. *Queer French: Globalization, Language, and Sexuality Citizenship in France*. Ashgate, 2007.
Reader, Keith. *The Marais: The Story of a Quartier*. Liverpool UP, 2020.
Redoutey, Emmanuel. "Géographie de l'homosexualité à Paris." *Urbanisme*, no. 325, 2002, pp. 59–63.
Ross, Andrew Israel. *Public City/Public Sex: Homosexuality, Prostitution, and Urban Culture in Nineteenth-Century Paris*. Temple UP, 2019.
Sibalis, Michael. "Urban space and homosexuality: The example of the Marais, Paris' 'Gay Ghetto.'" *Urban Studies*, vol. 41, no. 9, 2004, pp. 1739–58.

CHAPTER EIGHT

Carving out space in the city
LGBTQ+ pride as a queer *lieu de mémoire*

Luke L. Eilderts[1]

This chapter argues that lesbian, gay, bisexual, transgender, and queer+ (LGBTQ+) Pride demonstrations – commonly referred to in French as "la Marche des fiertés" [Pride March], "la Pride," or, less frequently, "la Marche des visibilités" [Visibility March] – function as queer *lieux de mémoire* [sites of memory]. Through their repeated enactment, these events express what Achille describes as "an urgent need to (re)assess the potential of a gradual and palimpsestic rewriting of the *roman national* [national narrative]" (25). Indeed, in Pierre Nora's influential collection of people, places, ideas, and objects that compose France's national narrative, one encounters a rather stark silence when it comes to non-heteronormative subjects or themes. Drawing inspiration from Étienne Achille, Charles Forsdick, and Lydie Moudileno's 2020 edited volume *Postcolonial Realms of Memory* this chapter asks that we broaden our understanding of France's national narrative by uncovering previously hidden or ignored sites of memory. Appearing in cities and towns during the summer months, French Pride demonstrations create spaces for LGBTQ+ individuals to become visible while also forging collective memories and traditions among its participants and viewers. Moreover, these queer *lieux de mémoire* have multiplied across France

---

[1] I would like to thank the editors of this volume for their valuable critiques of this chapter. I would also like to thank the organizers of Strasbourg's *Marche des visibilités* for their work and activism year after year.

and are no longer limited to large cities such as Paris and Lyon, further underscoring the growing presence of a French LGBTQ+ community and its place within the *roman national*.

Appearing in the early 1980s, Nora's influential concept of *lieux de mémoire* is a framework that explores the ways in which collective memory is preserved, transmitted, and symbolically represented in society. According to Nora, these sites are physical or symbolic places where a community's historical consciousness is concentrated and perpetuated. Nora's project has received criticism for its "silences" and "absences" while also "implying not only an exclusively republican and 'Hexagonal' conception of history but also a classic, if not narrow, perception of national memory" (Achille, Forsdick, and Moudileno 4–6). By focusing on the universal, Nora's project underscores how this concept privileges normative expressions of desire, sexuality, and gender identity rather than advancing a broader and more open understanding of them. Pride parades and demonstrations, through their repeated occupation of physical space as well as their commemorative practices, serve as both tangible repositories and figurative supports of collective memory, thereby allowing LGBTQ+ people to connect with and reflect upon their history (Nora 18–19). While Nora may be forgiven for not including a chapter on la Marche des fiertés – the Parisian event that most closely resembles it today only began in the last few years of the 1970s – it can no longer be overlooked.

What, then, makes a "queer" *lieu de mémoire*? My understanding of the term "queer" is informed by two overarching threads, which often intertwine with one another. On one hand, "queer" designates that which is odd, does not conform, and is at times "just plain wonky" (Ahmed 565). On the other, "queer" can also serve as an umbrella term that encompasses sexuality or gender identities that stand in opposition to dominant sexual and gender norms. While the term has carried a negative connotation and long served as an insult, it has also been reclaimed by some who wish to affirm their oppositional stance in relation to heteronormativity and traditional social structures (Whittington 157–59). A queer *lieu de mémoire* might therefore distort time and space (Halberstam 70–75), while highlighting forms of kinship beyond traditional models of the heteronormative family and nation (Caron 196–206).

Demonstrations like Paris's Marche des fiertés LGBT+ [LGBT+ Pride March] have their roots in what had previously been known as la Gay Pride or La Lesbian et Gay Pride, but whose use by event organizers in

France has nearly disappeared due in large part to trademark concerns (Bassingha). Moreover, as progressive understandings of sexual and gender identity have become more fluid, complex, and intersectional since the sexual liberation movements of the 1960s and 1970s, the terms used to designate minoritized sexual communities have grown to echo that complexity with additional letters being added to the LGBTQ+ acronym (e.g., "Q"ueer, "Q"uestioning, "I"ntersex, "A"sexual, and the "+" symbol representing the inclusion of people who may not identify with any of the listed categories). For some activists and scholars, however, the desire for inclusivity has resulted in a kind of "alphabet soup" that obscures the expressions of human sexuality and gender identity more than it illuminates them (Budhiraja, Fried, and Teixeira 131–34). Indeed, gender and sexuality are but a part of the complex intersectionality of human identity (Provencher, *Queer Maghrebi French* 257–66). Pride demonstrations, therefore, are not a solution to all the challenges faced by LGBTQ+ people. Additionally, not everyone who positions themselves against or outside heteronormativity sees themselves reflected in the event or the terms used to define it (Robineau 153). As an organizing concept, Pride has been critiqued by activists and scholars for its limited and limiting possibilities (Halperin and Traub 8–11), and the strategies for gaining political and social rights have often been questioned for championing normative views on sexuality and gender. I would argue, however, that as long as LGBTQ+ people remain targets of hate crimes and discrimination, Pride demonstrations can serve as a powerful, albeit imperfect tool for social change.

While the spark that led to the modern world-wide phenomenon that we know today often simply as Pride has its origins within the United States of the late 1960s, the ritual of commemorating it has traveled the world, especially in the global industrialized north. Reflecting on the worldwide adaptation of Pride, Peterson, Wahlström, and Wennerhag point out that "[d]espite its origins in the US, the tradition has become translated into new contexts to suit different national and local settings" (2). That idea of "translation" into a specifically French context can be seen with the beginnings of what would eventually become La Marche des fiertés in Paris. Traced back to the actions of the *Front homosexual d'action révolutionnaire* (FHAR), which was "bathed in the revolutionary legacy of 1968 and the feminist movement" (Weeks 46), this militant group participated in the traditional May Day marches alongside labor unions starting in 1971 and continuing until 1977 (Filleule 287; Sibalis, "Gay liberation comes to France" 272–73). After this moment, the *FHAR* and other activist organizations preferred to stage a separate event in late June, the traditional time period when the Stonewall riots are commemorated. As Michael Sibalis explains, "[e]ver since 1977 (with one exception) the march has taken place on a Saturday in late June, thereby commemorating the Stonewall Riots of June 27, 1969, when gays on Christopher Street in New York City resisted a police raid and launched the American gay liberation movement" ("'La Lesbian and Gay Pride' in Paris" 51).

The event's symbolic power as a turning point in the fight for sexual liberation might be what has become one of its most influential features. The momentum to commemorate this event does not appear to be slowing either as the number of Pride demonstrations and events continues to increase all while symbolic and physical violence against LGBTQ+ people remain a disturbing reality. Moreover, while France experienced what might be interpreted as its own founding moment of "gay liberation" – on March 10, 1971, approximately 30 activists interrupted Ménie Grégoire's popular weekday radio show, the topic of which was "l'homosexualité, ce douloureux problème" [homosexuality, this painful problem] – it is not this event that is commemorated today (Sibalis, "Gay Liberation Comes to France"). Interestingly, an interactive theatrical production of this nearly forgotten event was staged at *Les Célestins Théâtre de Lyon* in May and June 2024 (Célestins Théâtre de Lyon).

In "Between memory and history: *Les Lieux de mémoire*," a translation of the opening chapter to his multi-volume collaborative project, Nora engages with the symbolic quality of *lieux de mémoire* and the competing narratives of memory imposed from above against that which bubbles up from below.

> If, finally, we were most concerned with the symbolic element, we might oppose, for example, dominant and dominated *lieux de mémoire*. The first, spectacular and triumphant, imposing and, generally, imposed – either by a national authority or by an established interest, but always from above – characteristically have the coldness and solemnity of official ceremonies. One attends them rather than visits them. The second are places of refuge, sanctuaries of spontaneous devotion and silent pilgrimage, where one finds the living heart of memory. (Nora 23)

While local Pride parades may not be controlled *a priori* by a "national authority," one might argue that the various national, regional, or local organizing committees, whether they are large and with a long reach, such as those found in the metropolises of the world, or those more grass-roots organizers in smaller cities and villages, often provide a *mot d'ordre*, an "established interest." For example, the president of Strasbourg's 2008 organizing committee shared in an email exchange that "[n]ous n'avons rien contre la fête, mais nous nous refusons à réduire nos démarches politiques et militantes à une parade" [We have nothing against partying, but we refuse to reduce our political and activist actions to a parade] (Labaste). However, as Katherine McFarland Bruce suggests, "[m]ore so than other protests, Pride really belongs to the marchers and spectators that participate. While paid and volunteer organizers do tremendous work year-round to take care of the financial, legal, and organizational details of putting on a large event, they give remarkably little direction about the events' message or the behavior of participants" (7–8). In many respects, Pride celebrations allow for LGBTQ+ people to come together in a surprisingly visible and spectacular fashion. It creates a space where they can participate in a myriad of acts, and where participants may have different goals and aspirations for their participation. While some may choose to attend in order to advance a political or social cause, others may be more persuaded by the possibility of dressing up and dancing along to the music, and either group might take advantage of the possible social encounters to be had. This reinforces what Bruce advances in that individual participants, the ones who show up and take part in the march, are the ones who really "own" the event, despite the organizers' contours or guidelines. Moreover, the role of "marcher" and "spectator" often becomes blurred as participants move in and out of the parade, observing one moment and joining in the next (Bruce 8). As we explore the complex dynamics of Pride celebrations, it becomes evident that while participants may resist centralized control, the influence of organizing committees remains palpable through the posters, flyers, and other linguistic messages displayed throughout the march. Turning our attention to a regional manifestation can help shed some light on the intersection of LGBTQ+ visibility as well as some of the local and national sociopolitical dynamics.

Instead of focusing on the capital, I would like to consider a regional event, the *Marche des visibilités homosexuelles, bisexuelles et transgenres* [The Gay, Lesbian, Bisexual and Transgender Visibilities March] in Strasbourg. The regional capital's march presents a compelling example of French republican anxieties triggered by the threat of explicitly visible non-heteronormative sexualities in the public sphere. Moreover, the region of Alsace has traditionally been a stronghold of the political right since World War II (Barth), as well as exhibiting a slightly stronger, albeit waning, religious affiliation than the rest of the country (Wydmusch). While Paris's march is the oldest and most well-attended of the summer Pride marches in France, the growth in regional Pride events, of which summer 2022 saw the largest number of parades and demonstrations since their creation, underscores that the French national narrative can no longer ignore its LGBTQ+ citizens.

The beginning of Strasbourg's Pride events serves as an interesting departure point to highlight how French republican political discourse was used to question the event's very existence. As described in their 2003 book *La culture gaie et lesbienne*, Anne Rambach and Marine Rambach recount that in April 2001 a colloquium called "Écrire les homosexualités" [Write Homosexualities] was scheduled to take place thanks in part to the support of the mayor's office. With the election loss of Catherine Trautmann (Parti socialiste) to Fabienne Keller (Union pour la démocratie française), the mayor's office did what Rambach and Rambach called an about-face, refusing even to allow the municipal magazine to cover any events linked to the LGBTQ+ Strasbourg community (50–53). In a 2002 interview that appeared in the LGBTQ+ magazine *Têtu*, Keller stated that Pride marches are too grounded in a sexual identity, and that she felt that such an event conflicted with French ideals of citizenship.

> Dans les Gay Pride que j'ai vues, notamment à San Francisco, il y avait des choses choquantes, excessives. Ce qu'on nous montre dans ces manifestations appartient à la vie privée, un domaine à respecter. Il faut être extrêmement vigilant. Franchement, à titre personnel, je ne pense pas que cela facilite l'intégration des homosexuels dans la société. Cette affirmation très forte, presque violente, est une manière de se différencier des autres et de s'en écarter. Ce n'est pas la bonne méthode pour s'intégrer. (Nicolas 11)

> [In the Gay Pride parades that I have seen, notably in San Francisco, there were some shocking things, excessive. What is shown to us in these demonstrations belongs to private life, a domain to be respected. One must be extremely vigilant. Frankly, I personally do not think that this helps facilitate the integration of homosexuals into society. This very strong affirmation, almost violent, is a way to differentiate oneself from others and to move away from them. This is not the right method for integration.]

Keller's stance on demonstrations of non-normative sexualities like the ones she saw in San Francisco reveal several points that will be recognizable to anyone familiar with French discourse on republican universalism. The drive to silence the voices of LGBTQ+ individuals and reduce the public visibility of their bodies in the name of upholding an ideal "unmarked" French sexual citizenship underscores how the discourse of French nationhood has long aimed at suppressing difference within the Republic (Provencher, *Queer French*; Gunther; Bell and Binnie; Richardson; Stychin). Furthermore, Keller draws connections among French and American Pride demonstrations, highlighting what she sees as a particularly extreme example in San Francisco. Her narrative presents these events as a part of a larger, almost unified expression of LGBTQ+ enthusiasm and activism. In her hesitation to support such an event in the Alsatian capital, Keller implies that Pride demonstrations, even for those who would normally not approve of them, are linked together forming a queer, traveling *lieu de mémoire*. Despite her reticence, the event was allowed to proceed during the summer of 2002 and has continued every year since (excluding the summer of 2020 when the COVID-19 pandemic halted most gatherings).

While interest and participation in the demonstrations have waxed and waned over the years, their continued presence on French soil as well as the increase in the number of demonstrations and locations across the globe (e.g., Nyanzi) may be indicative of what the editors of this volume advance is "the development in France of multi-faceted communities and their ability to create collective cultural meaning and memory" (Bouamer, Provencher, and Schroth 5). LGBTQ+ people continue to occupy, disrupt, and queer public spaces year after year, thereby forging their own traditions and their own memories. While participants will change from one Pride season to the next and from one parade to another, the events themselves are able to claim a kind of filiation with other Pride parades and demonstrations, not only forming connections to a larger French LGBTQ+ community, but to a transnational one as well. In 2008, for example, the organizing committee invited a small delegation of Turkish LGBTQ+ activists to participate as guests of honor not only in the march but also in some of the workshops, symposia, and other social activities planned during the week leading up to the Saturday parade. More recently, in 2023, the organizing committee further strengthened its connections to the transnational LGBTQ+ community by highlighting on its website threats to the community not only in France but also in places like Algeria, Hungary, Qatar, Russia, and the United States (FestiGays. net, *La Marche*).

In some of their most widely distributed materials and flyers, the organizers of Strasbourg's *Marche des visibilités* create an interesting virtual space where their calls to action and their use of imagery spurs their readers to enter into a kind of dialogue or reflection on the LGBTQ+ community (FestiGays.net, "Les 20 Ans de Festigays"). On every one of the flyers produced since 2002, the slogan "*Liberté, Égalité, Visibilité*" [Liberty, Equality, Visibility] appears. By transforming the motto of the French Republic, organizers claim their own space within the nation. The absence of *fraternité* [brotherhood] and the inclusion of *visibilité* suggests that LGBTQ+ people might not feel they have a place within the Republic, that the idea of *fraternité* has been denied to them. Indeed, as Mona Ozouf explains, for some, *fraternité* recalls the violent and exclusionary reactions during *la Terreur* [the Terror] of the early 1790s, where the word suggested "exclusion" (101). Furthermore, the rejection of *fraternité* could also be due to its religious connections, although this interpretation is less likely since the word's "evangelical halo" was removed through its redefinition to align more with "solidarity" during the Third Republic (Ozouf 109–10). Instead, by highlighting visibility, they point out their own invisibility within the Republic.

The flyers often contain language that evokes not only the idea of an LGBTQ+ community and its past, present, and future, but also some of the social and political issues facing the local community around the time of that year's march. In 2007 and 2008, for example, issues of both physical and mental health were highlighted through the slogans "ÉGALITE, PRÉVENTION/MAINTENANT DES ACTES!" [Equality, Prevention/Actions Now!] (2007) and "ADO TRANS HOMO/ DU MAL-ÊTRE AU SUICIDE/AGISSONS!" [Teen Trans Homo/From Angst to Suicide/Let's Take Action!] (2008). Others speak to the struggle against phobias linked to non-normative sexual and gender identities not only between implied straight and LGBTQ+ peoples, but also among LGBTQ+ people themselves: "HOMO/TRANS/BIPHOBIE/STOP À L'HYPOCRISIE!" [Homo/Trans/Biphobia/Stop the Hypocrisy] (2006); and "UNI(E)S CONTRE L'HOMOPHOBIE ET LA TRANSPHOBIE" [United against Homophobia and Transphobia] (2010). In the lead up to and after the vote on the *Mariage pour tous* [Marriage for all], as well as the many debates on what constitutes a family, the organizers emphasized the importance of these political and social rights: "À QUAND LES MÊMES DROITS?" *[When will there be the same rights?]* (2011); "L'ÉGALITÉ N'ATTEND PLUS!" *[Equality no longer waits!]* (2012); "*Vive les marié·e·s*, MAIS la lutte continue" [Long live the newlyweds, but the struggle continues] (2013); À QUAND UN MONDE RAINBOW?" [When will there be a rainbow world?] (2014), where the word "rainbow" references the rainbow flag as an international symbol of LGBTQ+ movements; and "NOS FAMILLES MÉRITENT VOS DROITS" [Our families deserve your rights] (2018). In this last example, the use of the possessive adjectives "nos" [our] and "vos" [your] creates a sharp separation between the LGBTQ+ people who feel their families do not benefit from the same rights as others.

Several flyers evoke the history of Strasbourg's march, calling upon its readers not only to reflect on the past, but also to place it within the genealogy of the larger LGBTQ+ rights movement. For the 40th anniversary of the Stonewall riots, the 2009 flyer stressed the idea of togetherness and community while also encouraging readers to remember: "ENSEMBLE, se souvenir pour mieux agir" [TOGETHER, remember in order to take better action]. What readers are asked to remember, however, remains cleverly open, since "se souvenir" lacks an object. For 2016, the flyer reads "liberté/égalité/visibilité/15 ans de lutte!" [liberty/equality/visibility/15 years of struggle!], which references the 2001 events canceled by the mayor's office. The 2021 flyer includes a list of years and the events associated with them, such as the 1969 Stonewall Riots, the first Pride demonstration in France in 1977, the removal of "homosexuality" from the list of mental illnesses in 1990, the 1999 vote on the *Pacte civil de solidarité (PaCS)* [civil solidarity pact, or civil union law], the 2010 declaration that trans identity is no longer a mental illness, and the 2013 *Mariage pour tous*. All of these events are topped by the phrase *"La lutte continue"* [The struggle continues], reminding readers that the march towards equal political rights and social change remains ongoing. Furthermore, if we apply Peterson, Wahlström, and Wennerhag's notion of the translation of Pride, we can see in these examples that, while the founding event is the Stonewall riots, several of the other events might only resonate with a French audience (e.g., *PaCS*, *Mariage pour tous*).

Varying from year to year, the flyers often include stylized representations of raised fists or hands (2007, 2010, 2017, 2021), which suggest protest and, when in a group, a collectivity or collective act. In 2007, for example, the reader sees the fraying edges of a rainbow flag that, instead of coming apart, rise together and appear as fists. Highlighting some of the political and social issues occupying the minds of the organizers in the lead up to an election cycle, the 2017 flyer portrays outstretched arms depositing ballots with words like "SANTÉ" [health], and "PMA" [medically assisted procreation] into a transparent voting urn.

While many of the images used in the flyers do not specifically reference the city or region in which the march takes place, there are a few exceptions. Most notably in 2005, for example, the flyer displays a stork with peacock tail feathers in the colors of the rainbow. At first, the image does not appear out of the ordinary. As one of Alsace's most recognizable symbols, the stork and its likeness are found throughout the region. Moreover, the use of rainbow colors on a flyer advertising a Pride demonstration does not appear out of place. Upon closer inspection, however, the queerness of this creature becomes more apparent. In a clever juxtaposition, the artist has created a hybrid creature, one that not only references the region with the image of the stork, but also the LGBTQ+ movement through the flamboyant plumage of the peacock made even more outrageous with its rainbow colors.

These bits of paper, flyers and posters scattered from the departure point to the eventual destination, represent the traces and fragments of a collective LGBTQ+ memory. Tucked away in one's personal space, proudly used as a bookmark, or safely archived in a scrapbook, these flyers recall the participants' connection to the larger LGBTQ+ community no matter how loosely it may be constructed. Moreover, the event and its repetition in the numerous other marches not only in France but across the globe forge a kind of shared memory and tradition, even if that memory differs by location, language, and local geography. Yet, through their almost disposable nature, these cultural ephemera might also disturb the notion of traditional *lieux*. The turnover of cultural and political trends, the changing understandings of sexual desires and gender identities, the growth in experiences mediated through or captured by social media and the Internet may unsettle the permanence often associated with traditional sites of memory. Moreover, these traces may be rendered invisible, albeit unintentionally, by the city's street maintenance program. While attending the 2008 parade, for example, I could not help but reflect on the irony of what unfolded at the end of the procession: just after the passing of the last float and marchers, street cleaners appeared and swept up nearly every trace of the event. While one of the main goals of the march is to give visibility to LGBTQ+ people, as soon as they were gone, the city appeared to wash them away in an effort to return the spaces they occupied to their normal functions as quickly as possible. What was most likely done out of practicality seemed to mirror the French republic's incapacity or unwillingness to see difference.

To close, I would like to return to Étienne Achille's argument mentioned at the beginning of this chapter and propose that, like colonial histories, demonstrations such as Pride also ask us to "(re)assess the potential of a gradual and palimpsestic rewriting" of national narratives in order to make LGBTQ+ history "accessible." Through an examination of the posters and flyers studied here, we see how these objects emerge as contributors to the changing contours of national memory. Moreover, just as Pride demonstrations remind spectators that French LGBTQ+ people exist, those same demonstrations allow LGBTQ+ people a way to forge collective memories and traditions that inform and influence the writing and rewriting of the *roman national*.

Works cited

Achille, Étienne. "Playing Devil's Advocate." *Francosphères*, vol. 10, no. 1, June 2021, pp. 9–25.
Achille, Étienne, Charles Forsdick, and Lydie Moudileno. "Introduction." *Postcolonial Realms of Memory: Sites and Symbols in Modern France*, edited by Étienne Achille, Charles Forsdick, and Lydie Moudileno. Liverpool UP, 2020, pp. 1–19.
Ahmed, Sara. "Orientations: Toward a queer phenomenology." *GLQ: A Journal of Lesbian and Gay Studies*, vol. 12, no. 4, 2006, pp. 543–74.
Barth, Elie. "Alsace, terre de droite." *Le Monde.fr*. June 18, 2004.
Bassingha, Esther. "Marche des fiertés: pourquoi ne dit-on plus 'gay pride'?" *CNEWS.fr*. June 23, 2023.
Bell, David, and Jon Binnie. *The Sexual Citizen: Queer Theory and Beyond*. Polity, 2000.
Bouamer, Siham, Denis M. Provencher, and Ryan K. Schroth. "Introduction: Queering *Lieux de mémoire*." *Queer Realms of Memory: Archiving LGBTQ Sites and Symbols in the French National Narrative*, edited by Siham Bouamer, Denis M. Provencher, and Ryan K. Schroth. Liverpool UP, 2025, pp. 1–23.
Bruce, Katherine McFarland. *Pride Parades: How a Parade Changed the World*. New York UP, 2016.
Budhiraja, Sangeeta, Susana T. Fried, and Alexandra Teixeira. "Spelling it out: From alphabet soup to sexual rights and gender justice." *Development, Sexual Rights and Global Governance*. Routledge, 2010, pp. 131–44.
Caron, David. *My Father and I: The Marais and the Queerness of Community*. Cornell UP, 2009.
Célestins Théâtre de Lyon. "L'Homosexualité, ce douloureux problème." *Les Célestins, Théâtre de Lyon*. https://billetterie.theatredescelestins.com/event/197737-lhomosexualite-ce-douloureux-probleme.

FestiGays.net. "Les 20 ans de Festigays." *FestiGays.net.* https://festigays.net/les-20-ans-de-festigays/.

———. *La Marche.* https://festigays.net/marche-des-visibilites/.

Filleule, Olivier. "Lesbian and Gay Pride." *Dictionnaire des cultures gays et lesbiennes*, edited by Didier Eribon. Larousse, 2003, pp. 287–88.

Gunther, Scott. *The Elastic Closet: A History of Homosexuality in France, 1942–Present.* Palgrave Macmillan, 2009.

Halberstam, Jack. *The Queer Art of Failure.* Duke UP, 2011.

Halperin, David M., and Valerie Traub, eds. *Gay Shame.* U of Chicago P, 2009.

Labaste, Youssef. *Réponse à ton interview.* February 23, 2008.

Nicolas, Christian. "Strasbourg: Fabienne Keller." *L'Agenda de têtu*, no. 15, February 2002, pp. 10–11.

Nora, Pierre. "Between memory and history: *Les Lieux de mémoire.*" Translated by Marc Roudebush. *Representations*, vol. 26, 1989, pp. 7–24.

Nyanzi, Stella. "Queer pride and protest: A reading of the bodies at Uganda's first gay beach pride." *Signs: Journal of Women in Culture and Society*, vol. 40, no. 1, September 2014, pp. 36–40.

Ozouf, Mona. "Liberty, equality, fraternity." *Realms of Memory: The Construction of the French Past*, edited by Pierre Nora and Lawrence D. Kritzman. Translated by Arthur Goldhammer, vol. 3. Columbia UP, 1998, pp. 77–114.

Peterson, Abby, Mattias Wahlström, and Magnus Wennerhag, eds. *Pride Parades and LGBT Movements: Political Participation in an International Comparative Perspective.* Routledge, 2018.

Provencher, Denis M. *Queer French: Globalization, Language and Sexual Citizenship in France.* Ashgate, 2007.

———. *Queer Maghrebi French: Language, Temporalities, Transfiliations.* Liverpool UP, 2017.

Rambach, Anne, and Marine Rambach. *La Culture gaie et lesbienne.* Fayard, 2003.

Richardson, Diane. "Constructing sexual citizenship: Theorizing sexual rights." *Critical Social Policy*, vol. 20, no. 1, 2000, pp. 105–35.

Robineau, Jeanne. *Discrimination(s), genre(s) et urbanite(s): la communauté gaie de Rennes.* Harmattan, 2010.

Sibalis, Michael. "Gay liberation comes to France: The *Front homosexuel d'action révolutionnaire* (FHAR)." *French History and Civilization: Papers from the George Rudé Society*, edited by Ian Coller, Helen Davies, and Julie Kalman, vol. 1, 2005, pp. 265–76.

———. "'La Lesbian and Gay Pride' in Paris: Community, commerce and carnival." *Gay and Lesbian Cultures in France*, edited by Lucille Carins. Peter Lang, 2002, pp. 51–66.

Stychin, Carl F. "Sexual citizenship in the European Union." *Citizenship Studies*, vol. 5, no. 3, 2001, pp. 285–301.

Weeks, Jeffrey. "Gay liberation and its legacies." *The Ashgate Research Companion to Lesbian and Gay Activism*, edited by David Paternotte and Manon Tremblay, 2015, pp. 45–57.
Whittington, Karl. "Queer." *Studies in Iconography*, vol. 33, 2012, pp. 157–68.
Wydmusch, Solange. "L'Evangélisme alsacien: lieux et contours." *Actualité des protestantismes évangéliques*, edited by Christopher Sinclair. Presses universitaires de Strasbourg, 2002, pp. 43–69.

CHAPTER NINE

Queering the *périph'*
New sites for queer memory in contemporary French cinema

James S. Williams

In the short film *Quatre Fromages/The Edge* (2019), directed by David Chausse and shot as if in real time in the northern Paris *banlieue* of Saint-Denis,[1] a chance encounter takes place between a young Maghrebi pizza delivery guy (Aïmen Derriachi) and a trans Franco-Chinese dancer (Yuming Hey). They have found themselves locked out together on the rooftop of a tower block. After a mutually suspicious and aggressive start based on rushed judgments and contemptuous preconceptions – the dancer thought the delivery guy was going to jump off the edge after becoming upset about a failed delivery; he dismissed them as a deviant alien – the two learn to relate to each other with lively banter and humor embracing cultural and sexual difference. A space of play with cultural, sexual, and ethnic identity is opened up that encompasses language – teasing each other with ethnic stereotypes while declining to divulge their first names – as well as artistic appreciation. The dancer will invite the delivery guy to listen to their music on their headphone; he will eventually freely compliment them on their dancing. He also reveals, to their approval, the dream he harbors of setting up a voluntary network of community support operating outside the metropolitan corporate sphere.

In the final scene, after occupying opposed cinematic fields, the pair sit together on the edge of the roof facing the same direction and eating the

[1] Included in *The French Boys 4*.

undelivered pizza – the opportunity to reflect on their explosive meeting. A slow, wide-angle zoom-out allows the two to admire the dense concrete skyline and branch of the Seine stretched out majestically below them in the warm glow of the setting sun. Hence, although unfolding in a circumscribed area above the streets and so at one remove from daily reality, *Quatre Fromages* presents the *banlieue* as a shared, open, heteroclite, *aesthetic* realm that upends its conventional depiction as faceless, desolate, and disconnected. Further, it provides new relational markers and the seeds of intersectional *banlieusard* [*banlieue* dweller] memory: the promise of fresh kinds of affective connection and alliance and a potential new communal network of social exchange.

I start with this exciting and propitious vision of a queer *banlieue* because it swims so beautifully against the tide of most French films about queer life in the working-class *banlieue*, which tend towards hard-hitting, fervently violent, often salacious, genre-driven dramas shot in naturalistic and highly graphic fashion. A representative example is *7ème ciel/In Seventh Heaven* (2013), a short by Guillaume Foirest set in a *cité* [housing project] in Champigny-sur-Marne, a southeastern suburb of Paris in Val-de-Marne, which follows the everyday life of a young *beur* [a person of Maghrebi origin born and living in France], visibly tortured by having to hide his sexuality.[2] Sofiane (Redouane Behache) is existentially lost: at once homophobic and gay, tough and vulnerable, by day riff-raff, by night hustler performing S/M tricks with a wealthy, older white client a car-ride away. In conflict with his family and trying vainly to stem the rage of his friends towards perceived others, he is pushed to the edge, eventually running through the *cité* in tears and revealing his true sexuality to his nonplussed girlfriend on the phone. The final shot leaves him in limbo: neither of the two traditional options for queer *banlieusards* of color, particularly of Muslim background – stay firmly hidden in the closet or escape – seems possible. The closing credits duly acknowledge two controversial recent books that made visible for the first time Arab queer intimacy: *Homo-ghetto* (2009), an investigative report on homosexual life in the *banlieue* by Franck Chaumont, former Beur FM editor-in-chief, which presents gays and lesbians in the *cités* dramatically as "les clandestins de la République" [the stowaways of the Republic];[3] and *Un homo dans la cité* (2009), a personal account by

---

2 The short *7ème ciel* is available for streaming on the 2019 compilation film *French Touch: Between Men* (FilmDoo).

3 Mehammed Mack argues incisively that in Chaumont's "restrictive sexual

Brahim Naït-Balk detailing the descent into hell, then liberation, of a gay man of Maghrebi background.[4]

Quatre Fromages emphatically refutes the general characterization of working-class *banlieues* as a generalized non-place operating under the law of silence and violence, that is, as a racialized, homophobic zone off-limits for out queer people and effectively outside the boundaries of queer French citizenship. Indeed, the film directly counters the often sensationalist news reporting of the *banlieue* as a volatile, even lawless, zone of brutal hypermasculinity, misogyny, and indiscriminate sexual violence (including gang rapes of young women).[5] It also declines the pornographic gaze, the other side of the fantasmatic coin of metropolitan phobia and speculation about the *banlieue*. I'm thinking in particular of the websites of ethnic gay porn and violence like citebeur.com perpetuating (white) stereotypes of Arab and Black *lascars* [thugs] – part of the multiplicity of cultural representations that, as Mehammed Mack argues in *Sexagon: Muslims, France, and the Sexualization of National Culture* (2017), both reflect and produce postcolonial France as a kaleidoscope of sexual obsessions (notably the supposed "virility cultures" of Franco-Arabs rendering Muslim youth as both sexualized objects and unruly subjects).

At the root of the general stigmatization of the *banlieue* and the scapegoating of communities of immigrant origin as always and already outside the purview of French citizenship – regardless of where the individuals within these communities were born – is, of course, partition: it is separated off from the city and segregated in a manner perpetuating the rigid colonial mapping of space (for example, the *indigènes* consigned to the plantations). Taking into account the status of many *banlieusards* as descendants of *indigènes* in French colonial history, Hervé Tchumkam, in *Postcolonial Realms of Memory* (2020),

---

liberation" the "desire to melt into the (sexual) Republican fabric is assumed, and desires for sexual *non*-assimilation are thus never entertained" (47) (original emphasis).

4 Other powerful examples of the subgenre of short films about queer oppression in the *banlieue* include Yohann Kouam's *Le Retour* (2013), set in the northeastern Paris *banlieue* of Bobigny, and Nathan Carli's *Malik* (2018), shot in nearby Bagnolet.

5 See, for example, Cathy Guetta's investigative report, *La Cité du mâle*, broadcast by ARTE on September 29, 2010. The title makes a play on the homonyms "*mâle*" (male) and "*mal*" (evil), suggesting a link between an overabundant masculinity in the *cités* and a predisposition to do wrong.

uses Pierre Nora's concept of *lieu de mémoire* to argue that the *banlieues* now stand out as a site of memory in their own right, precisely because their treatment by the state is reminiscent of French colonial history characterized by repressive measures such as racial profiling, prohibition of the veil, and the creation of anti-crime squads (101). His conclusion that France should rehabilitate the *banlieues* as sites of French national memory as part of the general project of healing the wounds of the colonial past is incontrovertible: "they [the *banlieues*] are not only *lieux de mémoire* but can also constitute the ultimate site where both the French state and its citizens of African heritage can converge around a common memory" (107).

Yet Tchumkam's approach is premised on the universalizing heterosexual presuppositions of Nora's *lieu de mémoire*, which effectively precludes difference and diversity.[6] It raises the question how might the *banlieue* be screened as a fully inclusive space in a way that dethrones and queers the exclusionary contours of the *lieu de mémoire*. Put differently, how might cinema, the focus of my study, actively resist what Éric Fassin has termed the overdetermined, false opposition between the *centre-ville* and *banlieue* (*intra muros* vs *extra muros*), which triggers further pernicious binaries such as "homosexual ghetto" and "homophobic ghetto" – all based on the lazy, racist assumption that the working-class, multiracial *banlieue* is an indecipherable, barren wasteland devoid of and resistant to (white) "French" culture?[7]

In what is developing as a crucial aesthetic and political project by the Algerian-born film producer of *Quatre Fromages*, Hakim Atoui, to queer the *banlieue*,[8] his debut feature-length film of the following year, *La Première marche* (2020), a documentary co-directed by (white) French reporter Baptiste Etchegaray,[9] took further the short's ambition to frame the *banlieue* as an affirmative site of queer collective memory. It recorded the preparations for the first ever Marche des Fiertés (Gay Pride) in

6 See the editors' introduction.

7 See Fassin. For accounts of the place of queers in the *banlieue* within French media discourse and the French cultural imaginary, see Amine (in particular 116–47) and Lotem.

8 Another short produced by Atoui called *Scred* (2017), shot in Aubervilliers, and again directed by Chausse (assisted by Simon Frenay), explores the smoldering internalized homophobia that erupts between two (white) male acquaintances living in the Paris *banlieue* (the title is *verlan* [backslang] for *discret*).

9 The DVD released in 2021 by Outplay Films includes an interview with the directors.

Saint-Denis on June 9, 2019, organized by a group of four young student activists at Paris 8 University Vincennes-Saint-Denis. Taking place three weeks before Paris Gay Pride, the Marche des Fiertés was both a festive and militant event. Walking the short route through central Saint-Denis with the main banner in inclusive French script reading "Banlieusard·e·s & fièr·e·s" [*Banlieue* Dwellers & Proud], the thousand or so participants sought expressly to combat the media's denigration of the *banlieue*. The square of the Basilica of Saint-Denis was transformed into an unprecedented queer "village" – a free, open space of local associations and ad hoc groupings and alliances corresponding to the organizers' egalitarian wish not to have the march headed by chosen officials. On the program was a drag queen workshop and an after-party with the queer collective "Sœurs Malsaines" (Wicked Sisters). In one fell swoop the working-class *banlieue* was revealed as a new, vital, inclusive, and intersectional locus of queer visibility.

As a queer documentary about an ethnically diverse queer collective, namely the Saint-Denis Ville au Cœur association founded by the four students (Luca Poissonnet, Annabelle Redortier, Youssef Belghmaidi, and Yanis Khames), *La Première marche* offered a queer response (conscious or not) to Nabil Ben Yadir's big-star drama *La Marche* (2013), which recreated the historic 1983 *Marche pour l'égalité et contre le racisme* [March for Equality and Against Racism] from Marseille to Paris. Yet it is specifically as the manifestation of a new type of queer *banlieue* film – rather than simply for its relevance as a faithful documentary record of a historical queer event in the *banlieue* – that *La Première marche* is so important, as it is directly concerned with the mission of queering the place of the *banlieue* in the French visual sphere. Its explicit *parti pris* is to provide an authentic portrait of queer everyday lives in their local, multi-ethnic, cultural habitat over an extended period of time, thus illustrating the *banlieue* as a space of lived daily experience, engaged political debate about personal/public identity, and far-reaching social change.

In what follows, I will assess the cinematic and political stakes of *La Première marche* in inaugurating a new platform of queer French film memory rooted in the working-class, multi-racial *banlieue*. I will argue that the extraordinary ambition of the first Marche des Fiertés in the *banlieue* – a groundbreaking step in reversing the negative terms of representation of the *banlieue* as peripheral to notions of the *patrimoine*, and, in so doing, creating a site of queer memory in a domain where there has ostensibly been none before – is extended by the film itself, which dissolves the standard demarcation between center and *banlieue* mapped as an opposition between visibly queer and repressed or clandestine queer. By presenting the *banlieue* instead as a privileged site for interrogating national identity and advancing what the editors of this volume propose suggestively as "the reinstitution of a living queer citizenship,"[10] *La Première marche* contributes to the construction of a new, collective, postcolonial queer memory – one that serves to rewrite the French national narrative. To gain a full measure of the film's potential value as a queer *lieu de mémoire* mobilizing the spatial dimension of memory, I will compare it with *Homme au bain/Man at Bath* (2010) by established queer *auteur* Christophe Honoré, a drama anchored in documentary aesthetics and one of only a small handful of feature-length films that have resolutely crossed the *périph(érique)* to celebrate queer life and intimacy in the multicultural spaces of the *banlieue*.[11]

Spaces for queer memory: New coordinates, new openings

Focusing on the six months of preparation for the Marche des Fiertés, *La Première marche* follows close-up over 70 minutes the four main activists and their friends and associates as they negotiate the many logistical challenges posed by the march with energy, passion, and defiance. Eschewing an authoritative voice-over, this grass-roots, DIY-style, and entirely self-funded film, shot with only one digital camera, feels at once intimate and casual, moving forward in time haphazardly as it records not only public actions but also private, incidental moments of amusement, tension, and occasional desultoriness. We are made privy to a new generation of queer protest: smart, eloquent, ardent, globally aware, well-versed in the arguments around homonationalism and transphobia (the work of Jasbir Puar is confidently cited), and wise not only to how *banlieusards* are racialized and stigmatized but also how secularists weaponize homosexual rights to attack "backward" practicing Muslims (as if one cannot be both queer and Muslim).

The student activists start off with the same core understanding as Tchumkam of the colonial determinants of the *banlieue* – indeed, the history of colonization flows inescapably through some of their personal stories. Yet while they would surely espouse the idea that the *banlieues*

---

10 See the editors' introduction.
11 A DVD of *Homme au bain* was released by Lumière in 2010.

"ultimately stand out as sites of a shared memory, which is nothing less than the communal memory of all French citizens, regardless of their race or origin" (Tchumkam 107), their response is to establish their own particular ideological framework for discussion and action. They are acutely aware of their own difference: not only do they not correspond to the mediatized image of the *banlieusard* as the unemployed and disengaged other choosing to withdraw from official scrutiny of the Republic and refuse its desires for universalism and transparency (they are, after all, social sciences students with aspirations), but also their very queerness makes them feel doubly other and marginalized in the *banlieue* setting. Their key terms are intersectionality, inclusivity, and *territoire* – both the geographical territory of Saint-Denis and queer territory as a construct. Moreover, they display no putative immigrant need to identify with the host country: the only flag in evidence is the global Rainbow flag, as opposed to the *Tricolore* or a flag indicating their postcoloniality. In fact, belonging is expressed in the film in staunchly local rather than national terms, and there is direct resistance to pre-set Republican notions of identity, even though the activists are working firmly within the mainstream political and administrative system and not revolting against it (the march was directly supported by Saint-Denis City Hall).[12]

Underpinning *La Première marche* is a spatial politics based on the specificity of locale and neighborhood that undermines any simple conception of the *banlieue* as an anonymous, amorphous, undifferentiated mass. This strategy of particularizing the *banlieue* and reorienting the viewer's perception of *banlieusard* space entails assiduously tracking the bodies of queer residents in circulation. No time is wasted on conventional establishing shots, and the film's very lack of artfulness and stylistic effects, together with its clear commitment to a mobile, wide-angle, inclusive frame, ensure that the *banlieusards* are fully seen and heard. The camera leads the viewer around central Saint-Denis and, in the spirit of free access, enters a motley array of domestic and institutional spaces that are visited and revisited: sitting room, balcony, stairwell, train station, RER car, roadside, campus café, board room,

---

12 Saint-Denis is, of course, rich with the signs of Republican and colonial memory. The march started at Place de la Résistance-et-de-la-Déportation, proceeded down the rue Gabriel-Péri, turned into the rue de la République, before finally reaching the square of the Basilica, which houses a royal necropolis dating back to Francis I.

Europe 1 radio studio, second-hand clothes store, etc. Official settings like the City Hall chamber are visibly queered, with at one point the electronic display board being used to communicate a message about homonationalism. We are taken also to Aubervilliers with Youssef who makes a chance connection in a café with a female waitress when she announces that she, too, is originally from Rabat. We then move on to his apartment for an impromptu conversation during which he confides he found life difficult and "neocolonial" in the Moroccan capital (a city, we note, where colonial urban planning cast the poorest to the ultraperiphery),[13] while also disclosing self-ironically that he suffers from the "colonial syndrome" of dating only white men.

The effect of this at once aleatory and multifocal vision of the queer everyday is to de-dramatize the *banlieue* – in direct contrast to the punctual flashpoints of violence and rioting relayed by the media in search of stories of death, violence, and terrorism, but also to those *banlieue* films (gay or straight) detailing fear, trauma, and despair. Indeed, the film dares to suggest that merely recording the details of everyday queer life in the *banlieue* is already to initiate a filmic space of and for queer memory.

A similarly understated cinematic approach to the *banlieue* is taken in *Homme au bain*, set between Gennevilliers, a working-class suburb to the north-west of Paris, and New York (Paris itself barely features). Splicing together video footage of the U.S. release of Honoré's 2009 drama, *Non ma fille, tu n'iras pas danser/Making plans for Lena*, and a short commissioned by the Théâtre 2 Gennevilliers, the film presents a gay couple breaking up: after Emmanuel (played by celebrated porn star François Sagat) sexually assaults his film-maker lover Omar (Omar Ben Sellem), the latter asks him to vacate the apartment by the time he (Omar) gets back from a week-long promotional trip to New York. Omar's high-jinks in Manhattan are intercut into a documentary-like record of the uber-muscled Emmanuel at a loose end in Gennevilliers having bored sex with chain-smoking skinny young men living in the same tower block or close by. The very first image embeds the film in an unprettified concrete landscape of blocks, the humdrum setting for its frank and direct portrayal of queer *banlieusard* life conveyed in a social-realist idiom.

The commune of Gennevilliers has become (in)famous, of course, for being the place of abode of Chérif Kouachi, one of the two brothers

---

13 See Ossman and Terrio.

of Algerian background behind the *Charlie Hebdo* attacks in Paris in January 2015. It is also a familiar site of homophobic attacks and persecution: in November 2018, a young gay *beur* called Lyes Alouane talked directly to the media about his daily experience of abuse and aggression.[14] Less well known, however, is that Gennevilliers is a site of queer art history. The film's title is a reference to the 1884 canvas of male nudity by Impressionist painter Gustave Caillebotte, who resided in Gennevilliers after completing it, and who died there in 1894. Caillebotte's interest in the male nude, set in a modern context, has been linked to his own presumed homosexuality since his subject matter repeatedly involved virile workers, muscular rowers, and male bathers. Honoré's film is arguably a modern rendition of the painting *Homme au bain* – Emmanuel will even draw a large romantic portrait of Omar on the walls of their shared apartment.

Yet, crucially, the cultural references in Honoré's film are rich and mixed, including references not only to French art, literature, and song, such as Francis Lacombrade's *La Classe des garçons* (1980) or the music of Charles Aznavour, but also to American songs and culture. The presence of the cult American novelist Dennis Cooper playing an aging, queer artist living upstairs in the same block underscores the at once transnational and transcultural dimension of the *banlieue*, amplified by the free use of English, as when Emmanuel takes a taxi with a bilingual girlfriend via the *périph'* to Porte de Clignancourt. While acknowledging the drawback of a white American character moving into a *banlieue* apartment to be closer to the raw "ethnic" masculinity he fetishizes, Mack rightly argues that *Homme au Bain* depicts the *banlieue* "as a relative paradise of spontaneous sexual opportunity and unchallenged homophilia [...] understood in the sense of loving the same sex and loving those who are culturally or socially similar, a nonpejorative way of referring to *communautarisme*" (Mack 225).

But more is at stake in *Homme au bain*. As in *La Première marche*, but in a very different register, Honoré provides a vivid and compelling sense of the queer everyday: Emmanuel goes food shopping, casually picks up men, shaves his and other's body hair, does the housework while donning an apron in a self-conscious parody of suburban boredom. For Honoré is keen to show how gay men habitually function: the way they look at each other, feel, have sex, or fantasize, as in the sequence where Emmanuel applies strips of yellow tape to the face

---

14 See Daboval.

of an Omar-lookalike. It is not simply that the isolation and solitude of *banlieue* life are being reclaimed and redeemed as queer. Rather, the *banlieue* is experienced naturally as a porous, multi-layered, and non-threatening space of encounter and surprise where distinctions such as *milieu* [in the gay scene] vs *hors-milieu* [out of the gay scene] do not apply, offering thus the potential to experiment and pursue freely one's desires, including also the drive for queer coupledom (albeit unsuccessful here). Moreover, in a film where queer border crossings take the additional form of moving between different media (film, video, painting), the *cité* is queered formally through the continually shifting perspectives of public space enjoyed simultaneously outside, at ground level, and inside, from within the high-rise apartment. In both *Homme au bain* and *La Première marche*, the *banlieue* cannot be fixed conceptually as a uniform non-place on the urban periphery – rather, it appears an immense, loose amalgam of lived spaces and proliferating socialities that interweave organically over the course of time. By slowing down the pace and insisting on duration, the two films capture the intersubjective spaces and rhythms of shared, queer experience, so allowing the processes of embodied queer memory to take hold.

Transformative queer memory

In different yet complementary ways, *Homme au bain* and *La Première marche* are reframing and resetting Paris's traditional negative other – its sub-urban fringes – as an evolving nexus of collective cultural memory in contemporary France through the dynamic processes and movements of queer intermixing. By establishing cinematically new queer sites of cultural memory through the visibility of the queer body in free movement, and by allowing cultural *mixité* to reverberate queerly in a shared, hybrid, open frame of cultural mediation, they offer, like the short *Quatre Fromages* hailed at the start, new figurations of community in France beyond the officially sanctioned parameters of *intégration*. Such cultural remapping of *banlieue* space as defiantly transnational, intersectional, and queer reflects an intrinsic understanding of film as a necessarily "impure" and potentially transformative medium of memory, and it lays the basis for a new, queer, audiovisual reconfiguring of the *lieu de mémoire* as defined by Nora. This radical cultural move is all the more significant for the fact that, while the momentous march in Saint-Denis galvanized in turn the organizers of the Marche des Fiertés

LGBTQI+ (formerly Paris Gay Pride) to start the 2021 march in the nearby *banlieue* of Pantin, a follow-up event entitled Pride des Banlieues had to be postponed until June 2022 due to the Covid pandemic. Yet through in-person and virtual screenings across France, notably the annual Paris Festival du Film LGBTQI&+++ Chéries-Chéris, *La Première marche* has continued to provoke fertile dialogue and exchange, for example, a documentary produced by the Conseil Départemental de la Haute-Garonne entitled *Banlieusards et Fiers, histoire d'une marche des fiertés* [*Banlieue* Dwellers and Proud: Story of a Gay Pride] featuring the two directors.[15] Indeed, my analysis has shown that queer memory is never more alive and transformative than when it is actualized in the material present – that is, when it is not just retrospective (honoring the past) but also prospective (imagining a better future).

The cinematic move to open up new *banlieusard* spaces for shared, collective, queer memory corresponds in part to what the activist Yanis calls for in *La Première marche*, namely a sustainable structure of queer community and engagement in the *banlieue*. But it also contributes to a wider cultural project in France to visualize the *banlieue* differently, in particular its ultra-male aspects. Mohamed Bourouissa's revelatory images of Paris *banlieue* life in *Périphérique* – his breakthrough series of photographs produced in 2005–2008 during an extreme period of social disturbance in the fight against inequality – are another such manifestation. With friends and acquaintances, Bourouissa restaged lived moments of both public and private daily life that played explicitly with the operations of memory and reinvented the visual archive as an intersectional *lieu de mémoire*. As the films studied have shown, cinema, too, has the power to generate progressive, collective sites of cultural memory and resistance, with the potential to disrupt and ultimately reshape the French national narrative, by foregrounding the fluid complexities and affective contours of queer lives in the *banlieue* and revealing radiant new forms of queer citizenship.

Works cited

Amine, Laila. *Postcolonial Paris: Fictions of Intimacy in the City of Light*. U of Wisconsin P, 2018.

---

15 See *Banlieusards et Fiers, histoire d'une marche des fiertés*, available on the YouTube channel of the Conseil départemental de la Haute-Garonne.

Atoui, Hakim. *Scred*. France, 2017. Short. In *The French Boys 4*. Feature Film. NQV Media, 2022.

Atoui, Hakim, and Baptiste Etchegaray. *La Première marche*. France, 2020. Feature Film. Outplay Films DVD, 2021.

Bourouissa, Mohamed. *Périphérique*. Loose Joints, 2021.

Carli, Nathan. *Malik*. Feature Film. France, 2018. Georges Films.

Chaumont, Franck. *Homo-ghetto*. Le Cherche Midi, 2009.

Chausse, David. *Quatre Fromages/The Edge*. France, 2019. Short. In *The French Boys 4*. Feature Film. NQV Media, 2022.

Conseil départemental de la Haute-Garonne. *Banlieusards et Fiers, histoire d'une marche des fiertés*. YouTube, 2020. www.youtube.com/watch?v=z46Z_LEB0Q0.

Daboval, Adeline. "L'homophobie gagne du terrain en banlieue." *Le Parisien*. November 10, 2018.

Fassin, Éric. "Homosexual city, homophobic banlieue?" *métro politiques*. March 9, 2011. Translated by Christina Mitrakos. Web.

Foirest, Guillaume. *7ème ciel/In Seventh Heaven*. France, 2013. Short. In *French Touch: Between Men*. Feature Film. FilmDoo, 2019.

Guetta, Cathy. *La Cité du mâle*. ARTE, September 29, 2010.

Honoré, Christophe. *Homme au bain/Man at Bath*. Feature film. France, 2010.

———. *Non ma fille, tu n'iras pas danser/Making plans for Lena*. Feature film. France, 2009.

Kouam, Yohann. *Le Retour*. France, 2013. Short. In *The French Boys 2*. Feature film. NQV Media. France, 2021.

Lotem, Itay. "'L'homosexualité? ça n'existe pas en banlieue': The indigènes de la République and gay marriage, between intersectionality and homophobia," *Modern and Contemporary France*, vol. 27, no. 2, 2019, pp. 205–21.

Mack, Mehammed Amadeus. *Sexagon: Muslims, France, and the Sexualization of National Culture*. Fordham UP, 2017.

Naït-Balk, Brahim (with Florence Assouline). *Un homo dans la cité*. Calmann-Lévy, 2009.

Ossman, Susan, and Susan Terrio. "The French riots: Questioning spaces of surveillance and sovereignty." *International Migration*, vol. 44, no. 2, 2006, pp. 5–21.

Tchumkam, Hervé. "Banlieues." *Postcolonial Realms of Memory: Sites and Symbols in Modern France*, edited by Étienne Achille, Charles Forsdick, and Lydie Moudileno. Liverpool UP, 2020, pp. 101–108.

III
Icons and Figures

CHAPTER TEN

Cult graves and queer memory

Melanie C. Hawthorne

It is a paradox, of course, but one that bears repeating, that so much of life depends on death. Indeed, the dead have so much work to do, it's a wonder they get any time to rest in peace. The dead lead busy lives, two of them, to be precise, according to Thomas Laqueur in his study, *The Work of the Dead* (2015), "one in nature, the other in culture" (10). In this sense, we all have a stake in burial culture, and the raw cultural material of the past is potentially available to every member of society to draw from, but different individuals and groups will make different use of that material. Relationships to the dead can take many forms, and they can be structured, and even manipulated, beyond the level of the individual to further certain agendas, to encourage certain identities, and to impose ideological structures that serve different groups.

The injunction to *remember* the dead (and the recognized ways of doing that) makes the exercise part of Pierre Nora's project on *"lieux de mémoire,"* where he examines the role collective memory can play in the formation of group identity. The "co-(m)memoration" (the remembering together) of the dead is a major theme in public memory in general, and a structuring element of community. Multiple essays collected in the volumes of *Les Lieux de mémoire (Realms of Memory)*, edited by Nora, testify to the importance of the role of the dead in forging a sense of shared values among the living. The topics include the Pantheon, Victor Hugo's funeral, royal tombs, and the "famous dead," and I would cite in particular Antoine Prost's essay "Monuments to the Dead," in the second volume, "Traditions," as illustrating this point.

Nora's interest is in the shaping of such a collective identity at the national level (French, in particular). Nationalism may favor the inclusion of many, but it operates by the exclusion of a few. Critics have questioned whether national identity (French or other) is so monolithic, suggesting that Nora has overemphasized one version of "France" at the expense of others. Which France does Nora represent, and who is excluded from this definition?[1] Sexual minorities have often been targeted for exclusion from national discourse, for a variety of reasons. At the height of the "Lavender" scare in 1950s America, for example, it was considered "unpatriotic" to be "homosexual" (the label favored at the time). It was feared that such sexual nonconformity might make the individual identify with trans- or supra-national groups that threatened national interests in the same way that communism was perceived to do.[2] Which means that those identities tended (and still tend) to be excluded from the publicly endorsed sites where the work of national remembering was carried out. Thomas Dunn has pointed out some of the forms this erasure has taken, from public (i.e., collective) memorials – what he refers to as "monumental memory" – to school textbooks that silently present even the youngest children with an unquestioned heteronormative perspective (Dunn).[3]

Despite these examples of "forgetfulness" in remembering – to paraphrase this current volume's introduction (Bouamer, Provencher, and Schroth 13) – death has always played a distinct role in the life of gay and queer subcultures, just as it has for other minority groups. An obvious contemporary example might be the role of the AIDS crisis at the end of the twentieth century in inspiring political activism, but there are many older and less obvious ways the dead unite the living. Heike Bauer, for example, argues that "queer suicide and violent deaths are part of a traumatic collective experience, markers of the potentially lethal force of heteronormative ideals and expectations but also complex sites of shared identification and resistance" (37).

1 For example, Marcel Detienne, *L'identité nationale, une énigme* (Gallimard, 2010).

2 For a consideration of the ways that gay identities might even transcend the national level, see, for example, Woods where he coins the term "Homintern" by analogy with "comintern" (communist international) to capture the sense that gay people may form supra-national affiliations precisely because they are often excluded from what is considered proper national (and nationalistic) characteristics.

3 For a discussion of "monumental memory," see, for example, Dunn, chapter 1, "'Making Do' with Heterosexual History." For a discussion of the heteronormative dominance of school curricula, see Dunn, chapter 4, "Imagining GLBTQ Americans."

She exhumes the archives of German sexologist Magnus Hirschfeld to illustrate how "individual suffering contributed to the shaping of a collective sense of homosexual identity," citing, for example, the impact of Oscar Wilde's death on men who identified with him as well as interest in suicides among the medical community at the turn of the nineteenth century (38). The point is further illustrated by a classic film of the period, *Anders als die Andern* (*Different from the Others*) released in 1919, which opens with the scene of a man scanning the morning papers for reports of "unexplained" deaths that he interprets as suicides by people like him (he later commits suicide when he is blackmailed on account of a homosexual relationship) (50). Given the shame and despair that often beset the gay man (or woman) who risked persecution from doctors, priests, and police, suicide was unfortunately an all-too-common response, but the deceased might, one imagines, bequeath a gift to his friends by bringing them together at his funeral and by providing a place where like-minded individuals might sympathize. Perhaps funeral-crashing could be read as a queer alternative to the heterosexual phenomenon of wedding-crashing, but this is not the place to pursue that possibility.

Instead, I wish to examine a more contemporary extension of the social exploitation of the dead through a form of taphophilia, specifically in the way queer celebrity graves become cult sites that enable the creation and expression of a sense of community, albeit a diffuse and distanced one. I first took on this topic in an article "You Are Here," in which I considered the issue of how one can have nostalgia for something or someone you have never known in the first place (what Alison Landsberg calls "prosthetic memory"), suggesting that part of what fuels such affect is the way marginal subjects process "trauma without drama" (Hawthorne, "You Are Here"). All the dead have a role to play in shaping the experience of the living (ontology is "hauntology," as Derrida would have it), but the focus here will be on a subset of the possibilities created by spaces that memorialize the famous. It's one thing to think about graves that are meaningful to an individual person (family graves and the like), but another to think about a more collective, "public" experience, especially one that unfolds at a single point but at different moments in time.

For those who don't feel represented by, or in, the mainstream, subcultures have their own spaces that might be invisible to "straight" culture except in ghostly form (Gordon). An analysis of some lesbian, gay, and queer spaces, comparing and contrasting two French "cult" gravesites in different parts of Paris, through discussion of the tributes left at the grave of Oscar Wilde (Père Lachaise cemetery) and of Renée Vivien (Passy cemetery) will illustrate yet another way that coming together around death can forge communal bonds. Neither of these cult figures was French by birth, though both died in France – making it, in a sense, their adopted homeland. The communities imagined here, then, transcend national boundaries.[4] Setting aside the national question, their graves may instead offer insight into the role the dead have played in shaping gay, lesbian, and queer identities in the recent past.

To begin with, the monumental grave of Oscar Wilde (1854–1900) has been famous almost since its inception, though Wilde was initially buried elsewhere, humbly banished to the more liminal cemetery of Bagneux south of the "périphérique," in a "provisional" grave. In July of 1909, however, his remains were transferred to the Père Lachaise cemetery in northeast Paris, a necropolis that was developed specifically as a tourist destination, generating foot traffic that brought attention to his resting place.[5] With an imposing – and some would say shocking – sculpture by a major artist, Jacob Epstein, the grave was bound to draw the eye of anyone passing, regardless of whether they came with the intention of paying tribute to Wilde or were merely on their way to elsewhere.

The tomb has long inspired discussion and debate. Epstein's large sculpture of a stylized naked male figure was unveiled in 1914 by the controversial figure Aleister Crowley, and the nudity was a source of conflict from the start. The conspicuous genitalia were covered by a plaque for the unveiling, but that was soon removed (Epstein was angry at the censorship), and the sculpture was quickly and repeatedly defaced, castrated, and censored. Opinions differed as to whether the ablations were carried out by admiring souvenir hunters or what were imagined to be outraged little old ladies attacking the offending parts with umbrellas. Meanwhile, the site gained a reputation as a cruising place. In later years, the "sphinx" (as the sculpture came to be called) was covered in lipstick

---

4 On the intersection of gender, sexuality, and nationality, see Hawthorne, *Women, Citizenship, and Sexuality*.

5 That the cemetery was created as a "destination" site is evident from the efforts made to "seed" the necropolis with celebrity graves. For example, the cemetery was only created in 1804, yet it contains the remains of Abelard and Héloise, who died in the twelfth century; obviously, they were consciously brought from elsewhere. The remains of playwright Molière were also transferred for a similar reason: to attract visitors.

kisses, more clearly readable as signs of tribute, but no less damaging in their long-term effect. To mark the centenary of Wilde's transfer to a celebrity cemetery, the tomb was scrubbed clean and a protective transparent shield was installed around it in 2011. All of this has been well documented and written about elsewhere, so I want to focus on a different topic here and explore the grave's role as a kind of "message board."

In addition to removing parts of the sculpture and adding kisses, visitors leave things that take many forms. Over the course of the last two decades, I have made regular visits to Wilde's grave in order to document some of these tributes. Although my visits are not systematic in any way (no attempt to visit on the same day each year, or at the same time, for example) and do not constitute anything like a scientific sample, they give some idea of the kind of material to be found there. Each year that I have been able to travel to Paris, I make a point of spending an hour or two beside Wilde's grave. I make notes on the people that I see come and go, and on what they do. I document through photographs in as much detail as possible what has been left at the grave. The following descriptions are based on those notes, and the year given in parentheses refers to the year in which I took a particular photograph or note that supports the observation.

Many "offerings" take the form of favorite quotations from Wilde and his works. One visitor scrawled "l'importanza di essere Oscar!" on the tomb, for example (2008). Another wrote "women wearing malve [mauve] always have a history," from *The Picture of Dorian Gray* (2012). These quotations and references to Wilde's work ("Art for art's sake! 3.4.8"; 2008) demonstrate a familiarity with his writings and not just his life and create a kind of canon of "fan favorites." These selected excerpts may echo well-known citations, but this does not preclude more idiosyncratic choices.

Many people leave flowers, of course, among other typical objects left at graves, but they also leave less traditional offerings that have personal meaning. These can be roughly subdivided into two categories. First are the things that look as though they were chosen specifically and brought intentionally by the visitor to honor Wilde. A postcard bearing the slogan "Greetings from Reading" (with four exciting views of cars and roads, 2015) seems a premeditated reference to Wilde's time in Reading Gaol, for example. And a Pol Rémy "champagne" bottle is unlikely to have ended up there by happenstance (2017).[6] Whether the bottle was

---

6   Produced in Burgundy, Pol Rémy is technically a sparkling white wine, not a true champagne.

opened and drunk elsewhere, whether it was opened on the spot and poured on the grave as a libation or drunk as a toast by visitors, or left full and opened by others, the details don't matter, and indeed the fact that such objects invite the viewer to supply a narrative is part of the cultural work that they do. Did the person who gifted this bottle (full or empty) intend to evoke the chicken and champagne dinners that Wilde offered to rent boys, the "feasting with panthers" (Croft-Cooke) ascribed to Wilde? Whether the visitor to the grave thinks of this association or misses it entirely and thinks only of champagne as a conventional toast, a connection is made between the donor and the viewer.

The other category offerings consists of what might be called "found objects." These appear to be the result of more spontaneous gestures, impulses inspired by the moment. One finds oneself in front of the tomb, perhaps one sees all the things that others have left, and one casts around for something one can add. (The desire to imitate the behavior of others, to "join in," is the very scaffold of community as it is in the process of formation.) The inherent value of the object one leaves is not the point; indeed these contributions often take the form of trivia. Thus, people leave pebbles (perhaps in a nod to Jewish tradition, though Wilde was not Jewish, but also because pebbles are plentiful and usually ready to hand in a cemetery); used Metro tickets (a dying trend, now, since they are being phased out by the RATP); small coins (bigger denominations only invite theft); band aids (2012); even sugar cubes that one might have casually picked up at the last café one visited (2008); in short, the kind of thing one might happen to have in one's pocket that is easy to part with. Some silver foil wrapped around a stick (a dead flower stem?) and a piece of fruit (Apple? Peach? Impossible to tell now that it has rotted; 2015), ribbons tied around a post of the protective shield and a small, a microfiber, cloth (the kind used for cleaning eyeglasses or phone screens) tied into a knot ("don't forget"?), and even a tube of lipstick itself (all 2017) indicate other creative answers to the question "What do I have that I can part with?" The significance of these tokens is not the value of the gift, nor the prior thought that went into it, but the fact that through the gesture one is engaging with a wider community one feels called upon to acknowledge. One is adding one's two cents (sometimes literally) to the construction of a group of people centered on Wilde but not simply about Wilde. One leaves things for others to see, and while one may never meet those others in person (indeed the anonymity of the enterprise is part of its structure), one engages in an inherently collective activity.

The intentionality of the gesture is illustrated in the written messages that are left "for" Wilde, but that are available for other visitors to read. Some messages are signed, for example. Silvia, Sara, and Alberto added their names on 23/02/08 (according to their date), but Sara, Pao, Lola, and Olly got there first in 2006. Tom and Faye drew their names inside a heart. Emile Zola also signed the wall of the tomb, somewhat improbably, but there is no reason to suppose that the majority of names are not genuine, especially as they are usually first names only. Sometimes the visitors indicate where they are from. Thus, in 2007, one enthusiast scrawled "Viva México" on the side of the tomb, while another drew a pair of lips, dating it 22/3/07 and signing it (?) "<u>s-s-n-a</u> [space] <u>a-e-j-i-u Spain</u>" (underlined twice). In 2008, another fan wrote, "love from Australia XX," while someone else testified that "[name illegible] from Brazil was here," to which someone in different handwriting added "de Venezuela." The word "Uruguay" lies next to "♥ from Kentucky." And "Laura Weir" left a handwritten note on a piece of lined paper (torn out of a notebook?) to say, "Thank you from Scotland. May God rest your soul." Thoughtfully, she added an "X" and dated it: 29/5/08. In 2009, I spotted a message in Japanese inscribed in red lipstick (I don't read Japanese) and "Moscow 2008" in Russian (I do read Cyrillic). This is just a sample from a series of random visits over a few years, but they illustrate one function of the "bulletin board" nature of such tributes. They are letting you know that if you are part of the Oscar Wilde fan club, you have friends all around the world, even if you have never met them.

While these messages may at one level be intended for Wilde, at another, they are also public statements meant for other, living, visitors. Some messages are signed, like those discussed above, many remain anonymous. But either way, they testify to a desire to communicate. In this sense, the gravesite itself acts as a kind of "hyphen" (Mireille Rosello's word) connecting two parties, putting them in communication with each other.[7] While Rosello's focus is on ethnic connections that create a transnational Maghreb, the grave of Oscar Wilde, an Irish writer-in-exile buried on French soil, brings a different community into being, replacing national identity with a transnational sense of belonging.

The grave of Renée Vivien, the pseudonym of Anglo-American writer Pauline Mary Tarn (1877–1909), is similarly supra-national, but in other

---

7 On the "hyphen," see Rosello 130.

respects, it offers a study in contrasts. Certain fundamentals remain the same, such as the sense that Vivien was a sexual pioneer who was shunned for her "shameful" choices. In her poems and short stories of the first decade of the twentieth century, Vivien was one of the first women to write openly and unapologetically about same-sex female eroticism and was a pioneer of lesbian identity. In particular, she resurrected the role of Sappho as not just a role model for aspiring women writers, but as a sexual forerunner, free from the concepts of guilt and sin (since she lived in pre-Christian times). Despite the superficial tolerance of *Belle Époque* Paris, Vivien was all too familiar with discrimination, and indeed she wrote about her feelings of being persecuted (see, for example, the poem "le pilori"), which means that just as gay men may have identified with Wilde's suffering, lesbians could find a kindred spirit in Vivien. Her early death and tortured image lend themselves to this vision of her as a martyr figure.

Despite these parallels, Vivien's grave, topped by an ornate gothic chapel with stained glass windows, does not enjoy the same public attention as that of Wilde. For one thing, its location in Passy cemetery to the west of Paris, far off the beaten track despite its proximity to the Eiffel Tower, puts it largely out of sight of tourists. Although Passy Cemetery has its share of the famous dead (Claude Debussy, Edouard Manet, Berthe Morisot), few people take the time to visit. Yet Vivien's grave attracts cult attention, and it too functions in a similar way as a message board, though on a smaller – but still international – scale.

As in the case of Wilde, I have visited Vivien's grave regularly, recording and documenting (in both notes and photographs) its use. Two general observations seem important at the outset. The first is that while the Père-Lachaise cemetery has a constant stream of visitors and is in itself a tourist destination, I rarely saw anyone else at the Passy cemetery, let alone anyone who looked like a tourist. Because the location is off the beaten track, people rarely "stumble across" Vivien's grave. The few mentions of the cemetery in tourist and online materials rarely include her as one of the cemetery's "famous dead."[8] If people come to her grave in Passy, it's because they already know what they are looking for.

---

8 A Google search for "Passy cemetery" leads first to the Wikipedia cemetery site that fails to give her real name (so is of no help in locating her grave in the cemetery itself), followed by a blog, entitled frenchmoments.eu, which does not mention Vivien at all. Third on the list is atlasobscura.com, which lists such minor celebrities as "noted French aviators Costes and Bellonte, aircraft designer Henry

Cult graves and queer memory   167

The second point to make is that Natalie Clifford Barney, the rich American heiress and salon hostess who was Vivien's sometime lover and who was also a pioneering figure in lesbian history, is also buried in Passy cemetery just a short distance from Vivien.[9] Her grave presents a distinct contrast to that of Vivien, however. For many years, Barney's grave has remained austere, with few or no flowers or other tributes.[10]

The lack of attention to Barney's grave highlights the extent to which Vivien's attracts a cult following (perhaps because, unlike Barney, Vivien died young and is often compared to the "poètes maudits" of French literature). Over the years, the grave has received many offerings of various sorts. As in the case of Wilde's tomb, there are gifts and tributes that seem to demonstrate intentionality. Of course, flowers are always a common choice, but violets in particular make a frequent appearance because of their central role in Vivien's work. (She had a close friend named Violet when growing up, but Violet died young, and Vivien mourned her the rest of her life.) Lilies are also a popular choice of flower, both because of the association between lilies and death generally, but also perhaps because Vivien was known to favor them. But other objects have also found their way to her grave: a framed picture of a cross-dressed Vivien, a heart on a stick, a melancholy cherub figurine playing a guitar (Vivien was fond of music), even a Santa Claus have all endured the elements during many seasons in a planter at the foot of the tomb.[11]

Written messages, too, show a desire to make a statement. Some messages are placed out of easy reach, inserted high up behind the grill or folded multiple times and wedged in a corner, as though meant to remain private; but others are left in plain sight. A commercially produced greetings card depicting a heart with an arrow through it

---

Farman and American silent screen star Pearl White (star of 'Perils of Pauline')," but fails to mention Vivien.

9 As a measure of Barney's fame, it is worth recalling that when the feminist artist Judy Chicago set out to pay tribute to the most important historical female figures in her 1970s multi-media feminist artwork, the "Dinner Party," Natalie Barney earned a place while Renée Vivien did not.

10 An exception was the recent commemoration of the fiftieth anniversary of her death, in February 2022, when her grave was covered with flowers and sprinkled with rose petals.

11 More recently, in 2022, the planter was no longer "front of house," having been removed to the back of the chapel where it was invisible to the casual visitor, but the figurines were still there, albeit in an advanced state of decomposition.

drawn in the sand on a beach has two handwritten messages on the other side. One is a poem dated "24/02/2007 – mercredi 'des cendres.'" The second, dated "07/03/2007 – Sainte Félicité," wishes "double bonne fête à ma félicité/Que ces quelques fleurs t'apportent le Bonheur/Rendez-vous peut-être avant l'Eternité." In the top right-hand corner of the same card: "Pauline, ♥ je t'aime" (2007; note that this message is directed to the poet using her real name, rather than her pseudonym). A postcard of a "Girl with Stylet, called Sappho," remains blank, but the reference to Sappho, a poet Vivien revered, translated, and sought to imitate, is perhaps all the message the donor intended (2014). A hand-drawn card of a woman in profile, with wild hair, looking much inspired by the work of art nouveau poster artist Alphonse Mucha, appeared in 2011. Inside, the message is inscribed to "Pauline/Renée" and reads "Thank you for providing a portal so that we of the future can take prolonged strolls through your psyche. Your work is wonderful and I hope my English translations do it justice."

The centenary of Vivien's death, 2009 (she died in 1909 at the age of only 32), brought renewed attention to her final resting place. A card depicting two hands holding red roses in the shape of a heart, and dated "11/11/2009," includes a poem, "A Renée Vivien" (note the use of the pseudonym rather than the intimacy of using the "real" name), and is signed with an email address: cyane_2009@yahoo.fr (no longer an active address as far as I can tell). Just before the covid pandemic hit, in the summer of 2019, someone wrote out a quotation from "Lettres à Kérime 1905," as follows: "Je suis reconnaissante à la vie de m'avoir accordé un si beau bonheur, un rêve si extraordinaire. Car jamais un poète ne vécut un songe plus adorable: jamais aucun poète n'aura une aussi merveilleuse maîtresse. Je t'adore" [I am grateful to life for having granted me such beautiful happiness, such an extraordinary dream. For never did a poet live a more adorable dream; never will any poet have such a marvelous mistress. I adore you].[12] This reference to a lesser-known text by Vivien suggests someone more deeply acquainted with Vivien's work, but the fact that such a lengthy quotation, unlikely to be recalled from memory, is written casually on a piece of paper evidently torn from a notebook (the square perforations are still visible) suggests that it was prepared ahead of time and not a spontaneous recollection.

---

12 This particular offering left enough information that it allowed me to track it back to the work of Melanie Davis, a Canadian artist and jeweler with the goal of translating the works of Vivien into English. See her website www.valkyria.ca.

Still, not everyone who comes calling has thought ahead about what to bring, so again there are examples offerings that appear to be afterthoughts. One variation on the Metro ticket/coin token gift seen at Vivien's grave is a Japanese stamp discretely affixed to a corner of the iron gate of the tomb (face value: 80 yen) in 2012. It is hard to know if this was simply an ordinary stamp that the visitor happened to have handy (assuming s/he was from Japan), or if this was a knowing allusion to the role of *japonisme* in Vivien's life and work (she had an important collection of Asian art and published a collection of Asian short stories called Netsuké in 1904, for example). Either way, it testifies to, once again, the international dimension of the virtual community of admirers.

One element in evidence at Wilde's tomb but lacking at Vivien's is that of graffiti. References to Vivien's work and the names of visitors (when mentioned) are written out on pieces of paper, not scrawled on the walls of the tomb itself, which remain respectfully pristine. Despite the stereotype of "lipstick lesbians," there were no kisses on the tomb until 2023 (and even then the smooches numbered only two), and no evidence of attempts to deface the memorial or take souvenirs by removing pieces. While the tomb did briefly boast its own mailbox (2010), this addition was short lived, and in general the tomb is well maintained and respected. That the grave is near to the administrative offices may or may not be a factor: "disrespectful" treatment of the grave would quickly be noticed at Passy, whereas Père Lachaise is too big and busy for much surveillance.

Despite some differences, both cult graves serve as places where a queer community can meet and forge a sense of shared identity. The "message board" function appears to be the primary mechanism for the expression of this collective sense of queer memory. Positive messages counter the dominant narratives of these figures as morally reprehensible; demonstrate the existence of numerous people from all over the world who share a different perspective; create a kind of "canon" of the most resonant writing; and, generally, create a queer-affirmative space. Mireille Rosello has described some of the identifications made possible by graves.[13] While she focuses on fictional examples in novels and films, her treatment of the theme draws attention to an important aspect of these "performative encounters" (the subtitle of her book). Invoking the discourse of speech act theory, Rosello underscores the way that a

---

13 See Rosello, *France and the Maghreb*, especially chapter 5, "Ghostly Encounters: On Forbidden Processions and on Listening to the Dead" (pp. 128–64).

performative act actually makes something happen, for real. If I say, "I promise to remember you," the utterance of the words is itself the action of the promise, not just a verbal description accompanying some other event. In this sense, all the messages and tributes left at the graves discussed here – as at graves more generally – are performative: they do something. Beyond serving as gestures of respect toward the deceased, such acts forge connections among the living; they help to create and affirm a sense of community

There is yet another use to which these sites can increasingly be put in the twenty-first century, and that is the background for "selfies." Tracking images on social media is beyond the scope of this study, but I would like to highlight one anecdotal experience that speaks to how attitudes towards queer cult graves have changed over the last few decades. When I began my study, around 2003, visitors to Oscar Wilde's tomb tended to come in small groups (individuals, couples, small groups of maybe three or four friends), and they were mostly subdued and discreet in their behavior (consulting maps of the cemetery, quietly reading guidebooks, examining the grave, talking amongst themselves). For sure, some of the shame of being openly associated with Wilde had already dissipated, but the visits did not seem exactly festive or occasions for celebration. But I noted a distinct change during my observation in 2015. Monday, June 15, was in many ways a typical, slow, weekday morning, but for the first time (in my experience) I witnessed a large school group visit to Wilde's grave. The students appeared to be high school age (i.e., minors), accompanied by a French-speaking tour guide, who addressed them. An adult who seemed to be their teacher translated into (American) English, mentioning explicitly that Wilde was gay, but referring also to his literary work. All of which was startling enough as a sign of changing times (the teacher did not seem to fear that exposing the young people in her care to a potentially pernicious influence would get her into trouble), but the class then proceeded to pose in front of the tomb for a series of group photos that seemed to have "official" sanction. Everyone seemed comfortable to be recorded in this setting, no doubt one of many images that would later be shared with parents and family to illustrate "what I did on my school trip to Paris." Such nonchalance would have been unthinkable even a few decades ago (and may become unthinkable again soon if current "don't say gay"-type legislation is widely taken up). On the one hand, the behavior was a welcome sign of changing attitudes; an openly gay Oscar Wilde was now safe for young minds, and acknowledging his sexuality did not preclude an appreciation of his work. On the other hand, it suggests that the cult status of his tomb may be shifting. If <u>everyone</u> goes there, can it continue to function as a special place, a "crypto" crypt? Which raises the question of what happens to sites of memory that function for subcultures when the sites cease to be knowledge reserved for a few. Perhaps continued observations of these cult graves will reveal something of an answer as we see what becomes of these sites in the rest of the twenty-first century.

Meanwhile, the use made of these cult grave sites raises questions about Nora's project of foregrounding national identity formation. If a nation turns its back on its queers (through discrimination and hostile legislation, for example) and the queers respond with self-exile (Wilde, Vivien), this mutually reinforcing dynamic of exclusion perpetuates the perception that queers are fundamentally disloyal to the nation, that their cosmopolitanism represents a threat, and even makes them a national security risk (the lavender menace). Cult graves, while firmly located on a specific national soil, can function as a site for disembodied exchanges that go beyond the national to create supra-national networks of affiliation. In this context, what should we hope for? Should Nora's ideas about group identity formation be updated and repurposed in a postnational moment to create citizens of the world rather than of individual nations? Or should the nation, if it is to survive as a concept, embrace its former outcasts (as it has the once-scandalous Josephine Baker)? Would France, as a nation, ever embrace the remains of Oscar Wilde in a similar move? I shall keep an eye out for the day I see graffiti on Wilde's tomb that cries "Au Panthéon!"

Works cited

Bauer, Heike. *The Hirschfeld Archives: Violence, Death, and Modern Queer Culture.* Temple UP, 2017.

Croft-Cooke, Rupert. *Feasting with Panthers: A New Consideration of Some Late Victorian Writers.* Holt Rinehart Winston, 1967.

Detienne, Marcel. *L'Identité nationale, une énigme.* Gallimard, 2010.

Dunn, Thomas R. *Queerly Remembered: Rhetorics for Representing the LBGTQ Past.* U of South Carolina P, 2016.

Gordon, Avery F. *Ghostly Matters: Haunting and the Sociological Imagination.* U of Minnesota P, 1997.

Hawthorne, Melanie. *Women, Citizenship, and Sexuality: The Transnational Lives of Renée Vivien, Romaine Brooks, and Natalie Barney.* Liverpool UP, 2021.

———. "You are here." *Dix-neuf*, vol. 16, no. 1, 2012, pp. 87–111.
Johnson, David K. *The Lavender Scare: The Cold War Persecution of Gays and Lesbians in the Federal Government*. U of Chicago P, 2004.
Landsberg, Alison. *Prosthetic Memory: The Transformation of American Remembrance in the Age of Mass Culture*. Columbia UP, 2004.
Laqueur, Thomas. *The Work of the Dead: A Cultural History of Mortal Remains*. Princeton UP, 2015.
Prost, Antoine. "Monuments to the Dead," in *Realms of Memory: The Construction of the French Past*, vol. 2, *Traditions*, edited by Pierre Nora and Lawrence D. Kritzman. Translated by Arthur Goldhammer. Columbia UP, 1997, pp. 307–30.
Rosello, Mireille. *France and the Maghreb: Performative Encounters*. UP of Florida, 2005.
Woods, Gregory. *Homintern: How Gay Culture Liberated the Modern World*. Yale UP, 2016.

CHAPTER ELEVEN

Abdellah Taïa's *transfilial* memories of Genet's tomb in Larache

Denis M. Provencher

France has officially commemorated many of its writers, like Molière, Hugo, and Balzac, as members of its *grands écrivains* and keepers of its *roman national* [national narrative]. These men lie at rest in Le Panthéon, Père La Chaise, or other official cemeteries, which is a testament to their status as national figures deemed worthy of commemoration. As Melanie Hawthorne illustrates in our volume (see the previous chapter), Pierre Nora's multi-volume *Les Lieux de mémoire* (1984–92) includes several chapters on the "role of the dead" in national memory, with entries on Le Panthéon, Hugo's funeral, and royal tombs. However, the scholarship in the Nora tradition has largely overlooked French writers like Jean Genet, who may or may not have earned the same "literary prestige" (Ducournau) of other French and Francophone authors. Genet's "queer" novels do not recount, for example, an upstanding heteronormative version of the Republican narrative with his characters who simultaneously embody poetry and profanity, sainthood and criminality, martyrdom and treachery. He remains both a literary and figurative "orphan of the state" – erased from official commemoration and buried in a modest grave in a Christian Spanish cemetery in the small coastal town of Larache, Morocco.

At the same time, Genet's burial site, one which he chose willingly out of love for Larache, and its resident Mohammed Al-Katrani, continues to fascinate writers, pilgrims, and tourists, and this current chapter will illustrate how it functions today as both a "sacred" and a "profane" site filled with "transfilial" memories. I define transfiliation as a transgressive model of kinship and belonging that involves knowledge transfer or memory sharing, which is transmitted over time and space, and which can involve both LGBTQ-identified (queer) and non-LGBTQ-identified individuals. Transfilial sites of memory are both multidirectional (Rothberg, Sanyal, and Silverman) and intersectional (Crenshaw; Provencher, *Queer Maghrebi French*), and are not necessarily specific to queer individuals. While Achille, Forsdick, and Moudileno do not explicitly argue that postcolonial realms of memory are intersectional, they do state that Nora's project reflects "a certain French incapacity and/or unwillingness to engage with the inherent and undeniable imbrication of the colonial in the *roman national* [national narrative]" (5–6; my emphasis). Hence, my chapter aims to argue how we need to expand on this "imbrication" to include multiple groups that contribute to the *roman national* through their differences. Moreover, and as we will see, while realms of memory have largely been associated with an understanding of the past through present eyes, transfilial sites of memory are largely forward-focused, projecting multiple identities and groups into a future where they can potentially live productively together.

In what follows, I focus my analysis on queer Moroccan author Abdellah Taïa, arguably the first North African writer to declare his homosexuality publicly in the media in 2007, and how he has memorialized Genet's burial site in both his cinematic work, *La Tombe de Genet/ Genet's Tomb* (2008), and his postings on Facebook and Instagram social media accounts (2022). In part one, I analyze his 12-minute short film *La Tombe de Genet*, which pays homage to Genet and Larache. This includes an examination of how the film resonates aesthetically with Genet's own oeuvre and how it also functions intertextually in relation to other oral, literate, and visual texts. In part two, I examine Taïa's social media postings from a recent visit to Larache, and Genet's tomb, where he inserts himself visually into the digital commemoration. As we will see, the short film and the social media postings have implications for how we understand transfilial memory formation and transmission across time and space for both LGBTQ-identified and non-LGBTQ-identified communities, as well as how we decolonize French national memory.

La Tombe de Genet (2008)

The signification of "Genet" as queer archetype has evolved, mutated, and migrated from the space of metropolitan France (Provencher, *Queer French* 80) to other parts of the Francophone and non-Francophone world in broader global contexts, and Taïa's work in general, and short film in particular, must be contextualized a bit in this set of cultural productions. For example, a series of international publications – including Edmund White's *Genet: A Biography* (1993), Leo Bersani's *Homos* (1995), Tahar Ben Jelloun's *Jean Genet, menteur sublime* (2010) as well as international visual productions like Rainer Werner Fassbinder's *Querelle* (1982), Todd Haynes's *Poison* (1991), and John Waters's iconic character "Divine" in films like *Pink Flamingos* (1972) – have venerated Genet as a global queer icon and as an outlaw who embodies both sacred and profane elements. Taïa follows in this tradition and honors Genet as the queer archetype in several publications that include a special issue of *Nejma* on "Jean Genet, un saint marocain" (2010–11), a chapter, "De Jenih à Genet," in *Le rouge du tarbouche* (2004), and his essay "Genet, Abdallah et moi" (discussed more fully below). These written accounts have helped to set in motion Taïa's process of literary veneration of Jean Genet as a Moroccan saint who embodies both the sacred and the profane. In 2008, Taïa travels for the first time to Larache, and Genet's tomb, and, as we will see, his cinematic commemoration resonates forcefully with the queer archetype of "Genet."[1]

The celebration of a queer Genet in Larache is seen and felt throughout Taïa's "chaotic" (Boulé 181), low-budget, color film, which he produced with a hand-held camera. In Genet-like style, Taïa and his camera "cruise" or wander like a *flâneur* through the largely empty Larache, with a series of scenes set in its alleys, streets, cemetery, and port. As scholar Jean-Pierre Boulé writes: "Le film est composé d'images en couleur, sans dialogue, ou voix off, sans intrigue" [The film is composed of color images, without dialog or voice over, without plot] (180).[2] This recalls many silent encounters or mono-syllabic verbal exchanges between characters in Genet's own novels (Bullock and Provencher) and also Genet's own silent short film *Un chant d'amour* (1950).[3] Apart from

---

1   Taïa produced and released *La Tombe de Genet* as a bonus track on the French-language (region 2) DVD of *L'Armée du salut/Salvation Army* (2013).
2   All English translations are my own.
3   Indeed, the silent aspect of this film contributes to the commemorative effect

occasional local residents laughing, birds chirping, and wind blowing, Taïa's film successfully captures Genet's own aesthetics. Moreover, during an interview with the author, Taïa explains to me that holy burial sites of saints in Morocco are places of both pilgrimage and prostitution and are often accepted as such by the general public. Taïa relies on this local system of social semiosis to successfully incorporate queer Genet into Moroccan sainthood (Provencher, "Interview").

As mentioned above, prior to producing this film, Taïa had published two written and non-experiential accounts of Genet's tomb – "De Jenih à Genet" (2004) and "Genet, Abdallah, et moi" (2010; but written before the 2008 visit to Larache) – which inform the film. In these texts, the author draws primarily from his imagination and the secondhand knowledge of Genet he received respectively from his mother's cousin, Malika ("De Jenih à Genet"), and his mother, M'Barka ("Genet, Abdallah, et moi").[4] Boulé situates *La Tombe de Genet* in relation to these two texts: "L'important […] c'est que sa visite avait déjà eu lieu dans son imaginaire et avait fait l'objet d'un double travail d'écriture. La suite logique était donc de l'écrire à nouveau sous forme de film" [What's important […] is that his visit had already taken place in his imaginary and had been the object of a double work of writing. The logical follow-up was hence to write it again in cinematic form] (180). It is important to note that while Taïa's strong and real-life female relatives Malika and M'Barka are not LGBTQ-identified, they are still described as "en dehors des lois" [outlaws] ("Genet, Abdallah, et moi" 11), or as "female revolutionaries," with their own "queer tales of liberation" (Provencher, *Queer Maghrebi French* 170–80). It is unclear if Malika or M'Barka have their own first-hand experience with Genet or his tomb, but they share in the popular fervor surrounding Genet that is already at work in Morocco concerning sainthood, and this transfer of information to Taïa involves a form of "transfilial" memory of a queer figure (Genet) from Taïa's non-LGBTQ-identified female elders to him as queer child. Hence, transfiliation and transfilial memory-making are transnational, transgressive, and intersectional processes (Provencher,

when we recall the commemoration practice of holding a minute's silence for someone with the expression, "une minute de silence pour …" [a minute of silence for …]. I'd like to thank Siham Bouamer for this important remark.

4 See Heyndels as well, for excellent analyses of Taïa's written accounts of Genet's tomb.

Queer Maghrebi French 20, 47) and Taïa's commemorations of Genet and Larache are equally transfilial.

A film viewer who is unfamiliar with Genet's queer novels and characters or with Taïa's writings may have a difficult time deciphering this short film as a product of transfiliation related to Genet and Larache, or as an extension of either Genet's or Taïa's previous work. This may be one reason why this short film was only made available commercially for purchase as a bonus on the French DVD (region 2) of *L'Armée du salut*. Indeed, this raises questions about queer memory transfer for the audience and Taïa's own sources of memory. The Moroccan author possesses knowledge of the French author and his burial site from both oral sources (cousin and mother) and literate sources during his own discovery of Genet's writing after college. Unlike many queer sites of memory-making, which often occur from inside a group of LGBTQ-identified individuals, the first sources of Taïa's memory are derived from his straight female relatives and their own understanding of Moroccan sainthood, which includes contradictory elements. Hence Taïa "sutures himself" (Landsberg 2) into this larger history of familial transmission or "postmemory"[5] along with his own literary discovery and combines them with filmmaking to commemorate a former time and place loved by Genet. Similarly, Taïa takes what he learned from M'Barka and Malika and combines this with his own knowledge of Genet and cinema to create a transfilial memory of Genet and Larache for a new generation of followers. Although the film does not rely on flashback in the sense of transporting the spectator back in time chronologically, its documentary effect on Larache, and Genet's grave, gives it a quality that "has the capacity to carry viewers to faraway places and alternate temporalities" (12). Its silent feature also recalls earlier periods of cinema such as "travel film," for example, which

---

5 Drawing on Marianne Hirsh's concept of "postmemory," Horvat argues: "For queer people, what Hirsch terms 'familial postmemory' has rarely been possible. However, this does not mean that queer postmemory is not passed on" and she argues that "media such as film and television play a crucial role in creating such postmemory" (4). Horvat also contends that queer memory is "shaped in greater measure by on-screen representation than other types of minority community memories, which do not have to deal with the same obstacles to familial memory transfer" (4). Similarly, Çaliskan argues that post queer memory emerges where "alternate forms of family and time can be formed through memories that unexpectedly become inheritable" and are "familiar and strange at the same time" (271).

relied less on narrative, and offered viewers "actual footage from such distant and inaccessible places as India, Arabia, Japan, and Africa" (12). Hence, viewers unfamiliar with Genet's and Taïa's work may have some familiarity with documentary and travel cinema, and this may assist them in decoding *La Tombe de Genet*.

Breaking from the film's silence, Taïa inserts two inter-diegetic titles to guide his viewer: (1) "Un jour, l'écrivain français Jean Genet (1910–1986) sera un saint au Maroc. En juin 2008, je suis allé à Larache à la recherche de sa tombe" [One day, the French writer Jean Genet (1910–1986) will be a saint in Morocco. In June 2008, I went to Larache in search of his grave]; and (2) "Prison de la ville de Larache" [Prison in the city of Larache]. Although *La Tombe de Genet* captures both the cemetery and the prison introduced by these two inter-diegetic titles, those are not the only sites of memory in the film. Of course, Taïa and his camera linger in the cemetery and at Genet's tomb by focusing on the gravestone, the surrounding wildflowers, the coastline, and the prison situated behind the cemetery. Hence, the director stages again the sites of the cemetery, the grave, and the prison in quiet dialogue with many of Genet's own works, images, and themes (Boulé 183). However, the camera then tracks Taïa's wandering to an edge of town to document the rocks where swarms of young men and boys are jumping into the ocean for a swim. The spectator also observes young men getting in and out of boats that most likely carry them to the opposite bank. Although this segment lacks an inter-diegetic title, it remains significant to the overall aesthetic and message of the film because Taïa seems to be documenting Genet's own longing for Morocco and its young men. The director uses the haptic gaze (Bruno) of the camera's eye, meaning it lingers longingly in close proximity to these youthful bodies, approaching them in a way in which the human hand is forbidden from touching them. Taïa goes on pilgrimage in Larache and hopes to make an offering to Genet, somewhat similar to what Hawthorne illustrates in our volume, but which "consistera à enregistrer la vie, la jeunesse et les corps des jeunes Larachois" [will consist of recording life, youth, and the bodies of these young men of Larache] (Boulé 185). This provides the spectator a visual experience that commemorates Genet's poetic queer gaze and desire while also memorializing the French author's belonging in a space where he always felt a sense of filiation with Arab men. Taïa successfully combines pilgrimage and cruising in his film to reinforce Genet's Moroccan sainthood as a combination of these contradictory elements.

Indeed, Taïa also puts his film in conversation intertextually – if not explicitly then implicitly – with other cultural productions pertaining to queerness and queer characters in Larache. For example, in Rémi Lange's film, *The Road to Love/Tarek el hob* (2003), the two main queer Maghrebi French characters Karim (university student) and Farid (flight attendant), fall in love in Paris and share the reading of Genet's oeuvre as an expression of their own love. Near the end of the film, after engaging in a pilgrimage to Larache and Genet's tomb, they declare their commitment and consecrate their relationship, which recalls and rewrites the marriage tradition of the Bedouin, a series of nomadic Arab communities.[6] Early on in the film, Lange casts Taïa as himself (a young gay Moroccan writer), who serves as an informant to Karim during a school assignment on documentary film, which suggests that the director had already identified Taïa as a transfilial voice to be included in *Tarek el hob*.

In contrast to Lange's film, and unlike Karim and Farid, Taïa does not visually insert his own body in the pilgrimage in *La Tombe de Genet*. Hence, in terms of memory-making in the film, Taïa does not rely on his own direct contact with Genet, but rather on transfilial memory and other visual representations that circulate in the technological age through mass media consumption. Taïa's transfilial voice and cinematic eye are thus related to what scholar Alison Landsberg refers to as "prosthetic memory," which she defines as memories that are: "not strictly derived from a person's lived experience" (Landsberg 25) and that "circulate publicly, and [...] [are] experienced with a person's body as a result of an engagement with a wide range of cultural technologies" (25–26).[7] This resonates with the contention that transfilial memory functions across communities. For example, the individual who sees or receives a transgressive memory of Genet and Larache has the ability

---

6 Queer Moroccan author Rachid O. includes a fictional account of a trip to Genet's tomb in his chapter "Luc," in *Plusieurs vies* (1996). However, in Rachid O.'s account, the Frenchman Luc searches for Genet's tomb, and his Moroccan lover serves as his accompanying guide.

7 Landsberg offers examples such as the memories of the Holocaust and memories of slavery in the United States, and argues that they do not belong solely to Jews or African Americans respectively (2). Hence, prosthetic memories do not deal solely with identity politics for a particular community because they can speak to anyone who views the film. Landsberg also argues that: "the construction of prosthetic memories might serve as the grounds for unexpected alliances across chasms of difference" (3).

to then reshape their own subjectivity and politics (2), and this can also affect the broader viewership and how they choose to remember and commemorate a literary and historical figure. In sum, as we have seen in this section, Taïa takes the former "Saint Genet" of Jean-Paul Sartre and turns him into a "Saint in Morocco," for whomever would like to know and remember him.[8] *La Tombe de Genet* invites in new pilgrims and cruisers from different communities to incorporate these images into their own "archive of experience" (9), by "creating a portable, fluid, and non-essentialist form of memory" (18). Taïa's *La Tombe de Genet* functions as a transfilial site of memory that relies on transgressive and transformative forms of filiation, which have the potential to create new intersectional solidarities and communities in these sites of memory-making (Carrée).

Taïa's *Facebook* and *Instagram* visits to Larache

Abdellah Taïa announces a real-life follow-up visit to Larache, and Genet's tomb, 14 years after having directed *La Tombe de Genet*. On June 20, 2022, the author posts the following text in French on his Facebook account. He writes:

> LA TOMBE DE JEAN GENET. Hier, à Larache, j'ai vécu un moment magique avec mon ami Soufiane Hennani. A Tanger, nous avons pris le grand taxi pour aller à Larache nous recueillir sur la tombe "musulmane" de l'extraordinaire écrivain JEAN GENET (1910–1986). Notre Saint. Notre Patron. Notre inspiration. Notre GRAND AMOUR. Sa tombe est tellement belle, tellement poétique, tellement émouvante. Elle donne directement sur la mer: l'Océan Atlantique. Soufiane a dit que Jean Genet nous aimait: il a ouvert toutes les portes de la ville de Larache devant nous. Nos cœurs. Nous avons rencontré la merveilleuse et douce RAHMA. Nous avons adoré Saïd qui, de loin, a suivi tout de notre rituel inventé pour Jean Genet. Nous avons parlé avec Saïd. Nous avons pris des selfies avec Saïd. Et nous avons prié pour lui, aussi… Larache est sublime. SUBLIME. Dans les années 70, Jean Genet a aimé dans cette ville un homme: MOHAMED EL KATRANI. Il l'a suivi dans son monde. Et il

---

8   While Sartre first venerated Genet as a writer, and existential homosexual and criminal, in *Saint Genet, comédien et martyr* (1952), this process was conducted partially through a highly problematic psychoanalytical frame that relied on the flawed notion of "arrested development" for homosexuals during an era in France when homosexuality remained criminalized.

a voulu être enterré pas loin de lui et de sa famille. Allez marcher dans les rues magnifiques de Larache et vous comprendrez immédiatement pourquoi cet immense écrivain a choisi cette ville comme dernière station. Soufiane a dit: Il nous regarde, Jean Genet. Oui, depuis très longtemps, Jean Genet nous regarde. Et nous aime… Notre vénération pour lui est éternelle… Je vous envoie toute la baraka de Jean Genet et tout l'Amour de Larache… Abdellah Taïa

[THE TOMB OF JEAN GENET. Yesterday, in Larache, I experienced a magical moment with my friend Soufiane Hennani. In Tangiers, we took a shuttle van to go to Larache to spend some time in silent contemplation at the "Muslim" tomb of the extraordinary writer JEAN GENET (1910–1986). Our Saint. Our Patron. Our Inspiration. Our GREAT LOVE. His tomb is so beautiful, so poetic, so moving. It directly faces the sea: the Atlantic Ocean. Soufiane said that Jean Genet loved us: he opened all the gates of the city of Larache before us. Our hearts. We met the marvelous and sweet RAHMA. We loved Saïd who followed from afar our invented ritual for Jean Genet. We spoke with Saïd. We took selfies with Saïd. And we prayed for him, also… Larache is sublime. SUBLIME. In the seventies, Jean Genet loved in this city a man: MOHAMED EL KATRANI. He followed him in his world. And he wanted to be buried not far from him and his family. Go walk in the magnificent streets of Larache and you will immediately understand why this immense writer chose this city as a last stop. Soufiane said: He is watching us, Jean Genet. Yes, for a long time. Jean Genet watches us. And loves us… Our veneration for him is eternal… I send you all the baraka of Jean Genet and all the Love of Larache… Abdellah Taïa]

In this posting, Taïa composes a homage to Genet and Larache, and attaches four accompanying bright color photographs (see Figures 11.1–11.4), all of which, as we will see below, make intertextual references to his earlier written and visual accounts. The Facebook message reads much like a love letter where the author explains the "invented ritual" and the "magical" trip he and Sofiane took, and describes the city, its people, Genet's tomb, and Genet's love and *baraka*. Abdellah and Sofiane take the shuttle from Tangiers almost as if to accomplish "time travel," which brings them back to Larache of the 1970s and Genet's love for El Katrani. Upon their arrival, they interact with local residents, who, like Genet, show them affection and love. Although the photographs and trip are dated from 2022, they function in a similar way to *La Tombe de Genet* by offering a documentary and ethnographic effect or a flashback. Moreover, like protagonists Ali and Abdellah in "De Jenih à Genet" (Taïa, *Le rouge* 49), Sofiane and Abdellah sit in silent contemplation

182 Queer Realms of Memory

Figure 11.1 Abdellah Taïa walking in Larache

and admiration. Again, these intertextual references rely on forms of transfilial memory that Taïa has acquired either through transfilial memory (from his aunt or mother) or from prosthetic memory of what he has experienced in producing his own visual account of Genet's tomb and Larache, or from other commercially available accounts, including Lange's *The Road to Love/Tarek el hob* (2003).[9]

What is striking about this Facebook posting is how Taïa visually inserts himself for the first time into his narrative of Genet. For example,

---

9 In *Celui qui est digne d'être aimé*, Taïa also writes about giving a presentation on Genet and not mentioning El Katrani, which he subsequently regrets. This and the Facebook post seem to serve as a corrective to Taïa's earlier oversight. I would like to thank Ryan Schroth for directing me to this additional intertextual reference.

Figure 11.2 Abdellah Taïa sitting at Genet's tomb

in Figure 11.1, Taïa crosses a street in Larache, wearing a blue and white striped djellaba, black sneakers, and sunglasses, with the slaughterhouse Matadero in the background, which also appeared in *La Tombe de Genet* (Boulé 182). Boulé reminds us that this Spanish-language reference signals to the viewer the colonial past of the region (182); Taïa, walking in front of this building, subtly underscores how he resituates Genet as a site of memory in the postcolonial context of today's Morocco. Other spectators and visitors are also visually present in this version of the tale. For example, in Figure 11.3, Sofiane smiles and sits on the tomb, similarly wearing a djellaba, and embraces the gravestone for the camera. The hug is a powerful image that documents the feelings of love Taïa underscores in his written Facebook message and it also archives the affective feeling pilgrims and "cruisers" like Sofiane hold for Genet. It is a visual example of the memory that the Facebook posting instills

184 Queer Realms of Memory

Figure 11.3 Sofiane Hennani sitting at Genet's tomb and hugging the gravestone

in its viewers since neither the author, Taïa, nor his friend Sofiane have ever met Genet personally nor do they have first-hand memories of him. Yet, because of one's own ability to read Genet's work and connect transfilially to Genet's cultural production and Taïa's other written and visual accounts, the spectator can potentially enter into an imagined community with them. Moreover, in Figure 11.4, a man, most likely Saïd, as described in the accompanying written post, sits on the wall along the coast of Larache, wearing a T-shirt, a hoodie, a baseball cap, jeans, and sneakers, and smiles directly at the camera. Just as Genet was attracted to Larache, and fell in love with one of its locals, El Katrani, Taïa as the new narrator is enamored with and "loves" Saïd, according to his posting. Moreover, like the camera in *La Tombe de Genet*, which wanders and hovers over the bodies of young men, Saïd now follows from a distance and watches Abdellah and Sofiane in this

Genet's tomb in Larache 185

Figure 11.4 Saïd sitting on a wall along the coast in Larache

site of pilgrimage and prostitution. The form of transfilial memory that gets passed from queer elder (Genet) to queer child (Taïa), will in turn allow the author to share this memory through photography with his viewers. Taïa also constructs an authentic transgressive tale by bringing newer local characters into the center of the narrative and creating parallels between these real-world people and fictional characters from his previous written versions.

Taïa's posting on his Instagram account is not completely identical to the Facebook posting discussed above. While the written text on Instagram is identical, the posting includes a slightly different and expanded set of images. It includes, among others, an additional photo of Taïa sitting on a columned wall, as well as photos where Taïa sits on Genet's tomb looking toward the camera (Figure 11.2), a photo of a woman (perhaps Rahma) who appears in a local domestic scene and looks directly at the camera, and another photo where two anonymous men with their backs turned to the camera walk down the path along the cemetery. It is interesting to note that many of the photos include individuals who look directly at the camera and the spectator. This reinforces a message of a coherent protagonist or sovereign subject who engages directly with the spectator and uses the camera's "eye" as a form of alternative language to create community and shared memory about Genet and Larache. In this way, Taïa is able to highlight both the "hypervisible and unsayable" (Grandena 83) that has historically categorized the queer mythmaking associated with the archetype of "Genet."

Taïa also includes a final picture (Figure 11.5) of three men and a dog sitting on or swimming along the rocks in Larache, which again intertextually references *La Tombe de Genet* and gives additional authoritative voice to the narrative through its documentary or ethnographic effect. While the spectator cannot fully understand the Instagram post without having seen *La Tombe de Genet*, the current Facebook and Instagram postings – unlike the film, which had limited commercial distribution – have the potential for far broader circulation, enabling the transfer of memory and the commemoration of Genet for a transfilial, intersectional, and global audience.

Taïa engages actively with his friends, fans, and followers on Facebook and Instagram in constructing this site of transfilial memory. Therefore, the responsibility of loving Genet and Larache does not fall on one individual. In the written text, Taïa relies on the use of "we" to include all of his Facebook connections in the transmission of memory and commemorative act. Moreover, at the end of the written text on Facebook and Instagram, Taïa emphasizes how he wants to transmit Genet's *baraka* to others, similar to the way he had been transformed after being touched by Genet in previous versions (in "De Jenih à Genet" 50). Taïa, who relies on previous written accounts along with the tools of cinema and photography, is able to rewrite the transfilial tale for a transgressive and transnational audience of friends, fans, and followers on Facebook and Instagram. Taïa's personal feelings about Genet on social media become public postings that serve as new sites of memory for others. As Landsberg explains, "privately felt public memories [...] develop after an encounter with a mass cultural representation of the past, when new images and ideas come into contact with a person's own archive of experience" (19). The reader of Facebook and Instagram, at least the one who is connected to Taïa, now has the potential to enter

Figure 11.5 Men and a dog sitting and swimming on the rocks in Larache

et tout l'Amour de Larache... Abdellah Taia #abdellahtaïa #abdellahtaia #abdelataia #abdelátaia #abdelàtaia #abdelàtaïa #abdelataïa @editionsduseuil @editionspoints #morocco #morocco #larache #jeangenet #tanger #tangiers #lgbtq #arabspring

Figure 11.6 Instagram Hashtags

into the narrative alongside Abdellah, Sofiane, Rahma, and Saïd. In fact, we see that the number of clicks used to like (910 total), comment on (74 total), and share (40 total) Taïa's Facebook page, and to like (1,250 total) and comment on (110 total) Taïa's Instagram page are significant.[10] They also become part of a site of memory that will be digitally archived

---

10 I recorded these figures on June 7, 2023, and it is possible that these numbers may increase over time.

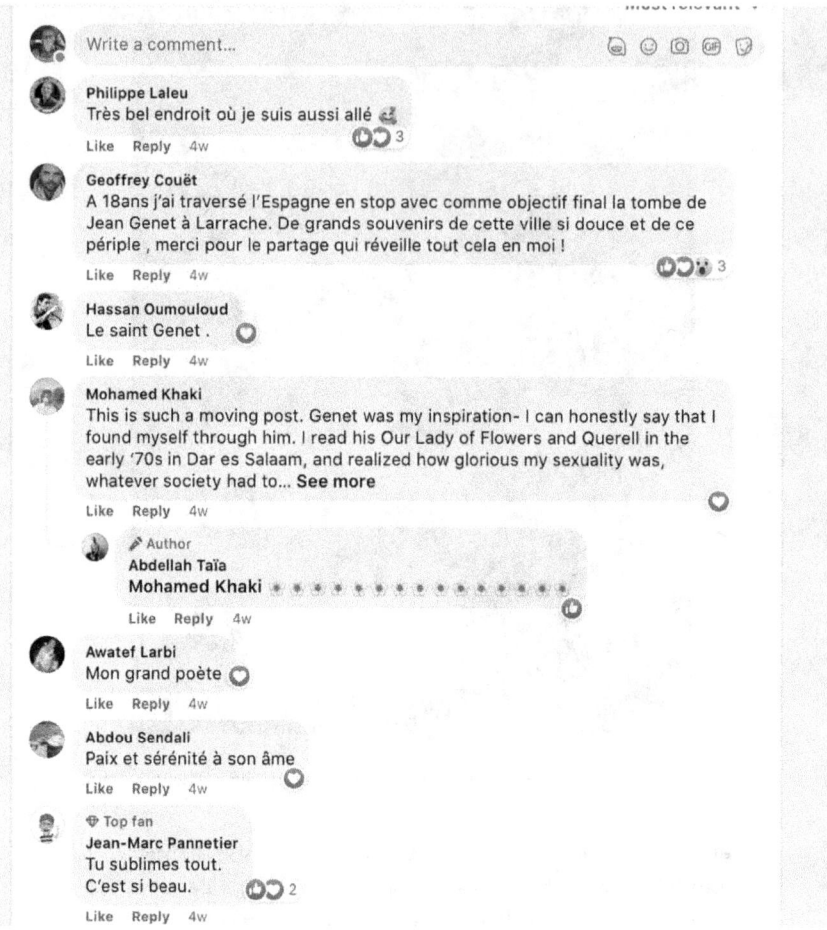

Figure 11.7 Facebook comments

into the future (Figures 11.6–8). The vast majority of Facebook and Instagram followers like and support Taïa's postings, with messages of love for Genet as a saint and inspirational writer. In addition, they mention Patti Smith's video visit to Genet's tomb, and Juan Goytisolo, a Spanish author, and Genet's friend, who is also buried in Larache. They also praise Taïa for his posting and his own writings, and several followers express love and appreciation in multiple languages for him by using heart emojis or other icons. Only one message posted to the thread on Facebook draws the reader's attention to the anti-Semitic and racist

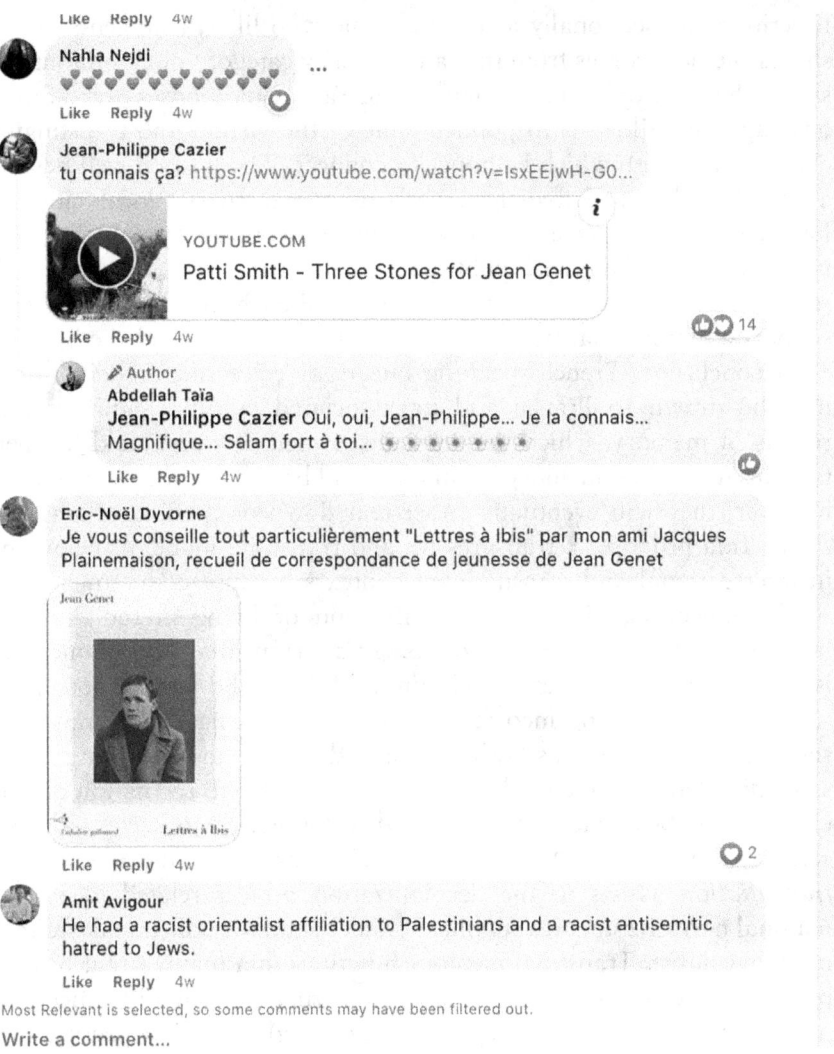

Figure 11.8 Facebook comments

stances Genet supposedly displayed in some of his writing, which has also been documented in recent scholarship (Amin). As Landsberg reminds us: "Two people watching a film may each develop prosthetic memory, but their prosthetic memory may not be identical" (21). The same is true for the photographic image in this unfolding and dynamic site of memory of Genet and Larache. Indeed, this site of transfilial memory functions intersectionally as not everyone who likes, comments on, or shares the post comes from the same identity category or community or shares the same opinions. In Figure 11.6, Taïa also proposes over a dozen hashtags that allow us to ponder some of the virtual and translingual communities with which he hopes to connect. These reach well beyond a LGBTQ-identified audience, with references to the local cities of Larache and Tangiers as well as with Morocco at large, the Arab Spring movement, and the French publishing world. Taïa's site of memory will remain dialogic in a way that many official French sites of memory that support a national narrative have not traditionally accomplished.

In conclusion, French-speaking queers of color like Abdellah Taïa may be drawn to France and its associated cultural signifiers and realms of memory, which they first discovered in stories told by their families (transfilial memory) or in films and books (prosthetic memory); however, they will eventually either tear down or decolonize many of them. Taïa proposes a transgressive and transfilial model of belonging in intersectional and transnational contexts because of his own sense of disconnection with or disidentification of living in the diaspora between France and the Maghreb. Taïa's transfilial site of memory is both "faithful" to Genet and "unfaithful" to the nation, not in the sense of remembering incorrectly, but by venerating Genet transgressively and transfilially as both a saint and sinner, and operating in the same dissident way Genet did, which is unfaithful to the nation and its empire. The fact that Genet is buried in Larache, Morocco, and Taïa celebrates him as a "Moroccan Saint," helps us to understand how *transfiliation* assists in the decolonization project related to French national narratives, which Achille, Forsdick, and Moudileno take to task in their volume. Transfilial memory functions in a manner that has the potential to draw in various communities that embody difference to a new form of universalism (Suaudeau and Niang) that is intersectional by definition and forward-looking, allowing us all to find new narratives by which to live together in the future.

Works cited

Achille, Étienne, Charles Forsdick, and Lydie Moudileno, eds. *Postcolonial Realms of Memory: Sites and Symbols in Modern France*. Liverpool UP, 2020.

Amin, Kadji. *Disturbing Attachments: Genet, Modern Pederasty, and Queer History*. Duke UP, 2017.
Ben Jelloun, Tahar. *Jean Genet, menteur sublime*. Gallimard, 2010.
Bersani, Leo. *Homos*. Harvard UP, 1995.
Boulé, Jean-Pierre. *Abdellah Taïa, la mélancolie et le cri*. Presses universitaires de Lyon, 2020.
Bruno, Giuliana. *The Atlas of Emotions: Journeys in Art, Architecture, and Film*. Verso, 2018.
Bullock, Barbara E., and Denis M. Provencher. "The linguistic representation of femininity and masculinity in Jean Genet's *Notre-Dame-des-Fleurs*." *French Cultural Studies*, vol. 12, no. 1, 2001, pp. 43–58.
Çaliskan, Dilara. "Queer postmemory." *European Journal of Women's Studies*, vol. 26, no. 3, 2019, pp. 261–73.
Carrée, Roland. "Des morts et des hommes: vie et mémoire de Jean Genet au Maroc." *middleeasteye.net*. July 15, 2022.
Crenshaw, Kimberlé. "Demarginalizing the intersection of race and sex: A Black feminist critique of antidiscrimination doctrine, feminist theory and antiracist politics." University of Chicago Legal Forum, 1989, pp. 139–67.
Ducournau, Claire. "Literary prestige." *Postcolonial Realms of Memory: Sites and Symbols in Modern France*, edited by Étienne Achille, Charles Forsdick, and Lydie Moudileno. Liverpool UP, 2020, pp. 63–70.
Fassbinder, Rainer Werner. *Querelle*. Feature film. France, 1982.
Genet, Jean. *Un chant d'amour*. Short. France, 1950.
Grandena, Florian. "Zooming in, coming out: Languages in Olivier Ducastel and Jacques Martineau's *Ma vraie vie à Rouen/The True Story of My Life in Rouen* (2003)." *Studies in French Cinema*, vol. 9, no. 1, 2009, pp. 75–86.
Haynes, Todd. *Poison*. Feature film. France, 1991.
Heyndels, Ralph. "Ecrire le tombeau de Jean Genet. Instants rêvés dans le cimetière espagnol de Larache: Abdellah Taïa et Rachid O." *Toutes les images du langage Jean Genet*, edited by Frieda Ekotto, Aurélie Renaud, and Agnès Vannougvong. Schena Editore, 2008, 91–101.
———. "Entremêlements narratifs sur la tombe de Jean Genet, Abdellah Taïa et Rachid O." *Travaux de littérature*, vol. 22, *La littérature française au croisement des cultures*, 2009, pp. 473–81.
Hirsch, Marianne. *The Generation of Postmemory: Writing and Visual Culture after the Holocaust*. Columbia UP, 2012.
Horvat, Anamarija. *Screening Queer Memory: LGBTQ Pasts in Contemporary Film and Television*. Bloomsbury, 2021.
Landsberg, Alison. *Prosthetic Memory: The Transformation of American Remembrance in the Age of Mass Culture*. Columbia UP, 2004.
Lange, Rémi. *The Road to Love/Tarik el hob*. Feature film. France, 2003.
Nora, Pierre, ed. *Les Lieux de mémoire*, 3 vols. Gallimard, 1984–92.

O., Rachid. *Plusieurs vies*. Gallimard, 1996.

Provencher, Denis M. "Abdellah Taïa's *transfilial* myth making and unfaithful realms of memory." *Abdellah Taïa's Queer Migrations: Non-Places, Affect, and Temporalities*, edited by Denis M. Provencher and Siham Bouamer. Lexington Books, 2021, pp. 219–55.

———. "Interview with Abdellah Taïa." June 7, 2023.

———. *Queer French: Globalization, Language, and Sexual Citizenship in France*. Ashgate, 2007.

———. *Queer Maghrebi French: Language, Temporalities, Transfiliations*. Liverpool UP, 2017.

Rothberg, Michael, Debrati Sanyal, and Maxim Silverman. "Editors' note. *Nœuds de mémoire*: Multidirectional memory in postwar French and francophone culture." *Yale French Studies*, vol. 118/19, 2010, pp. 1–2.

Sartre, Jean-Paul. *Saint-Genet, comédien et martyr*. Gallimard, 1952.

Smith, Patti. *Three Stones for Jean Genet*. 2014. www.youtube.com/watch?v=IsxEEjwH-Go&t=9s.

Suaudeau, Julien, and Mame-Fatou Niang. *Universalisme*. Anamosa, 2022.

Taïa, Abdellah. *L'Armée du salut*. Points. 2013.

———. "Genet, Abdallah, et moi." *Les Passions de Jean Genet*, edited by Ralph Heyndels. Schena Editore, 2010, 11–15.

———. "Jean Genet, un saint marocain." *Nejma: Revue littéraire*, winter 2010–11.

———. *Le rouge du tarbouche*. Ségier, 2004.

———. *La Tombe de Genet*. Points. 2008 (published alongside *L'Armée du salut*, 2013).

Waters, John. *Pink Flamingos*. Feature film. USA, 1972.

White, Edmund. *Genet: A Biography*. Vintage, 1994.

CHAPTER TWELVE

The Chevalier d'Eon

Todd W. Reeser

Like many French people with whom I have spoken, the Chevalier d'Eon came to my attention via pop superstar Mylène Farmer's 1987 hit song, "Sans contrefaçon" ["Without a Doubt"; literally, "Without Forgery"]. The speaker asks their mother: "Pourquoi je suis pas un garçon?" [Why am I not a boy?] but then proclaims: "Sans contrefaçon je suis un garçon" [Without a doubt, I am a boy] – a phrase repeated over and over. The speaker notes that they "do their own thing" [je n'en fais qu'à ma tête] and announces: "Un mouchoir au creux du pantalon, je suis chevalier d'Eon" [With a handkerchief in the crotch of my pants, I am the Chevalier d'Eon]. The reference to this pre-modern historical figure looks to denote a transgender child assigned female at birth who does not identify with that gender. His experience of gender is not invented or fake but constitutes currency to be employed in the gendered economy of everyday life.

Charles d'Eon de Beaumont, known as the Chevalier d'Eon (1728–1810), was assigned male at birth, but then they largely passed as a woman later in life.[1] Many people of the time believed, however, that d'Eon was assigned female at birth and had dressed and passed as a man in the first part of their life because their father wanted a boy after a series of daughters were born – a narrative that d'Eon propagated. After their death in London, where they had been living since 1785, a doctor examined their body and proclaimed that the Chevalier had male organs. Historians have documented d'Eon's life in detail and

---

1 Given the gender complications in the life of d'Eon, I use they/them pronouns here, with the understanding that such pronouns did not exist at the time.

their relation to gender (e.g., Marilyn Morris; Kates, "D'Eon"; Kates, *Monsieur*; Frank; Pinsseau). D'Eon may well have been what we now call intersex, transgender, non-binary, or genderqueer, or they may have been cisgender and assumed a new gender presentation for feminist ends, as a virile woman proving gender equality. Or, d'Eon may have been attempting to further their career with French royalty by acquiescing to gender change as requested. What interests me here, however, is not how d'Eon defined their gender, but how they function as a queer site of memory. While visiting the Chevalier d'Eon Museum in d'Eon's hometown Tonnerre in Burgundy, the guide (a self-identified descendant of the Chevalier) remarked that today various groups claimed the Chevalier as one of theirs. The gays want them to be gay, trans folk want them to be trans, lesbians want them to lesbian, the guide noted. Though he was talking about today, something similar could be said diachronically: d'Eon has been remembered in a wide variety of ways in the service of both queer and cisnormative ideologies. Oddly, although d'Eon is moderately well known as a historical figure in France, they have not been understood as any kind official *lieu de mémoire* because the figure is taken as marginal, not part of any national narrative. To consider d'Eon as a site of memory reinscribes a specific history of queerness into French national narrative, recognizing what may already be in sight but not seen. Because d'Eon's queerness cannot be easily categorized or defined in modern terms, it may be hidden, as moderns cannot easily recognize d'Eon in legible terms.

Another reason for the diffuse reception of d'Eon is that despite all the biographies in existence none has been definitive, and d'Eon has functioned after death as a sign of gender more than as a historical subject. As a 1968 article about the "enigma of the Chevalier d'Eon" in a regional newspaper published near d'Eon's home estate notes concerning their life, "en dépit des travaux sérieux parus sur la matière" [despite serious works that have come out on the topic], the public is "plutôt ami 'des histoires' que 'de l'Histoire'" [a friend of "stories" more than of "history"] (Larcher). The collection over more than 200 years of *histoires* in the plural have themselves become d'Eon, and as *lieux de mémoire* replacing memory with stories, as Nora puts it, they are "multiple yet specific; collective and plural yet individual," since "history belongs to everyone and to no one," particularly in this case around "the cult of the dead" (3, 16). The gender and the body of d'Eon "have no referents in reality" but "are their own referents – pure signs" (19). Although d'Eon's genitalia were certified after death and although the baptismal record is housed at the town hall in Tonnerre, their true sex was put into question during and after their lifetime, with some even questioning whether the doctor actually saw what he documented that he saw. In 1836, biographer Frédéric Gaillardet published what looked to be a comprehensive biography, supposedly based on authentic materials in the archives, with the title *Mémoires du chevalier d'Eon*, but a number of elements of the narrative turned out to be made-up. D'Eon did in fact write parts of an autobiography, but they remained in the archives (now in the Brotherton Collection at Leeds University), until they were published in 2001 in an English translation (D'Eon, *Maiden*). Yet even d'Eon's autobiographical text cannot be taken at face value since they were crafting an *histoire* about their true sex as female. Although numerous letters and other writings in d'Eon's hand are held in archives in France and England, the fragmented nature of the texts contributes to the inability to come to final conclusions about gender, normativity, and queerness. Yet, the lack of consensus also permitted later thinkers to categorize d'Eon's gender according to their will, transforming the figure for their own ideological purposes.

Categorizing d'Eon

The most influential remembrance of all is likely English sexologist Havelock Ellis's 1905 chapter on "Eonism" in *Studies in the Psychology of Sex* (translated as *Etudes de psychologie sexuelle*). Ellis defines d'Eon's type as "people who took pleasure in behaving and dressing like the opposite sex and yet were not sexually inverted" (1), meaning not what we would now call "homosexual." For Ellis, d'Eon is "probably the most conspicuous of these historical personages" (1) as they had no sexual relationships and "had adopted feminine dress on his own initiative and became commonly regarded as a woman" (2), thereby "fulfilling a deep demand of his own nature" (3). Along with Ellis, numerous French publications in the mid-twentieth century suggest that the category of Eonism is not a modernist invention but is embedded in the French tradition (e.g., Lhermitte). Another figure, the Abbot of Choisy, from the seventeenth century, cited by Ellis (3–4), but also in other sources (e.g., Lhermitte 97), helps to confirm that d'Eon is not some strange queer exception in France but indicative of some kind of metamorphosis embedded in the French past. To remember gender in a French context is not necessarily to remember people with a single gender presentation over the course of their life course nor to remember people whose gender aligned with the sex assigned at birth.

Consequently, mid-twentieth-century discourse on "*transsexualité*" makes frequent reference to the figure, as reimagined beyond Ellis. Writing a monograph on the invention of the category of *transsexualité* in France, I have frequently come across references to d'Eon in popular and medical discourse. The first publicly recognized French transsexual, Michel-Marie Poulain, includes a chapter titled, "Le Chevalier d'Eon," in the narrative of her life (Marais 100–104). Poulain is reminded by people around her and by her official papers that she was assigned male at birth and is taken as a man, but she sees herself as female and wonders if she is a monster. What offers her solace and inspiration, however, is the story of d'Eon, "une image heureuse, simple, conciliante" [a happy, simple, and reassuring image] (104). To avoid suffering, Poulain decides to keep d'Eon in mind as a comforting role model, and the image of d'Eon recurs in dreams (155). In what is very likely the first French film about transsexuality, Gaveau's *Adam est ... Eve* (1954), the main character – whose name at the beginning of the film is Charles Beaumont – becomes Charlotte Beaumont after a stay at a gender reassignment clinic in rural France (see Reeser "Transsexuality"). The citation of d'Eon's names is not random: the gender transition – though not exactly the same as d'Eon's, which did not of course include medical intervention – refers back to the Chevalier as the only available reference for transsexuality at the time.

Contemporaneous medical discourse takes up the seemingly stable category as well. Delay et al. (385) begin a case study with a discussion of *éonisme*, the Chevalier serving as the ultimate example, along with the court of Henri III and Louis XIV's brother's entourage (see also Abécassis 177; Gardien-Jourd'heuil and Gardien 56). As the category of *transsexualité* becomes more visibly articulated after the 1950s, *éonisme* is increasingly a debated concept, at times incorporated into the new medicalized category and at times distinguished from it. In his 1978 thesis, Valensi takes into account the analysis of d'Eon's handwriting, concluding that he is fully male (40–46). Valensi sees a "sorte de délire" [a kind of delirium] in d'Eon's identification as a woman, "faisant de lui selon les critères actuels un transsexuel" [meaning that he is a transsexual, according to the current definition] (67). Transvestism in this case was "le début d'un authentique transsexualisme" [the beginning of a bona fide transsexualism] (67). In a 1961 psychological treatise, Aimes takes "modern Chevaliers D'Eon" as transsexuals – men who want to be women and seek surgery (149). The reconsideration of d'Eon in the twentieth century is predicated on the widespread belief that d'Eon – as Dascotte-Mailliet's 1957 novel–biography put it – belonged "à deux époques, comme elle semblait appartenir à deux sexes" [to two eras, as she belonged to two sexes] (207). D'Eon was the complicated, uncategorized early modern figure as well as the figure that could be adjusted to the era of transsexuality where they also "belonged" (or were made to belong).

Contesting categories

Not everyone took d'Eon as a transsexual in an early modern figure's body, however. Their gender was hotly debated – by doctors, historians, and artists. In 1958, Lemay devotes an entire article to arguing that "le Chevalier d'Eon n'était pas Eoniste" [the Chevalier d'Eon was not Eonist], that Ellis's appellation is "erroneous," and that legends enter into popular "habit" where they remain (205). Using texts from the eighteenth century to prove his point, Lemay writes that the term that should be used is *"transvestisme"* since d'Eon was "neutralized" and told to take on a female role, which he accepted but "definitely took no pleasure in" [n'y prenait certainement aucun plaisir] (206). In a substantial medical dissertation from 1956, Colla notes that d'Eon does not fit in the category of "habitual transvestism" since they "s'être servi du travesti plutôt que l'avoir subi" [used transvestism rather than underwent it] (12).

A 1957 television show, *Enigmes de l'histoire*, about d'Eon, includes a debate between two men who argue over whether d'Eon was a man or a woman, with one of them arguing that the doctors who attested to male genitalia after death may have been bought off ("Chevalier"). At the very end of the show, the men invite viewers to write in and say whether d'Eon was a man or woman ("Envoyez-nous donc votre réponse"). Such a televised debate allegorizes the broad, diachronic debate about d'Eon and the inability finally to know not only their sex, but also their gender. A few years after Gaveau's transsexual film, Jacqueline Audry's more well-known film, *Le Secret du Chevalier d'Eon* (1959), portrays the version of their life in which they were born female but assigned male at birth by their father. D'Eon is clearly played by an actress (Andrée Debar) loosely dressed as a man, with her inability to pass part of the dramatic irony and comedy of the film. The two films made within a few years of each other, then, can be taken as a cinematic dialogue, a kind of debate over d'Eon: did they go through a deep transformation, or were they ultimately one sex dressed as the other?

In *Le Chevalier d'Eon et son problème psycho-sexuel* (1966), Cadéac approaches the biographical evidence skeptically. Acknowledging the autopsy, he wants to go beyond exterior appearance as evidence, since the possibility of "divers états intersexuels" [various states of intersexuality] (5) must be considered. But he also asks whether d'Eon was perhaps a "véritable travesti" [true transvestite] (6), and whether abnormal anatomy is the cause of this mental state. He concludes, however, by noting that their cross-dressing was a result of their own character, despite the fact that "il souffrait de cet état ambigu auquel la nature l'avait condamné" [he suffered from the ambiguous status that nature had condemned him to], while "en perpétuelle lutte avec lui-même" [in perpetual struggle with himself] (191). Cadéac carefully notes in his conclusion that this case is definitely not "*transsexualisme*" (194), but a condition caused by internal conflict itself.

In other cases, gender categories themselves are taken as problems or they are ignored entirely. Already, in Frédéric Gaillardet's preface to the first biography of d'Eon, in 1836, the question of sex and of gender is posed, with no answer offered or desired: "De ces deux personnes quelle fut la vraie? De ces deux sexes, de ces deux genres, quel fut le simulé?" [Of these two people, which one was the real one? Of these two sexes, of these two genders, which one was fake?] (VI). Was the Chevalier, Gaillardet asks, ultimately a man, a woman, or both together? Words denoting unknowing, like enigma, are used to refer to D'Eon (VII), but it is the need to be one sex or gender that is really enigmatic. The author verifies having seen the unambiguous birth records certifying maleness but then hypothesizes as to whether there had been a "fausse énonciation de sexe" [false declaration of sex] (12) and some "secret" (13).

Following this tradition of unknowing in the twenty-first century, d'Eon becomes a recurring reference beyond binarized sex categories and transsexuality, connoting queer, non-binary, or trans* identities. In a 2009 dance piece, *Eonnagata* (Guillem, Lepage, and Maliphant), the fluidity of gender is represented via corporeal artistic movement. Lavrillier's experimental video, *Le Chevalier d'Eon*, interprets the figure as transgender/queer inspiration in the media age. The popular video game *Assassin's Creed: Unit* includes the figure of d'Eon, who explains that they are a master swordsman but dressed in women's clothes, with no explanation about gender offered. Maupré's two-volume graphic novel, *Le Chevalier d'Eon*, includes some queer moments. Instead of the closure of genital inspection that proves maleness, the novel ends with a man in the streets of London telling another that d'Eon will be buried in Middlesex, a name denoting an in-between space outside the gender binary. Silvestre's *Chevalier d'Eon: agent secret du Roi* makes the biography available to young adult readers in non-reductive terms. In a sense, recent remembrances of d'Eon such as these – and innumerable others – return back to the historical context before twentieth-century medical discourse and modernist sexology attempted to categorize non-normative gender in pathological terms. In the absence of labels, something very queer emerges from considering d'Eon contextually – the more biographical details and the more interpretations that are presented, the queerer their life seems to be. D'Eon ultimately incarnates our inability to know premodern gender. Precisely because of this representational variety and the inability to ever pin gender down, d'Eon queers remembrance itself at the same time as they embody French historical queerness.

Archiving d'Eon

D'Eon is not simply the composite of texts and images that circulate in French cultural memory, for d'Eon has also been archived officially. I hypothesized when beginning to work on d'Eon that as archives are key to the construction of realms of memory, and as an archiving impulse has increased in modern times (Nora 8–10), queerness must be held in the archives somewhere. How then can one approach the archives queerly, bringing out what is trapped in the archival closet? As Charles Morris urges us in a study of the queer archive, in order to "make [...] an indelible mark on the public record and public discourse," we need to continually "cruis[e] in vexed pursuit of the elusive artifacts of our queer histories" (148). It was in this spirit – searching for what may or may not exist in places that may or may not have what I seek – that I visited sites with archives, to gain a sense of what it means to archive d'Eon. Were the physical places where d'Eon's traces remained, queer? Or could they be made queer by queer scholars such as me? Significant papers from and about d'Eon are housed in the Archives Nationales in Pierrefitte in the suburbs of Paris, in the Municipal Library of Tonnerre, and in special collections at the University of Leeds. Papers that I examined included letters, inventories, bills of sale, and autobiographical fragments prepared for possible publication. Cruising through innumerable boxes, files, and papers did not lead me anywhere that historians had not already gone. What did emerge, however, was affect. As a scholar who has undertaken decades of archival work in France, I felt a queerness liberated from the past as I cruised papers. Already knowing d'Eon's life story, I felt a kind of queer frisson as I viewed the Chevalier's handwriting, and documents referring to d'Eon in the masculine *and* the feminine. Reading bills of sale or invoices led me to imagine how the objects purchased might relate to gender. In Leeds, I read through autobiographical texts with great interest, hunting or waiting perhaps for something queer to jump out at me, something that had not yet been noticed by anyone. But nothing new appeared in these "elusive artifacts," only the feeling that I was touched by something queer that had been archived and was placed in front of me by a librarian. Discussing the archive, Nora talks of our "superstitious respect and veneration for the trace [that] negates the sacred but retains its aura" (9). Rephrasing Nora, I might say that for me

Figure 12.1 The Chevalier d'Eon outside the train station, Tonnerre, Burgundy
Photograph by author

Figure 12.2 Lycée Chevalier D'Eon, Tonnerre
Photograph by author

the archival traces of d'Eon retain the aura of early modern queerness, queering the categories of gender with which I live on a daily basis. I was in touch with premodern queerness in a way that I had never been before – precisely because I had trouble locating any earth-shattering or direct form of queerness that would explain gender. I was forced to leave behind my modern categories of gender to enter another world, one that haunted me with its non-categorization and its specific details.

I paid two visits to Tonnerre to better understand how physical vestiges of d'Eon's life relate to memory, since d'Eon returned to Tonnerre as a woman before moving to London. What vestiges of their life remained for French people or for foreign tourists like me to see and experience today? And how do they relate to queerness? Upon leaving the train station, I found a larger-than-life cutout of the Chevalier displayed in a square (Figure 12.1), a testament to their valor while presenting as a woman. A local real estate agency was named "Chevalier d'Eon." I found local wines named after the Chevalier in a wine shop. On the gate outside the local high school was a sign with the school's name "Lycée

Chevalier D'Eon," along with "Liberté, Égalité, Fraternité," and the image of Marianne (Figure 12.2).

I visited the town hall to see first-hand d'Eon's baptism record. Their birthplace nearby is marked with a plaque. I visited the home where they lived, now the *Musée du Chevalier d'Eon*, open on a guided tour conducted by a self-described descendant of the Chevalier, who knows everything about d'Eon's life and about every object in the museum. The objects displayed (paintings, clothing, swords, etc.) were so numerous that it was difficult for me to keep track of what had belonged to d'Eon and what had not. A sign out front advertising the museum depicted d'Eon as a woman on one side and as a man on the other.

The local municipal museum houses a series of objects relating to d'Eon as well, photos of which the town archivist graciously sent me. The whole site of Tonnerre, it seemed to me, as a visitor, was a monument to this queer figure from France's past. I imagined d'Eon walking around town, visiting parks and the like. Queerness, I felt, is not just housed in the Marais in Paris or other urban locations, but in this rural village as well. On one level, this space embodied the idea that queer memory is disseminated through French geographies and just has to be located.

What struck me after my visits, however, was that Tonnerre was simultaneously a non-site of memory. I was confused about why the village was not better known as a queer site across France and beyond, why folks wanting to go on an LGBTQIA+ pilgrimage were not flocking to this city. Why were its restaurants and hotels not filled up with tourists seeking queer sites, I wondered, as I sat almost alone in my hotel's dining room? D'Eon is popular in Japan, thanks to manga and animated features about the figure, so why were Japanese tourists not coming to visit Tonnerre? While visiting the municipal library one afternoon and speaking to a librarian about their collection and about the local reception of d'Eon, I asked her what the locals thought of them. They don't know really know much about them, she told me, and then she walked into the main area of the library to ask a group of students who attended the Lycée Chevalier d'Eon what they knew about the Chevalier. Not much, it turned out. One student sheepishly volunteered that d'Eon was a spy. Another noted something similar. But nothing about gender, nothing related to gender transition. Perhaps d'Eon was taken as a gender spy, entering into one gender to learn clandestinely about it, but that was not the student's line of thought. I have had similar experiences with other French people as well, when I ask them if they know d'Eon. Even well-educated French people might not know them. If it is institutions that do not allow for the queerness of historical figures to become publicly known, French educational institutions clearly had a hand in this invisibility. No one that I have met has ever recounted learning about d'Eon in a French school. If d'Eon functions as a realm of memory, it is not in the same way as Joan of Arc. They saw themself as similar to Joan of Arc (the "Maiden of Tonnerre," like the Maiden of Orleans), but whereas moderns see Joan of Arc as a national realm of memory (as Nora does), they definitely do not see d'Eon that way, even on a lesser scale.

What though of d'Eon's physical remains? I had read on a grave-finding website that d'Eon was buried in the St. Pancras Old Churchyard in central London, but the exact whereabouts of the grave were not given. I set out to find the grave, wandered around the graveyard hunting for the burial site, only eventually to find a large memorial stone listing a series of names with a fence barrier in front that barred me from approaching. Presumably d'Eon's body had been moved, perhaps because of the nearby train lines, or perhaps for some other reason. In what, I thought, should have been a queer site of memory – resembling, say, Oscar Wilde's tomb in Père Lachaise cemetery in Paris – I was left with uncertainty. I did not know where d'Eon's body was. Their endpoint was marked by a monument that didn't denote anything. There was nothing queer here, it was as normative a marker as any other that I could see on that sunny June day.

This inability to find d'Eon's burial place in the cemetery, I thought, allegorized a modern relation to d'Eon's gender. It was ultimately impossible to locate. Unable to connect to d'Eon, I was left with a sense of distance from this queer past, unlike the connection I had felt in the archives. Nora tells us that "we feel a visceral attachment to that which made us what we are, yet at the same time we feel historically estranged from this legacy" (7). Even though d'Eon might seem contemporary, a kind of pre-modern figure in a twenty-first-century body, belonging to two époques, there is also something alienating about a figure who functioned in another categorical system than the Anglo-American sex/gender system that I am so used to being part of. Nora writes that "the past is a world from which we are fundamentally cut off. We discover the truth about our memory when we discover how alienated from it we are" (12). If "we seek not our origins but a way of figuring out what we are from what we are no longer" (13), for me d'Eon is not only a queer origin for queer or transgender modern subjects, and a sign that queer has always already been inside France, they are also a sign of what gender is no longer – a unique figure in a less binarized and cisgender world, which allowed them to be the enigma that they were.

Works cited

Abécassis, Albert, and Michel Berthon. "Sur un cas d'inversion sexuelle avec travestissement." *Médecine légale et dommage corporel*, vol. 30, no. 1, 1949, pp. 177–80.
Aimes, Alexandre. *Pour comprendre les changements de sexe*. Expansion scientifique française, 1961.
Assassin's Creed Unity. Computer game. Ubisoft, 2014.
Audry, Jacqueline. *Le Secret du Chevalier d'Eon*. Feature film. Éditions René Chateau Vidéo. France, 1959.
Cadéac, Marcel. *Le Chevalier d'Eon et son problème psycho-sexuel, considérations sur les états psycho-sexuels et sur le travestisme*. Maloine, 1966.
"Chevalier d'Eon." Episode of television series, *Enigmes de l'histoire*, Channel 1. August 13, 1957.
Colla, René. "Le Travestissement habituel." PhD thesis, University of Paris, 1956.
Dascotte-Mailliet, Paule. *L'Etrange demoiselle de Beaumont*. A. Fayard, 1957.
Delay, J., P. Deniker, T. Lemperière, and J.-C. Benoit. "Histoire d'un travesti: L'Eonisme." *L'Encéphal*, vol. 43, no. 5, 1954, pp. 385–98.
D'Eon de Beaumont, Charles. File: BC MS CHEVALIER D'EON/02. Papers of Charles Chevalier d'Eon de Beaumont. University of Leeds.
———. *The Maiden of Tonnerre*. Translated by Roland A. Champagne, Nina Ekstein, and Gary Kates. Johns Hopkins UP, 2001.
Ellis, Havelock. *Studies in the Psychology of Sex*. vol. 2. Random House, 1942 [1905].
Farmer, Mylène. "Sans contrefaçon." *Youtube.com*. Web.
Frank, André. *D'Eon chevalier et chevalière, sa confession inédite*. Amiot-Dumont, 1953.
Gaillardet, Frédéric, ed. *Mémoires du chevalier d'Eon*. 2 vols. Chez Ladvocat, 1836.
Gardien-Jourd'heuil, M.-P., and P.-E. Gardien. "Un cas de transvestisme." *Annales Médico-Psychologiques*, vol. 106, no. 1, 1948, pp. 52–58.
Gaveau, René. *Adam est ... Eve*. Feature film. Hollywood Boulevard Vidéo. France, 1954.
Guillem, Sylvie, Robert Lepage, and Russell Maliphant. *Eonnagata*. 2009.
Kates, Gary. "D'Eon returns to France: Gender and power in 1777." *Body Guards: The Cultural Politics of Gender Ambiguity*, edited by Julia Epstein and Kristina Straub. Routledge, 1991, pp. 167–94.

———. *Monsieur d'Eon is a Woman*. Johns Hopkins UP, 2001.
Larcher, A. "L'Enigme du Chevalier d'Eon passionne toujours les amateurs d'histoire." *L'Yonne républicain*. January 17, 1968, unpag.
Lavrillier, Carol Marc. *Le Chevalier d'Eon*. undated. Video. BNF. Notice FRBNF42265860.
Lemay, P. "Le Chevalier d'Eon n'était pas Eoniste." *Le Progrès médical*, vol. 10, May 24, 1958, pp. 205–206.
Lhermitte, François. "L'Eonisme." *La Semaine des hôpitaux*. January 6, 1954, pp. 97–98.
Marais, Claude. *"J'ai choisi mon sexe": Confidences de Michel-Marie Poulain*. Les Éditions de Fontvieille, 1954.
Maupré, Agnès. *Le Chevalier d'Eon*. 2 vols. Ankama Éditions, 2014–15.
Morris, Charles E. "Archival queer." *Rhetoric and Public Affairs*, vol. 9, no. 1, 2006, pp. 145–51.
Morris, Marilyn. "The Chevalière d'Eon, transgender autobiography and identity." *Gender and History*, vol. 31, no. 1, 2019, pp. 78–90.
Nora, Pierre. "Between memory and history." *Realms of Memory: Rethinking the French Past*, vol. 1, *Conflicts and Divisions*, edited by Pierre Nora and Lawrence D. Kritzman. Translated by Arthur Goldhammer. Columbia UP, 1996, pp. 1–20.
Pinsseau, Pierre. *L'Étrange destinée du chevalier d'Eon, 1728–1810*. Clavreuil, 1945.
Reeser, Todd W. "Transsexuality and the production of French universalism: René Gaveau's *Adam est … Eve* (1954)." *French Review*, vol. 91, no. 2, 2017, pp. 126–38.
Silvestre, Anne-Sophie. *Chevalier d'Eon: Agent secret du Roi*. Flammarion, 2013.
Valensi, Philippe. "Le Chevalier d'Eon: du transvestisme au transsexualisme." PhD thesis, University of Paris VI, 1978.

CHAPTER THIRTEEN

(Re-)defining the popular music "Gay icon" in media coverage of Dalida and Mylène Farmer

Chris Tinker

The concept of the "Gay icon" is well established in contemporary French media discourse, including the usage of terms such as *icône gay*, *icône gaie*, and *icône des gays*, as well as other related designations such as *icône queer* and *icône LGBTQ*. The question of what makes a potential Gay icon has also formed the subject of both academic and wider public debates. While considering that the term "has been dreadfully overused lately" (2), Georges-Claude Guilbert provides extensive discussion of the Gay icon in his 2018 book, which is subtitled *The (Mostly) Female Entertainers Gay Men Love*. For Guilbert, "The gay icon tends to be heterosexual. Sometimes she is a fighter, sometimes a long-suffering victim; in any case, she's a strong personality, who often ends tragically. She is a star, and no one becomes a star without encountering some pitfalls on the way" (6). Where female popular music artists as Gay icons are specifically concerned, Anthony Mathé's semiological study (2013) associates their status with particular themes in their songs, including desire, sex, provocation, transgression, ambivalence, inversion, dreams, celebration, spectacle, and corporality (100). This chapter explores how the mass media in contemporary France, particularly the written press, contribute towards representing and remembering two of the most prominent examples of female popular music Gay icons: one living, Mylène Farmer (b.1961), and the other deceased, Dalida (1933–87).

Following her early childhood in Quebec during the 1960s, Mylène

Farmer (birth name Gauthier; stage name Farmer after the U.S. actor Frances Farmer), grew up in the Parisian suburb of Ville-d'Avray. Since her first hit single, "Maman a tort" (1984), she has enjoyed enormous success as a performer and as a lyricist, particularly given her songwriting partnership with the composer and film/video producer Laurent Boutonnat. While Farmer is associated with spectacular stage shows and video clips, she is also represented by the media as a somewhat shy and reclusive figure. Dalida was born Iolanda Cristina Gigliotti to Italian parents and raised in Egypt before moving to Paris to develop her singing career in the mid-1950s (the name Dalida was settled upon following an earlier stage name Dalila). Barbara Lebrun's 2020 book-length study of Dalida highlights her early exoticism and Mediterranean, particularly Italian, and Latino-Caribbean influences, her association in the early to mid-1960s with a relatively safe "rock bon genre," and the melodramatic songs/performances of 1966–67, given her attempt to take her own life in 1967 (Dalida later died by suicide in 1987). Lebrun also considers Dalida's relationship with the Middle East and North Africa, including songs in Hebrew in the early to mid-1960s and her popularization in France of songs in Arabic from the late 1970s, as well as her engagement with 1970s French disco. In the case of Dalida, her contemporary media coverage, to use Cath Davies' terms, "acts as an effective summation of the construction of [the] star persona when alive, while also signaling the development of [a] posthumous media image" (193).

Media coverage of Dalida and Farmer as Gay icons displays features of celebrity journalism more generally identified by Annik Dubied: storytelling, the combination of news and entertainment, new releases and public pronouncements, the relationship between private and public lives, the disclosure of previously hidden information, the negotiation of social change, and the attributes of celebrities themselves ("L'information-people"; "L'information-people, entre rhétorique"). These include physical, visual, and behavioral characteristics, ordinary and/or extraordinary qualities, personal strengths and weaknesses, self-control (or lack thereof), and personal difficulties and motivations. In addition, to use Chelsea Reynolds's terms, the "importance of normalizing judgement to the news industry's professional ethos" (5) is relevant to coverage of Gay icons.

The media representations of Gay icons may also be viewed in terms of some of the key aspects of Queer theory, as articulated by Cervulle and Julliard, in particular sexuality as a subjective property, the homo/

heterosexuality binary and associated non-negotiable social structures, and heterosexuality as a form of public culture that gives substance to a hegemonic public. A re-conception of public debate, moving from the Habermassian notion of rational–critical public towards new forms of language, communication, and aesthetics of protest is a further relevant concern (Cervulle and Julliard 14–15). Moreover, as David L. Eng, Jack Halberstam, and José Esteban Muñoz comment, "the political promise of [Queer] reside[s] specifically in its broad critique of multiple social antagonisms, including race, gender, class, nationality and religion, in addition to sexuality" (1).[1] Christopher Pullen's concept of "new storytelling for gay and lesbian identity" (1) also highlights the potential, across various media forms, for "a shift from 'being' towards 'becoming'" (3–4) as part of a "post queer politics" (Ruffolo), emphasizing "the diverse, yet coalescent and mobile nature of individual storytellers, who [...] offer scope to the diversity of identity" (10).

In addition, and particularly within the context of this edited volume, media coverage of the Gay icon may be understood in contemporary France as processes of what Pierre Nora (1996) defines as "rememoration," a view of history that emphasizes: "effects" rather than "causes"; the "traces" left by "actions remembered"; the "interaction" of "commemorations"; "the construction of events over time" and "the disappearance and reemergence of their significations"; "perpetual reuse and misuse"; "influence on successive presents"; and "the way in which traditions are constituted and passed on" (xxiv). Furthermore, such coverage may be viewed in terms of "le quotidien" [everyday life], characterized, according to Étienne Achille and Lydie Moudileno (2018), by a series of contradictions, tensions, and frictions between "la liberté et la surveillance, l'hospitalité et le rejet, l'ordre et le désordre, l'oubli et la mémoire, le visible et l'invisible, le même et le divers, et bien d'autres encore" [liberty and surveillance, hospitality and rejection, order and disorder, forgetting and memory, visibility and invisibility, sameness and difference, and many others] (7–8).[2] Moreover, while Achille and Moudileno highlight within the postcolonial French context the "insidieuse" [insidious] Barthesian naturalization of bourgeois ideologies, as well as "le racisme dit 'ordinaire'" [so-called "casual" racism] and "micro-agressions dans l'espace public, professionnel et familial" [microaggressions in the public,

---

1 See also Leap 562; Provencher, "Stepping back" 411; and Provencher, *Queer Maghrebi French* 24.
2 For further discussion, see Provencher, "Abdellah Taïa" 224.

professional, and familial sphere] (11–13), our discussion of Gay icons might also consider the presence of naturalized, casual, and microaggressive forms of homophobia within the broader context of French republican universalism.

Gay icons: glamorized and/or troubled

Coverage of both Dalida and Farmer effectively reuses and perpetuates well-established myths of female Gay icons as glamorous (Davet; Fourny "Dalida"), including an association with a French *transformiste* cabaret tradition. Both figures are identified as particular inspirations and popular subjects for drag queens (Leherpeur; Fourny "Michou"; Pocréaux; "La Vraie vie"; "Léo Sullivan"; "Saint-Michou").[3] In one example of coverage, however, a 2010 *Sud Ouest* review of Gay nightlife and venues in Bordeaux (M.D.), glamorous stereotypes of Dalida are both highlighted and effectively played down. Indeed, the review describes one particular bar, L'Ours marin ["The Sea Bear], as "à mille milles du cliché paillettes-Dalida" [far from the glittery cliché associated with Dalida]. It also characterizes the place as a straight-friendly and non-ghettoized space, and its clientele in terms of an inclusive plurality of sexual and generational identities, while effectively giving representation to a distinct Bear identity.

Farmer, in particular, is characterized in terms of disorder, as a troubled personality whose personal and psychological difficulties appeal to Gay audiences ("Chanson française"; Combecave). Moreover, her own view of herself as sharing "une sensibilité exacerbée" [extreme sensitivity] (Magné) and "le sentiment d'être 'différent'" [the feeling of being "different"] (Randanne; B.C.) is represented.[4] Coverage of Dalida and Farmer also emphasizes the combination of glamor and psychological difficulties. Soline Pillet (*Toute la culture*) includes Dalida and Farmer in a list of "icônes tragiques" [tragic icons], characterized by "déboires personnels" [personal setbacks], a "destin tragique" [tragic destiny], or a "mal de vivre" [world weariness], which speaks to audience members who "se sentent en décalage dans leur société" [feel at odds with their own society] and who "confère à ces idoles une aura de martyre qui les fige pour toujours dans la postérité comme de mythiques

---

3 See Lebrun on Dalida's associations with drag in France (264–65).
4 See Guilbert on the psychological suffering of Dalida (54–55) and Farmer (73).

(Re-)defining the popular music 211

héroïnes dont le glamour et la féminité absolus sont sublimés par la souffrance intime" [give these idols an aura of martyrdom that preserves them forever in posterity as mythical heroines whose absolute glamor and femininity are enhanced by their personal suffering]. Dalida's biographer, David Lelait-Helo, also emphasizes in media interviews the combination of Dalida's glamor, psychological difficulties as well as Gay audience identification ("Dalida: Trente ans"; "Trente ans après").[5] In sum, while media coverage emphasizes the disorder and glamor associated with female Gay icons, a capacity to play down such glamor is also demonstrated.

Problematization of the Gay icon

While media representations contribute towards drawing consensus around the notion of the Gay icon, other examples of coverage generate tension or conflict. Media coverage situates both Dalida and Farmer within a broader genealogy of Gay icons in the world of entertainment: Dalida is compared by the fashion writer Alice Pfeiffer to the Italian singer Raffaella Carra, while Farmer is said to be a "reference" for the contemporary popular music star Héloïse Letessier (Christine and the Queens) ("La reine Christine"). In *Le Figaro* (2015) Mylène Farmer is, amongst others, regarded by Nicolas Ungemuth as following a successful marketing strategy established by David Bowie, which included bringing together "les adolescents mal dans leur peau, les parias, les hétéros frustrés, les gays refoulés ou non et tous les déprimés" [awkward teenagers, outcasts, frustrated heterosexuals, Gay people, whether they are repressed or not, and people suffering from depression].

In contrast, certain examples of coverage actively represent or resist the very term *icône gay* as narrow and limiting, highlighting instead the breadth of artists' audience appeal. For example, François Delétraz on Mylène Farmer's 2019 concert at La Défense arena observes that she has moved from being "l'égérie des gays" [the muse for Gay people] at the start of her career to attracting wider audiences today. Léna Lutaud comments with reference to Dalida's glamorous look, "La nostalgie fait recette, et pas uniquement auprès du public gay" [Nostalgia is all the rage; not only among Gay audiences]. On a *Franceinfo* blog,

---

5 See Lebrun on the identification between Dalida's suffering and her gay male audiences (254–55).

Anne-Claire Ruel (2020) looks beyond Farmer's status as a Gay icon so as to emphasize the over-riding impression of authenticity that she creates: "surtout une icône qui semble 'vraie'" [above all an icon who seems "real"]. Following the selection of Paris as the host city of the 2018 Gay Games, Clément Guillou (2013) views the event as an opportunity to redress a perceived imbalance in representations of Gay men: traditional sporting masculinities are emphasized rather than feminine and glamorous representations or stereotypical assumptions that all Gay men enjoy Farmer's music. An account by a fan of Mylène Farmer published in *Le Progrès* following one of her concerts in Paris during her 2019 residency also questions her exclusive identification with Gay audiences: "Avant, je n'assumais pas d'être fan, c'était la chanteuse pour gays" [Before, I wasn't comfortable being a fan; she was the singer for Gay people] ("À la sortie du concert"). While coverage certainly represents the visibility and development of Gay icons, same-sex desire is played down in favor of a bourgeois universalizing sameness based on hetero- and homonormative values.

Tensions over LGBTQ+ advocacy and activism

For Guilbert, "It is not necessary to raise awareness of LGBTQ+ issues, actively support LGBTQ+ rights, speak out against discrimination and homophobia, and be involved in AIDS charities to be a gay icon, but it helps" (5). Dalida is associated in coverage with LGBTQ+ advocacy and activism, her support for Gay Pride in France, the community radio station Radio Fréquence Gay (Du Fayet), and awareness-raising around or research into HIV and AIDS ("Sidaction est en deuil"). Attention is also drawn to the Gay men in Dalida's personal and professional entourage (Du Fayet).[6] In contrast, Farmer is represented in problematic terms in relation to ongoing debates regarding equal marriage in France. Press coverage reports on a fan's plea, originally published in *L'Express* in 2012, for the singer to take a stance ("Mylène Farmer, prenez position!").[7] Farmer's appearance at a state dinner at the Elysée attended

---

6 For further discussion of Dalida's gay male entourage, see Guilbert 53 and Lebrun 255–56; and for discussion of her active support for same-sex relationships, see Guilbert 53 and Lebrun 256–59.

7 See also Jean; Tronche; "Mylène Farmer, porte-parole"; "Mylène Farmer dévoile"; Grevet; and Duchatelle.

by then French president Nicolas Sarkozy and Russian president Dmitry Medvedev is also reported as causing consternation given ongoing concerns over a ban on pride events in Russia (Jean).

Dalida and Farmer feature in a media controversy concerning homophobia and, more specifically, *follophobie* [effeminophobia]. The controversy relates to an edition of the French television reality dating show, *L'Amour est dans le pré* (2018), in which the presenter, Karine Le Marchand, refers to a Gay male contestant as "viril" and as "yag," which she defines as a man who does not recognize himself in "la culture gay" ("la culture gay," viewed as synonymous with Farmer, Dalida, as well as Madonna) (Rouyer).

Coverage of Dalida and Farmer also represents and questions essentialist assumptions linking sexual orientation to cultural and musical tastes. A 2016 report in *Rue89*, discussing scientific research seeking to establish common characteristics of same-sex desiring people (features mentioned include having several older brothers, a counter-clockwise hair whorl, and a large penis, as well as being left-handed), takes enjoying Dalida's music as a given (Faure). Coverage in 2011 in the Swiss newspaper *Le Tribune de Genève* also reports on a controversial application, *Mon fils est-il gay?* [Is my son Gay?], which, in its own words, reportedly includes, "20 questions pour savoir si tout est bien en ordre avec votre fils" [20 questions to determine if all is well with your son], and which, according to the newspaper, relies on "un ensemble de clichés autour de l'homosexualité masculine. Si le jeune homme passe beaucoup de temps dans sa salle de bain, qu'il a des piercings et aime Dalida, Mylène Farmer et les comédies musicales" [a series of Gay male stereotypes: whether the young man spends a lot of time in the bathroom, has piercings, and likes Dalida, Mylène Farmer, and musicals] ("Dialogai demande").

Media coverage effectively mobilizes the female Gay icon in favor of LGBTQ+ rights in France and beyond (with Russia viewed as comparatively lacking) and in terms of controversies relating to effeminophobia and essentialist views of sexual orientation and cultural/musical taste. Thus far, we have seen that while coverage of the Gay icon as a site of meaning and memory-making generally maintains notions of disorder, visibility, and glamor, same-sex desire is on occasion played down. However, LGBTQ+ rights are effectively promoted in coverage while controversies concerning effeminophobia and stereotyping are reported.

Abdellah Taïa: Dalida as personal truth

A site of consensus and conflict, the Gay icon is also represented in everyday, personalized, and more open-ended terms, or in Mathé's formulation, "la qualification 'ouverte' de l'icône gay" [the "open" definition of the Gay icon] (99). In a *France Inter* radio interview with the Moroccan writer Abdellah Taïa on the publication of his 2019 novel *La Vie Lente* ("Dignité, Abdellah Taïa"), Taïa describes his own and his sisters' youthful admiration for Dalida, given, for example, her successful career in France, her integrity (retaining her accent and her "arabité" [Arabness]), her expressive qualities during performances ("le mélo, les larmes, la tragédie") [melodrama, tears, and tragedy], and her repetitive use of words that reminds him of his mother. Taïa highlights Dalida's capacity to reflect his own truth (Dalida represented "quelque chose qui disait de nous une vérité de nous portée en France et au-delà de la France" [something which revealed a truth about us that was delivered into France as well as beyond France]. The depth of meaning that Taïa found in Dalida and her tragic end ("le tragique dans lequel elle est entrée à la fin nous interpelle tous") is also contrasted with the limited, popular, "light-hearted folklore" surrounding her in France that emphasizes her gestural expression and association with disco music. For Taïa, while he and his sisters were aware that their dreams of Dalida – "star égyptienne" [Egyptian star] – were "des rêves de pauvres, que rien n'allait arriver" [dreams of poor people, and that nothing would ever change], singing the songs of others was still a possibility in response to "cette réalité d'avance condamnée" [this reality that was already doomed].

While Taïa's interview stresses the fundamental importance of same-sex desire to his sense of self ("Je suis pédé, homosexuel d'abord avant d'être écrivain, que le monde le veuille ou pas" [I'm Gay, homosexual first before being a writer, whether everybody likes it or not]), his personal response to Dalida, apart from his reference to her tragic end, represents a departure from established and dominant definitions of the Gay icon. Indeed, Taïa's *France Inter* interview provides an example of what Provencher refers to in *Queer Maghrebi French* as the "negotiation" of "cultural hybridity and flexible language, temporalities, and filiations" (15) as part of his own "becoming" (Pullen) – and represents a diversification in the representation of social class.

Conclusion

Media coverage of Dalida and Mylène Farmer maintains notions of the female Gay icon as glamorous, troubled, or a combination of both, and underlines the importance of audience identification. On occasion, however, questions are raised around the legitimacy of the Gay icon, essentialist and pathologizing views on same-sex desire, as well as the issue of effeminophobia. Dalida in particular is credited in coverage with specific examples of Gay advocacy and activism during her lifetime, while Farmer, as a living Gay icon, is the subject of scrutiny regarding her contribution to LGBTQ+ causes. Finally, Abdellah Taïa's radio interview situates Dalida in terms of a personalized, flexible, hybrid, Queer approach that views Dalida across national, cultural, generational, and class divisions. In sum, while media representations view female Gay icons in terms of "visibility" and "disorder," to use the terms of Achille and Moudileno, a tension between "hospitality" and "rejection" is generated, particularly where non-normative sexualities are concerned. Although some continuity with the past is maintained, contemporary media coverage of the Gay icon represents a *lieu de mémoire* characterized by an instability and ambivalence in meaning-making.

While this initial study focuses on "mainstream" press coverage produced in metropolitan France, future work on media coverage of Gay and other icons could focus on the extent of the "normalizing judgement" of particular media producers as well as on a broader range of media texts (including LGBTQIA+ press, cultural blogs, and fan websites) and their target audiences. Moreover, further research could take into account recent ethical developments in contemporary French journalism, namely the 2015 charter, "Les médias contre l'homophobie," produced by the Association des Journalistes Lesbiennes, gays, bi·e·s et trans et intersexes (AJL), and a 2014 toolkit for journalists, "Informer sans discriminer" [Inform without discriminating], which includes aims to promote respect; combat discrimination, hierarchized sexualities, erasure of LGBT people, racism, and sensationalism; and improve the quality of representations, specifically lesbian, gay, bisexual, trans, intersex, asexual, aromantic, nonbinary, and genderfluid. Finally, further engagement with Achille, Forsdick, and Moudileno's "transcontinental, transcultural, and [...] translingual" approach (9) will contribute towards generating a broader Francospheric and global understanding of mediated Gay icons.

Works cited

Achille, Étienne, and Lydie Moudileno. *Mythologies postcoloniales: pour une décolonisation du quotidien*. Honoré Champion, 2018.

Achille, Étienne, Charles Forsdick, and Lydie Moudileno. *Postcolonial Realms of Memory: Sites and Symbols in Modern France*. Liverpool UP, 2020.

"À la sortie du concert, j'étais en apesanteur." *Le Progrès*. June 21, 2019. NexisUni.

B.C. "Chanteuse triste et icône gay." *20minutes.fr*. August 25, 2008. Web.

Cervulle, Maxime, and Virginie Julliard. "Le Genre des controverses: approches féministes et queer." *Questions de communication*, vol. 33, no. 1, 2018, pp. 7–22.

"Chanson française." *Le Point*. September 17, 1999. NexisUni.

"La charte contre l'homophobie." Association des Journalistes Lesbiennes, gays, bi·e·s et trans (AJL). *Ajlgbt.info*. 2015. Web.

Combecave, Marion. "Barbra Streisand (Arte): Top 10 des chanteuses icônes gays." *Yahoo!Actualités*. April 16, 2017. Web.

"Dalida: Trente ans après sa mort, l'icône populaire de nouveau sur le devant de la scène." *Francesoir.fr*. January 5, 2017. Web.

Davet, Stéphane. "Ces chanteuses vénérées par les gays." *Le Monde*. February 17, 2017. Web.

Davies, Cath. "No mere mortal? Re-materialising Michael Jackson in death." *Celebrity Studies*, vol. 3, no. 2, pp. 183–96.

Delétraz, François. "Et soudain, Mylène Farmer descendit du ciel et marcha sur les eaux…" *Lefigaro.fr*. June 16, 2019. NexisUni.

"Dialogai demande le retrait de l'application Mon fils est-il gay?" *La Tribune de Genève*. September 23, 2011. NexisUni.

"Dignité, Abdellah Taïa." *France Inter*. March 13, 2019. Web.

Dubied, Annik. "L'information-people." *Communication*, vol. 27, no. 1, 2009, pp. 12–17.

———. "L'information-people, entre rhétorique du cas particulier et récits de l'intimité." *Communication*, vol. 27, no. 1, 2009, pp. 54–65.

Duchatelle, Mathilde. "Ça fait trente ans qu'on se connaît." *La Montagne*. March 25, 2014. NexisUni.

Du Fayet, Guilhem. "Dalida." *Cacti-magazine.fr*. April 11, 2018. Web.

Eng, David L., Jack Halberstam, and José Esteban Muñoz. "Introduction. What's queer about queer studies now?" *Social Text* 84–85, vol. 23, no. 3–4, 2005, pp. 1–17.

Faure, Guillemette. "Comment reconnaître un homo (sans son disque de Dalida)?" *Rue89*. November 3, 2016. Web.

Fourny, Marc. "Dalida: Les dix chiffres clés de sa vie." *LePoint*. January 11, 2017.

———. "Michou, le roi de Montmartre, est mort à 88 ans." *LePoint*. January 26, 2020.
Grevet, Jordan. "Mylène Farmer: 'Je préfère un mariage gay à un mariage triste.'" *Closermag.fr*. December 17, 2012. Web.
Guilbert, Georges-Claude. *Gay Icons: The (Mostly) Female Entertainers Gay Men Love*. McFarland, 2018.
Guillou, Clément. "Si vous vous demandiez à quoi servaient les Gay Games…" *Rue89*. October 8, 2013.
"Informer sans discriminer." Association des Journalistes Lesbiennes, gays, bi·e·s et trans (AJL). *Ajlgbt.info*. 2014. Web.
Jean. "Mylène Farmer prend position sur le mariage gay." *Evous.fr*. February 1, 2018. Web.
Leap, William L. "Queer linguistics, sexuality, and discourse analysis." *The Routledge Handbook of Discourse Analysis*, edited by James Paul Gee and Michael Handford. Routledge, 2011, pp. 558–71.
Lebrun, Barbara. *Dalida: Mythe et mémoire*. Le Mot et le reste, 2020.
Leherpeur, Xavier. "Les reines de la nuit." *L'Obs*. December 4, 2019. Web.
Lelait-Helo, David. *Dalida: Le mal d'aimer*. Archipoche, 2022.
"Léo Sullivan, un transformiste qui revendique son côté masculin." *La Voix du Nord*. October 31, 2013. NexisUni.
Lutaud, Léna. "Le mythe Dalida." *Lefigaro.fr*. January 8, 2017. NexisUni.
Magné, Régine. "De l'ombre à la lumière." *Sud Ouest*. December 18, 2004. NexisUni.
Mathé, Anthony. "Sémiologie de l'icône gay: les paradoxes du genre." *Communication & Languages*, vol. 177, no. 3, 2013, pp. 93–109.
M.D. "Le gay savoir." *Sud Ouest*. July 30, 2010. Web.
"Mylène Farmer dévoile son nouveau clip!" *LePoint.fr*. December 1, 2012. NexisUni.
"Mylène Farmer, porte-parole de la cause gay? 'Certainement pas.'" *Elle*. December 2012. Web.
"Mylène Farmer, prenez position sur le mariage gay." *Lexpress.fr*. November 14, 2012. Web.
Nora, Pierre. "Preface to English Language Edition: From *Lieux de mémoire* to *Realms of Memory*." *Realms of Memory: Rethinking the French Past*, vol. 1, *Conflicts and Divisions*, edited by Pierre Nora and Lawrence D. Kritzman. Translated by Arthur Goldhammer. Columbia UP, 1996, pp. xv–xxiv.
Pfeiffer, Alice. "Dans les coulisses de Projet Fashion." *L'Express*. March 3, 2015. Web.
Pillet, Soline. "Gay comme une icône." *Toute la culture.com*. January 9, 2010. Web.
Planes, Jean-Marie. "Il venait d'avoir 18 ans." *Sud Ouest*. July 8, 2001. NexisUni.

Pocréaux, Cyril. "La ville et ses coulisses; Pau." *Le Point*. March 8, 2007. *NexisUni*.

Provencher, Denis M. "Abdellah Taïa's *transfilial* myth making and unfaithful realms of memory." *Abdellah Taïa's Queer Migrations: Non-Places, Affect, and Temporalities*, edited by Denis M. Provencher and Siham Bouamer. Lexington Books, 2021, pp. 219–55.

———. *Queer Maghrebi French: Language, Temporalities, Transfiliations*. Liverpool UP, 2017.

———. "Stepping back from queer theory: Language, fieldwork, and the everyday in sexuality studies in France." *French Cultural Studies*, vol. 25, no. 3–4, 2014, pp. 408–17.

Pullen, Christopher. *Gay Identity, New Storytelling and the Media*. Palgrave Macmillan, 2012.

"La reine Christine; Événement. L'artiste nantaise Christine and The Queens est nommée dans cinq catégories des Victoires 2015." *Presse Océan*. February 13, 2015. *NexisUni*.

Randanne, Fabien. "Cher vs Mylène Farmer … Ce vendredi, c'est le duel des icônes gay dans les sorties musicales." *20minutes.fr*. September 28, 2018. Web.

Reynolds, Chelsea. "Casual Encounters: Constructing Sexual Deviance on Craigslist.org." PhD thesis, University of Minnesota, 2017. Web.

Rouyer, Marion. "Karine Le Marchand sort du silence après ses propos maladroits assimilant gay et fans de Mylène Farmer." *Gala*. January 24, 2018. Web.

Ruel, Anne-Claire. "Mylène Farmer, Icône Vraie." Fais Pas Com' Papa. *Francetv Info*. September 27, 2020. Web.

Ruffolo, David V. *Post-Queer Politics*. Ashgate, 2009.

"Saint-Michou de Montmartre fête ses 80 ans: 'Quelle belle soirée!'" *La Tribune de Genève*. June 21, 2011. *NexisUni*.

"Sidaction est en deuil." *Centre Presse* (Aveyron). March 24, 2011. *NexisUni*.

"Trente ans après sa mort, Dalida au cinéma et en hologramme." *Le Point*. January 5, 2017. Web.

Tronche, Jean-Frédéric. "VIDEO. Mylène Farmer ne veut pas être la porte-parole du mariage gay." *Nouvelobs.com*. December 2, 2012. Web.

Ungemuth, Nicolas. "Toutes les vies de Bowie." *Lefigaro.fr*. March 6, 2015. *NexisUni*.

"La vraie vie est sur scène." *Sud Ouest*. December 30, 2011. *NexisUni*.

CHAPTER FOURTEEN

Giovanna Rincon and *Acceptess-T*
Living archives of transgender solidarity in an age of homonationalism

Blase A. Provitola[1]

La succession des décès des personnes trans, elle est préprogrammée par une transphobie institutionnelle qui est bien cristallisée et qui est reprise aussi par la société. C'est bien tout ça qui pousse les personnes trans à s'ôter la vie. C'est ça aussi qui pousse beaucoup à se défouler quand les personnes trans cumulent d'autres facteurs d'exclusion. Et quand il s'agit de femmes trans, migrante et travailleuse [sic] du sexe, elle devient aussi la victime collatérale des politiques répressives et criminalisantes, des politiques racistes qui s'installent de plus en plus de façon décomplexée ici par la droite dure, voire par l'extrême droite qui est vraiment à l'attaque aujourd'hui sur cette question.

[The succession of deaths of trans people is preprogrammed by institutional transphobia that has crystallized and been taken up by society as well. All of that is what pushes trans people to take their own lives. That is what also pushes many to lash out when trans people accumulate other factors of exclusion. And when trans women are involved who are migrants and sex workers, they become the collateral victims of repressive, criminalizing, and racist policies that are embraced more and

---

1   I thank Giovanna Rincon for granting me an interview and reading a draft of this chapter. I also thank Simon Jutant and Elliot McCullough for their precious feedback.

more openly here by the Right and especially the Far Right that is really on the offensive today with this issue.]

Prominent activist Giovanna Rincon pronounced these words in 2021, a particularly deadly year for transgender people in France, at the annual *ExisTransInter* march for trans and intersex rights formerly known as *Existrans* ("Marche contre la transphobie").² She went on to affirm: "Donc nous, nous refusons d'être présentées comme des personnes trans, victimes et souffrantes. Nous refusons, par cette présence massive ici, à dire haut et fort que nous vivons heureuses et heureux d'être trans et nous ne souffrons pas de ce fait" [So we as trans people refuse to be presented as perpetually suffering and victims. We refuse, through our massive presence here, by saying loud and clear that we are happy to live as trans people, and that this does not bring us suffering]. Rincon's unwavering solidarity with trans people, migrants, sex workers, and those living with HIV – especially individuals at the intersection of these identities – is marked by a firm insistence on structural oppression and a refusal to reduce their experiences to narratives of victimhood.

Rincon has gained recognition for her work as co-founder and president of the Paris-based trans organization *Acceptess-T* (*Actions Concrètes Conciliants: Education, Prévention, Travail, Equité, Santé et Sport pour les personnes Trans*), spokesperson for both the Trans and Intersex Federation (*Fédération Trans et Intersexes*) and Union of Sex Work (*Syndicat du TRAvail Sexuel, STRASS*), and vice president of one of the Île-de-France chapters of the HIV/AIDS organization *COREVIH* (*Coordination de la lutte contre les infections sexuellement transmissibles et le virus de l'immunodéficience humaine*). In 2015, she was awarded Le Refuge/Institut Randstad's jury prize (Baudoin), and in 2018 she received an *Out d'or* prize from the Association of Gay, Lesbian, Bisexual and Trans Journalists (Le Breton; Manelli). If this contribution focuses in large part on her life's work, it is not to make her representative of any group's experiences, nor to allow her individual accomplishments to overshadow collective struggle – two phenomena to which she is vehemently opposed – but rather to highlight decades of community activism and solidarity. Along with so many others, Rincon strives to protect those lives systematically erased from the French

---

2 Since 1997, this march has been organized by the *Existrans* collective, which became the *ExisTransInter* collective in 2019 thanks to intersex rights activists. Marches prior to 2019 will therefore be referred to as *Existrans* marches for historical accuracy. All translations are my own.

national narrative. Because of her efforts to make their absences present, she constitutes a living realm of memory and a constant reminder that queer and trans rights must not come at the expense of such communities' most marginalized members.

To consider a living person a queer realm of memory is to question whether Pierre Nora's conception of temporality can apprehend the experiences of France's minoritized communities. The few historical figures included in his original project, like Charlemagne or Joan of Arc, are so woven into the fabric of national memory as to have become "symbolic [elements] of the memorial heritage of [...] the French community" (Nora xvii). A *lieu de mémoire* forms as memory congeals into the history of an imagined national community: "We feel a visceral attachment to that which made us what we are, yet at the same time we feel historically estranged from this legacy, which we must now coolly assess" (Nora 7). However, queer and trans approaches to temporality can allow for intimate emotional attachments to those who came before us or fight alongside us – attachments often felt with an immediacy that complicates the temporal distance inherent in Nora's project. Furthermore, such alternative temporalities can disrupt national "chrononormativity," or "the use of time to organize individual human bodies toward maximum productivity" (Freeman 3). Instead, what appears are often different forms of "queer time," or "models of temporality that emerge within postmodernism once one leaves the temporal frames of bourgeois reproduction and family, longevity, risk/safety, and inheritance" (Halberstam 6). Yet even as trans people disrupt linear conceptions of time and progress that feed the intertwined structures of nationalism and global racial capitalism, this does not mean that we must remain confined to the past or the fleeting present. Many of us experience time in a way that recalls José Esteban Muñoz's conception of queerness as "essentially about the rejection of a here and now and an insistence on potentiality or concrete possibility for another world" (1). And yet, if we seek to reject "a here and now" – an expression connoting the painful limitations of the present – then we must also look to current expressions of solidarity and worldbuilding that inspire us as we work towards a "then and there." Indeed, when faced with institutional forces that are so often synonymous with trans death, it is crucial to look to living trans people as a reminder that our existences are not only possible, but joyful and desirable. Giovanna Rincon is one such person for so many queer and trans people, and I am thankful to her for agreeing to a virtual interview with me in March 2022.

In the context of this volume, one must also be careful not to treat queer and trans as synonyms. Rincon finds sexual identity labels "pesante" [burdensome] because of their often-divisive role among trans people, some of whom recognize themselves in the sexual fluidity and progressive politics often associated with the term "queer," and some of whom reject the common assumption that they are necessarily queer simply because they are trans.[3] Though Rincon's sexuality, in her own words, "peut apparaître un peu hétéronormée" [may appear a bit heteronormative], she resists the heterosexualization enforced by legal and medical gatekeeping practices: "A tout prix, j'essaie d'éviter de donner cette idée comme quoi je reproduis en quelque sorte en tant que femme trans une espèce d'hétéronormalisation de ma propre identité" [I try at all costs to avoid giving the impression that, as a trans woman, I reproduce a form of heteronormalization of my own identity]. Though she does not necessarily see the umbrella term queer as "dépolitisant" [depoliticizing] for trans women, she resists "la nécessité de devoir porter une étiquette pour avoir une place au niveau psychoaffectif et psychosocial" [the need to adopt a label to find belonging on a psycho-affective and psychosocial level]. For community building purposes, she is therefore careful to differentiate between her "étiquette privée" [private label] and, as she puts it, "l'étiquette qui fait objet d'éponge pour pouvoir capter et respecter les communautés que nous défendons" [the label that serves as a sponge in order to attract and show respect for the communities that we defend]. Rincon's strategic relationship to sexual identity categories resists equating transness with queerness while also centering trans women's voices and experiences that have so often been erased from French queer and feminist histories.[4]

Rincon's trajectory also stresses the importance of migration in France's queer history. Born in 1969 in Bogotá to a family of few means, Rincon became aware of her difference from other children as early as age five. As she coped with both her father's violence and, as she puts it, "le regard intrusif des autres, qui jugeaient ma famille" [the intrusive gaze of others, who judged my family], Rincon quickly developed a sense of rebelliousness that, she clarifies, "ne s'est pas concentrée uniquement

---

3 Unless otherwise noted, quotes from Giovanna Rincon are from my interview with her. It was conducted in French, and all English translations are mine. Some very minor cosmetic edits have been made when transcribing this oral interview.

4 On the silencing of transgender voices within francophone feminisms, see Baril. For one example of a queer history that excludes trans people, see Martel.

sur moi-même ni sur mon identité de genre" [was not exclusively focused on either myself or my gender identity] (Funk 187). She left middle school when teachers and students alike harassed her for her femininity, yet in her neighborhood of Barrio Santander she managed to form a circle of friends who experimented with and exchanged information about non-normative gender expression. When she reached puberty, she took the matter of her transition into her own hands by pilfering her mother's birth control pills. Shortly thereafter, domestic violence drove her from home and onto the streets of Bogotá. She found support in another trans woman, Charlie, and a local man, Arturo, who provided food and shelter to LGBT minors rejected by their families. By age 15, Rincon was running her own hair salon, one of the only professional spaces available to trans women.

Rincon also became aware of early transgender media personalities who proved that such a life was possible: Brazilian model Roberta Close and Italian actress Eva Robin's.[5] "Elles sont devenues des modèles. C'est important d'en avoir, car ce sont eux qui nous donnent le courage…" [They became role models. It is important to have them because they are the ones who give us courage…] (Funk 189). However, when asked which figures represent sites of trans memory for her, she prioritized the local and everyday over international glamor:

> Même si [Robin's et Close] sont deux icônes du personnage trans, et qu'elles ont ouvert quand même l'espace de la visibilité trans en quelque sorte, je ne me suis pas non plus reconnue en ces deux personnages totalement. Ça m'a servi comme un point de repère, mais les premières personnes qui restent pour moi importantes dans ma mémoire, ce sont les femmes trans que j'ai rencontrées à Bogotá par la suite, c'est-à-dire à peu près quand j'avais quinze ans. C'est le moment où j'ouvre mon salon de coiffure. Je pourrais citer Samantha, Claudia, Angéline – des femmes trans qui étaient travailleuses du sexe et qui vivaient dans le quartier où j'avais mon salon de coiffure. Et aussi, dans ce même quartier, il y avait d'autres femmes trans qui avaient des salons de coiffure, et qui ont été pour moi les premières sources d'inspiration et de repères sur le plan vraiment du réel.

> [Even if [Robin's and Close] are two trans icons, and even if they opened up a space for trans visibility in a certain way, I didn't totally see myself in those figures either. That was a landmark for me, but the people who remain at the forefront of my memory are the trans women I met in

---

5 Robin's spells her last name with an apostrophe.

Bogotá when I was about 15. It was around the time I opened my own hair salon. I could cite Samantha, Claudia, Angéline – trans women who were sex workers and who lived in the neighborhood where my hair salon was. And also, in the same neighborhood, there were other trans women who had hair salons, and who were for me the first sources of inspiration and points of reference in terms of real life.]

Rincon's subsequent activism would draw on those women's techniques of information sharing and mutual aid.

At the age of 20, she received the HIV diagnosis that she describes as one of the most devastating and most politicizing moments of her life: "La séropositivité a complètement changé ma vision de la vie. Je ne me donnais plus le droit de reproduire la discrimination, ni envers moi-même ni envers les autres" [Being HIV positive completely changed my vision of life. I no longer allowed myself to discriminate, neither against myself nor against others] (Funk 190). With no treatment yet available, the doctor gave her three years to live. Three years later, she was fortunately still standing but knew that she would have to leave Colombia to gain access to adequate medical care and financial resources. In 1993, she migrated to Rome, where she joined a network of trans migrants who were mostly undocumented, sex workers, and HIV positive: "C'était une époque hyper violente, extrêmement raciste, où il y avait beaucoup d'abus de pouvoir de la police italienne envers les femmes trans étrangères, des agressions à coups de pied et de matraque. Combien de fois je me suis tue? Je me regardais dans le miroir et je me disais 'un jour ça ira, tu pourras parler'" [It was an ultra-violent, extremely racist time, with the Italian police abusing their power, targeting foreign trans women and assaulting them with kicks and billy clubs. How many times did I keep quiet? I would look at myself in the mirror and say, "one day it will be okay, you'll be able to speak up"] (Bardou). State-sanctioned neglect of the HIV epidemic killed many of the women she knew by refusing them treatment when they were among those in most urgent need of care.

In this bleak environment, Rincon found inspiration in activists to organize against medical discrimination. It was after doctors denied her access to lifesaving antiretroviral therapies that she first learned about the inspiring Italian sex work advocate and activist Pia Covre:

Et je suis allée à un hôpital public. Ils m'ont interdit l'accès aux antirétroviraux. Et figure-toi qu'à la télé un jour, Pia Covre a parlé et à l'époque il n'y avait pas de téléphones portables, il n'y avait rien. En bas [de l'écran] il y avait juste un numéro de téléphone parce qu'elle disait qu'elle défendait les droits des TDS [travailleuses du sexe] et que les antirétroviraux, il fallait les mettre à disposition et lutter contre la stigmatisation des putes et de l'épidémie. Et j'ai pris ce numéro de téléphone et je l'ai appelé parce que je venais de traverser une violence vis-à-vis de l'accès aux soins. Et quand j'ai appelé, j'avais la peur de ma vie d'appeler une personne cisgenre. L'unique lien qui nous rassemblait moralement c'était qu'on était toutes les deux dans la question de travail du sexe. Et ça a été phénoménal parce que sa réponse a tout de suite aussi fait un déclic en moi et ça m'a permis d'avancer beaucoup dans la lutte contre le sida après, parce que j'ai pu aussi me faire valoir mes droits au sein du système de santé italien. Et par la suite d'accompagner aussi beaucoup d'autres personnes trans en situation d'intersectionnalité afin de pouvoir accéder aux premiers traitements du VIH.

[I went to a public hospital and they denied me access to antiretroviral drugs. And then, wouldn't you believe it, one day on television I saw Pia Covre speak, and at the time, there were no cell phones, there was nothing. At the bottom [of the screen] was just a phone number because she was saying that she defended sex workers' rights, and that antiretrovirals had to be made available and the stigmatization of whores[6] and of the epidemic had to be fought. And I took down that number because I had just faced such a violent reaction when trying to access care. And when I called her, it was one of the scariest moments of my life calling a cisgender person. The only thing that connected us morally was that we were both organizing around the issue of sex work. And it was phenomenal because her response instantly made something click for me and allowed me to rapidly advance in my fight against AIDS afterwards, because I was also able to assert my rights within the Italian healthcare system. And then accompany many other trans people in intersectional situations so they could access their first HIV treatments.]

Despite Rincon's dedication to community organizing and mutual aid, she did not initially see herself as an activist for trans issues: "J'agissais en faveur de la communauté mais sans vouloir chercher à appartenir à une association" [I was acting in favor of the community but without trying to belong to any organization]. However, she became more explicitly politicized when, in 2000, she attended EuroPride in Rome, which paid homage to Latina trans activist Sylvia Rivera:

C'est là où j'ai connu l'histoire de Sylvia Rivera et ce qu'elle avait fait. C'est

---

6   The term "pute" [whore] has been reclaimed by many sex workers aiming to politicize their struggles.

là où j'ai pris conscience de ce que c'est le mouvement LGBT à la base politiquement parlant: ses origines, ses révoltes, et les icônes qui étaient derrière tout ça. Et c'est là où j'ai compris que cette reconnaissance, c'était en quelque sorte un mea culpa vis-à-vis de la question trans à l'intérieur de ce mouvement.

[It was there that I got to know Sylvia Rivera's story and all that she had done. It was there that I became aware of what the LGBT movement really was, politically speaking: its origins, revolts, and the icons who were behind it all. And it was there that I understood that this recognition was in part a kind of mea culpa vis-à-vis trans issues within the movement.]

Having acknowledged her hesitancy to speak out as a trans woman in queer spaces, Rincon began to get more involved in trans activism.

In 2002, Rincon traveled to the Salpêtrière Hospital in Paris to accompany and advocate for a longtime friend dying of AIDS-related complications. The only other advocate present was a member of the organization that Rincon would subsequently join: *Prévention Action Santé Travail pour les Transgenres (PASTT)*. Until 2007, she traveled back and forth between Paris and Udine, Italy, seeking out safer working conditions while also volunteering for *PASTT* before being hired as an employee. By 2007, she was living full time in Paris and attended her first *Existrans* march, which inspired both admiration and skepticism:

J'ai compris qu'il y avait une forme de transnationalisme qui était peut-être naïf, qui manquait de politisation, qui avait des objectifs purement orientés vers "Nous sommes françaises, et nous avons tels besoins." Et tous ces besoins-là étaient liés à la notion d'identité française. Et donc, pour moi, quand j'arrive dans ces marches-là, déjà je ne me reconnais pas. Je perçois l'importance de ce mouvement, je suis dans l'admiration parce qu'il existe, mais en même temps je ne peux pas m'empêcher de dire qu'il y a une forme de violence parce qu'en quelque sorte il y a une indifférence [qui] se traduit par l'exclusion, par le défaut de parole, et par le manque de conscience de réalités liées à l'intersectionnalité.

[I understood that there was a form of transnationalism[7] that was a bit naïve, that lacked politicization, whose objectives were purely aligned with "We're French and we have such-and-such needs." And all those

---

7 Rincon uses the term "transnationalism" as an extension of Jasbir Puar's term "homonationalism," to suggest that white, cisnormative trans subjects are starting to be granted certain limited rights within the nation-state, whereas other more stigmatized trans and gender-variant people are excluded. "Homonationalism" refers to such dynamics in relation to queer subjects (Puar 2007).

needs were linked to the notion of French identity. So, for me, I didn't see myself in those marches from the get-go. I sensed the importance of that movement, and I was in admiration of its existence, but at the same time I couldn't stop myself from saying that there was a form of violence, because in a certain way there was an indifference [that] translated to exclusion, an absence of voices, and a lack of awareness of realities related to intersectionality.]

Rincon was determined to make France's trans movement better represent its marginalized members, even though she remained reticent to speak about her own experiences out of a sense of pride: "Je ne tomberais jamais dans la victimisation devant personne" [I would never fall back on victimization in front of anyone].

During that period, Rincon was also inspired by her meeting with Hélène Hazera, a journalist and activist who has long been open about being trans, HIV positive, and a former sex worker. Though from different backgrounds, they shared political commitments inspired Rincon:

Je me suis dit, tant que je ne m'appropriais pas cette stigmatisation-là, je serais presque coupable de l'exclusion de l'intersectionnalité dans les luttes trans et autres. Tant que je ne prenais pas la parole et que je ne vivais pas de façon factuelle et claire qu'est-ce qui m'est arrivé à moi et d'où nous revenons, qu'est-ce qui va arriver aux futures générations trans? Quels sont les processus auxquels je vais participer pour [...] que cette notion d'identité trans française puisse s'approprier [ses] responsabilités collectives? Et je pense que c'est à travers ce processus en 2010 où il y a un déclic, une cristallisation, une forme de révolte, une forme de nécessité de dire c'est le moment de parler de tout ce que j'avais vécu dès 1990 dans l'histoire de la lutte contre le sida, dans le travail du sexe, dans la notion de l'immigration, la peur de la police, les violences policières...

[I said to myself that as long as I wasn't reclaiming that stigmatization, then I would practically be guilty of excluding intersectionality from trans and other struggles. As long as I wasn't speaking out and clearly owning what happened to me and where we were coming from, then what was going to happen to future generations of trans people? Which initiatives was I going to participate in so [...] that this idea of French trans identity would also be able to take up [its] collective responsibilities? And it was through that process in 2010 that something clicked and crystallized into a form of revolt, a need to say that it was time to talk about what I had been going through since 1990 throughout my involvement in the fight against AIDS, in sex work, in the issue of immigration, the fear of police, police brutality...]

Around the same time, Rincon also distanced herself from *PASTT* because she felt that trans women were sometimes treated as if they would inevitably be limited to sex work: "Comme s'il n'y avait même pas le droit de rêver à d'autres options" [As if they didn't even have the right to dream of other options] (Hazera and Rincon).

This led Rincon to co-found what has come to be one of the most radical and well-respected transgender organizations in France today: *Acceptess-T*.[8] Staffed almost entirely by trans people, *Acceptess-T* centers the demands of those living at the intersection of multiple marginalized identities. They support a wide range of causes and initiatives such as the free and voluntary change of gender markers, the suppression of gender markers from identity documents, the training of practitioners who work with trans and intersex populations, the end of gender segregation in sports, the financing of research on trans and intersex healthcare, respect for incarcerated trans people's rights, and the regularization of trans and intersex migrants ("Nos revendications"). *Acceptess-T* provides sexual health education and STI testing, access to housing, social assistance, legal services, French language classes, accessible spaces for socialization and physical activity, and a fund to support trans youth affected by the Covid-19 pandemic.

When *Acceptess-T* began participating in the organization of the *Existrans* march in 2010, it was the first time, according to Rincon, that an organization "portait la notion de l'intersectionnalité à la première personne" [brought forward the notion of intersectionality in the first person] in a way that would elevate all trans people: "il y avait une prise de conscience collective [...] qui toucherait par exemple les trans françaises issues de l'immigration, les trans françaises peut-être blanches mais qui sont pauvres, et d'autres et d'autres" [there was a collective understanding [...] that would impact French trans people from immigrant backgrounds, French trans people who may be white but are still poor, and many others]. In the face of universalism that systematically denounces marginalized communities' autonomous organizing as a form of threatening so-called "communautarisme" [communitarianism], Rincon emphasizes the struggles trans people share with other minoritized groups: "délit de faciès" [profiling] (Rincon, "Giovanna"),

---

8   According to *Acceptess-T*'s website, the organization was initially co-founded by Rincon and Chris Valle, who were then joined by Claudia Anjos, Gaby Corrales, Jennifer Cruz, Maire Dulong, Joana Machado, and Alexia Rivillas.

police brutality, state surveillance practices, the decimation of the welfare system through neoliberal labor reforms, and the 2016 law criminalizing sex work clients. At a time when gender-based oppression is often framed as an individual psychological issue, *Acceptess-T* helps trans people politicize their experiences and transforms them into collective action. Rincon's interviews repeatedly stress structural violence: "Everyday transphobia is denounced, but what about state transphobia?" (Ballet). Nowhere has that been clearer than in her tireless fight for justice in the face of trans death.

Death often feels omnipresent for members of the trans community. Since 2020, 16 trans people are reported to have died by suicide in France, all of them aged 30 or under: Doona Jué (aged 19), Luna Avril Mabchour (17), Nicolas Abunahle Taleb Salem (26), Sté, Tristan Frémont (19), Jay Hoarau (16), Sasha Chiron (22), Samuel Boutry (20), Tal Piterbraut-Merx (29), Adrien Baptiste Luckas, Gwenn Agathe Linski (27), Mirza-Hélène Deneuve (alias Julles, 26), Bobby Melon (24), Maël Eden Paufert (30), Roz (24), and one individual whose name was not reported (aged 15) ("Remembering Our Dead").[9] According to the Trans Murder Monitoring project, at least 13 trans women have been murdered in France since 2011: Cassandra Flores Zapata (aged 39), Mylène (42), Lucha Zarate Vilcas (53), Niurkeli Carguaitongo (33), Vanesa Campos (36), Jessyca Sarmiento (38), Paula Migeon (50), Ambre Audrey Istier (49), Ivanna Macedo Silva (31), Beatriz Souza/Bastos (38), and three other individuals whose names were not reported. The fact that most of these trans women were sex workers and/or migrants reflects international statistics: for trans people murdered in Europe in 2023, 94 percent were women, 78 percent were sex workers (compared with 48 percent worldwide), and 45 percent were migrants ("Trans Murder Monitoring Resources").[10] Indeed, it is crucial for memorial practices to lend visibility to those interlocking aspects of identity, lest accounts of anti-trans violence be "deracialized" such that "the narrative allows Whites to deny the ways in which we/they enable and benefit from the ongoing legacy of colonial and racialized violence" (Lamble 35). Rincon and organizations such as *Acceptess-T* fight to ensure that race, class, and immigration status remain central when remembering lives lost.

9 Ages included when available. Name list last consulted November 17, 2023.
10 Statistics on sex workers and migrants are based on victims whose occupations and migration status were reported at the time of their death.

Considering the persistent cultural association between transness and death (especially for trans women of color), I asked Rincon how she balances the commemoration of death with the need for trans joy. Indeed, one sociological study has used the term "joy deficit" to name the absence of happiness and positive affect in scholarship on the lives of trans people and other minoritized groups: "This deficit is particularly troubling as joy is vital to human well-being, can sustain people experiencing and mobilizing against oppression, and helps make life worth living" (Shuster and Westbrook 2). How do we honor the memories of so many lives lost without sending the message that to be trans is to be, as Rincon has put it, reduced to a "bombe à retardement" [ticking time-bomb] (Rincon, cited in Enda 44)? For Rincon, the answer lies in using mourning as inspiration for meaningful collective action: "politiser davantage la transphobie, politiser nos mort·e·s, c'est l'unique stratégie pour mettre la société face à la responsabilité de cette transphobie à laquelle tout le monde participe" [further politicizing transphobia, politicizing our dead, is the only strategy that makes society confront its own responsibility for this transphobia in which everyone is implicated] (Rincon, cited in Enda 44). This is evident in the ways that she and other trans activists have fought to ensure that those who murdered Vanesa Campos in the Bois de Boulogne in 2018 be brought to justice.

When I concluded our interview by asking if she would like to share any memories of trans joy, she offered up two moments encapsulating Michael Rothberg's insistence that "Solidarity [...] is a frequent – if not guaranteed – outcome of the remembrance of suffering" (Rothberg 11). Her first memory was one of hope arising in the wake of the staggering number of suicides among trans youth in 2021. When people came together to commemorate their lives, she realized that parents and other family members of the deceased were increasingly showing up to demonstrate their support for the trans community and ensure the respect of their loved ones' memories so that they would not be, to borrow Rincon's formulation, "deux fois assassinées" [murdered twice] (Rincon and Jutant 170). This marks a notable shift, since trans suicides have so often stemmed from family abuse or neglect:

> On se rend compte que ces jeunes personnes trans étaient soutenues par leurs familles, et que leurs familles pleurent leur départ. Et que leurs familles à leur tour continuent à se battre contre la transphobie institutionnelle qui ne souhaite pas respecter ni le genre ni le prénom choisi de [la personne décédée]. Et pour moi, c'est là où il y a vraiment un changement. Ça me rend très rassurée et ça me donne beaucoup de joie.

[We're realizing that these young trans people were supported by their families, and that their families are mourning their passing. And that their families are in turn continuing to fight institutional transphobia that respects neither the gender nor the chosen name [of the deceased]. And for me, that is where there is real change. It reassures me and brings me great joy.]

Unlike the socially enforced promises of happiness that, as Sara Ahmed has argued, perpetuate the violence of the status quo, this joy stems from an adamant refusal to fall in line and accept the unacceptable (Ahmed 2010).

Rincon's second memory was from the trial of Vanesa Campos's murderers in January 2022, where she was called in as an expert witness. The two primary accused were sentenced to 22 years in prison for "meurtre en bande organisée" [pre-meditated gang murder] ("Meurtre de Vanesa Campos"). For Rincon, however, the sentence itself was not what constituted true progress:

> Pour la première fois, ça arrive dans le système de justice en France où un membre d'une communauté parmi les plus stigmatisées a le droit de dire quels sont les déterminants qui préconstruisent tout ça au-delà du fait qu'il y a des coupables qui ont assassiné Vanesa Campos. Et que tous ces déterminants sont préconstruits par l'indifférence institutionnelle, par les lois répressives, par la pénalisation et la criminalisation du travail du sexe [...]. Pour moi, dans ce procès, il y a un évènement historique, mais pas parce que nous avons réussi à faire condamner ceux qui ont assassiné Vanesa Campos. Ma satisfaction la plus grande, c'est que non seulement nous avons réussi à faire valoir ses droits et les droits de ses collègues qui étaient victimes, mais aussi les droits de leurs familles [...]. Et le fait que ma parole – qui est une parole collective – soit considérée, c'est pour moi aussi un élément qui rentre dans l'histoire du mouvement LGBT, du mouvement trans, [et des mouvements pour les droits des travailleuses du sexe] [...]. Avec le nombre de médias qui se sont occupés de l'affaire, il y a eu une forme de compréhension, une forme de sensibilisation, un moment de cristallisation autour des droits des personnes trans, ce qui renvoie un message humanisant vis-à-vis de la communauté trans. Et donc historiquement, pour la première fois dans notre mémoire, nous installons notre place et une parole sérieusement argumentée et incontournable, une parole – la mienne et celle d'*Acceptess-T* – qui aujourd'hui est devenue nécessaire.

[It was the first time in the French justice system that a member of one of the most stigmatized communities had the right to say that there are determining factors that constructed all of this in advance, beyond the fact that there were people guilty of murdering Vanesa Campos. And that all of these factors are constructed by institutional indifference, repressive laws, and the penalization and criminalization of sex work [...]. For me, this trial was a historical event, but not because we succeeded in getting Vanesa Campos's murderers sentenced. My greatest satisfaction is that we not only managed to assert her rights and the rights of her colleagues who were victims, but also the rights of their families [...]. And the fact that my word – which is collective – was taken into consideration, that for me also becomes part of the history of the LGBT movement, the trans movement, [and sex workers' rights movements] [...]. In the numerous media outlets that covered the story, there was a form of understanding, a form of sensitization, a moment of crystallization around trans issues, which sends out a humanizing message vis-à-vis the trans community. And so, historically, for the first time in our memory, we have laid claim to a space and to a thoughtful and vital voice – my own as well as that of *Acceptess-T* – whose necessity has finally been recognized.]

Documenting the ongoing fight to create a future free from trans murder and suicide is also a way of honoring those who have left us prematurely. This piece is dedicated above all to their memories, which are kept alive through the many annual vigils held worldwide for Transgender Day of Remembrance as well as through countless other individual and collective memorial practices.[11] At the same time, my decision to focus on a living trans person in this contribution questions the temporal distance built into Nora's *lieux de mémoire*. Queer and trans people should know that we need not be victims of tragedy to be valued and remembered, and we should consider those still among us to be living sites of memory from whom we can learn and draw inspiration. I also hope that this contribution will push researchers and archivists to center not just trans voices, but especially those who are sex workers, migrants, and/or HIV positive. By refusing to reproduce the exclusions inherent in Nora's project, this chapter, like the work of Rincon and

---

11 Transgender Day of Remembrance (TDOR) is an annual international event that takes place on November 20 to memorialize transgender people who have been murdered. It first began in 1999 in the United States in response to the murder of Black transgender woman Rita Hester in Boston the previous year. Though local events honoring TDOR typically include candlelit vigils and reading the names of the deceased aloud, they also often include other political and cultural practices such as marches, poetry readings, movie screenings, art exhibits or installations, and panel discussions. For further historical background and an analysis of TDOR as a form of necropolitical community building, see Steinbock 2019.

Acceptess-T, draws attention to the absences through which officially recognized identities in France – be they national or sexual – continue to be constituted.

Works cited

Ahmed, Sara. *The Promise of Happiness*. Duke UP, 2010.
Ballet, Virginie. "Une violence au quotidien et à tous les niveaux." *Libération*. April 3, 2019. Web.
Bardou, Florian. "En France, Giovanna Rincon en résistrans." *Libération*. June 28, 2019. Web.
Baril, Alexandre. "Francophone trans/feminisms: Absence, silence, emergence." *TSQ: Transgender Studies Quarterly*, vol. 3, no. 1–2, 2016, pp. 40–47.
Baudoin, Karine. "Prix Le Refuge Institut Randstad 2015: ACCEPTESS-T lutte contre l'exclusion sociale des citoyen(ne)s trans." May 15, 2015. www.karinebaudoin.com/ftp/communique_lerefuge_150515.pdf.
Enda, Sil. "Politiser nos mort·e·s pour mettre la société devant ses responsabilités. Rencontre avec Giovanna Rincon de *Acceptess-T*." *Les AssiégéEs*, vol. 3, March 2019, pp. 42–44.
Freeman, Elizabeth. *Time Binds: Queer Temporalities, Queer Histories*. Duke UP, 2010.
Funk, Mason. "Giovanna Rincon: Militante transgenre." *C'est ça, notre liberté: 50 ans de lutte LGBTQ+ de Paris à New York*. Translated by Nino S. Dufour. HarperCollins, 2021, pp. 187–92.
Halberstam, Jack. *In a Queer Time and Place: Transgender Bodies, Subcultural Lives*. New York UP, 2005.
Hazera, Hélène, and Giovanna Rincon. "Bogota-Paris, portrait d'une présidente Trans." *Minorités*, no. 104, October 22, 2011. www.web.archive.org/web/20140118210822/www.minorites.org/index.php/2-la-revue/1198-bogota-paris-portrait-d-une-presidente-trans.html.
Lamble, Sarah. "Retelling racialized violence, remaking white innocence: The politics of interlocking oppressions in Transgender Day of Remembrance." *Sexuality Research & Social Policy*, vol. 5, no. 1, March 2008, pp. 24–42.
Le Breton, Marine. "Giovanna Rincon remporte l'Out d'or du coup de gueule pour nous avoir parlé de l'insécurité des femmes transgenres." *Huffington Post*. June 20, 2018. Web.
Manelli, Florent. "Giovanna Rincon." *40 LGBT+ qui ont changé le monde*. Éditions lapin, 2019, pp. 188–91.
"Marche contre la transphobie, 10 octobre 2021, Paris." *Sous les pavés l'archive* from Collectif archives LGBTQI. April 10, 2022. www.archiveslgbtqi.fr/archives-orales/.

Martel, Frédéric. *Le rose et le noir: les homosexuels en France depuis 1968.* 3rd Edition. Éditions du Seuil, 2008.

"Meurtre de Vanesa Campos: les deux principaux accusés condamnés à vingt-deux ans de réclusion criminelle." *Le Monde.* January 29, 2022. Web.

Muñoz, José Esteban. *Cruising Utopia: The Then and There of Queer Futurity.* 10th Anniversary Edition. New York UP, 2019.

Nora, Pierre. "Preface to English Language Edition: From *Lieux de mémoire* to *Realms of Memory*." *Realms of Memory: Rethinking the French Past*, vol. 1, *Conflicts and Divisions*, edited by Pierre Nora and Lawrence D. Kritzman. Translated by Arthur Goldhammer. Columbia UP, 1996, pp. xv–xxiv.

"Nos revendications." *Acceptess-T.* www.acceptess-t.com/nos-revendications.

Puar, Jasbir K. *Terrorist Assemblages: Homonationalism in Queer Times.* Duke UP, 2007.

"Remembering our dead – Reports." *Remembering Our Dead.* www.tdor.translivesmatter.info/reports.

Rincon, Giovanna. "Giovanna, femme transgenre, humiliée par la police en plein milieu de l'aéroport." *StreetPress.* March 7, 2017. Web.

———. Personal interview. March 13, 2022.

Rincon, Giovanna, and Simon Jutant. "Transféminicides: des violences de genre spécifiques?" *Cahiers du Genre*, vol. 73, no. 2, 2022, pp. 161–75.

Rothberg, Michael. "Introduction: Between memory and memory. From *Lieux de mémoire* to *Nœuds de mémoire*." *Yale French Studies*, vol. 118/19, 2010, pp. 3–12.

Shuster, Stef M., and Laurel Westbrook. "Reducing the joy deficit in sociology: A study of transgender joy." *Social Problems*, 2022, pp. 1–19.

Steinbock, Eliza. "The early 1990s and its afterlives: Transgender nation sociality in digital activism." *Social Media + Society*, vol. 5, no. 4, 2019. Web.

"Trans murder monitoring resources." *Transrespect versus Transphobia Worldwide.* www.transrespect.org/en/trans-murder-monitoring/tmm-resources/.

IV

Alternative Archives: Literature and Cinema

IV

Alternative Archives, Literature, and Cinema

CHAPTER FIFTEEN

Archives of desire

Viewing *cinéma colonial* as a queer *lieu de mémoire*

Barry Nevin

Introduction: Memory, queer spectatorship, and French cinema

This chapter examines how *lieux de mémoire* can persist not just as a physical form or source but also as an immaterial, digital platform, and how *cinéma colonial* may be considered a queer realm of memory. *Cinéma colonial* was one of the most popular genres of the *entre-deux-guerres*, during which numerous films took French North Africa as their setting, often focusing on French-born individuals who either imparted their putatively superior spiritual values to indigenous communities or yielded to desires forbidden in the metropole (Crisp 31–71). This genre was especially important to the empire's consolidation of the colonies as a *lieu de mémoire* in the popular imaginary since "[t]hose in France who saw North Africa in the 1920s and 1930s almost always saw it on film" (Ungar 35).

Cinematic genres may initially appear to sit uncomfortably within Pierre Nora's concept of *lieux de mémoire* since he emphasizes the tangibility and physical durability of his chosen *lieux*, essentially arguing that their "most fundamental purpose is […] to materialize the immaterial" ("Between" 19). In contrast, although not all films remain equally accessible (some remain confined to archives or are considered lost), the "fluidity of consumption" in the present era of digital media convergence has decreased the importance of cinemas and physical media to film spectatorship (Hayward 129). However, the third volume of Nora's project includes proverbs, tales, songs, and conversation, and in the same volume, he defines the *lieu de mémoire* as "toute unité significative, *d'ordre matériel ou idéel*, dont la volonté des hommes ou le travail du temps a fait *un élément symbolique du patrimoine mémoriel* d'une quelconque communauté" [any significant entity, whether material or conceptual in nature, which human will or the work of time has rendered a symbolic element of the memorial heritage of any community] ("Comment écrire" 20; my italics). *Cinéma colonial* can therefore be considered a *lieu de mémoire*. More specifically, it belongs to what Étienne Achille, Charles Forsdick, and Lydie Moudileno call "immaterial sites" (9, 13) while also functioning as one of the "transmissible" sites that Robert Guégan (22) distinguishes from the "fixed sites" of memory constituted by physical monuments.

The modes of memory afforded by this transmissibility and immateriality are key to how *cinéma colonial* engenders what Alison Landsberg terms "prosthetic memory." Through such memories, which Landsberg links chiefly with technologies of mass culture, the spectator "does not simply apprehend a historical narrative but takes on a more personal, deeply felt memory of a past event through which he or she did not live" (2) and which informs the spectator's experience of the present. The resulting memories, Landsberg adds, not only "become part of one's personal archive of experience" (26), but also potentially "create shared social frameworks for people who inhabit, literally and figuratively, different social spaces, practices, and beliefs" (8). As a facilitator of prosthetic memory, *cinéma colonial* functioned (and continues to function) as a privileged conduit to French colonial history's iconic figures (Maréchal Lyautey in *Les Hommes nouveaux* [L'Herbier, 1936] and Catholic missionary Charles de Foucauld in *L'Appel du silence* [Poirier, 1936]), major sites (Sidi-Bel-Abbès in *Le Grand Jeu* [Feyder, 1934] and the Casbah in *Pépé le Moko* [Duvivier, 1937]), territories (particularly Morocco, Algeria, and the Sahara), and various institutions (political, religious, commercial, and otherwise). Cinematic renderings of the colonies' peoples, places, and practices crystallized an imperialist consciousness that connected the metropolitan imaginary to the past and present of *la plus grande France*, and the films in question have ultimately outlasted the colonized settings they originally purported to represent.

The extent to which this genre offered sexual minorities opportunities to identify with queer fictional characters is an important matter due to

France's highly conditional tolerance of queer communities between the world wars. On the one hand, "sodomy" was officially decriminalized by the Napoleonic Penal Code of 1810, and the interwar period gave homosexuality a stronger public voice than ever in literature, notably in the pages of Marcel Proust's *Sodome et Gomorrah* (1921) and André Gide's *Corydon* (1923). Meanwhile, famous drag balls held during Lent in the Magic City dance-hall and the Salle Wagram reified Paris's interwar image as Europe's nerve-center for homosexual life, especially after Nazism restricted Berlin's hitherto-vibrant homosexual scene (Tamagne 50–52). It is nonetheless true that, "[q]uite apart from those who did not feel that this glamorously transgressive world represented their own homosexuality, there were many who barely knew of its existence" (Jackson 32). Furthermore, for much of the French public, male homosexuality reenacted France's traumatizing loss of manpower during World War I (Dean 144), and up until directly anti-gay legislation was ratified in 1942 (under the Vichy regime) it remained widely accepted that the principle means of becoming homosexual was "through contamination during the vulnerable years of adolescence" (Gunther 32).

At first sight, French interwar cinema appears to have failed spectators seeking to identify with queer characters or to escape prejudice, if only provisionally. Film scholar James S. Williams observes that, even prior to the 1942 law, "[a]ny whiff of same-sex sexuality had to be nipped in the bud immediately to pass the censor" (246) and that queer characters tended to be "predominantly negative and often highly crude, fetishizing stereotypes and archetypes" (253), such as the *folle* (or "effeminate") played by Géo Forster in Jean Renoir's *La Règle du jeu* (1939) and the *poupée* (or "doll") played by the young and flashily dressed François Simon in *Circonstances atténuantes* (Jean Boyer, 1939). Yet Williams also observes a considerably more nuanced queer aesthetic in the work of acclaimed queer auteurs such as Marcel Carné (*Les Enfants du paradis*, 1945), Jean Cocteau (*Orphée*, 1950), and Marcel L'Herbier (*Le Bonheur*, 1934), and advocates further research on "fresh, proliferating lines of queer lineage and allegiance" (271). Bringing the queerness of *cinéma colonial* into sharper focus through Nora's and Landsberg's respective frameworks allows us to deepen our awareness of the "queer mainstream" discussed by Williams (263), to recognize the historicity of our own queer desires, and to go part of the way in completing what the editors of this volume describe as "the 'jigsaw puzzle' of an otherwise invisible or undocumented set of queer lives, feelings, and memories" (Bouamer, Provencher, and Schroth 19).

Both *cinéma colonial* and the *outre-mer* were major sites of queer embodiment during the interwar period. In an invaluable overview of generic conventions in *cinéma colonial*, Colin Crisp observes that relationships among characters – whether between "inter-racial" couples, or white, metropolitan-born individuals – could sometimes "promote the French nation as the highest embodiment of civilization" (40) but that romantic pairings could also "seek to speak, under cover of 'foreignness,' of erotic excesses which cannot be figured as a legitimate part of any society, even French society" (39). Queer sexualities were considered one such excess, and they could be implied in a French colonial context precisely because they were constitutive of the exotic otherness with which colonial culture was associated between the world wars. France's colonial troops were frequently associated with situational homosexuality, partly because hot climates were believed to spark sexual excesses (a claim dating back to Antiquity) and partly because of the extensive periods endured by all-male troops in barracks and on campaigns, where military comradeship among soldiers "could and did veer off into sexual intimacy" (Aldrich, *Colonialism* 3). Although many of the most retrograde and pernicious aspects of *cinéma colonial*, especially its essentialist understanding of sexuality, corresponded with the officially imposed histories that Nora ("Between memory and history" 23) associates unfavorably with *lieux de mémoire*, prosthetic memory's "unique ability to generate empathy" (Landsberg 24) transforms these films into occasionally valuable facilitators of queer spectator identification.

The two films analyzed in the remainder of this chapter have been selected because both were produced during the apotheosis of popular enthusiasm for the empire but differ markedly in terms of style and production context. Jacques Feyder's foundational colonial epic, *L'Atlantide* (1921), is an independent silent film that he directed largely in North Africa, whereas *Gueule d'amour* (1937) is a star vehicle that was produced in Germany for French audiences a number of years after the transition to sound, and whereas Feyder was a heterosexual *père de famille*, Grémillon was bisexual (Burch and Sellier, *The Battle* 173). Before proceeding, it is important to note that, much as "*lieux de mémoire* only exist because of their capacity for metamorphosis" (Nora, "Between memory and history" 19), any understanding of queer realms of memory demands a revised understanding of what the queer encompasses. Some scholars – notably Leo Bersani, Judith Butler, and Eve Sedgwick – seek to undermine norms and challenge normativity, including those produced by queer inquiry (Wiegman and

Wilson 3–4). However, without entirely disregarding the importance of anti-normative methodologies to constructions of the queer, other scholars have highlighted the radically transformative potential of purportedly "straight" sites through a productive focus on the non-normative (McCann and Monaghan 13–14). Although this chapter discusses the subject position that *cinéma colonial* created for queer and non-normative spectators, it does not claim that this is the only position (or memory) these films have historically offered viewers.

Masculinity and metacinema in *L'Atlantide* (1921)

Feyder's narrative centers on the fatal triangular relationship between two legionnaires and the queen of the fabled Atlantis. The film opens with a caravan locating Lieutenant Saint-Avit (Georges Melchior) barely alive in the Sahara. Following a period of convalescence in Timbuktu, during which he experiences a series of hallucinations, he returns to Paris. He is subsequently stationed in Hassi-Inifel, Algeria, where he recounts the events that led to his near-fatal trek through the desert. An extended flashback reveals his experience of becoming acquainted with his superior, Captain Morhange (Jean Angelo), happening upon Atlantis, and falling prey to its queen, Antinéa (Stacia Napierkowska), who compels him psychedelically to kill Morhange prior to his own escape.

Noël Burch and Geneviève Sellier briefly but perceptively identify a homosexual subtext in Feyder's film ("Representations" 122). Indeed, rather than falling unambiguously in love with Antinéa, Morhange calmly resists her advances, and Saint-Avit appears more romantically interested in his superior than in the Atlantean queen. The two men therefore reproduce the dynamics of the romantic triangle theorized by Sedgwick in *Between Men: English Literature and Male Homosocial Desire*, wherein two men's relationship with one woman tends to amplify the two men's homoerotic (and potentially homosexual) bond. Key to understanding Saint-Avit's sexual interest in Morhange is a process of identification and desire theorized by Leo Bersani, who writes that one's selection of a sexual partner "is an imitation – or rather, an identification with other desiring subjects" (*Homos* 60), and that while all love is homoerotic to the extent that partners desire to find themselves in the other, homosexual love involves a heightened "desire for sameness" (Bersani, "Aggression" 69).

242 Queer Realms of Memory

Both Saint-Avit and Morhange are in the French military and are characterized by a thirst for adventure, but Morhange is clearly established as the more experienced and more knowledgeable soldier. For example, while traveling through the desert, he recognizes etchings in a cavern as the Greek equivalent of "Antinéa" inscribed in Tifinagh (an Imazighen script) and indicates that Greek inscriptions have never been found at such a low latitude. Morhange is also portrayed as a more emotionally stable character: unlike Saint-Avit, his sexual desires do not frustrate him, and although he appears to effortlessly ignore Antinéa's allegedly irresistible sexual appeal, he does not clearly demonstrate feelings for Saint-Avit either. Furthermore, he is characterized as a more spiritually enlightened figure: we learn early in the film that, following an unspecified personal loss, Morhange spent a three-year leave of absence at a monastery, and even though Antinéa spitefully informs the mortally wounded Morhange that Saint-Avit struck him, Morhange prays for him to be forgiven.

Saint-Avit clearly respects and admires Morhange and insists on accompanying his superior to other Tuareg etchings, but his queer desire becomes evident when Antinéa, seeking to win Morhange's affection, confines him to her quarters while isolating Saint-Avit in his. The latter's imagined vision of Morhange embracing Antinéa (Figure 15.1) indicates not only that Saint-Avit desires Morhange (Nevin 355), but also

Figure 15.1 Saint-Avit imagines Morhange and Antinéa together

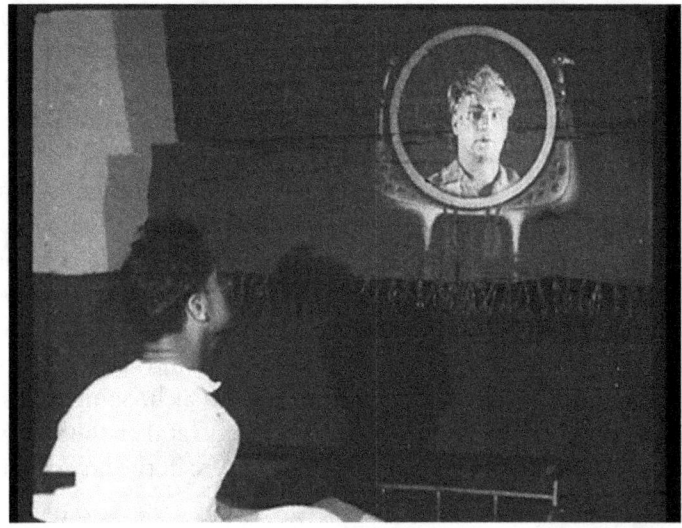

Figure 15.2 A delirious Saint-Avit "sees" Morhange

that he envies both Morhange's ability to attract Antinéa and what he mistakenly perceives as Antinéa's ability to satisfy Morhange's heterosexual desires. Morhange essentially functions as a Lacanian ego ideal for Saint-Avit, and although Saint-Avit's attack on his object of queer affection is committed under the influence of Antinea's drug, this attack is simultaneously an assault on what Saint-Avit perceives as his own queer otherness and, ironically, on how this prevents him from fully emulating the captain.

Viewing the two men's queer rapport through Laura Mulvey's theory of visual pleasure uncovers a revealing metafilmic perspective on Saint-Avit's hallucinations in Timbuktu. While recovering in a ward, he imagines a gong that increases in size. On this gong, a series of images appears: Antinéa, the injured Morhange (Figure 15.2), her cat, Morhange once again, and a skull. The widening circle of the gong that contains the images envisioned by Saint-Avit evokes how an iris imitates the opening of a camera's lens in silent cinema (such as this film's opening shot of Antinéa). Feyder's composition indicates that, even after Saint-Avit has killed his double, Morhange continues to function as a Mulveyan "screen surrogate" (12). In this respect, Saint-Avit's vision of Morhange is a projection of his own queer desire and also of his threefold lack: Saint-Avit has passively served as Antinéa's instrument of revenge, has killed an object of desire in whom he has perceived a superior version of himself, and has proven himself manifestly incapable of suppressing his traumatic memories. Saint-Avit's claim at the end of the film that he is returning to Atlantis because he is obsessing over Antinéa ("Depuis trois ans, je ne sais plus rien d'ELLE," he declares, "Mais je la vois, je lui parle!" [I have learned nothing of HER in three years; but I see her, I speak to her!]) is unconvincing. In his series of visions, she appears only once. Even then, she wears an intimidating mask which contrasts markedly with other scenes where her face is fully visible or is partially hidden behind the colonialist trope of a sexually suggestive veil (see Shohat 32–33). Her costume in this hallucination suggests that, first and foremost, she reminds Saint-Avit of his lack. Atlantis now constitutes a queer realm of his memory in his own mind. As such, Saint-Avit's sexual frustration compels him to revisit the site of his fatal encounter with his own queerness and to permanently relinquish life in the heteronormative metropole.

Queering the gaze in *Gueule d'amour* (1937)

Like *L'Atlantide*, *Gueule d'amour* centers on an erotic triangle involving two men and one woman. Lucien (played by Gabin), a non-commissioned officer of the spahis who is idolized by women, meets Madeleine (Mireille Balin), an attractive, upper-class woman who spends one night with him but refuses to leave her aging protector. Once demobilized, Lucien becomes a typesetter and locates her in Paris. However, she rejects him, and he realizes that he is no longer a figure of adulation without his uniform. After she becomes engaged to Lucien's military comrade, René (René Lefèvre), he demands that she break off her engagement, but when she threatens to tell René that Lucien forced her to do so, a despondent Lucien strangles her. At the end of the film, Lucien admits to René that he killed Madeleine, and René escorts him to the train station, where Lucien begins his journey to Africa.

Despite the film's seemingly heterosexual thrust, there is a moment during Madeleine and Lucien's first evening together when the narrative subtly confirms its investment in a queer gaze. The camera elegantly tracks them as they leave their table in a casino until they exit the frame. It then recedes and pans left as they re-enter the frame on the left. Afterwards, the camera pans right, following them as they walk towards the exit. The camera subsequently pans left again and pauses on two men who stand looking towards people dancing in the casino

Figure 15.3 Two anonymous male characters look ahead in the casino

as music played by a band reaches a climax (Figure 15.3). Although the two men's backs face the camera, the foregrounding of this stationery homosocial pairing is striking in a room dominated by animated male–female couples dancing and by the conspicuous absence of the film's two stars. Through the gradual and unexpected emphasis placed on these two men, this moment sensitizes the spectator not only to the generation of a space of gay male spectatorship, but also to the idea that queer vantage points may exist on the periphery of a film, even if these are not explicitly acknowledged within the narrative from the outset.

The sexual implications of this sequence are telling from an Orientalist perspective because even though Grémillon's film (unlike *L'Atlantide*) is set only in French locations – Orange, Cannes, Châteauneuf-du-Pape, and Paris – the relationship between queer identity and colonial life remains key to how the film encourages the spectator to empathize with Lucien. Two elements of Gabin's star persona are key to this positioning. First, for film scholar Ginette Vincendeau, his narratives produce "une surdétermination de son statut d'objet du regard" [an overdetermination of his status as object of the gaze] (227), and this objectification incorporates an erotic element for characters and spectators alike, whether male or female. Second, Gabin embodies what Vincendeau influentially describes as "le degré zéro du masculin" [the zero degree of masculinity], and he therefore derives his virility from how he contrasts with characters around him, such as Madeleine's implicitly gay butler, rather than through a consistent deployment of innately "masculine" characteristics (271). Hence, although Madeleine "incarne pour Lucien (et pour le spectateur) la beauté et la richesse dans leurs aspects les plus séduisants" [embodies the most seductive aspects of beauty and riches for Lucien (and for the spectator)] (Sellier 26), Lucien competes with her as an erotic and feminized object, notably through his grammatically feminine nickname – "Gueule" (a colloquial term for "face") – and the decorative role played by the spahis, whose uniforms and weapons were obsolete within their "régiment à fonction surtout ornementale" [regiment with a primarily ornamental role] (Vincendeau 194).

Lucien's awareness of (and satisfaction with) his own objectification is especially evident in two early scenes. The first is the film's opening scene, as the eagerly anticipated spahis arrive to the adulation of predominantly female crowds and a medium shot frames him smiling smugly on horseback. The second is when he pauses with René to observe a photo of himself behind a shop window (Figure 15.4). In the photograph, Lucien stands unassumingly, his gaze turned upward and his hands in his pocket. Both of these examples connote Lucien's passivity and, in doing so, evoke Richard Dyer's observation that the physically inactive male body's visual appeal is a potentially feminizing force that can only be counterbalanced by the suggestion of action (128). Lucien's failure to embody an active vision of masculinity also manifests itself through his helplessness in his scenes with both Madeleine and René. During one of his most romantic moments with Madeleine, she places her hand on Lucien's cheek and kisses him, prompting him to declare, "Je ne prévois jamais le mot que vous allez dire ni le geste que vous allez faire" [I can never predict what you're going to say or the move you're going to make], emphasizing his lack of agency. Later, shortly after admitting to René that he has killed Madeleine, Lucien remains incapacitated and frustratedly beseeches his comrade, "Je sais plus où j'en suis! Je comprends plus rien! [...] Dis-moi ce qu'il faut faire! Mais aide-moi! Dis-moi ce qu'il faut faire! Dis-moi! Dis-moi ce qu'il faut faire" [I don't know where I am anymore! I don't understand anything at all! [...] Tell me what to do! Just help me! Tell me what to do! Tell me! Tell me what to do]. Paralyzed by indecision, Lucien can only seek a solution from someone whose emotional restraint and loyalty offer him the reassurance and practical guidance he needs to escape after murdering Madeleine.

Male homosocial bonding and the concomitant extrusion of disruptive

Figure 15.4 René and Lucien view Lucien's photograph

women were already established tropes in French cinema by this point in the decade (Burch and Sellier, *The Battle* 75), especially in Gabin's films (Vincendeau 236). While Lucien is not coded as an unambiguously homosexual character, Grémillon directs this homosocial tendency towards pointedly queer territory by progressively relegating Lucien's female admirers and Madeleine to the margins of both his and René's lives. Two successive scenes disrupt the heterosexual thrust of Lucien's relationship with these women early in the film. Shortly after arriving in Orange, Lucien rejects an invitation from a besotted young woman, then the narrative cuts to a shot of René entering Lucien's bedroom while the latter is calmly outstretched on his bed and smoking a phallic cigar. Although a subsequent shot of Lucien's bed reveals pictures of women affixed to his wall, the delayed revelation of this décor only partially mitigates the destabilizing effect of framing and editing across these two scenes. Grémillon reiterates both Lucien's passivity and this incomplete neutralization of queer desire shortly after Lucien strangles Madeleine and arrives at René's home. The distraught Lucien clings to René's hand, establishing a degree of queer physical and emotional intimacy only partially undercut by his hysterical declaration that "Je l'aimais, René. Je l'aimais plus que toi! Je l'aimais autant que toi! T'entends!" [I loved her, René. I loved her more than you! I loved her as much as you! Do you hear?] Therefore, much like Saint-Avit's claim that he is motivated by a heterosexual romantic attachment at the end of *L'Atlantide*, Lucien's statement cannot entirely sublimate the queer underpinnings of his relationship with René, which ultimately constitutes Lucien's pretext for murdering Madeleine.

Grémillon accentuates the queerness of the two men's relationship in the film's final scene when René accompanies Lucien to the train station in Orange. The window frame, through a vertical line in its center, confines René and Lucien within separate visual sections, but René disrupts this rigid demarcation when he embraces Lucien (Figure 15.5). Grémillon stresses the homoerotic intimations of this moment by cutting to a shot of René's hand affectionately placed on Lucien's wrist as the latter leans out through his carriage window and panning the camera as the train begins to depart. This understated *mise en scène* eloquently retains our view of the two men within the frame until Lucien descends from the carriage's footboard. Whereas this scene in the station, like the aforementioned moment in René's home, emphasizes the tactile and sexually ambiguous bond they share, the film's final shot frames Lucien's outstretched hand bidding farewell aboard the train as his (and our) view of René recedes ineluctably into the distance.

For Williams, "[i]t is a quietly shattering scene alive with queer possibilities but cannot go anywhere – it is already over before it has manifested itself into being" (258). Indeed, there is a sense that their

Figure 15.5 René embraces Lucien

relationship beyond the closing shot will be defined exclusively by nostalgia and exile. However, corresponding with the textual operations of prosthetic memory, this scene generates vital possibilities for spectator identification, chiefly through the trope of doubling already seen in *L'Atlantide*. Vincendeau observes that male doppelgängers frequently serve as Gabin's contrasting foil or antagonist (222–24). The physical differences between the imposing Lucien and the slight René are transcended by their common emotional sensitivity, their debatable love for Madeleine, and their commitment to one another before the train leaves, all of which render both men "degré zéro" embodiments of masculinity who are drawn to one another in a Bersanian process of self-identification and desire. As a result, the space for queer spectatorship evoked in the casino now includes the narrative's two central male characters. Ultimately, although each man's relationship with Madeleine is crucial to *Gueule d'amour*'s fatalistic thrust and to Lucien's progressive psychological degeneration, the bond between these two men is nonetheless co-extensive with the film's internal challenges to heterosexual romantic conventions.

Conclusion

Viewing *cinéma colonial* as a queer *lieu de mémoire* allows us to advance Williams's goal of "cultivat[ing] forms of embodied queer spectatorship and intensity" (273). Both *L'Atlantide* and *Gueule d'amour* explore the queer gaze by deploying framing and metafilmic motifs as key structuring principles of *mise en scène* and integrating the Sedgwickian triangulation of desire into a motif of doubling. On the one hand, one must concede that these films shy away from clearly designating homosexuality and even constitute cautionary tales regarding queer relationships, the castrating force of vindictive women, and the colony's reputed pathological disruption of heterosexuality. Furthermore, both films feature a queer male character driven to commit a sexually motivated (and arguably anti-heterosexual) murder. Yet, by resisting the reductive, readily recognizable types identified by Williams and situating queer identities on the threshold between homosexuality and non-normative heterosexuality, these films portray queerness as an inclusive and ambiguously embodied aspect of human identity. In other words, these films are both complicit in and resistant to the homosexual discourses produced by a French cinematic culture that was patriarchal, heterosexist, imperialist, and Orientalist.

Because these films persist as an increasingly accessible queer realm of memory, they continue to provide sexual minorities with a vantage point on the past, all the better to determine our progress as individuals and communities in search of progressive representation. Nora's framework encourages us not only to reconsider film's role as an archive of prosthetic memory, but also to identify coherence, correspondences, and contradictions across the queer identities produced by *cinéma colonial* and French cinema in general as we probe the question of what queer film spectatorship potentially involves.

Works cited

Achille, Étienne, Charles Forsdick, and Lydie Moudileno. "Introduction." *Postcolonial Realms of Memory: Sites and Symbols in Modern France*, edited by Étienne Achille, Charles Forsdick, and Lydie Moudileno. Liverpool UP, 2020, pp. 1–19.

Aldrich, Robert. *Colonialism and Homosexuality*. Routledge, 2002.

———. "Colonial man." *French Masculinities: History, Culture and Politics*, edited by Christopher E. Forth and Bertrand Taithe. Palgrave Macmillan, 2007, pp. 123–40.

Bersani, Leo. "Aggression, gay shame, and Almodóvar's art." *Is the Rectum a Grave? And Other Essays*. U of Chicago P, 2010, pp. 63–82.

———. *Homos*. Harvard UP, 1996.

Bouamer, Siham, Denis M. Provencher, and Ryan K. Schroth. "Introduction: Queering *Lieux de mémoire*." *Queer Realms of Memory: Archiving LGBTQ Sites and Symbols in the French National Narrative*, edited by Siham Bouamer, Denis M. Provencher, and Ryan K. Schroth. Liverpool UP, 2025, pp. 1–23.

Burch, Noël, and Geneviève Sellier. *The Battle of the Sexes in French Cinema, 1930–1956*. Translated by Peter Graham. Duke UP, 2014.

———. "Representations 1920–50: Gender representations in French fiction films." *The French Cinema Book*, edited by Michael Temple and Michael Witt. BFI Palgrave, 2018, pp. 119–26.

Crisp, Colin. *Genre, Myth, and Convention in the Classic French Cinema, 1929–1939*. Indiana UP, 2002.

Dean, Carolyn J. *The Frail Social Body: Pornography, Homosexuality, and Other Fantasies in Interwar France*. U of California P, 2000.

Dyer, Richard. "Don't look now: The instabilities of the male pin-up." *Only Entertainment*. Routledge, 2002, pp. 122–37.

Guégan, Xavier. "Transmissible sites: Monuments, memorials and their visibility on the metropole and periphery." *Sites of Imperial Memory: Commemorating Colonial Rule in the Nineteenth and Twentieth Centuries*, edited by Dominik Geppert and Frank Lorenz Müller. Manchester UP, 2015, pp. 21–38.
Gunther, Scott. *The Elastic Closet: A History of Homosexuality in France, 1942–Present*. Palgrave Macmillan, 2009.
Hayward, Susan. *Cinema Studies: The Key Concepts*. Routledge, 2023.
Jackson, Julian. *Living in Arcadia: Homosexuality, Politics, and Morality in France from the Liberation to AIDS*. U of Chicago P, 2009.
Landsberg, Alison. *Prosthetic Memory: The Transformation of American Remembrance in the Age of Mass Culture*. Columbia UP, 2004.
McCann, Hannah, and Whitney Monaghan. *Queer Theory Now: From Foundations to Futures*. Red Globe Press, 2020.
Mulvey, Laura. "Visual pleasure and narrative cinema." *Screen*, vol. 16, no. 3, 1975, pp. 6–18.
Nevin, Barry. "French military masculinities and the birth of *Cinéma colonial*: Triangulating queer desire in Jacques Feyder's *L'Atlantide* (1921)." *Modern & Contemporary France*, vol. 29, no. 4, 2021, pp. 341–66.
Nichols, Ben. *Same Old: Queer Theory, Literature and the Politics of Sameness*. Manchester UP, 2020.
Nora, Pierre. "Between memory and history: *Les Lieux de mémoire*." Translated by Marc Roudebush. *Representations*, vol. 26, 1989, pp. 7–24.
———. "Comment écrire l'histoire de France?" *Les Lieux de mémoire*, vol. 3, *Les France*, book 1, edited by Pierre Nora. Gallimard, 1992, pp. 9–32.
Sedgwick, Eve Kosofsky. *Between Men: English Literature and Male Homosocial Desire*. Columbia UP, 2015.
Sellier, Geneviève. *Jean Grémillon: Le cinéma est à vous*. Méridiens Klincksieck, 1989.
Shohat, Ella. "Gender and culture of empire: Toward a feminist ethnography of the cinema." *Visions of the East: Orientalism in Film*, edited by Matthew Bernstein and Gaylyn Studlar. Rutgers UP, 1993, pp. 19–66.
Tamagne, Florence. *A History of Homosexuality in Europe: Berlin, London, Paris, 1919–1939*, vol. 1. Algora, 2003.
Ungar, Steven. "Split screens: *La Maison du Maltais* as text and document." *Cinema, Colonialism, Postcolonialism: Perspectives from the French and Francophone Worlds*, edited by Dina Sherzer. U of Texas P, 1996, pp. 30–50.
Vincendeau, Ginette. "Gabin unique: le pouvoir réconciliateur du mythe." *Jean Gabin: Anatomie d'un mythe*, edited by Claude Gauteur and Ginette Vincendeau. Nouveau monde, 2006, pp. 123–300.
Wiegman, Robyn, and Elizabeth A. Wilson. "Introduction: Antinormativity's queer conventions." *differences*, vol. 26, no. 1, 2015, pp. 2–22.

Williams, James S. "Looking through the rearview mirror: Queer interzones in French cinema, 1895–1945." *The Oxford Handbook of Queer Cinema*, edited by Ronald Gregg and Amy Villarejo. Oxford UP, 2021, pp. 245–80.

CHAPTER SIXTEEN

Le lieu de drague comme lieu de mémoire, or cruising, cinema, and colonial vestiges

Jules O'Dwyer

> Un plan de ville, c'est un territoire de chasse. Et draguer, une manière de le lire.
>
> — Guy Hocquenghem, *Le Gay voyage*

Cruising grounds and queer memory

What might it mean to think the relation between Pierre Nora's conception of the *lieu de mémoire* and that most emblematic space of gay life, the *lieu de drague*, or cruising ground? What concerns come in or out of view when we elect as our object of inquiry those evanescent spaces in which men have historically met other men? Those illicit sites of public sex that are mutable, ever shifting, and adapting in response to external factors (whether the disciplinary force of the police, processes of gentrification, the enduring effects of the HIV/AIDS crisis); those spaces that, while imbued with a dense historicity, contain no memorial plaques; and those zones of queer activity that often pass under the radar, or remain hidden in plain sight, impervious to the gaze of the general public?

Along with the figure of the closet, which constitutes the primary scene of sexual self-identification, the cruising ground occupies a privileged position in the topoi of gay life. While much ink has been spilled on the shifting spatial parameters of sexual encounter (such as the move away from physical locations and toward online platforms), these discourses, which emphasize the waning fortune of the analogue cruising ground in a digital age, often have the effect of piquing historical curiosity in the physical sites of queer encounter through time. The threat of cruising's supposed obsolescence, that is, has catalyzed interest in queer spaces, ranging from site-specific excavations of minor and untold histories through to nostalgic reflections on an erstwhile "golden age" of cruising.

Building on important work in French queer studies, from Denis Provencher's "mapping of gay Paris as a realm of memory" and Michael Sibalis's historical account of the French capital's "queer zones" to Lawrence Schehr's interest in how cinema queerly re-inflects France's social and cultural geographies, this chapter takes as its focus the urban cruising ground – or *lieu de drague* – which I situate both within the local environment of a Parisian neighborhood and the national context of France (Provencher 154; Sibalis; Schehr). To set in motion this investigation, I want to start by drawing out the theoretical stakes of this endeavor in broader terms.

Cruising history

Gay cruising is a spatial practice that involves wandering through a given environment with an eye attuned to furtive sexual possibilities. It entails waiting, watching, and interpreting the traffic of gazes among subjects, as well as responding to often-encrypted gestural codes. While cruising resembles the spatial practice of *flânerie* that has become a touchstone in modernist conceptions of urban life (Baudelaire, Benjamin), the purposefulness of cruising, which Hocquenghem in the opening epigraph suggestively terms "la chasse" [the hunt] (9), helps to distinguish it from more erotically disinterested modes of urban exploration.

The practice of cruising negotiates numerous tensions. Approached as a mode of relationality, cruising has offered for some queer thinkers a sense of anchorage, belonging, and "interclass contact," to use Samuel Delany's term (111), while for others its allure lies in its temporary suspension of identity and "training in impersonal intimacy," to draw on the language of one of its other foremost theorists, Leo Bersani (60). In geographical terms, the spatiotemporal coordinates of cruising zones are often insistently specific (they are often the product of local factors and historical contingencies). Yet, by this same token, these ephemeral spaces are also potentially everywhere. The cruising ground's capacity to mediate the twin registers of the general and the particular extends, moreover, to questions of memory and history. For while cruising grounds are spaces of immanence – their affective force palpably registered in the ipseity of the "here" and "now" – a more speculative notion of cruising has been powerfully invoked by figures such as José Esteban Muñoz to gesture to a deferred future: a "then and there" yet to come.

And despite the cruising ground's context specificity, it often exerts a *transhistorical* pull on the gay imaginary. Consider, for instance, the expansive historical reach of previous accounts of cruising. In *Queer Space: Architectures of Same-Sex Desire*, Aaron Betsky (1997) considers architectures of homosexuality from the ancient Greek gymnasium to New York's Studio 54 nightclub. In *The Poetics of Cruising*, literary scholar Jack Parlett (2022) traces lines of continuity from the poetry of Walt Whitman through to the hook-up smartphone application Grindr. And in his "intimate history of a radical past time," Alex Espinoza (2019) interleaves his potted history of cruising – spanning from the Greeks to the present-day, by way of 1970s San Francisco – with his own experiences. While some of these writers take care not to level historical particularities, the scope of these accounts indicates the affective pull of the past in the present. The anonymity associated with the socio-sexual practice lays the ground for envisaging the imagined community of men who came before them. Much recent writing has sought, then, to understand the practice of cruising as simultaneously tangible and ephemeral, while the spaces that serve as its backdrop paradoxically figure a marker of historical continuity and an index of change.

If Pierre Nora's theory of *les lieux de mémoire* was felt as an urgent response to the erasure and suppression of minor histories at a particular juncture marked by a crisis of historicity, then perhaps the recent groundswell of interest in *les lieux de drague* responds, in part, to a similar set of anxieties. (Though, to be sure, in the latter case, these anxieties are also propelled by the collective effects of neoliberalism, gentrification, and historical amnesia surrounding the HIV/AIDS crisis.) Put schematically, the concerns that preoccupy the burgeoning field of queer history include: how queer histories are told, whose histories are told, and how to assemble *plural* histories from archives of experience that are often structured by silence. (The double valence of the French *histoire*, which encompasses both the singular story and collective history is particularly helpful here.) Indeed, if the frangibility of cruising grounds – spaces that often leave little by way of a trace – allegorizes the tenuous place that anonymous sex occupies within narratives of queer history that are increasingly vying for cultural legitimacy, then I would wager that these spaces are also powerful insofar as they figure an alternative to sanitized accounts of a queer spatial imaginary.

Let us now turn to the cultural context of France, which constitutes my focus here. In his historical study of public sex, *Backward Glances* (2003), Mark Turner writes of how the "cruiser rubs up against the *flâneur*" – a figure whose cultural significance has enjoyed a much more sustained scholarly exegesis (7). Given that Paris is the *flâneur*'s native soil, I am interested in how these generative frictions might be articulated in texts that explore microhistories of urban cruising in France's capital. In what follows, I propose to examine the filmmaker Vincent Dieutre's attempts to map queer memory in the city of Paris by taking as my primary focus his short film *Bonne Nouvelle* (2001). As we will see, Dieutre's film offers a microhistory of Parisian spaces that rubs against the grain of pre-existing literary and cultural depictions of the French capital. In *Bonne Nouvelle*, the figure of the gay cruiser, who is embodied by the filmmaker himself, supplants the archetypical *flâneur*, thereby pointing to generally overlooked ways of seeing Paris. Dieutre does not shy away from questions of public sex, drug use, and clandestine immigration – themes that rarely figure in culturally sanctioned visions of the city of light. In the foregoing analysis, I am interested in what this framing of "marginal" urban spaces can reveal to us about a constellation of social concerns that include sexuality, but extend to questions of race, geopolitics, and postcoloniality. Put another way, I am interested in thinking about the *lieu de drague* as a realm of memory that is freighted with intersectional baggage.

Nora's project of uncovering *les lieux de mémoire* – a metonymic mode of investigation that both attends to the accretion of memory in communal spaces and treats overlooked sites as historical reserves of social life – might offer a promising way into thinking about these ephemeral histories of same-sex intimacy. Yet, by reading Dieutre in tandem with Nora, and critical work that has emerged in the wake of his project, I hope to emphasize the pitfalls, as well as the promises, contained in such an approach, to reflect on the sexual and racial politics of cruising in French gay culture more generally. But before doing this, I briefly want to unpack some of the challenges of thinking about queer spatiality in a Parisian context.

Gay Paris

In keeping with the rigid and remarkably unchanging geography of Paris after Haussmann, France's capital is quite stratified in terms of its sexual offering and where one looks for it. In terms of park spaces, the Tuileries is in the mind of many synonymous with gay cruising, while the Bois de Boulogne's longstanding association with transgender sex work has long occupied a privileged place in the Parisian imaginary (Sibalis 18; Provencher 155–91; Ross). Yet, if these queer zones attain a self-evident resonance in the minds of many, the longer history of these socio-sexual practices remains occluded from historical memory.

While France's Sodomy Laws were repealed in 1791, against a broader backdrop of revolution, Michael Sibalis (1999) notes that this only applied to sex in the private domestic sphere. Public sex would be heavily policed by vice squads (*brigades de mœurs*), established in the early nineteenth century, and men engaged in public sex would be charged with laws pertaining to hygiene and indecent exposure. It is in police records, Sibalis notes, that the archival trace of queer sex would likely be found. Writing against the grain of Foucault's repressive hypothesis, Andrew Israel Ross (2019) has more recently explored the "sexual management" of the French capital in the nineteenth century, paying attention to the ways that authorities have regulated and zoned the city's sexual provision against a shifting backdrop of urban expansion and, from the second half of the century, Haussmanization.

Sibalis's and Ross's accounts suggest that cruising zones were essentially dynamic; their locations would shift over time, responding to social, technological, and urban developments. For example, while Paris's arcades were places of cruising in the mid- to late nineteenth century, they gradually became less important compared to railway stations, for example, whose heavy footfall would offer new possibilities for what Baudelaire calls "bathing in the multitude". Other spaces, such as the banks of the Seine, remain as popular now as in the eighteenth century (Sibalis 22). In his microsociological study titled *Lieux de drague* (2002), Bruno Proth suggests that by the early twenty-first century, the privileged "scènes et coulisses d'une sexualité masculine" [scenes and backstages of masculine sexuality] would include: the RER station, the quays of the Seine, the borders of a canal, and the woodlands on the outer edges of Paris – thereby corroborating this vision of change and continuity through time.

Cinema – an indexical art form that archives space and place and offers us the tools for its queer reimagining – provides a compelling window into thinking about the shifting use of space across time. And French queer cinema, as I argue elsewhere, offers a rich archive of space's counter normative repurposing. The work of documentary filmmaker Vincent Dieutre, in particular, sheds light on many of the topics raised above. His films, which exhibit a formal debt to art cinema antecedents Chantal Akerman and Jean-Luc Godard but infuse this docupoetic tradition with a distinctly homoerotic charge, have explored the minor histories of cruising across the spaces of Europe. Most famously, his peripatetic film *Leçons de ténèbres* (1999) interwove its meditations on cruising with an account of Caravaggist aesthetics by following the trajectory that the Old Master forged throughout Europe (Utrecht, Rome, Naples) while temporarily alighting on these cities' cruising grounds along the way. Dieutre's lesser-known Paris-based projects, *Jaurès* (2012) and *Bonne Nouvelle* (2001), have taken these eponymous districts as their focus, telling the histories of local spaces in ways that blend the public and the private – imbuing public space with queer memories and practices so as to bring out little known stories hiding beneath the surface. If, as Nora argues, the crisis of history within the late twentieth century necessitated, on the part of the cultural historian, a pivot away from an overarching "Histoire" to more contingent "mémoires" to gain access to new forms of social life, then Dieutre offers us a model for undertaking this memory work. In my analysis of *Bonne Nouvelle*, which I propose we treat as a cinematic corollary to Nora's project, I want to explore both the merits and limits of using the analytic prism of homosexuality as a means of accessing previously untold urban histories.

Bonne nouvelle

Working within a long tradition of essay films that turn to the Parisian streetscape to anchor their forms of ideological critique (e.g., Agnès Varda, Jean Rouch), Dieutre's *Bonne Nouvelle* documents the underbelly of the eponymous neighborhood to delaminate a picture postcard view of Paris; the series of urban cinematic snapshots (or "clichés" in French) that *Bonne Nouvelle* presents to us figure an attempt to resist cliché. Dieutre's is a film that wants, pre-emptively, to avoid the trap of the tourist gaze, turning his attention to the forms of queer and migrant life that often lie out of frame. The film's image track is composed of a

Le lieu de drague comme lieu de mémoire   259

sequence of largely static shots that present various oblique corners of the neighborhood. Through Dieutre's use of voiceover narration, these interstitial urban scenes are transformed into realms of memory that crystallize the traces and residues of a queer lifeworld. And they are equally haunted by historical absences and evocations of lost loved ones. Much like the filmmaker's own fallible memory, the spaces that Dieutre displays are structured by gaps, riddled with lacunae, and subject to the ruinous vicissitudes of time.

The film opens with an epigraph set against a black background that reads: "la métropole matérialise, en même temps que la perte intégrale de la communauté, l'infinie possibilité de son regain" [the metropolitan materializes the infinite possibility of revival of the community, at the same moment as its integral loss]. Though the aphorism itself is torn from the pages of *Tiqqun* – a short-lived journal published by a critical-theoretical collective in 1990s Paris, who saw themselves as the descendants of the Situationist International – the intellectual tradition that grounds Dieutre's urban vision stems further back in time. Mutely summoning the specters of Charles Baudelaire, for whom cities elicit a contradictory sense of excitement, anxiety, and anomie (among the other affects that animate the "modern" condition), and Walter Benjamin, for whom city spaces oscillate dialectically between states of ruin and renewal, the filmmaker frames the social spaces of his own "metropolis" as fragile and fleeting in equal measure. In an ode to Baudelaire's *Tableaux parisiens*, *Bonne Nouvelle* is comprised of a web of urban fragments, a record of fleeting sense-impressions, that, when stitched together, evoke the neighborhood's distinctive affects and structures of feeling.

Early on in the film, we are introduced to Dieutre's predilection for cruising. He dwells in passageways, circles the local squares, exchanges incipient glances with pedestrians on densely packed thoroughfares. The spoken text also introduces us to a string of unseen characters; Youssef, Dieutre's "amant turc du mardi" [Tuesday's Turkish lover]; Wajberg, a young cocaine trafficker that the filmmaker encounters outside a café; Farid, a hairdresser whose touch he longs for; and a nameless figure sleeping in the doorway of the filmmaker's apartment block whom he names "Le mort de l'escalier" [The dead man on the stairs]. These invisible figures, summoned only by voiceover narration, are the film's primary characters, forming part of the neighborhood's queer demimonde.

Dieutre's ambition seems fairly clear: to archive, in cinematic form, a patchwork of past encounters and fleeting memories within a clearly delimited urban space. Yet, given that the characters whom Dieutre and the other voiceover narrators describe in sensory detail are never shown on screen, this entails what the filmmaker calls "un travail de reconstruction" [a work of reconstruction], or an interpretative labor of reconciling the two registers of voice and image. By laying these intimate, and often sexual, stories over images of sites of passage (e.g., Métro steps, alleyways, indoor arcades), the profilmic geography is suffused with an ephemeral, but nonetheless palpable, eroticism. As the camera lingers on specific locations, the camera's gaze aligns with Dieutre's own position; every open space that appears in front of the camera is a potential cruising zone, every gesture a potentially encrypted social signal. The filmmaker reinflects the memorial logic established in Nora's project by imbuing physical spaces with queer memories and bringing into consciousness untapped archives of experience that have geophysical coordinates but leave little by way of a trace. While Nora's work often extends beyond physical sites or spaces, Dieutre takes seriously the topographic dimension of this project, or what Paule Petitier describes as "le lien de la mémoire et de l'espace, la prédilection de la mémoire de s'incarner dans des lieux" [the link between memory and space, memory's tendency to embed itself in spaces] (103).

Eroticism, exoticism, racial occlusion

While the Parisian tableau that I have so far painted is legible according to the dominant idioms of modernist urban theory, there is another (altogether more troubling) dimension to *Bonne Nouvelle* that I want to bring into view: an uneasy crack in the film's representational logic that emblematizes a longstanding fault line in French gay culture. For if Dieutre's film queerly inflects the Norassian project, then it still exhibits the shortcomings that have been levelled against this same project: its glaring lacunae and occlusions surrounding questions of race and religion, colonial legacies, and geopolitical positionalities (Achille, Forsdick, and Moudileno). To introduce this more contentious aspect of the film, one need look no further than its first chapter. Here, the image track contains footage of unsuspecting passers-by on the Boulevard Bonne Nouvelle, while the voiceover recounts one of Dieutre's diary entries: One day, while walking along an adjoining street, he runs into a man, Youssef, whom he first cruised in the nearby Rex Club, an evening before. Yet on this occasion the man initially fails to reciprocate the filmmaker's erotic gaze. Dieutre explains: "Habitué à ces accès de désir soudains qui rythment mes promenades sur le boulevard, je me retourne" [Accustomed to such fits of desire, which routinely punctuate my strolls along the boulevard, I turn around]. Realizing that Youssef is now following him, he launches into a phenomenologically rich description of the ensuing cruising encounter: "Du coup la vie devient plus dense, le temps plus épais" [All of a sudden, life acquires added density, and time thickens]. The voiceover evokes in granular detail the interpersonal dynamics between both men: the interplay of furtive gazes; the subtleties of body language; and the choreography of glances and gestures set to the metronome of the filmmaker's increasingly quickening heartbeat. Later slipping through the door of his apartment building, Youssef initiates the start of a string of sexual encounters that would continue, with regularity, over the coming months:

> Youssef était l'amant turc du mardi, ponctuel et performant. Jamais je n'ai obtenu ou demandé adresse ni téléphone, jamais je n'ai donné le mien. J'ai simplement fini par comprendre qu'il traînait place du Caire pour travailler au noir dans les ateliers du Sentier et ma curiosité s'est arrêtée là.
>
> [Youssef became my Turkish lover on Tuesdays. He was punctual and he performed well. Never did he divulge his home address or telephone number, and nor did I. Ultimately, I inferred that he hung around the Place du Caire, he was an undeclared worker in one of the workshops in Sentier, and my curiosity stopped there.]

The sexual politics that underwrite the scene point to an ethical quandary that is worth dwelling over. How are we to interpret Dieutre's lack of curiosity here? A charitable interpretation of this passage would likely invoke Youssef's right to opacity and anonymity. Indeed, theoretical accounts of cruising typically stress that its ethical potential lies in its resistance to an epistemological will to know the other. However, as Dieutre goes on to mention the precarity of the racialized subject, noting that Youssef "doit à nouveau baiser sa femme" [must once more go home and fuck his wife], it becomes clear that this pseudo-anonymity is hard to reconcile with what Tim Dean calls cruising's "distinctive ethic of openness to alterity" (176). Dieutre's choice not to flesh out this figure's personhood, aside from evoking the conspicuous markers of his ethnicity, mirrors problems surrounding race in French thought in general, and queer culture in particular.

Let us start with the first, more general, charge. In one of the most trenchant critiques of Pierre Nora's project and the author's "colonial aphasia," Ann Laura Stoler draws on a recent example of contemporary writing, Kamel Daoud's *Meurseault, contre-enquête* (2014), which marks an attempt to fill in "the emptied space of the Arab" that lies at the heart of Camus's canonical novel, *L'Etranger* (Stoler 123). In *L'Etranger* – a text whose place at the heart of the French *patrimoine* is assured – the underdeveloped character of the "Arab" (who is rendered a mute specter, a prop, and is instrumentalized as a narrative catalyst) exemplifies a reductive engagement with racial difference that, for Stoler, speaks to broader patterns of thought entrenched within French culture, as well as a "warped reckoning with the colonial histories that saturate the fabric of contemporary France" (124). Such representational dynamics are particularly pronounced in the context of France's queer culture. Indeed, it is another Camus – the controversial gay writer Renaud Camus (whose "dry" descriptive prose Dieutre (2007) cites as inspiration for his work) – that offers the most striking example of how the queer artist's sexual partners, or "tricks", can be reduced to racialized typologies, a tendency that remains an enduring trope in French gay life writing. As scholars such as Kadji Amin (2017), Joseph Boone (2014), and Mehammed Mack (2016) have shown, with reference to the work of André Gide, Jean Genet, and Roland Barthes, among others, there exists within the French gay *récit* a foundational ambivalence toward the politics of race. As Maxime Cervulle and Nick Rees-Roberts note in *Homo Exoticus: race, classe et critique queer* (2010), these instances of writing share a common feature: "l'énonciateur reste toujours le même: l'homosexuel blanc occidental" [the speaker always remains the same: the gay white western subject] (15). Such a charge, I argue, applies equally to Vincent Dieutre.

As the subsequent "chapters" of *Bonne Nouvelle* continue to entwine themes of gay sex, ethnic difference, and urban marginality through frank first-person diaristic testimonies, two other rhetorical strategies grow increasingly apparent. First, Dieutre uncritically extends his exploration of the district's multicultural character to its sexual offering. For instance, the long static frames comprising shots of alleys and passageways are presented against a sonic bed that captures "Eastern" music and calls to prayer. The ambient soundscape of the film thus connotes an otherness that bleeds into its sexual politics: eroticism and exoticism grow increasingly entwined. Such strategies of framing, which ought to be read within this longer tradition in French gay cultural production to conflate the mapping of foreign lands with the exploration of non-white bodies, do little to interrogate the power dynamics that underwrite these social encounters. Second, *Bonne Nouvelle*'s curation of a string of chance meetings – sexual or otherwise – with subjects on society's fringes (drug addicts, homeless persons, undeclared workers) seeks both to arrogate toward, and to confer upon, the filmmaker himself this same marginal status. This strategy, which resonates with what Amin terms the politics of "erotic coalition" (78), demands us to probe the ethical limits of the filmmaker's affinity with, or subjective appropriation of, a given neighborhood's "character."

When read against its grain (which is to say: against the grain of its narrator's voice and his authorial intention), *Bonne Nouvelle* raises important questions about the place that the white gay subject occupies within the constellation of social themes that the film takes as its documentary subject. To bring the broader Parisian literary context back into view, then: just as the normative dimensions of *flânerie* (predicated on the luxury of idleness, the right to public space, the freedom of unobstructed walking) has been subject to productive criticism by virtue of its gendered blind spot, I want to suggest that the queer cognate to this spatial activity, *la drague*, entails its own racial and geopolitical biases that are worthy of interrogation. To be sure, the frictionless access to urban space that we are granted in *Bonne Nouvelle* represents a thoroughly partial perspective. Not only does Dieutre present a spatial archive of living memory by drawing out the queer experiences that accrete and amass in particular locations, but his film also exemplifies and indexes broader patterns of thinking that subtend the (white) French queer canon. When read as a case study for "queer realms of memory," the film is instructive (in a negative sense) insofar as it reproduces once again the shortcomings of Nora's normative whiteness, as well as inviting urgent questions about the merits and limits of turning to sexuality as a primary analytic rubric.

But what might a historical approach to queer spaces that is more attuned to issues of difference look like? Perhaps a partial answer to this question might be found by returning to the streets around Bonne Nouvelle themselves – *la Rue D'Aboukir, La Place du Caire* – and taking seriously the histories of colonial conquest to which these street names allude, as well as exploring how these histories helped shape the ground upon which modern France, and its queer cultures, now stands.

Works cited

Achille, Étienne, Charles Forsdick, and Lydie Moudileno. *Postcolonial Realms of Memory: Sites and Symbols in Modern France*. Liverpool UP, 2020.

Amin, Kadji. *Disturbing Attachments: Genet, Modern Pederasty, and Queer History*. Duke UP, 2017.

Bech, Henning. *When Men Meet: Homosexuality and Modernity*. Translated by Teresa Mewquit. U of Chicago P, 1997.

Bersani, Leo. *Is the Rectum a Grave? And Other Essays*. U of Chicago P, 2010.

Betsky, Aaron. *Queer Space: Architecture and Same-Sex Desire*. William Morrow, 1997.

Boone, Joseph Allen. *The Homoerotics of Orientalism*. Columbia UP, 2014.

Cervulle, Maxime, and Nick Rees-Roberts. *Homo Exoticus: race, classe et critique queer*. Armand Colin, 2010.

Daoud, Kamel. *Meursault, contre-enquête*. Actes Sud, 2014.

Dean, Tim. *Unlimited Intimacy: Reflections on the Subculture of Barebacking*. U of Chicago P, 2009.

Delany, Samuel R. *Times Square Red, Times Square Blue*. New York UP, 1999.

Dieutre, Vincent, dir. *Bonne Nouvelle*. Short. Shellac Sud, 2001.

———. "'Et plus si affinités…': Le trick comme figure de la modernité au cinéma." *La Rencontre*, edited by Jacques Aumont. Presses universitaires de Rennes, 2007, pp. 37–55.

———. dir. *Jaurès*. Documentary film. Jour2Fête, 2013.

———. dir. *Leçons de ténèbres*. Feature film. Les Films de la Croisade. France, 1999.

Espinosa, Alex. *Cruising: An Intimate History of a Radical Pastime*. The Unnamed Press, 2019.

Hocquenghem, Guy. *Le Gay voyage. Guide et regard homosexuels sur les grandes métropoles*. Albin Michel, 1980.

Mack, Mehammed Amadeus. *Sexagon: Muslims, France, and the Sexualization of National Culture*. Fordham UP, 2017.

Muñoz, José Esteban. *Cruising Utopia: The Then and There of Queer Utopia*. New York UP, 2009.

Parlett, Jack. *The Poetics of Cruising: Queer Visual Culture from Whitman to Grindr*. U of Minnesota P, 2022.

Petitier, Paule. "*Les Lieux de mémoire*, compte-rendu." *Romantisme*, vol. 63, 1989, pp. 103–10.

Proth, Bruno. *Lieux de drague: scènes et coulisses d'une sexualité masculine*. Octarès, 2002.

Provencher, Denis M. *Queer French: Globalization, Language, and Sexual Citizenship in France*. Ashgate, 2007.

Ross, Andrew Israel. *Public City/Public Sex: Homosexuality, Prostitution, and Urban Culture in Nineteenth-Century Paris*. Temple UP, 2019.

Schehr, Lawrence R. "Fragmented territories: AIDS and Paris in *Les Nuits Fauves* of Cyril Collard." *French Forum*, vol. 34, no. 1, 2009, pp. 53–65.

Sibalis, Michael. "Paris." *Queer Sites: Gay Urban Histories since 1600*, edited by David Higgs. Routledge, 1999, pp. 10–37.

Stoler, Ann Laura. *Duress: Imperial Durabilities in Our Times*. Duke UP, 2016.

Turner, Mark. *Backward Glances: Cruising the Queer Streets of New York and London*. Reaktion, 2003.

CHAPTER SEVENTEEN

A queer rewriting of history
The case of Leïla Slimani's *Le Pays des autres*

Maxime Foerster

Introduction

Reflecting on the monumental success of *Les Lieux de mémoire,* Pierre Nora observes that the dialectics between memory and history have led to a new trend in contemporary literature:

> Memory has never known more than two forms of legitimacy: historical and literary. These have run parallel to each other but until now always separately. At present the boundary between the two is blurring [...]. History has become our replaceable imagination – hence the last stand of faltering fiction in the renaissance of the historical novel, the vogue for personalized documents, the literary revitalization of historical drama, the success of the oral historical tale. (24)

What Nora calls the "spectacular bereavement of literature" (24) is, in fact, a new momentum – one in which authors recognize that there is no spontaneous memory, and that literature can not only contribute to the will to remember but also help erect a realm of memory against erasure and oblivion.

As far as sexual minorities are concerned, since their lives have been systematically erased from the official History, with a capital H, committed authors from various countries have engaged with the dialectics between history and memory in order to reinscribe the fate of queer people in the patriarchal narratives of the history of the Nations. The publication of *The Prophets* by Robert Jones Jr., in 2021, which focuses on the lives of two male slaves in love on a plantation in antebellum America, illustrates this orientation of literature towards memory and, more specifically, the project to represent through fictional characters the lives of queer people who were made invisible by History. In 2020, the Franco-Moroccan author Leïla Slimani published *La guerre, la guerre, la guerre*, the first volume of a trilogy entitled *Le pays des autres* (translated and published a year later under the title *In the Country of Others*, vol. 1, *War, War, War*), which is partly inspired by her own family based on the marriage between her French maternal grandmother with a Moroccan soldier serving in the French army in World War II. Inspired by her passion for American western films and southern gothic literature, Slimani shared in an interview that she applied the historical novel to her family in order to create a Moroccan saga à la Faulkner ("Le grand entretien, avec Leïla Slimani"). At the beginning of the novel, recently married Mathilde and Amine settle on a farm near Meknes in the late 1940s, a time when Moroccans are getting ready to fight French colonialism and achieve their independence.

In *Queer Nations, Marginal Sexualities in the Maghreb*, Jarrod Hayes argues, based on the analysis of francophone literature from Morocco, Algeria, and Tunisia, that "nations are like fictions; they are, in fact, supported by narratives: history, narratives of origin, tales of heroism" (12), and that literature plays an essential role in both the construction and deconstruction of the national narratives. While the nationalistic state intends to promote a uniform and patriarchal narrative ("Islam is my religion, Arabic is my language, Algeria is my fatherland" [1]), authors counter official history by articulating in their novels alternative narratives leading to a complex and evolutive Nation:

> In rewriting the Nation, many authors repeat official narratives with a difference. This proliferation of roots opens the Nation to those who do not share the official version of identity and makes it a more heterogeneous space where marginalized citizens can also plant roots. This heterogeneity is also sexual; if there is something oppressive about the Nation, there is also something queer about it. (Hayes, *Queer Nations* 15)

The rewriting of the Moroccan Nation takes place in Slimani's trilogy as she uses a fictional account of her family romance to represent a heterogeneous nation in terms of origins (Morocco, France, Hungary), religions (Islam, Catholicism, Judaism), languages (Arabic, French), and sexualities (heterosexuality, homosexuality). The title of the trilogy, *In the Country of Others*, poses the nation as a choral assemblage where distinctive and dissident voices contribute one way or another to the complex dynamics of a national community seen as a constant work in progress. Whereas Hayes opposes in *Queer Roots for the Diaspora* the mangrove (intricate network of rhizomatic roots) to the family tree (traceable roots), Slimani has recourse to another botanical allegory to represent the heterogeneity of the Nation: a strange tree is growing on Amine and Mathilde's farm, called a *citrange*, resulting from the grafting of an orange tree onto a lemon tree. The *citrange* represents not only the *métissage* of Amine and Mathilde's family tree, but also the intersectional hybridity at the heart of the Moroccan Nation.

This chapter will focus on Mourad, the Moroccan soldier who met Amine in the French army, served him, and fell in love with him. Once he is back from Vietnam, where he fought a second war for France, Mourad is hired by Amine to work on the farm as his foreman. By creating the character of Mourad, a Moroccan Muslim from a lower class who is in love with another Moroccan man, Slimani inserts a "gay" character in her narrative of the Moroccan Nation. As neither the narrator nor the character uses the word gay, quotations will be used to express the anachronism of the term when applied to Mourad. While the depiction of male homosexuality in Morocco has traditionally focused on westerners coming to Morocco for sexual tourism (Jean Genet, Paul Bowles, Tennessee Williams), the originality of *In the Country of Others* is that it represents a Moroccan man in love with another Moroccan man without the mediation of a white western person. Mourad met Amine in France, while serving in the French army, but the text does not link Mourad's love for Amine with the impact of France over him. His love can be said to be indigenous because it does not result from an exposure to a western discourse on homosexuality. His fate, illustrated in the first and second volumes (*Regardez-nous danser* was published in France in 2022, and then in 2023 in England under the title *Watch Us Dance*) of the trilogy, shows that sexual minorities existed in Morocco regardless of French colonialism and that their struggle to survive was often tragic. The last part of the chapter will reflect on the stakes of rewriting History for Moroccan contemporary society.

Mourad, an indigenous "gay" character

Although Mourad is the main "gay" character in the first volume of *In the Country of Others*, he is not the only trace of queerness in the novel.

Amine and Mathilde, who suffer from isolation on their remote farm, are happy to befriend a couple of westerners who also settled in Meknes: Corinne and Dragan. While Corinne is a French woman who suffers from not having children, her husband, Dragan, is a Jewish doctor who ran away from Hungary, Germany, and finally France in order to avoid anti-Semitic persecutions during the 1930s and World War II. He started working as a doctor in a private clinic in Casablanca but ended up moving to Meknes for the following reason:

> In the white town on the Atlantic coast he'd found employment as a doctor in a well-known clinic. He'd earned plenty of money, but the director's reputation and the nature of the operations he was performing had ended up making him quit. They'd decided to move to Meknes, with its easygoing atmosphere and its orchards

> "What sort of operations were they?" asked Mathilde, intrigued by Corinne's conspiratorial tone. [...]

> "Rather extraordinary operations, if you want my opinion. Did you know that people come from all over Europe for that? The doctor is either a genius or a madman, but apparently he's capable of transforming a man into a woman!" (129)

While the reader might think this anecdote concerning Dragan's trajectory is an incongruous invention on the part of the author, it actually relies on a historical fact. The Clinique du Parc, located in Casablanca, is the place where Georges Burou, a French gynecologist, has pioneered gender affirming-surgery for transwomen.[1] A master of vaginoplasty, Burou became the preferred surgeon for the first wave of transwomen who could afford the cost of the trip, surgery, and long recovery in Casablanca.[2] By including this information, Slimani gives a concrete example of how Morocco has been a hospitable and transformative place for transwomen from all over the world when very few people knew about this new kind of surgery.

Lucien is another gay character who appears briefly at the end of

---

1   More details about Georges Burou and his impact of the history of transgenderism are available in Foerster's *Elle ou lui? Une histoire des transsexuels en France*.

2   Slimani makes an anachronistic error, though, as she situates Burnou's surgeries in the late 1940s or early 1950s, when they were not performed before the late 1950s.

A queer rewriting of history 271

the first volume but whose situation is also emblematic of Morocco as a place of escape for gay men. Working as an employee in a photography store, Lucien has a rough interaction with Amine when this latter discovers in the window display of the store a photograph of his sister Selma in love with a stranger and a foreigner (Alain Crozières, a French man working as a pilot for an airline company). Ashamed by the public display of his sister's emotions, Amine enters the store, confronts Lucien, and demands that the picture be removed and given to him. Lucien does not want any trouble and surrenders the photograph right away. The reader finds out that he came to Morocco to run away from trouble:

> Lucien didn't want any trouble. He'd left France after being blackmailed, and he'd come to this new world – a world just as mean as the old one, but with better weather – with the idea of sticking to his vows to be discreet. He'd heard far too much about the Arabs' sense of honor to dare provoke them. "Touch their women and you'll regret it," a customer had told him just after he opened the studio. No risk of that, Lucien had thought. (*War, War, War* 260)

Blackmail has been a classic way of ruining the reputation of closeted men in France, resulting in suicides, bribes, or, such as in Lucien's case, emigration. By including characters such as a Hungarian Jew (Dragan) or a French gay man (Lucien), Slimani reminds her readers of the significant migration to Morocco of vulnerable people who needed a refuge from anti-Semitism and homophobia. But by introducing a character like Mourad, she means to show that the diversity of Morocco also comes from the inside.

In *The Apparitional Lesbian*, Terry Castle raises a key question concerning the representations of sexual minorities: "Why is it so difficult to see the lesbian – even when she is there, quite plainly, in front of us? In part because she has been 'ghosted' – or made to seem invisible – by culture itself" (4). Although lesbians are not represented in Slimani's saga, Castle's remarks are also applicable to all subjects of non-normative sexualities. For instance, the creation of Mourad breaks this pattern of invisibility by giving a name, a voice, and a destiny to a subaltern person.

Mourad's feelings for Amine are not just sexual, his attraction being driven by love and devotion. Once he came back to Morocco, instead of adjusting to social and sexual norms by marrying a Moroccan woman and starting a family, he realized he could not live without Amine and, like a ghost from the past, ends up knocking on his door, looking like a haggard soul. Out of charity and loyalty for his former aide-de-camp, Amine invites him to stay on the farm and work as a foreman. Although Mourad's love will not be returned and he will have to keep his desires secret, at least he will get to live in the shadow of his beloved:

> He had no right, he thought, to bring his sins here, to stain these people's lives with his secrets. In his bed Mourad felt ashamed of not having told Amine everything. When he discovers the truth, Mourad thought, he'll kick me out, insult me, accuse me of taking advantage of his generosity.
>
> Mourad wished he could put his hand on Amine's and let his head rest on his commander's shoulder, breathe in his scent. He wished that their embrace, on the doorstep, could have lasted forever. He'd pretended, like the hypocrite he was, to be delighted to see Mathilde and the children, but in fact he'd have preferred it if they weren't there, if there'd been nobody in this house but him and the commander. (*War, War, War* 204)

Mourad becomes the queer ghost haunting the heteropatriarchal family as his company makes everybody uncomfortable around him and he is doomed to live with feelings of shame and self-hatred for his homosexuality. Feeling like an impostor, he cannot help but dream of the love that dare not speak its name in Morocco in the early 1950s. The way he manages Amine's workers is so harsh that he does not earn their respect and becomes an isolated figure, with no friends and no family: "Mourad treated the laborers with military strictness, and in less than three weeks the whole village hated him" (207). It is not clear whether Mourad's treatment of Amine's workers comes from his military discipline or as a defense mechanism to hide his homosexuality and avoid stigmatization. His love for Amine is carried like a burden because there is no hope of reciprocity and it must remain a shameful secret.

On the other side, does Amine know or suspect Mourad's feelings for him? The text remains ambiguous about the origin of Amine's growing awkwardness, but a turning point in Amine's treatment of his former aide-de-camp takes place in an episode at a brothel. Amine first took Mourad to a bar where they both got drunk, and then he took him to a brothel so that they could enjoy the services of female sex workers. Concerned by Mourad's state of isolation, Amine tried to get him out of his shell with a mix of alcohol and sex, but the result was a disaster as Mourad was not able to have sex with a woman. He failed the test of heterosexuality, offended the sex worker, and was thrown out of the brothel. This failure helps Amine make a decision:

> The next day he told the laborers that the foreman was ill, and he couldn't help feeling sad when he saw relief and joy on their faces. When Mathilde offered to look after Mourad, give him some medicine, her husband replied coldly that he only needed rest. "I think we should find him a wife," Amine added. "It's not good to be so alone." (250)

Acting with a sense of his patriarchal duties, Amine understands it is time to "fix" Mourad by coercing him into marriage. The text does not reveal if Amine is aware of Mourad's sexual situation but he is certainly not in denial about the fact that there is something problematic with his friend.[3] It is not socially acceptable for a man to remain single and Mourad will face contempt if he does not start a family. In a dramatic plot twist, Amine forces his younger sister, Selma, to marry Mourad at the end of the novel. According to Amine, she has disgraced herself and tarnished his honor by having an affair with a French man, so she also needs to be fixed. A good reputation is essential for Amine, so he cannot let his sister flirt with whomever she wants, especially with non-Muslim and non-Moroccan men. Selma's quest for agency and sexual freedom is crushed by her brother (in spite of being married himself to a French woman who did not convert to Islam) when he forces her to marry Mourad. This arranged marriage between a closeted "gay" man and a rebellious woman shows how Amine intends to enforce the basic rules of patriarchy. The institution of marriage remains the key strategy to impose social and sexual norms over dissident subjects such as single men and independent women.

The marriage between Selma and Mourad is a bitter and unhappy one, but at least honor and reputation are saved, especially with the birth of Sabah in the second volume (*Watch Us Dance* 52). One reason why the marriage was rushed is because Selma was pregnant by a French man, running the risk of wearing the equivalent of the scarlet letter in her community. Ironically, Mourad becomes a father and is temporarily perceived as a valid heterosexual man while he has never touched Selma. Since the first day of their wedding, Selma and Mourad do not sleep together: "When the house was ready Mourad felt proud, but it didn't change his habits. At night he left the big bed to Selma while he slept on the floor" (*War, War, War,* 274). While Mourad is proud to have purchased an expensive and large wooden bed, thinking it will please

---

3 Interestingly, the word *friendship* is never used to describe Amine and Mourad's relationship.

Amine that he treats his sister generously, he cannot bring himself to share any intimacy with his wife.

In the second volume of the trilogy, as years go by, workers keep despising Mourad and know that his marriage is a parody. His homosexuality became an open secret as rumors circulate about his mores: "They all hated Mourad, so that was why they had claimed to see him, on the Azrou road, picking up boys and leading them in secret to fornicate in the cedar woods" (*Watch Us Dance* 80). He dies early and tragically, crushed by stones while working at the bottom of a well. The narrator leaves space for doubt and suggests that Mourad's death is a death à la Pasolini (who was murdered in ambiguous circumstances, possibly a homophobic crime):

> The police were called. The officer, looking suspicious, asked Amine if he had any reason to believe that it had not been an accident. Arms dangling, mouth tight with nerves, Amine stammered a response. Of course it was an accident! What was the policeman insinuating? That someone might have wanted to kill Mourad? (*Watch Us Dance* 92)

His funeral, like his marriage, was a sad parody. As Amine was afraid that people would desecrate his grave (due either to his sympathy for France or his stigmatized homosexuality), he decided to leave his corpse in the well and organize a funeral without Mourad's body (*Watch Us Dance* 95). The well, by opposition to the empty and official grave, becomes the queer *lieu de mémoire*, the place of the rotting queer cadaver and the source of its persistent memory. Although Mourad disappears early in the second volume of the trilogy, he becomes a haunting ghost for both Selma and Amine after his death: "As a dead man, Mourad became a confidant, almost a friend, who no longer judged her. And she understood then what it had been impossible for her to see while they had lived together: this man's loneliness. His suffering" (*Watch Us Dance* 96). It took Mourad's death for Selma to realize that her husband was as much as a victim as she was, and the communication and empathy that were never there when he was alive are finally expressed now that she is haunted by him. The same haunting affects Amine: "He also talks with Mourad, whose ghost glides over the estate and whose memory weighs on his heart with all the heaviness of remorse" (*Watch Us Dance* 309).

As Hayes has shown in *Queer Nations*, repression of the sexual minorities leads in return to their spectral return, haunting the literature and the narratives of the Nation: "Maghrebian novels expose the queer ghosts that haunt the Nation; they also conjure up these ghosts to haunt it" (19). By choosing to narrate the life of Mourad and inscribe his fate in the saga of the Moroccan Nation, Slimani has erected a literary monument, a *lieu de mémoire* to all the "gay" men whose lives have been erased from Moroccan History. This realm of memory is strategic as the recognition of the existence of sexual minorities in Morocco before its independence paves the way for their recognition and inclusion in Morocco today and tomorrow.

Rewriting history is all about the future

As authors produce historical novels, they dispute the patriarchal and nationalistic propaganda of the state by providing alternative narratives on the diversity of the Moroccan Nation. And as their literary works become hospitable to voices that were silenced and oppressed because of their queerness, they enrich and complicate the national family by rewriting the story of the marginal members who were seen as a threat to heterosexuality as a political regime and were never given a chance to speak for themselves. Slimani uses the historical novel to give a voice back to the subaltern.

The stakes of these literary contributions to the making of Morocco is to have a direct impact on its contemporary society, pleading for less hypocrisy about the existence of sexual minorities in the Nation. As Morocco has been enforcing a systematic repression of sexual minorities in the name of the defense of a national idiosyncrasy, authors such as Slimani have produced works that deconstruct the myth of a fixed and uniform culture, denounce the consequences of this witch hunt (one can think, for instance, of the violent critical reception of the film *Much Loved* in 2015, leading the main actress to leave Morocco for her safety), and respect the dignity of the victims of the patriarchal order. In the preface to her book *Sex and Lies*, in which anonymous Moroccan women recount their stories of oppression, Slimani argues for an inclusive and evolutive understanding of culture: "Listening to these women, I became determined to shine a light on the reality of this land, which is far more complex and more troubled than we are led to believe" (15). Although *Sex and Lies* is a collection of personal stories and *In the Country of Others* is a historical novel, Slimani achieves the same goal with these two different genres: showing the diversity of the Nation, emphasizing its complexity, and giving a voice to those who are silenced.

> But when women in miniskirts are being accused of gross indecency, when homosexuals are being lynched in broad daylight, then we urgently need to consider shaping a new society that can unite us and enable us to avoid these kinds of outrages. [...] We must stop giving in to the temptation to wash our hands of the matter, to the lazy definition of our culture and identity as fixed, supra-historical facts. We are not the same as our culture; rather, our culture is what we make of it. (17)

This constructivist definition of culture is essential for Slimani's project to include sexual minorities and recognize their dignity. Far from being a given package of fixed values and patriarchal propaganda, culture is what we make of it because it results from constant power struggles and exchanges across social classes, genders, languages, religions, and sexualities. By having recourse to the genre of historical novel, Slimani makes a point of showing that Morocco does not have to become queer because it has always been queer in the first place.

Works cited

Ayouch, Nabil. *Much Loved*. 2015.

Castle, Terry. *The Apparitional Lesbian: Female Homosexuality and Modern Culture*. Columbia UP, 1993.

Foerster, Maxime. *Elle ou lui? Une histoire des transsexuels en France*. La Musardine, 2012.

"Le grand entretien, avec Leïla Slimani." Fête du livre de Bron. March 10, 2021. *YouTube.com*. Web.

Hayes, Jarrod. *Queer Nations: Marginal Sexualities in the Maghreb*. U of Chicago P, 2000.

———. *Queer Roots for the Diaspora: Ghosts in the Family Tree*. U of Michigan P, 2016.

Jones Jr., Robert. *The Prophets*. G. P. Putnam's Sons, 2021.

Nora, Pierre. "Between memory and history: *Les Lieux de mémoire*." Translated by Marc Roudebush. *Representations*, vol. 26, 1989, pp. 7–24.

Slimani, Leïla. *In the Country of Others*, vol. 1, War, War, War. Penguin Books, 2021.

———. *Sex and Lies: True Stories of Women's Intimate Lives in the Arab World*. Penguin Books, 2020.

———. *Watch Us Dance* (*In the Country of Others*, vol. 2). Faber & Faber, 2023.

CHAPTER EIGHTEEN

Fatima Daas's *La Petite Dernière* (2020)
A fugitive *lieux de mémoire* for the undercommons

Siham Bouamer

Scholars in postcolonial studies have critically examined the dynamics inherent to memorialization processes, often motivated by the imperative to challenge narratives that have historically excluded marginalized identities and histories. For example, in *Postcolonial Realms of Memory* (2020), Étienne Achille, Charles Forsdick, and Lydie Moudileno critique Pierre Nora's narrow focus, noting his failure to address (post)colonial histories. Their work emphasizes not only the importance of recognizing such *lieux* to understand the colonial past, but also to shed light on more contemporary issues and the invisibilization of postcolonial identities in France. They argue:

> These issues are central to discussions of French identity, or what some would call "Frenchness", especially at a time when the increasing hybridization of France – not least in terms of ethnicity and religious affiliations – raises questions about current understandings of republicanism and how this ideology fits (or does not fit) the socio-cultural realities of the early twenty-first century. (2)

While their observations are significant for the study of postcolonial memory, adopting a more intersectional approach, including considerations of queer memory, allows us to further complicate categories like "Frenchness" by challenging traditional conceptions of belonging and identity, as well as what it means to "fit" within the French republican ideology and its national discourse.

For that reason, I propose to examine Fatima Daas's debut auto-fictional novel *La Petite Dernière* (2020). The book recounts the story of Fatima, a young Muslim lesbian woman who lives in a Parisian *banlieue* with her Algerian immigrant parents. Throughout a complex narrative, the protagonist navigates the multiple parts of her identity, reflecting on her attraction to women, her Muslim faith, and her role as the daughter of immigrants. The novel breaks new ground by offering a voice to a queer woman, a perspective that is often marginalized in narratives about French Maghrebi individuals. While literary figures like Nina Bouraoui have indeed paved the way, Daas's perspective as a first-generation French woman from a Muslim migrant family offers a fresh perspective.

Daas addresses the invisibility of experiences like hers in several interviews. She explains that she always felt that "she did not exist" because of the lack of representation in France of individuals like her – "lesbian, Muslim woman, with an immigrant background" (Ayuso). Probing the question, "How do we shape ourselves when we have absolutely no representation?" Daas reveals that writing *La Petite Dernière* was not just a personal endeavor but a collective effort, as the "we" indicates, to create visibility for those with similar experiences. Indeed, insisting on literature as a space for collective intervention, Daas explains, "J'avais pas envie de faire un journal intime mais de la littérature" [I didn't want to write a diary, but literature], and stresses the importance of "faire exister ce [lesbienne et musulmane] personnage dans la littérature française" [bringing into existence this [lesbian and Muslim] character in French literature] (*French Institute UK*).

This approach leads me to reflect on her act of writing as part of a memorialization process within France's national narrative. In particular, I propose to consider *La Petite Dernière* as a *lieu de mémoire* that challenges Nora's conceptualization through the inclusion of narratives that are often marginalized, specifically those related to postcolonial and queer identities. Within that framework, literature becomes a crucial site for this memorialization process. This is what Oana Panaïté argues in her chapter on archives in *Postcolonial Realms of Memory*. Indeed, she identifies literature as "a restorative site that lays claim to the truth of the archive by supplementing its scarcity, correcting its falsehoods, or making up for its complete absence" (29–30). While Panaïté's observations provide valuable insights, it is important to expand and nuance her arguments to fully understand the complexity of *La Petite Dernière* as a site of memory. Much like the broader framework of *Postcolonial Realms of Memory*, queer identities remain invisibilized. Additionally, I take issue with the idea of postcolonial literature as a *restorative* site of memory – a term that does not recognize that these archives develop concurrently and independently to official ones.

Instead, I propose considering *La Petite Dernière* as a *fugitive* site of memory. Indeed, I argue that Daas's text can be situated within what Fred Moten and Stefano Harney (2013) call "the undercommons," which they define as social spaces where marginalized voices, to resist dominant structures, find alternative ways of living and being together in their fugitivity. At the core of the undercommons is "fugitive planning," a decentralized and informal collective act that aims to create liberated forms of knowledge – and by extension, memory-making. As such, the undercommons become an archival source that exists, to borrow from Jack Halberstam's opening essay to Moten and Harney's *The Undercommons*, beneath (in clandestinity) and beyond (in transgression) official ones.[1] This approach rejects the idea of restoring or reforming existing structures and instead promotes "a gathering in the break of all those already broken voices" (132). Brokenness, as a quality that brings together all fugitives, including disabled, poor, racialized, queer people, becomes a foundation to "tear [...] shit down completely and build something new," and, in the process, "refuse to ask for recognition" (151). This project of embracing brokenness is particularly relevant in the French context and can help us understand intersectional identities like Daas's within the framework of universalism, central to discourses on France's national narratives.[2]

Moten and Harney identify specific physical spaces but also attribute a social value to texts where we can trace the undercommons (108). Within those spaces, people engage in the work of "study," which Halberstam summarizes as "a mode of thinking with others separate

---

[1] Halberstam's preface, "The wild beyond: With and for the undercommons," can be read alongside his latest book, *Wild Things: The Desire of Disorder* (2020), in which he draws an analogy between colonialism and heteronormativity, two structures that impose order, and where wildness – embodied by racialized and queer subjects – needs to be controlled. He recognizes wildness as "a chaotic force of nature, the outside of categorization, unrestrained forms of embodiment, the refusal to submit to social regulation, loss of control, the unpredictable" (3).

[2] See Julien Suaudeau and Mame-Fatou Niang's *Universalisme* (2022). They advocate for a new form of universalism, one that recognizes intersectional identities like Daas's, through the metaphorical image of *Kintsugi* – a repaired broken vase in Japanese culture (10–11).

from the thinking that the institution requires of you" (11). In the first part of this chapter, I will demonstrate how Daas asserts this conceptual approach through writing, using it as a form of study where she embraces her brokenness outside the bounds of traditional educational and literary conventions. Through this process, she invites others to join her in what Moten and Harney call mutual "debt," a concept that must be understood beyond the financial sense to encompass a broader social and moral dimension. Considering the power dynamic involved in the debt/credit process, they argue for the importance of valuing the debts to our communities and refusing those due to institutions. They explain: "when you enter into the social world of study [...] you start to lose track of your debts and begin to [...] build them in a way that allows for everyone to feel that she or he can contribute or not contribute to being in a space" (109). As I will show in the second section of this chapter, Fatima attempts to find in social spaces – lesbian and Muslim communities – potential undercommons, but faces up to the reality of oppressive indebtedness that requires her to negate part of her identity to achieve real credi(bility) within the group.[3] By sharing the process through which she gets rid of those debts to "build something new," *La Petite Dernière* serves as a guide towards the undercommons, a fugitive *lieu de mémoire* that can be passed on.

Towards the undercommons: brokenness in writing

Virginie Despentes, in her brief commentary on *La Petite Dernière*, explains (2020): "Le monologue de Fatima Daas se construit par fragments [...]. Ici l'écriture cherche à inventer l'impossible: comment tout concilier, comment respirer dans la honte" [Here, writing seeks to invent the impossible: how to reconcile everything, how to breathe in shame]. Despentes identifies here different, but related, characteristics that distinguish Daas's writing. One of the most striking features of *La Petite Dernière* is indeed its distinctive, fragmented style. This is evident in the non-chronological flashbacks and the incorporation of various genres – letters, text messages, song lyrics – within the narrative. This fragmentation is also largely attributed to a specific stylistic choice: the

---

3 I use the word "credi(bility)" here and throughout the chapter as a play on words that evokes Moten and Harney's concepts of debt/credit and the notion of legitimacy in the groups where Fatima seeks refuge.

deliberate use of short sentences, often at the beginning of each new section that can be identified with the repetition of "Je m'appelle Fatima" [My name is Fatima]. In these opening lines, the protagonist reveals different facets of her identity in unexpected ways, including her asthma. Daas discusses in an interview that she intentionally incorporated breathing as a motif to symbolize the discomfort she experiences in society:

> Typographiquement dans le texte il y a des blancs, il y a des silences, il y a vraiment ce jeu-là autour de la respiration. Dans un second temps, l'asthme ce n'est pas anodin si je l'ai mis, ça va aussi avec le fait de ne pas trouver sa place, de manquer d'air, d'étouffer dans une société excluante." (Stroia 161)
>
> [Typographically in the text there are blanks, there are silences, there really is this play around breathing. Secondly, it is not insignificant that I included asthma; it also goes with the fact of not finding one's place, lacking air, suffocating in an excluding society.]

This condition, with its episodic nature, mirrors Daas's fragmented narrative style and serves as a metaphor for her fugitive resistance in living and expressing herself authentically and freely within a society that often seeks to constrain and define her; in other words, strangle her.

Fatima often talks about her asthma, saying, "Je suis porteuse d'une maladie invisible" [I carry an invisible illness] (37). Here, "je suis porteuse" [I carry], despite it being a common expression to describe an illness, suggests a sense of control, strength, and agency over her condition. Furthermore, reflecting on the causes that contribute to her asthma attacks, she explains, "Il m'a fallu du temps pour savoir que mes crises respiratoires pouvaient être déclenchées par des émotions" [It took me a while to realize that my asthma attacks could be triggered by emotions] (12). The recognition of her emotional triggers and the importance of conveying them through her writing style is an important aspect of the undercommons. The concept of hapticality, described by Moten and Harney as "the capacity to feel through others, for others to feel through you, for you to feel them feeling you," is central here.[4] They note that this feeling, inherent to the undercommons, "is not regulated, at least not successfully, by a state, a religion, a people, an

---

4 See Denis Provencher's chapter, "Abdellah Taïa's *transfilial* memories of Genet's tomb in Larache," in this volume, and his reference to cinematic and the digital haptic gaze.

empire, a piece of land, a totem" (98). Fatima's writing exemplifies this process, as she transmits her feelings and experiences and allows others to connect and empathize with her narrative. Accepting to "respirer dans la honte" becomes an active endeavor to resist dominant literary and social structures.

The fact that Fatima inconsistently adheres to her treatment becomes a symbolic gesture towards cultivating this resistance. She reveals:

> Je m'appelle Fatima.
>
> Je suis asthmatique allergique.
>
> Les médecins disent que je ne prends pas "sérieusement" mon traitement.
>
> Il m'arrive d'oublier mon traitement.
>
> De décider d'arrêter de le prendre à cause des effets indésirables.
>
> De décider d'arrêter de le prendre pour d'autres raisons. (20)
>
> [My name is Fatima.
>
> I have allergic asthma.
>
> The doctors say that I don't take my treatment "seriously."
>
> Sometimes I forget to take my treatment.
>
> I decide to stop taking it because of the side effects.
>
> I decide to stop taking it for other reasons.]

She identifies here specific reasons for her inconsistency with medical advice – whether forgetting or intentionally stopping due to side effects. However, by stating "pour d'autres raisons" [for other reasons], she alludes to a more covert purpose that we can identify in the lines that follow the above passage. She explains:

> Ils disent qu'oublier mon traitement, c'est refuser de prendre soin de moi, de mon corps, de ma santé.
>
> « Ils »: ceux qui ont essayé de me faire comprendre ma maladie, que je ne comprends pas.
>
> [...] celles et ceux que j'ai croisés dans les hôpitaux avec leurs blouses blanches ou bleues, celles et ceux qui m'ont appris à respirer correctement, comme les autres. (20)

> [They say that forgetting my treatment is refusing to take care of myself, my body, and my health.
>
> "They": those who have tried to make me understand my illness, which I do not understand.
>
> [...] those I met in hospitals with their white or blue coats, those who taught me to breathe correctly, like everyone else.]

Intentionally neglecting her treatment reflects her intention to reject being passively defined by doctors or societal expectations. Her defiance against "Ils" [They], the medical authorities, emphasizes her individuality and her refusal to conform to being "comme les autres" [like the others] at the risk of not being taken "seriously." While here it refers to the medical realm, she faces a similar struggle regarding "seriousness" in another space, this time more directly related to her writing for which she, in line with Moten and Harney's "fugitive planning," "refuse[s] to ask for recognition" (151).

Moten and Harney argue, through the examination of the commons of the university, that educational spaces are deeply entrenched in capitalist and colonial logics. They insist on the processes of exclusion, commodification, and marginalization that such an institution perpetuates (22–43); a critique that Fatima echoes in *La Petite Dernière*. After high school, she joined *hypokhâgne* (a preparatory class) but soon found the structure oppressive. She writes:

> Je dois:
>
> Travailler plusieurs heures après chaque journée de cours.
>
> Apprendre par cœur des dates, des définitions.
>
> Me taper des khôlles, lire et commenter des textes écrits exclusivement par des hommes blancs hétéros cisgenres. (72)
>
> [I have to:
>
> Work several hours after each day of classes.
>
> Memorize dates and definitions.
>
> Take oral exams, read, and comment on texts written exclusively by white, heterosexual, cisgender men.]

Hypokhâgne in France is known for preparing students for entrance to the École Normale Supérieure (an elite institution in higher education), a process of "professionalization," that, as Moten and Harney discuss, strips away the radical and transformative potential of education (30–36). Fatima's experience exemplifies their criticism on several levels. The rote memorization of dates and definitions and the extensive hours of study reflect the standardization and commodification of knowledge. Her use of "je dois" [I have to] highlights the fact that such an institution aims to produce compliant subjects to reinforce capitalist and colonial systems. This system fails to recognize or include the contributions and perspectives of marginalized groups, as evidenced by the narrow focus on certain texts that makes it difficult for students like Fatima to see themselves reflected in their studies and in the institution.

This ostracism is further demonstrated when Fatima recounts a specific instance during her first year at *hypokhâgne*. A professor confronted her and accused her of cheating, alleging she had not written her own assignment. This episode led to her profound disillusionment with the system. She reveals:

> Puis j'ai réalisé que prouver, démontrer, me rendre légitime, montrer ce que je valais n'était pas le lot des autres élèves qui étaient à l'intérieur, au chaud. Personne n'avait à argumenter pendant dix minutes, en t-shirt, dans le froid, pour prouver qu'il avait bien mérité un dix-sept sur vingt.
>
> Un mois plus tard, j'ai arrêté la prépa.
>
> Je ne suis pas allée en médecine.
>
> Je n'ai pas intégré Sciences Po.
>
> J'ai écrit. (74)
>
> [Then I realized that proving, demonstrating, making myself legitimate, showing my worth was not something the other students, who were warm inside, had to do. No one had to argue for ten minutes, in a t-shirt, in the cold, to prove that they truly deserved a 17 out of 20.
>
> A month later, I quit the preparatory class.
>
> I did not go to med school.
>
> I did not get into Sciences Po.
>
> I wrote.]

Interestingly, through her description of her feelings when she is taken to task, she uses vocabulary related to legality. This reflects, as Moten and Harney argue when comparing the university to prison, the punitive nature of the institution and the alienation of those who refuse to comply (41–42). Instead of continuing in a system that criminalizes her, she chose to pursue writing – a form of self-expression that exists outside educational boundaries.[5]

Despite the limitations of educational systems, Moten and Harney see potential for opposing their structures at the margin, yet within their walls, where informal practices of knowledge production can happen. Despite having left institutional education, Daas continues to intervene in the French school system. In an interview, Daas, when prompted to comment on her writing style as a way of "resisting [...] classicism," reflects on her role in transmitting a certain liberatory form of learning:

> I think a flowery style makes writing inaccessible. Yet if anything should be accessible to everyone, it's writing. It's the easiest thing to do. You can go anywhere, take a pen or a phone, and write. When I do events in middle schools and high schools with young people, there's a sense of gratitude because they think *even I could do this*. And I'm happy – I don't take that badly. On the contrary: it's super that young people say to themselves "If I want to write something, I could do that too. I can write in the style I want." (Moroz)

Through her writing and engagement with young people, Daas invites them to join her in fugitive study. She encourages them to accept their "brokenness" by showing them that it is possible to integrate a style deemed unconventional, or not credi(ble), in literature.

Joining the undercommons also implies a certain labor, one that consists of, Moten and Harney explain, "picking stuff up" and "taking turns doing things for each other" (109). This idea ties into the metaphor of debt and credit. Fatima notes that the students she met felt a sense of "indebtedness" ("gratitude") for her intervention in their lives, but it is now their turn to "pick stuff up." *La Petite Dernière* serves as a guide for those who wish to find the path towards the undercommons, by showing how to shed debts towards literary conventions but also, as I will show in the second part of this chapter, communities where one can be tempted initially to seek refuge.

---

5 See Frances Egan's article "Making space for queer Muslim women: (Dis)orientation in Fatima Daas's *La Petite Dernière*." Drawing on the work of Sara Ahmed, Egan examines different spaces in *La Petite Dernière*, including the classroom, to show how Fatima "inhabit[s] familiar sites" to create disorientation (162).

A guide to liberation from bad debts

In the first part of my examination of *La Petite Dernière*, I discussed educational and medical spaces that have historically marginalized racialized and queer communities. In this section, I examine Fatima's experience with two other spaces that initially seem to be potential undercommons where she can seek refuge: lesbian hubs and groups as well as the mosque, each representing a facet of her identity. Through this exploration, she aims to find acceptance for the brokenness that this duality creates. However, as I will demonstrate, her attempts to establish a form of "study" within these frameworks ultimately fail, leaving her with unresolved conflicts. This failure can be analyzed through Moten and Harney's metaphor of institutional debts, which perpetuate a power dynamic between debtors and creditors. These oppressive structures dictate which identities are deemed credi(ble) and impose the number of debts required to gain acceptance – one that Fatima is unable to pay without abandoning one part of her identity as a lesbian and Muslim woman.

To understand these power dynamics, let us first examine Fatima's involvement in lesbian groups where she seeks solidarity. With one of her lovers, Cassandra, she discovers queer spaces in Paris:

> On s'est immergées dans le monde lesbien, les afterworks en non-mixité, les soirées Barbieturix, les soirées queers à La Java.
>
> Je pensais ces espaces comme des refuges. (83)
>
> [We immersed ourselves in the lesbian world, the non-mixity afterworks, the Barbieturix parties, the queer parties at La Java.
>
> I thought of these spaces as refuges.]

Initially, Fatima views these hubs of lesbian life and culture in Paris as "refuge," and hence potential undercommons. However, the use of the past tense in "je pensais" suggests a shift in her perception. In addition, the shift from "we" to "I" indicates the difference between Fatima's experience with the group and Cassandra's. Indeed, despite the fact that Cassandra "n'avait rien d'une lesbienne, ni les codes vestimentaires, ni les valeurs communautaires, ni une ambition féministe surdimensionnée" [did not look like a lesbian, neither the dress codes, nor the communitarian values, nor an oversized feminist ambition] (83), it is Fatima who is ostracized in that space.

Fatima's involvement with people from an LGBTQ activist group further validates her negative experience:

> Cassandra et moi, on s'était mises en arrêt pour la Gay pride.
>
> Une amie militante, qui m'avait entendue me vanter, m'a attrapée par le bras pour me corriger.
>
> – La PRIDE, Fatima! Ne dis pas la Gay pride, tu invisibilises les lesbiennes et tout le reste de la communauté en disant Gay pride.
>
> [...]
>
> J'apprenais avec elle.
>
> J'ai remplacé la Gay pride par la pride.
>
> Cassandra et moi, on ne savait pas encore que, étant lesbiennes, il y avait tout un monde à adopter ou à avorter. (84)
>
> [Cassandra and I stopped work for the Gay Pride.
>
> An activist friend, who had heard me bragging, grabbed my arm to correct me.
>
> – PRIDE, Fatima! Don't say Gay pride, you make lesbians and the rest of the community invisible by saying Gay pride.
>
> [...]
>
> I was learning with her.
>
> I replaced Gay pride with pride.]
>
> Cassandra and I didn't yet know that, as lesbians, there was a whole world to adopt or abort.

At first sight, this space seems to offer Fatima some of the foundations of the undercommons. It is a place of study ("learning with") where she feels "indebted" for the feedback she receives. However, a discernible power dynamic permeates this exchange, breaking the pact of the undercommons and threatening Fatima's credi(bility). For instance, the forceful grabbing of Fatima's arm is an explicit physical assertion of power, but there are more covert elements at play too. For example, the accusation that Fatima contributes to the invisibility of lesbians by using the expression "Gay pride" paradoxically highlights her own marginalization within the group. The expectation to either "adopt or abort" a "whole world" reflects a model of inclusion that necessitates the exclusion of certain aspects of her life. "Adopting" suggests the formation of new familial bonds within the group, but it also implies a conscious decision to sever – symbolized by the violent connotation of "avorter" – potential connections with her own family, including her religion. In other words, this space determines which part of her identity is credi(ble) and ultimately imposes a binary view of her identity, which, as I will further develop at the end of this chapter, Fatima rejects.

Cassandra, unlike Fatima, does not have to symbolically "abort" her family to fully embrace queer spaces. Fatima reveals that her lover "quitte Toulouse pour Paris, laissant derrière elle ses parents et ses petits frères" [left Toulouse for Paris, leaving behind her parents and younger brothers], but she immediately corrects her statement: "Je dis 'laissant derrière elle,' mais Cassandra n'a rien laissé" [I say "leaving behind," but Cassandra didn't leave anything] (84). She points out a deeper realization of Cassandra's privilege: "Quitter le domicile sans s'en vouloir, sans être pour autant une grosse merde, sans avoir la sensation en franchissant la porte, pendant le déménagement, et des années plus tard, d'avoir trahi l'ensemble de ses valeurs familiales à cause d'une seule mauvaise décision" [Leaving home without self-reproach, without being a big shit, without feeling like a traitor to one's family values, when walking out the door, during the move and even years later, because of a single bad decision] (85). In this context, Cassandra's privilege lies not just in her physical ability to move from one regional city to Paris, the gay and lesbian central capital, but also in her emotional freedom to do so without guilt or debts. It is important to note that Fatima does not declare that she is burdened by debts imposed by her family but by her "valeurs familiales." More than a structural obligation, these values, in particular Islam, are integral to her identity, and she does not wish to discard them. Instead, she seeks a way to reconcile them with her queerness.

In addition, Fatima's reluctance to "avorter" her ties with her roots stems from the complex dichotomies imposed by societal norms and colonial mindsets. In an interview, Daas criticizes the binary thinking that, "Tu n'es pas une assez bonne lesbienne si t'es musulmane et de l'autre côté tu n'es pas une assez bonne musulmane si t'es lesbienne" [You're not a good enough lesbian if you're Muslim, and, on the other hand, you're not a good enough Muslim if you're a lesbian]. She rejects the notion that these identities are incompatible. In the same interview, she notes that criticism often comes from those questioning her queerness as a Muslim rather than her Muslim identity as a queer person. Daas elaborates, "Mais c'est en fait sauver la petite lesbienne maghrébine musulmane de ce qu'elle pense être vrai, être bon. C'est de la pure et dure colonisation" [But it's actually saving the little Maghrebi Muslim lesbian from what she thinks is true, what is good. It's pure and simple colonization] (Stroia 166). She suggests that France's national narrative portrays Islam as oppressive, and France as liberatory, a perspective rooted in colonial legacies that she does not want to reinforce. As such, she challenges the narrative of "coming out" that would require her to abandon one identity for another. For Fatima, this is not as simple as moving to Paris, like Cassandra, to join the lesbian communities. Instead, it implies a continuous negotiation, involving multiple "comings and goings," with Islam and her family.

I use the expression "coming and going" in reference to Denis Provencher's (2017) reflections on what he calls "modern coming out" of queer Maghrebi French men, who, born in or having migrated to France, mobilize artistic and linguistic strategies to build and assert their queer identities in France. These strategies, which aim to navigate transcultural and transnational temporalities, include "transfiliation" and the "flexible accumulation of language" – two forms of community-making and liberated self-expression that align with some of the foundations of the undercommons. Unlike other queer artists such as Abdellah Taïa and 2Fik, identified by Provencher as individuals who successfully employ such tactics, Daas does not explicitly assert, "Je suis lesbienne et musulmane" in her book. Fatima even reveals in the novel: "À aucun moment je ne dis les mots 'gay' ou 'lesbienne'; je dis 'ils' par pudeur" [At no point do I say the words "gay" or "lesbian"; I say "they" out of modesty/shame] (138). Although she makes this comment to describe a conversation about homosexuality in Islam with her mother, her avoidance of these words permeates the entire book. Fatima uses the word "lesbienne" sparingly (only eight times), and never directly in relation to herself.

This pattern resonates with Provencher's concept of the "impossible je," which describes individuals who "have not (yet) acquired the 'flexible language' or the economic and cultural capital in an urban setting." Provencher elaborates that "impossible subjects" stand out by "us[ing] statements that highlight the collective with the subject pronouns 'we' and 'they,' as well as topic sentences that underscore subjects like 'my family,' 'the country,' and 'my religion,'" alongside a "series of disconnected 'je' statements" ("Farid's impossible 'je'" 113). At first glance, those features are similar to Fatima's approach in *La Petite Dernière* and could reflect her attachment to the debts she owes her family and her Muslim community at the expense of the self. Unlike the impossible subjects, Daas possesses the cultural capital, as exemplified by her writing *La Petite Dernière*. However, she faces another challenge that hinders her ability to declare "je suis lesbienne et musulmane": her gender. I am not suggesting that Islam is inherently oppressive to women, which would reinforce the colonial mindsets she opposes. Rather, her gender presents an additional layer of complexity in accessing the language of Islam necessary for a "flexible accumulation of language," a challenge she navigates and overcomes through her work.

During one of her several visits to the mosque, she seeks a form of collective "study" with the imam to get validation about the fact that being both homosexual and Muslim is possible. To frame her question, she pretends it is for "une amie lesbienne musulmane" [a lesbian Muslim friend] and asks the imam for advice on "comment la conseiller, comment faire pour qu'elle ne se sente pas excommuniée" [how to advise her and how to help her not feel excommunicated] (128). While it is clear she is seeking guidance on reconciling both identities, the imam suggests repentance and declares homosexuality a sin. He recommends several spiritual actions, known as *thawab*, such as fasting and prayers, which in Islam are considered a sort of "debt" that, if performed, would restore her credi(bility). Fatima is tempted to confront him because "l'homosexualité féminine n'est pas abordée dans le Coran" [lesbianism is not addressed in the Quran]. While she does not directly challenge him, it is understood that she discredits his interpretation. Later, she reflects on the authority of the imam, paralleling her experiences with medical institutions – "L'imam, c'est aussi un docteur. Il est paternaliste, il répète qu'il faut prendre sérieusement le traitement et ne pas l'arrêter" [The imam is also a doctor. He is paternalistic, repeatedly emphasizing that the treatment must be taken seriously and not stopped] (169). She also compares her experience with him to educational authority figures – "Entrer dans le bureau de l'imam, c'est entrer dans le bureau du proviseur. J'ai encore fait une bêtise, une erreur, je vais être sanctionnée" [Entering the imam's office feels like entering the principal's office. I've messed up again, made a mistake, and I'm going to be punished] (170). This suggests that while she has tried to follow the imam's recommendations, the framework provided does not include people like her, who are criminalized within that space. She stops treatment and leaves *hypokhâgne*, with one goal: writing. Similarly, writing becomes her solution, a place where she can address female homosexuality and being Muslim.

Although she discredits what the imam says, she finds some value in his suggestion. She pauses in the narrative to reflect internally on his allusion to homosexuality as "une épreuve" [a trial] in her faith. Rather than interpreting it strictly according to its dictionary sense, she offers her own definition:

Une épreuve: nom féminin.

Événement douloureux, malheur.

Expérience à laquelle on soumet une personne qui est susceptible d'établir la valeur positive de cette qualité.

Difficulté qui éprouve le courage de quelqu'un, qui provoque chez lui de la souffrance. (128)

[A trial: feminine noun.

A painful event, misfortune.

An experience to which a person is subjected, likely to establish the positive value of this quality.

A difficulty that tests someone's courage, causing them suffering.]

While I have translated "épreuve" as "trial," which, in a religious context, describes overcoming difficult times that can lead to sin, it can also be interpreted differently: as a medical or school test, both of which have caused Fatima difficulties and suffering but have also led to a positive outcome, writing, for which "une épreuve" can take the meaning of a draft.

Interestingly, in the first line of her definition, where she specifies the gender of the word, we can locate the source that ultimately helps her find answers. Beyond grammatical specificity, she ascribes a feminine quality to her trial or, more specifically, to overcoming it. After all, when Fatima describes her "debts" towards Islam, she does so through the fact that she "porte le nom d'un personnage symbolique" [bears the name of a symbolic character in Islam], the first daughter of the prophet Mohamed. This indebtedness to the feminine also reflects in her relationship with another woman. Even though she holds similar views to the imam on homosexuality, her mother allows space for Fatima's self-expression and negotiation of her identity. Fatima notes, for example, that her mother attempts to show empathy for queer people, which allows her to contest some of her mother's initial statements.

This dynamic ultimately encourages Fatima to share the "épreuve" (draft) of her book's (*La Petite Dernière*) plot with her mother: "Ça raconte l'histoire d'une fille qui n'est pas vraiment une fille, qui n'est ni algérienne ni française, ni clichoise ni parisienne, une musulmane je crois, mais pas une bonne musulmane, une lesbienne avec une homophobie intégrée. Quoi d'autre?" [It tells the story of a girl who isn't really a girl, who is neither Algerian nor French, neither from Clichy nor Parisian, a Muslim, I believe, but not a good Muslim, a lesbian with internalized homophobia. What else?] (187). Ultimately, the way Fatima presents her narrative exemplifies a flexible accumulation of language, which allows her to navigate and detach from rigid identity categories to reflect the complex aspects of her own identity. She asserts, like Abdellah Taïa and 2Fik, whom I have previously mentioned, the fact that it is possible to be Muslim and a lesbian, outside definitions of what constitutes a credi(ble) – "une bonne" – one. It also manifests in the use of the structure "ni... ni," which, drawing on Françoise Lionnet and Shu-mei Shih's (2005) critical concept of "minor transnationalism," should be seen as a refusal to accept binary thinking and simplified narratives of hybridity and postcolonial identities that ultimately reduce the complexity of her intersectional identities and undermine the possibility of community building.

Conclusion: quoi d'autre?

The concept of "minor transnationalism" allows me to return to my initial criticism of the limitation of examining Daas's *La Petite Dernière* as simply a postcolonial realm of memory. It also enables me to conclude with a reflection on "trans" as an important marker of Daas's work. Her statement in the description of her book, "Ça raconte l'histoire d'une fille qui n'est pas vraiment une fille," first confirms Fatima's expression of her gender ambiguity throughout the novel, indicating, for example, that she does not relate to the clothing and social codes associated with the gender assigned to her – perhaps the reason why she does not use the word "lesbian" directly to describe herself. More broadly, embracing transness is also a refusal of fixity, essential for the fugitive planning of the undercommons. Moten and Harney explain this as a process of "regendering and transgendering" to resist forms of governance (50).

My primary interest lies in the concept of "regendering" to understand Fatima's choice to avoid the use of the "je" pronoun. This choice is not a strategy to conceal her identity or a characteristic of an "impossible subject," but rather an assertion of the "elle," which is not about affirming her gender but is similar to Sara Ahmed's approach of regendering her work by refusing to cite white men – as an opposition to academic patriarchal white structures – and exclusively using the feminine third person. This methodology is part of a politic of "[c]itation [a]s feminist [and queer] memory" (*Living a Feminist Life* 15). She explains:

> Citation is how we acknowledge our debt to those who came before; those who helped us find our way when the way was obscured because we deviated from the paths we were told to follow. In this book, I cite feminists of color who have contributed to the project of naming and dismantling the institutions of patriarchal whiteness. (17)

This act of citation is integral to the project of the undercommons, which thrives on the recognition and celebration of marginalized voices that challenge dominant paradigms. By offering an "elle" to her readers, Daas leaves a trace in the feminist and queer memory path, creating a space where new forms of knowledge and resistance can flourish, ones that we will be able to cite – in other words, to follow. However, we cannot forget that Daas follows a path carved by others. My reference to Provencher's work is an acknowledgment of Daas joining the transfilial relationships of others who have made strides to create new ways for Queer Maghrebi French authors and artists to express themselves. Daas is, after all, "La petite dernière," which she uses to describe the fact that she is the last child in her family, but also the last one in that literary family.

I cannot conclude without acknowledging my indebtedness to Black studies, which are central to the undercommons. Black critical thought has played a pivotal role in challenging France's national narrative and creating fugitive paths for marginalized voices to establish their own *lieux de mémoire*. Cited by Moten and Harney, Édouard Glissant is particularly relevant to the work I have endeavored to accomplish in this chapter. Moten and Harney draw on Glissant's idea of "consenting not to be a single being" to suggest that the work of the undercommons is inseparable from community building (154) – a concept highly relevant to Daas's refusal of the individual "je." Glissant's work has helped shape our editorial efforts to challenge Nora's conceptualization of *lieux de mémoire*. His intellectual peer, Patrick Chamoiseau – though only mentioned here in this conclusion – has also been influential in my examination of Daas's work. Explaining the concept of *traces-mémoires*, Chamoiseau writes:

> Les mémoires irradient dans la Trace, elles l'habitent d'une

présence-sans-matière offerte à l'émotion. Leurs associations, Traces-mémoires, ne font pas monuments, ni se cristallisent une mémoire unique: elles sont jeu des mémoires qui se sont emmêlées. Elles ne révèlent pas de la geste coloniale mais des déflagrations qui en ont résulté. Leurs significations demeurent évolutives, non-figées univoques comme celles du monument. Elles me font entendre-voir-toucher-imaginer l'emmêlée des histoires qui ont tissé la terre. (*Écrire en pays dominé* 120)

[Memories radiate in the Trace, they inhabit it with an immaterial presence offered to emotion. Their associations, Traces-memories, do not create monuments, nor crystallize into a single memory: they are the interplay of intertwined memories. They do not reveal the colonial gesture but the explosions that resulted from it. Their meanings remain evolving, unfixed, and ambiguous, unlike those of monuments. They make me hear-see-touch-imagine the entanglement of histories that have woven the land.]

La Petite Dernière serves as a vehicle for these *traces-mémoires*, through which personal and collective narratives intermingle and evolve. Her approach diverges from a singular historical narrative to engage with complex intersectional identities. Daas's engagement in the literary landscape also prompts me here to consider the concept of a *tracée littéraire*, an approach through which the *traces-mémoires* are expressed and communicated in literature. Patrick Chamoiseau and Raphaël Confiant reflect on the development of the *tracée*, which they describe as "nocturne, à moitié clandestine" [nocturnal, and semi-clandestine] (*Lettres créoles* 35). In other words, these narrative forms demand decoding because they are not immediately evident; they demand an affective connection, primarily accessible to those familiar with marginalized perspectives. It is a narrative that must not only be interpreted but also transmitted – two tasks that I aimed to undertake in this chapter and which I hope others will continue to accomplish.

Works cited

Achille, Étienne, Charles Forsdick, and Lydie Moudileno. *Postcolonial Realms of Memory: Sites and Symbols in Modern France*. Liverpool UP, 2020.
Ahmed, Sara. *Living a Feminist Life*. Duke UP, 2016.
Ayuso, Julia Webster. "People like her didn't exist in French novels. Until she wrote one." *New York Times*. November 19, 2021.

Chamoiseau, Patrick. *Écrire en pays dominé*. Gallimard, 1997.
Chamoiseau, Patrick, and Raphaël Confiant. *Lettres créoles. Tracées antillaises et continentales de la littérature: Haïti, Guadeloupe, Martinique, Guyane, 1635–1975*. Hatier, 1991.
Daas, Fatima. *La Petite Dernière*. Notabilia, 2020.
Despentes, Virginie. Endorsement on the back cover of Fatima Daas, *La Petite Dernière*. Notabilia, 2020.
Egan, Frances. "Making space for queer Muslim women: (Dis)orientation in Fatima Daas's *La Petite Dernière*." *Australian Journal of French Studies*, vol. 60, no. 2, 2023, pp. 160–74.
French Institute UK. "In conversation with Fatima Daas." *Youtube.com*. March 11, 2022. www.youtube.com/watch?v=jwX58artzqQ.
Halberstam, Jack. "The wild beyond: With and for the undercommons." Stefano Harney and Fred Moten, *The Undercommons: Fugitive Planning & Black Study*. Minor Compositions, 2013, pp. 2–12.
———. *Wild Things: The Desire of Disorder*. Duke UP, 2020.
Harney, Stefano, and Fred Moten. *The Undercommons: Fugitive Planning & Black Study*. Minor Compositions, 2013.
Lionnet, Françoise, and Shu-mei Shih. *Minor Transnationalism*. Duke UP, 2005.
Moten, Fred, and Stefano Harney. *The Undercommons: Fugitive Planning & Black Studies*. Minor Compositions, 2013.
Moroz, Sarah. "An unsentimental education." *Book Forum*. January 6, 2022. https://bhaskars2.sg-host.com/2021/01/page/3/.
Nora, Pierre. "Between memory and history: *Les Lieux de mémoire*." Translated by Marc Roudebush. *Representations*, vol. 26, 1989, pp. 7–24.
Panaïté, Oana. "Archives." *Postcolonial Realms of Memory: Sites and Symbols in Modern France*, edited by Étienne Achille, Charles Forsdick, and Lydie Moudileno. Liverpool UP, 2020, pp. 23–33.
Provencher, Denis M. "Farid's impossible 'je.'" *Journal of Language and Sexuality*, vol. 5, no. 1, 2016, pp. 113–39.
———. *Queer Maghrebi French: Language, Temporalities, Transfiliations*. Liverpool UP, 2017.
Stroia, Adina. "Entretien avec Fatima Daas." *Contemporary French and Francophone Studies*, vol. 27, no. 2, 2023, pp. 158–70.
Suaudeau, Julien, and Mame-Fatou Niang. *Universalisme*. Anamosa, 2022.

CHAPTER NINETEEN

Emotional geographies, queer realms of memory
Act Up-Paris and *120 battements par minute* (2017)

Ryan K. Schroth

In this chapter, I am interested in exploring the intersection of affect, space, and queer memory within Robin Campillo's important 2017 film, *120 battements par minute* (*120 BPM*). The film, as I will demonstrate, visualizes several key spaces that were central to early AIDS activism in France. By examining what queer and critical geographers have called "emotional geographies" (Davidson and Milligan), I aim to trace the ways in which a consideration of these spaces and the emotions that inevitably contour them might influence and even produce novel forms of queer memory-making. I also want to highlight how, by considering space alongside affect, these emotional geographies are made political, especially durng the affectively ambivalent early period of the HIV/AIDS epidemic. Finally, I will show how Pierre Nora's foundational distinction between history and memory might map onto (or not) these emotional geographies as they constitute and construct specifically queer *lieux de mémoire*.

From the outset, it must be stated that Nora and his contributors do not speak of affect in contemporary terms, but it is nonetheless present in the historian's massive multi-volume *Les Lieux de mémoire* (1984–92). For example, in the third volume, Mona Ozouf discusses the "feeling" of fraternity in "Liberté, égalité, fraternité," while Robert Morrissey demonstrates how a sense of French national feeling was first forged in the Middle Ages by Charlemagne. (In today's parlance, both of these examples discuss the affective experience of belonging.) Nora himself, in his now famous introduction to the first volume, only briefly speaks of affect when he discusses collective remembering, stating that as a process it is "affective et magique" [affective and magical] (25). Nora's comments betray a normative way of thinking about affect: that it is "mystical," and thus inexplicable, excessive, and immaterial. Indeed, much of the secondary literature that Nora's project has inspired subscribes to this understanding of affect (Veyrat-Masson; Legg). One notable outlier, however, is Nison (2019), who locates a sense of affect at the very center of memorialization, arguing that an object or space becomes a *lieu de mémoire* "quand il échappe à l'oubli, par exemple avec l'apposition de plaques commémoratives, et quand une collectivité le réinvestit de son affect et de ses émotions" [when it escapes forgetting, for example with the hanging of commemorative plaques, and when a collectivity reinvests it with its affect and emotions] (109). This chapter illustrates this concomitancy of memory and affect within queer *lieux de mémoire*.

If memory is at least partially an affective process, the same cannot be said for Nora's understanding of history. Indeed, at the heart of Nora's work is what seems to be a false (or at least unnecessary) dichotomy between memory and history. For Nora, history attempts to be objective (though it is not) because it is constructed through official narratives, shaped through historical study, and relies upon authoritative archives. It is inherently political because it involves the cataloguing of the history of the nation-state. However, this reliance on historical authority has, more often than not, meant that queer and other minoritized experiences were altogether forgotten or erased. Furthermore, Nora's distinction between memory and history implies a certain normative chronology: moving from the past (of history) to the present (of memory). In what follows, I will show how Campillo's film, through a scrambling of this chronology, further destabilizes the seemingly distinct boundaries of history and memory through an alternating focus on "legitimate" forms of history (e.g., documentary footage, official obituaries, etc.) and the recording of individual (fictionalized) queer stories. In the end, Campillo's film becomes a queer hybrid document that produces a politicized, embodied, and spatialized form of queer remembering through its deployment of queer affect and its inherent questioning of history and memory.

Act Up-Paris, as perhaps the most influential political organization working to record queer memory at the height of the HIV/

AIDS epidemic in France, was founded in 1989 by a group of French citizens, many of whom were seropositive. Following their American counterparts, they used the same spectacularly disruptive tactics, called "zaps." These political displays were often interruptive, direct-action protests, entailing perhaps "a lunchtime picket or unannounced 'office visit,' or maybe a disruption of a public meeting, fundraiser, or rally" (Goldberg 22). Leveraging the element of surprise, activists used air horns, whistles, chants, flags, signs, and even fake blood in their acts of nonviolent civil disobedience. One zap that the group often repeated was its famous "die-in," in which hundreds of activists would converge upon a spot and lie on the ground, impeding pedestrians and traffic, in an attempt to visualize the death and devastation caused by AIDS. Through their various political demonstrations, the group hoped not only to communicate their fear, sadness, frustration, and anger, but also to elicit the same types of emotional experiences in those who witnessed their actions.

This question of affect is indeed central to both AIDS activism, more broadly, and Act Up-Paris, in particular. One of the group's co-founding presidents, Didier Lestrade, in an interview that aired on France 24, described the affective experiences that gave birth to the Paris chapter, saying that Act Up was "une nouvelle manière de militer [...] surtout en créant des manifestations et des moyens de pression qui étaient absolument nouveaux. En fait, la peur était tellement réelle à la fin des années 90 qu'on a réussi à changer cette peur en activisme" [a new way to militate [...] above all through creating demonstrations and methods of pressure that were absolutely new. In fact, the fear was so real at the end of the 90s that we were able to change this fear into anger] (France 24). The organization was, in part, able to transform this fear into engaged activism through one of its guiding political principles: a deep commitment to valuing all minoritized groups at risk of contracting the deadly disease. Lestrade confirms the group's philosophy of intersectional inclusivity when he writes in *Act Up: Une histoire* (2022) that the group "a essayé de sortir les gays du trou sombre, en les amenant directement au cœur de la ville, en lançant des passerelles idéologiques avec les femmes, les hétéros, les toxicos, les précaires" [tried to get the gays out of this dark hole by bringing them directly to the heart of the city, by launching ideological bridges with women, heteros, addicts, the homeless] (18). In addition to demonstrating the affective landscape of queer life during the beginning of the AIDS crisis, as well as the potent mix of fear and sadness that marks this period, Lestrade also comments on how the group was able to take these negative affects and turn them into political anger and engagement through a philosophy of community and commonality.

While *120 BPM* serves as a fictional portrayal of the group, it indeed borrows from the organization's real-life history. For example, Sean (Nahuel Pérez Biscayart), one of the film's main characters, is inspired by Cleews Vellay, the second president of Act Up-Paris; Nathan (Arnaud Valois), Sean's lover, is based on Hugues Charbonneau, a vice-president of the organization; and the character Thibaut (Antoine Reinartz) was inspired by Lestrade (Vié). Clearly, Campillo's intention is not historical fidelity, but rather a blurring of the lines between what constitutes the historical and the fictional. Campillo challenges historical authority through the integration of several stories that are rich in emotion, namely fear, sadness, outrage, desire, and joy. These fictional narratives allow Campillo to portray (and perhaps incite) various affective responses for the viewer. This intermingling of affective narratives with the "official" history of Act Up-Paris, as well as Campillo's use of archival footage and "legitimate" sources, implicitly questions Nora's distinctions between history and memory, while offering something queer in between the two.

Emotional geographies: the spaces of queer memory in *120 BPM*

My study of the emotional geographies of *120 BPM* contributes to the growing body of literature on the film. Previous research has examined the film's depiction of political organizing (Gledhill; Pember) and its memorialization of queer AIDS victims (Wingrove; Troth). Benjamin Dalton (2022), on the other hand, explores the visualization of "(micro)biological landscapes and cellular processes" (194) in the film's imagery of atomization. Indeed, the film frequently employs tableaux that are composed of smaller repeating images: blood cells, confetti, raindrops, dust particles, and even bodies on the ground during the group's "die-ins." While Dalton understands these tableaux in relation to biological inquiry and the group's growing understanding of HIV virology, I am interested here in the ways in which these tableaux serve as filmic transitions between various spaces and times depicted in the film. By facilitating this movement, these transitions create a spatial and temporal map of mourning and memorialization that speaks to the larger emotional geography of queer AIDS activism during the early part of the pandemic.

In terms of affect, Brian Troth (2021) argues that the cultural trauma of the epidemic continues to haunt gay and queer communities, primarily due to unresolved mourning. He asserts that HIV/AIDS narratives often depict "negative feelings of disgust, shame, or guilt" (132). However, *120 BPM*, I would argue, uniquely emphasizes a range of emotions that includes outrage and joy. While "negative" affects are certainly present within the film, I am interested in how the film might move beyond narratives of disgust, shame, and guilt to include a sense of political outrage and even intense joy. My study, focusing on the intersection of space and affect, explores how the spatial and temporal orientations of affect might generate queer commemoration. Indeed, affects such as outrage and joy are directed outwards towards other bodies (rather than, say, the interior orientation of guilt). This simple (re)orientation imbues the film with a sense of transgression and political engagement that is concomitant with queer forms of memorialization. In addition to the film as a political act of resistance, Maxime Foerster and Daniel Maroun (2021) locate within it a sense of reparation that further counters more conventional AIDS narratives. They argue that the film "urge[s] the contemporary mainstream audience to resume a *travail de mémoire* concerning the worst years of the AIDS pandemic" (124). In short, this chapter examines this *travail de mémoire* while focusing on the spatiotemporal and affective dynamics that constitute it.

Below, I analyze the diverse spaces of affect found within the film in order to better understand how the film memorializes the HIV/AIDS pandemic in France. First, there is the lecture hall, where the organization's members actively thrash out, through democratic means, the political and social agendas of the group; second, there is the street, an important space for political demonstrations and the memorialization of the members the group has lost to the disease; third, the dance floor figures prominently throughout the film as a space of changing emotions, transitioning from anger, to joy, and finally to desire; and lastly, there is the bedroom, which is a space that is both erotic and memorializing. Through examining the ways in which space and affect come together in the film, we are also able to see how these emotional geographies produce novel means to remember and memorialize the losses of the epidemic.

The lecture hall: the heart of Act Up-Paris

In *120 BPM*, the members of Act Up-Paris meet in a university lecture hall for their weekly meetings where they set the political agenda of the organization. Their negotiations, as one might expect, are at times contentious, especially between the militant members of the group and those who are more moderate, evidenced by the division and infighting that takes place in the lecture hall. As the "heart" of the group, the lecture hall is closely aligned with anger, community, and blood. Indeed, from the throwing of fake blood during zaps to computer generated images of blood cells, the film draws on the imagery of blood to visually signify the group's untiring commitment to challenging forms of French universalism that value filiality over more communitarian forms of relationality. This blood serves to translate the group's anger and fear. The affective geography of the lecture hall is thus structured around this form of queer relationality, which is one centered not on "bloodlines" but rather on a "blood boiling" sense of anger that propels the group forward in its political commitments.

Indeed, one of the first scenes of the film illustrates this anger. A small group of activists interrupts a presentation by the *Agence Française contre la lutte du SIDA* (the AFLS, a governmental agency created by François Mitterrand that was notorious for its slow response to the AIDS epidemic). Suddenly, the zap goes wrong, when activists launch blood-filled balloons at the presenter, ultimately sieging the stage and handcuffing the speaker. Campillo splices together the actions of the zap with the heated debriefing that takes place after the event. While Sophie (Adèle Haenel) reminds the group that "on ne s'est jamais permis de menotter qui que ce soit pendant une action" [we've never allowed ourselves to handcuff anyone during an action] (00:08:19), the two activists responsible for the violence, Sean and Max (Félix Maritaud), argue that something had to be done because "l'action merdait" [the action was fucked] and the audience found their "petit numéro [...] folklorique" [little number [...] folkloric] (00:08:38).[1] This sequence serves as an introduction for the viewer to Act Up-Paris's political displays as well as a foundation for understanding the two factions at work within the association. Much of the content of the scenes that take place in the lecture hall focuses on the negotiation of these differing perspectives.

---

1 All translations are my own.

The lecture hall is an institutional space that is both a public and a private space where the intersectional, democratic philosophy driving Act Up comes to light. Despite their differences, the group's members are committed to several overlapping goals: first, to pressure the French government into actively responding to the AIDS crisis; second, to demand that private scientific and pharmaceutical companies share their latest research on the disease; third, to challenge the public's image of the disease as a "gay disease"; and, fourth, to provide preventative information to the groups at the highest risk for contracting the virus. Both factions seem to realize the importance of including other minoritized groups, such as hemophiliacs, drug addicts, and sex workers. This political commitment is visualized in the film through the diversity of the group's membership, which includes people of different ages and ethnicities, seropositive and seronegative people, trans people, people of different abilities, and so on. By forging intra-group political bonds, certain forms of relationality are created that, even if only temporarily, unite the queer community in surprising ways.

The emotional geography of the lecture hall, which serves as the group's de facto curia, is constructed through this sense of contention. The lecture hall, aligned as it is with the revolutionary spirit of May '68, comes to signify a challenge to France's national narrative. At the same time, it is also an institutional space that the activists figuratively "occupy," which charges it with a political energy that ultimately motivates their questioning of French national norms. In this setting, the division of the group mirrors one of the larger political debates taking place in France at that time: the debate around universalism and communitarianism. As the film repeatedly returns to the space of the lecture hall, we realize that it is here that the group, through prosocial strategies, plans their calculated attacks on the republican universalist framework of the French nation-state, which they collectively see as one of the overriding obstacles in their ongoing fight against HIV/AIDS. The lecture hall, described as the group's "heart," pulsates with a politics of identification that embraces diversity and dispersion (Watson 111). Anger, community, and blood structure this affective geography, where the group yearns for relationality beyond traditional "bloodlines," emphasizing a coalition built on difference. The blood used in their demonstrations symbolizes their outrage and the urgency of their actions, vividly representing both life and death amidst the spreading contagion. Blood will remain a central element, capturing the group's political commitments and urgency throughout the film.

The street: anger and mourning

In *120 BPM*, the public space of the street emerges as a central backdrop for Act Up's various political displays as well as its expressions of collective memory. The emotional geography of the street is centered on joy, outrage, and mourning. Campillo, in the sequences that take place in the street, alternates between shots from within the crowd and wider shots from above the crowd. The shots from above the crowd contribute to Campillo's imagery of atomization by focusing on the ways in which individual bodies come together to create a larger tableau. In the sequences in the street, the camera employs a combination of eye level and overhead shots, always focusing on the balance between the individual and the larger group.

One such example is the street demonstration that takes place after the death of a newcomer, Jérémie (Ariel Borenstein). The camera first focuses on the activists shuffling through the streets of Paris; we hear the air horns and whistles, as the camera pans up to show Jérémie's face and name on several signs hovering above the crowd. We realize that Jérémie has died, as group members hold signs in the shape of a cross, like tombstones floating above the crowd. The group chants "SIDA, on meurt / l'indifférence demeure" ["We're dying from AIDS / but the indifference remains"] (00:11:31). As Sean, at the center of the group, leads the chant, his voice cracks and he gestures emphatically, demonstrating a potent mix of outrage and grief. The group slowly advances through the streets of Paris in a solemn display of their collective and accumulated anger.

While this scene certainly works to memorialize queer AIDS victims by focusing on Jérémie's death, it is preceded by a sequence that powerfully remembers earlier political action in the street and ties it to the larger concerns of Act Up-Paris. Campillo constructs a stunning collage that retells the end of Jérémie's life by combining fictional moments with documentary footage of various Act Up interventions, including street demonstrations, images of their die-ins, and the interruption of a Catholic mass. The sequence is held together by a curious voiceover by Jérémie:

> Le mercredi 23 février 1848, le peuple est toujours dans la rue et quelques barricades ont été dressées. Un groupe d'une cinquantaine de manifestants se met en route vers le ministère des Affaires Étrangères, situé boulevard des Capucines. Mais ils trouvent le boulevard barré par les hommes du 14ème de ligne. Une torche à la main, un meneur s'avance,

menaçant, vers un lieutenant. Pensant l'officier en danger, un sergent tire. Croyant à un signal, la troupe ouvre le feu. Un peu plus tard, on relève seize morts et une quarantaine de blessés. Dès lors, la colère explose. Les corps des victimes sont chargés sur des charrettes et promenés à la lueur des flambeaux dans les rues de Paris. (01:08:06)

On Wednesday, 23 February 1848, the people were still in the streets and a few barricades had been set up. A group of about 50 demonstrators set off towards the Ministry of Foreign Affairs, located on Boulevard des Capucines. But they find the boulevard blocked by the men of the 14th line. Torch in hand, a leader advances, threateningly, towards a lieutenant. Thinking the officer is in danger, a sergeant fires. Believing it to be a signal, the troops open fire. A little later, 16 people are killed and some 40 injured. From then on, anger explodes. The bodies of the victims are loaded onto carts and paraded by torchlight through the streets of Paris.

Jérémie's words come from the description of an event that launched the French revolutions of 1848, entitled "La fusillade du boulevard des Capucines" [The shooting on the Boulevard des Capucines]. His narration ties together the *Révolution de février* [February revolution], which led to the end of the July Monarchy, with the contemporary political engagements of Act Up-Paris. These two different albeit similar situations, held together by the demands of the people for governmental action and a collective sense of anger, underscore the French government's neglect and inaction. In the description of the shooting, we notice that the casualties were unwarranted and caused by a literal jumping of the gun, which only serves to highlight the absurdity of the accumulating casualties caused by the AIDS disease. Jérémie's voiceover, combined with the documentary footage of Act Up, ultimately provides an important act of memorialization that visually combines the angry struggles surrounding France's republican universalist ethos with the question of revolution. Thus, while the film questions French republican universalism, it also simultaneously universalizes Act Up-Paris's political commitments by aligning them with other revolutions in French history. The association of the group with both an "official" form of history (e.g., the documentary footage; the February Revolution) and the images of Jérémie's physical decline in the hospital create an emotional geography that ultimately shifts and blurs historical narratives.

However, not all of *120 BPM*'s scenes that take place in the street are motivated by outrage. The Pride parade becomes a moment of group cohesion and joy as Act Up members party together in the streets. Sean suggests that some members of the group attend the parade as *pom-pom girls*. With whistles blaring, we see a group of about eight members dressed in American-style cheerleading uniforms, chanting, "Contre le SIDA, tu n'as pas le choix / Bats-toi, bats-toi, act up! [Against AIDS, you don't have a choice / Fight, fight, act up!] (00:52:17). Again, attentive to the dynamics between the group and individual characters, Campillo uses close-up shots at eye-level of smiling activists to drive home the pure joy that the members experience during the parade. As if to further visualize the importance of both individuals and the collectivity, the sequence contributes to the imagery of atomization as canons shoot confetti into the sky.

In another sequence from a later Pride parade, the group decides to build a float that will be "vraiment festif" [truly festive], allowing them to "danser dans les rues et en même temps [...] parler des traitements" [dance in the streets and at the same time [...] talk about treatments] (01:33:40). They construct a billboard-sized sign that says, in English, on one side, "Ignorance is your enemy," and on the other, "Knowledge is a weapon"; they surround the float with speakers and blare house music. The fact that their messaging is in English is a nod both to the American origins of Act Up and to the accessibility of English as a global language. This affiliation with the English language ensures that the film, in addition to challenging a universalized French national narrative, taps into a more global form of queer memory. In this sense, the film expresses a common sense of outrage that is often associated with the political organizing of queer groups. Indeed, more somber than the first scene, this Pride scene is nonetheless an expression of queer joy in its unique formulation of activism combined with celebration.

In short, the *120 BPM* scenes that take place in the streets serve as putting into practice the group's values, commitments, and objectives. The presence of Act Up-Paris in the street is meant to interrupt the status quo and French society's willful ignorance with regard to the realities of the AIDS crisis. The activists visually demonstrate, through their protests and pride celebrations, the disease's toll as they create an ambulatory queer *lieu de mémoire* that denounces the French government.[2] The emotional geography of the street is a movement between outrage and joy that is again celebratory while retaining the group's revolutionary

---

2   For more on ambulatory *lieux de mémoire*, see Luke Eilderts's chapter in this volume.

spirit. Here, they visibly and physically bring their challenging of the French national narrative into the streets.

The dance floor: community and catharsis

Directly following the Pride parade scenes, the core members of the group go dancing. Throughout the film, the emotional geography of the dance floor is anchored in a cathartic, high-energy dance that embodies the transition from outrage to joy that we identified in the street scenes. To the pulsating beat of house music, the activists purge themselves of the emotional burden of their various zaps. Still, Campillo uses various filmic techniques to remind the viewer that even these spaces of release are political for the activists. Indeed, Campillo employs a relatively horizontal and static camera here, which reinforces the group's egalitarian and intersectional mode of politics. Indeed, as Gledhill (2022) has argued, "this [camera] placement allows a more generalized, communal feeling to arise in the space" (138), which creates "a complex emotional and affective register in these moments, with a distinctly communal and prosocial atmosphere onscreen" (140).

Furthermore, as Watson (2022) has noted, the dance floor operates as a heterotopia, Foucault's (1967) concept of a space where seemingly contradictory elements come to cohabit. As a heterotopia, the dance floor exists both spatially and temporally outside of social norms, narratively sealing off the characters. The disco lights echo the imagery of atomization used throughout the film in their highlighting of various bodily elements of the dancing activists. The dance floor thus becomes a transformative space where group members express their emotions through dancing, jumping, and hugging, collectively exorcizing their pent-up frustrations with one another, the French government, French society, and the toll of the AIDS crisis.

Despite the catharsis that takes place on the dance floor, the threat of the present (i.e., life with HIV/AIDS) is always lurking for the members of Act Up-Paris. Indeed, while the dance floor is connected with "physical release from the despair of the present, [it] cannot ultimately keep it at bay" (Pember 154). In a stunning visualization of this constant reminder, Campillo constructs an elaborate visual transition from the dance floor back to the realities of the group's political work. At the end of the central dance scene, the camera focuses on the pulsating disco lights which slowly morph into dust particles, themselves dancing through the beams of light. As the music continues, these dust particles gradually transform into CGI-rendered blood cells. In a hard cut, the central blood cell is replaced with a hand-drawn image of an infected blood cell as we realize that we have been transported back to the space of the lecture hall and inserted into the middle of a scientific discussion about how the virus replicates itself. Harkening back to the group's intersectional political commitments, these "slippages between these plastic forms – dancing bodies to dancing particles to dancing cells to projected outlines – dehierarchize and horizontalize the forms" (Dalton 200). The imagery of atomization in the transition serves to move the viewer between the space of the dance floor and the lecture hall. Furthermore, the temporal movement achieved in the transition from the past of the dance floor to the present of the classroom mirrors the temporal dissonance inherent in Nora's conceptualization of history vs. memory, where memory is a sort of present recollection of the past. The visual change from dust to infected blood cell embeds the transition in the despair we often feel when we remember the AIDS crisis, while underscoring the invisibility of the virus when first contracted. Indeed, this "traveling" back and forth in temporalities is an example of how queer temporalities always already blur normative chronologies, further troubling Nora's conceptualizations of history and memory.

The bedroom: desire and memorialization

The final space we will discuss, the bedroom, figures prominently in the last third of the film. The emotional geography of the bedroom is focused, first, on the erotic nature of Sean and Nathan's growing relationship, but towards the end of Sean's life, the space becomes imbued with a deep sense of mourning and memorialization. Even as the space of the bedroom is portrayed as a realm of intimacy, the specter of the disease looms over the couple.

The first scene in the bedroom takes place after another dance scene. As Sean and Nathan dance together, the flashing lights begin to obscure their identities. The screen fills with dancing body parts. Gradually, the dancing bodies morph into Sean and Nathan's bodies entangled in bed. After an intimate moment, Nathan remarks on a photo of a younger Sean, which we learn was taken a year before Sean contracted the virus. This retelling of Sean's infection story overlays the erotic desire of the bedroom with the desire to remember. Here, the photo, illustrating

Barthes's (1981) conceptualization of the punctum, triggers the process of remembering, which is then contoured through an affective erotics. The photo further serves to "index," to borrow Margaret Iverson's terminology (2017), Sean's trauma associated with contracting the deadly virus. As a physical trace of Sean's memory, the photo archives the emotional geography of the bedroom which is founded on this overlapping of memory, erotics, and trauma.

After a brief stay in the hospital, Sean and Nathan decide to move in together. Here, the bedroom is associated with Sean's failing health, as his boyfriend and his mother (Saadia Bentaïeb) become his caretakers. The film takes a poignant turn when Sean asks Nathan to administer a lethal dose of a drug to end his life. As Nathan does so, his actions communicate his conflicted emotional state – an intense combination of sadness, fear, anger, and love. After Sean's heart has stopped, his mother and Max dress him and prepare him to be viewed. Sean's fragile and visibly emaciated body, in oversized clothes, is positioned as if lying in state. Slowly, in the middle of the night, the group's core members show up at the apartment. As they file past Sean's body and pay their last respects, the bedroom transitions into a mausoleum. This sequence recalls the earlier scenes in which Act Up members snake through the streets of Paris holding signs with images of deceased former members. The emotional geography of the bedroom functions through a sense of solemnity, as it turns the apartment into a queer Panthéon. A veritable *grand homme*, Sean is remembered and mourned through the assembling community of Act Up members.

Sean's death further unites the Act Up-Paris community. They set aside their philosophical differences and remember and mourn together. In this context, it is through death that community is formed. An important part of this memorialization project is the press release that the Act Up-Paris spokesperson prepares. They memorialize Sean in this way: "Sean faisait de la politique à la première personne. Il était folle, drôle, teigneux, vivant" [Sean was political in a unique way. He was gay, funny, wicked, alive] (02:09:37). The press release and Sean's obituary, as two examples of "official" historical documents, work to archive Sean's life and political work, while the group's insistence on the affective ("funny, wicked") further blurs the lines between history and memory.

(Re)membering Act Up-Paris: the real-world ramifications of the film

By way of conclusion, I would like to briefly consider the real-world consequences of Campillo's film, which drastically changed the organization of Act Up-Paris. In the years leading up to the film, Act Up-Paris had abandoned the disruptive interventions of the group's past in favor of focusing on its scientific expertise and its various prevention campaigns. The group's objectives had transformed in response to the arrival of new HIV tritherapies and PrEP (pre-exposure prophylaxis). However, following the film, Act Up-Paris saw a surge in membership, particularly by young militant activists experienced in antiracist and anticapitalist demonstrations, like *les Gilets jaunes* [the Yellow vests], *Nuit debout* [Up All Night], Black Lives Matter, and the Occupy movement ("Démission"). This new generation of activists worked to reinstate Act Up's former militant tactics and brought with it a renewed revolutionary spirit, clashing with the organization's leadership. Interestingly, in their effort to return to the group's past the organization was modernized by connecting it to contemporary, transnational social movements. In a sort of "self-fulfilling prophecy," the schism announced in the film and evidenced by the scenes of confrontation between the more militant and the more moderate members of the group had become reality.

In 2018, Act Up-Paris' two co-presidents, spokesperson, and a handful of seasoned activists resigned in a press release (Act Up-Paris), which allowed the new generation to take full control of the group. The resigned members created their own organization, *Les actupienNEs* [The Actupiens]. According to their website, they are:

> [F]ondamentalement ActupienNEs, dépositaires de ses luttes passées et récentes, attachéEs à son approche spécifique du combat par la prise en compte de toutes les dimensions médicales et sociales de l'épidémie et la parole des premierEs concernéEs en réponse à un pouvoir médical qui tend à reprendre le contrôle des savoirs sur nos vécus de séropos. ("Qui sommes-nous?")

> [F]undamentally ActupienNEs, custodians of its past and recent struggles, attached to its specific approach to the fight by taking into account all the medical and social dimensions of the epidemic and the voice of those first concerned by the response of a medical power that attempts to take control of our knowledge about our own experiences as seropositives.

Here, in direct opposition to the new leadership of Act Up-Paris, the resigned members position themselves as the "true" descendants of

Act Up. They describe themselves as the record keepers of the group's official memory. As descendants of the first generation of Act Up-Paris activists, they also (perhaps unwittingly) challenge first-hand accounts of the political organization, such as Lestrade's memoirs or Christophe Broqua's *Agir pour ne pas mourir!* (2006). However, whether from the point of view of the resigned members or the incoming leadership, it is clear that *120 BPM* both renewed public interest in the group and reinvested it with fresh political energy. The real-life ramifications of the film's release thus further blur Nora's distinction between history and memory.

Beyond its cinematic and critical success, the film makes clear a few lessons as we catalog queer realms of memory. Space, to varying degrees, is constitutive of most *lieux de mémoire*, but the film underscores, at least with regard to queer *lieux de mémoire*, the important role of both space and affect in sites of queer memory. It is indeed through affect that queer and minoritized individuals can produce novel forms of memory that go beyond – or move between – history and memory (Cvetkovich; Muñoz). The communication of this memory, as we see in the film, is at times contentious – filled with emotion – but it is nonetheless necessary with regard to queer memorialization. The emotional geographies of Campillo's film span Nora's sense of history and memory by combining personal stories, collective narratives, fictional and historiographical accounts, and archival documents. In this sense, it visualizes Halberstam's contention that the queer archive is a "jigsaw puzzle" (170). This interweaving of history and memory is, to be sure, a queer strategy that is at once tactical and compulsory. It allows queer memory to enter into dialogue with normative forms of memory-making and recording while valuing personal queer narratives and affective experiences. In troubling both history and memory, the film ultimately produces a queer *lieu de mémoire* that, beyond evoking affect and effectuating political change, reshapes the very history it represents.

Works cited

Act Up-Paris. "Où lutterons-nous maintenant contre le sida? Certainement plus à Act Up-Paris!" Press release. March 31, 2018. Web.

Barthes, Roland. *Camera Lucida: Reflections on Photography*. Translated by Richard Howard. Hill & Wang, 1981.

Broqua, Christophe. *Agir pour ne pas mourir!* Presses de Science Po, 2006.

Campillo, Robin, dir. *120 battements par minute.* Feature film. Les films de Pierre. France, 2017.

Cvetkovich, Ann. *An Archive of Feelings: Trauma, Sexuality, and Lesbian Public Cultures.* Duke UP, 2003.

Dalton, Benjamin. "Queer, plastic residues: Biological mutability and queer resistance in Robin Campillo's *120 BPM* (2017) and the work of Catherine Malabou." *Modern & Contemporary France*, vol. 30, no. 2, 2022, pp. 193–208.

Davidson, Joyce, and Christine Milligan. "Embodying emotion, sensing space: Introducing emotional geographies." *Social & Cultural Geography*, vol. 5, no. 4, 2004, pp. 523–32.

"Démission de l'équipe dirigeante d'Act Up-Paris." *Lemonde.fr.* April 2, 2018.

Foerster, Maxime, and Daniel Maroun. "The show must go on: HIV/AIDS studies and queer studies in twenty-first-century France." *Contemporary French Civilization*, vol. 46, no. 2, 2021, pp. 121–27.

Foucault, Michel. *Le corps utopique, Les hétérotopies.* Éditions Lignes, 2009.

France 24. "Act Up-Paris: La colère et la vie, un 'livre-document' retrace l'histoire du mouvement." *YouTube.com.* December 1, 2022.

"La Fusillade du Boulevard des Capucines." *À la découverte de l'histoire de France*, 2002. chrisagde.free.fr/histemprestrep/revolution1848a.htm.

Gledhill, Tom. "'House is not universal. House is hyper-specific': Dance music sequences and affect in *120 BPM* and *Eden*." *Modern & Contemporary France*, vol. 30, no. 2, 2022, pp. 129–44.

Goldberg, Ron. *Boy with the Bullhorn: A Memoir and History of ACT UP New York.* Empire State Editions, 2022.

Halberstam, Jack. *In a Queer Time and Place: Transgender Bodies, Subcultural Lives.* New York UP, 2005.

Iverson, Margaret. *Photography, Trace, and Trauma.* U of Chicago P, 2017.

Legg, Stephen. "Contesting and surviving memory: Space, nation, and nostalgia in *Les Lieux de mémoire*." *Environment and Planning D: Society and Space*, vol. 23, no. 4, 2005, pp. 481–504.

Lestrade, Didier. *Act Up: Une histoire.* Éditions La Découverte, 2022.

Muñoz, José Esteban. *Cruising Utopia: The Then and There of Queer Futurity.* New York UP, 2009.

Nison, Angéline. "La Reconstruction de la première guerre mondiale dans la photographie: L'exemple du Nord et du Pas-de-Calais." *Livraisons de l'histoire de l'architecture*, vol. 38, 2019, pp. 103–10.

Nora, Pierre, ed. *Les Lieux de mémoire*, 3 vols. Gallimard, 1984–92.

Pember, Alice. "The party is political: The moving politics of the queer dancefloor in *120 BPM* (2017)." *Modern & Contemporary France*, vol. 30, no. 2, 2022, pp. 145–60.

"Qui sommes-nous?" *Les ActupienNEs.* March 2018. Web.

Troth, Brian. "Haunted spaces: Trauma, mourning, and melancholia in the HIV epidemic in France." *Contemporary French Civilization*, vol. 46, no. 2, 2021, pp. 129–46.

Veyrat-Masson, Isabelle. "Entre mémoire et histoire: la Seconde Guerre mondiale à la télévision." *Hermès, La Revue*, vol. 1, no. 8–9, 1990, pp. 151–69.

Vié, Carolyn. "'*120 battements par minute* est un film très juste' explique l'ex-président d'Act Up-Paris." *www.20minutes.fr.* August 8, 2022.

Watson, Eleri Anona. "'L'idée d'une coalition': Derrida, Foucault, and the bumpy coalitions of ACT UP, Paris in Robin Campillo's *120 Battements par minute* (2017)." *Modern & Contemporary France*, vol. 30, no. 2, 2022, pp. 111–27.

Wingrove, Sarah. "Beyond 'la petite mort' – sex and death in *120 BPM*." *Modern & Contemporary France*, vol. 30, no. 2, 2022, pp. 227–39.

CHAPTER TWENTY

Haunted sites and haunted memories
HIV/AIDS temporalities in the contemporary French cultural memory

Daniel N. Maroun

"T'as pas le sida j'espère" [I hope you don't have AIDS] (Colby 3): a violent but emblematic reminder of the deferred phobia of HIV/AIDS that still looms in French cultural memory. The statement comes from journalist and activist Fred Colby's sister-in-law during one of his home visits to Miramas, France, in 2010. HIV/AIDS embodies a triadic semiotic configuration meaning that the virus and its syndrome represent material, symbolic, and functional aspects for French society. But the act of remembering this virus and the vociferous multiplicity of connotations associated with it creates an imbalance between the medical reality of the twenty-first century and the socio-sexual fear it still produces. Anchoring HIV/AIDS as a (queer) site of memory in the French cultural landscape forces us to confront its perpetual existence while reconciling the disproportional impact HIV/AIDS has had on queer populations since the 1980s. This chapter identifies how HIV/AIDS has carved out a queer realm of memory in the French socio-cultural landscape by analyzing the social and literary representations of the virus and how twenty-first-century individuals dialogue with its specter, producing a present memory that is anchored in the past.

A queer realm subverts a national discourse and stands in opposition to how Nora's *lieux* reinforced a national unity through the memory of symbolic sites. I contend that HIV/AIDS is a queer realm of memory because it opposes the collective national ideals that surround traditional realms; a queer realm is shared on the periphery and is inhabited by the marginalized and disenfranchised. Queer sites of memory destabilize the expectation of being a part of the dominant national discourse because of their identitarian unifying agent – in this specific case, sexuality. This chapter draws from two corpuses in order to show how social and literary discourse are mutually constitutive, both highlighting how HIV/AIDS continues to occupy the French socio-sexual psyche. It analyzes discourse in French newspapers *Le Monde* and *Le Parisien* to demonstrate how HIV/AIDS is still a deferred trauma, a pain from the past that continues to occupy sexual sociability in the present. Additionally, the chapter analyzes the works by millennial authors: Tristan Garcia's *La meilleure part des hommes* (2010), Arthur Dreyfus's *Histoire de ma sexualité* (2014) and *Journal sexuel d'un garçon d'aujourd'hui* (2021), as well as Constance Joly's *Over the Rainbow* (2021). The latter texts are examples of HIV/AIDS literature set in a post-2010 environment, one that reengages with the haunted past of the virus in a medically advanced contemporaneity, a post-tritherapy and post-PrEP environment.[1] Their storytelling brings a presence to a past, renewing the importance of HIV/AIDS discourse through a perpetuation of haunted trauma that takes its shape in various forms.

Haunted traumas are assorted configurations of trauma that all linger in anticipation of (re)visiting (i.e., haunting) through a reproduction of historical signs, signifiers, and significations of HIV/AIDS that endure. Therefore, in order to parse this concept of permanent haunting, I aim to show HIV/AIDS has become a bio-medical cultural realm of memory by presenting some examples that bring to the fore a confrontation between the trauma of the past and contemporaneity. This chapter employs the notion of an epistemology of haunting to survey the confrontations between the signifier of HIV/AIDS and its various cultural and contemporary significations.

---

1 Tritherapy is a form of antiretroviral therapy (ART) commonly used in treating HIV, aiming to slow the rate at which HIV can duplicate itself. A combination of three drugs (AZT) was used first in 1987. PrEP, or pre-exposure prophylaxis, is a medicine individuals can use before exposure to lower their chances of contracting HIV. PEP, or post-exposure prophylaxis, is medicine taken after possible exposure to HIV to prevent infection.

Deferred trauma: HIV/AIDS as a site of queer memory in culture and literature

Seismic shifts in cultural signification of the virus are why we can interpret HIV/AIDS as a queer realm of memory. This chapter therefore considers mutations in the temporality of HIV/AIDS as it travels from epidemic to endemic status (Gill-Peterson 279) in French society. This interval between epidemic and endemic gives space for a haunting to occur as biomedical advances impact cultural signification. To defer the trauma, as I propose, is to examine this tenuous relationship between the assumed present signification of HIV or AIDS and its torturous past. In this way, we can view haunting as the "remainder of the work of mourning" (Gill-Peterson 281) that impacts present negotiations of life with the disease.

Contemporary literary productions, like Tristan Garcia's *La meilleure part des hommes* (2010), Arthur Dreyfus's *Histoire de ma sexualité* (2014) and *Journal sexuel d'un garçon d'aujourd'hui* (2021), as well as Constance Joly's *Over the Rainbow* (2021), all share a discussion about the presence of an absence – that HIV/AIDS is assumed missing or embodying some sort of ghostly epidemiological matter that looms in the periphery.[2] Each of the aforementioned cultural artifacts deal with some sort of HIV "scare" wherein a protagonist must confront the reality of being seropositive. This confrontation inevitably leads to embracing the specters of HIV/AIDS cultural signification – what it meant, what it means, and how that meaning is negotiated with the past in the present.

The transition from epidemic to endemic for HIV/AIDS has given way to a slippery slope of mis-signification because the endemic status is the admission of a calculated distribution of death over a population. Consequently, this creates a misconception of a disease's perceived impact. Quite indicative of this shift is a 2021 article in *Le Monde* that features the testimony of a young adult woman, Andréa: "J'avais 22 ans et, pour moi, c'était quelque chose qui ne touchait pas les jeunes" [I was 22 years old and, for me, it was something that didn't affect young people] (Slavicek). Andréa's comment exemplifies how the interval between epidemic and endemic creates an expected temporality

---

2 Absence as a presence is also prevalent in examples of French AIDS cinema, such as Ducastel and Martineau's *Paris 05:59: Théo et Hugo* (2016) and Christophe Honoré's *Plaire, aimer et courir vite* (2018).

– a safe one, void of HIV/AIDS, because her generation has not had to face the virus head on. Colby shares a similar sentiment about HIV/AIDS in his 2019 autopathology: "Le sida, il ne passera pas par moi" [AIDS, I won't get it] (54) – an impossible reality, protected by his naivety. Andréa's aforementioned comment echoes Tristan Garcia's debut novel, *La meilleure part des hommes* (2010), when an older protagonist, Doum, critiques the younger generation: "Il y a aujourd'hui une nouvelle génération [...] un comportement différent" [Today there's a new generation [...] a different behavior] (44). Doum criticizes this new generation in how they approach sex and HIV, seemingly unaware of its past, ignorantly immune.

Garcia's novel serves as an example to show how intergenerational behavior may change but the intergenerational transmission of traumatic signification still exists. Take, for example, "Loïc," a 26-year-old seropositive man interviewed in *Le Monde*: "Ce n'est pas possible, je suis beaucoup trop jeune" [It's not possible, I am way too young] (Slavicek). Loïc's comment suggests that his youth should immunize him from the trauma of the past, from the virus itself. His comment stresses how HIV/AIDS is only coded by its past, but a past whose signification is linked to death: "Je pensais qu'il ne me restait plus longtemps à vivre" [I didn't think I had too long to live] (Slavicek).[3] His use of the imperfect underscores how his thought *was* one reality, but that other co-existing relations endure; that ontologically, his present is a negotiation between a shared past and a possible future with HIV/AIDS.

Andréa's earlier testimony in *Le Monde* brings to the fore the dialectic between past and present: "D'un coup, j'ai réalisé que ma vie allait changer et je me suis mise à pleurer. Je savais que je n'allais pas mourir demain. En revanche, j'étais terrifiée par l'impact du virus sur ma vie sociale et sentimentale" [Suddenly, I realized that my life was going to change and I started to cry. I knew that I wasn't going to die tomorrow. On the other hand, I was terrified of the impact the virus would have on my social and romantic life].[4] The specter of HIV/AIDS oscillates between the past and the present, making Andréa feel

---

3 In a documentary featuring Loïc, he adds, "Je me voyais pas avec le VIH; ça faisait pas partie du plan" [I didn't see myself contracting HIV; it wasn't a part of the plan] (LCP Assemblé Nationale). His statement demonstrates how queer male ontology negotiates with its HIV past such that his life plan now runs alongside HIV/AIDS.

4 Andréa's comment shares similarities with public health discourse that claims

the trauma of the past ("j'étais terrifiée") and how it dialogues with her present understanding of the virus ("je savais que je n'allais pas mourir demain"). Furthermore, it brings us back to the bearing HIV/AIDS has on an individual's sexual sociability because of its historical connotation, a plural signification. Since the early 2010s, there has been a cultural shift away from viewing HIV/AIDS as a true pandemic due to medical advances in tritherapies, PrEP, and PEP for queer and straight individuals. Yet, that does not change the ways in which HIV/AIDS continues to impact the "sexual sociability" (Møller and Ledin 147) that, in turn, informs prophylaxis usage like condoms, STI testing, and even serosorting – all in the guise of allowing individuals to reclaim a somatic pleasure in sex (148), without a moralizing fear that is often linked with HIV/AIDS. Andréa's statement represents the progress made from one affective state to another. Hauntology becomes a useful tool for examining this development because it is preoccupied with ontology – that is to say, the historical conditions or discourses about an individual's or concept's end status (Derrida, *Spectres de Marx* 31);[5] Andréa is thinking about her present and future, but based on the discourse of the past, something she would have never done if she had not contracted the virus.

The tension between past and present that the AIDS specter renews in seropositive individuals is also witnessed in the literary works of Arthur Dreyfus. Born in 1986, this millennial writes about his sex life *after* numerous preventative methods are available to stop the transmission of HIV. Despite this, however, he writes, in *Histoire de ma sexualité* (2014), about the apprehension surrounding gay sex: "Réunis dans un même lit [...] deux sexes se hérissent sous leurs caleçons bariolés. Bastien réfléchit un moment, avant de décliner: c'est trop dangereux" [Together in the same bed [...] two penises stood erect tented under their brightly colored underwear. Bastien considers for a moment, before declining: "it's too dangerous"] (Dreyfus 184). The narrator chimes in, stating, "Il n'a pas tort" [He's not wrong] (185), a reply which signals that something illicit and risky still looms in the background of gay sex in the early 2000s. AIDS still impacts the sexual sociability of individuals, where

---

people will live "near normal" lives (Murray 1–3), positing HIV as a manageable illness.
  5 Concerning hauntology, Derrida writes in *Spectres de Marx*, "Comment *comprendre* en effet le discours de la fin ou le discours sur la fin" [How do we actually understand the discourse of the end or the discourse about the end] (31).

their apprehension of the learned past impacts their present. In Dreyfus's same text, his friend Tango remarks: "C'est mon sida qui m'a rendu adulte" [My AIDS made me grow up] (255), a bold claim that transforms how we understands the juxtaposition of two temporalities, examined through the spectrality of AIDS: youth and seronegativity, adulthood and seropositivity, much like Garcia's protagonist Doum did earlier ("Il y a aujourd'hui une nouvelle génération" 44).

The specters of HIV/AIDS: haunting figures

The concept of hauntology, that is the return of a cultural or social past, provides a valuable tool for recognizing how previous HIV epistemologies loiter in contemporary cultural conceptions of the disease. Hauntology is thus a play between that which is present and that which is absent; it looks to the past to explain *a* present. Haunting is an epistemology of the present that is impacted by the social past; it differs from memory, because hauntology admits the existence of a figure that brings the past to a contemporaneity, forging "co-existing multiplicities of entangled relations" (Barad 264) where past, present, and future meet.

Hauntology's theoretical framework stems from Jacques Derrida and his discussion on Karl Marx. For Derrida, past experiences intermingle with future possibilities through the figure of the specter – a ghost or spirit, a *revenant* that keeps returning through repetitious acts. Derrida's specter is a "deconstructive figure" (Davis 375) that oscillates or hovers between presence and absence or life and death. Because of its deconstructive nature, the specter seeks to reveal a productive source of meaning. This is why Derrida suggests that intellectual tradition should aim to "parler *du* spectre, de parler *au* spectre, de parler avec *lui*" [talk *about* the specter, talk *to* the specter, talk *with* it] (Derrida, *Spectres de Marx* 32), so as to avoid associating specters and haunting with a false quest to uncover that which was previously secret or never discovered.[6] The specter deconstructs ontological understandings of existence. It can be a tool by which we are able to queer a realm of memory so

---

6 Derrida writes, "La littérature garde un secret qui n'existe pas, en quelque sorte [...] il n'y a pas de sens secret à chercher" [Literature keeps a secret that doesn't really exist [...] there is not any secret meaning to look for] (*Papier machine* 398).

that non-republican or peripheral communities can form a present temporality, a presence anchored in the memory.

The trauma and serophobia of HIV/AIDS haunts contemporary representations of life with HIV/AIDS because its spectrality has yet to reveal the possibility of the future. For journalist Fred Colby, talking about AIDS allows him to "contrôler le virus" [control the virus] (Colby 54) so as to forge an HIV/AIDS futurity that dialogues with the past reality of seropositivity. This is why we must speak *about*, *to*, and *with* the specter, so that we create queer futurities with HIV/AIDS. The Derridean specter is capable of emphasizing that which cannot be articulated with the lexicon of knowledge available to us. We are not aware of how cultural discourse will continue to represent HIV/AIDS, but we do know that it will be in dialogue with the past.

An example of this dialogue between past and present in French culture comes from HIV/AIDS survivor Maxime Journiac, in an interview from June 2021 with *Le Parisien*: "Je suis vivant, mais une partie de moi est morte" [I'm alive, but a part of me is dead], he claims, and later adds, "Je suis incapable de me projeter vers l'avenir" [I am unable to see myself in the future] (LeRoy). Journiac's claims of being alive, but part of him dead, highlights the dialectic between present (still alive) and past (but partly dead) that undergirds how the epidemic affected previous generations. It also demonstrates the "co-existing multiplicities of entangled relations" (Barad 264) that define hauntology because he is unable to see himself in the future *from* the present. Journiac's present is haunted by his past: "Je ne suis pas indemne. C'est un traumatisme au-delà de tout" [I am not unaffected. It's traumatic beyond all else] (LeRoy). His contemporaneity is defined by the trauma and wounds of his past and his future remains obscured by a present that must learn to negotiate with the specters of its past.[7]

This interview in *Le Monde* is a strong example of the crucial role that HIV/AIDS testimonials assume in a given culture, systemizing present meaning for the disease – a meaning that displays how contemporary representations will always embrace the past due to the displaced meaning of it in the present. HIV/AIDS is a queer realm of memory not

---

7 Journiac adds, "Bob est mort dans mes bras en juin 1986. C'était l'amour de ma vie, je suis veuf depuis" [Bob died in my arms in July 1986. He was the love of my life; I have been a widower ever since] (LeRoy). Journiac's statement about Bob in *Le Monde* showcases how his present is a constant reminder of what he is missing/lacking – Bob, his lover.

simply because of its rejection of the normative and national framework of Nora's *lieux de mémoire* but because present representations continue to invoke a past that haunts, whose presence is "un maintenant disjoint ou désajusté" [a disjointed or disadjusted now] (Derrida, *Spectres de Marx* 21). When the past implants or even supplants the present like it does for Loïc and Andréa from *Le Monde* earlier, its eerie ambulation in contemporary memory becomes a productive space for HIV/AIDS signification as the past, present, and future intermingle, forming a discursive queer realm for the virus.

In 2021, Dreyfus published *Journal sexuel d'un garçon d'aujourd'hui*, a literary rolodex of his sexual encounters. In it, he contracts syphilis but elects to write about AIDS instead: "J'ai pensé, comme toujours, au sida. Et comme toujours l'idée du sida s'est heurtée à l'idée de paternité" [I thought, like I always do, about AIDS. And, as always, the thought of AIDS clashes with the idea of family and fatherhood] (81). His use of "toujours" underscores the iterative affective practice that gay men face as they embrace gay sex – a gay ontology where the homosexual is consumed, waiting for his inevitable seropositivity. The specter of AIDS figuratively runs him over, forcing him to envision his future. Dreyfus continues, however, "Puis une piqûre m'a soigné [du syphilis] et j'ai recouvré mon sentiment d'éternité" [A poke cured me [of syphilis] and I regained my feeling of immortality] (81). The intersection of both futurity and HIV/AIDS is quite remarkable because the virus and its diagnosis was presumed to impede the future, quite literally to stop it through the early deaths of its victims. As the AIDS epidemic unfolded, queer cultural discourse and mores embodied an anti-futurity linked to the fatalistic outcome of the disease and bareback sex (Evans 136–37), but Dreyfus's quote highlights a certain hopefulness that can be employed as a method for queer orientation such that, as José Esteban Muñoz theorized, these queer populations can envision "networks of commonality and the structures of feeling that link queers across different identity markers" (47). The commonality, in this case, is the looming specter whose haunting brings together the past and present to share in community. It is through this lens that we can then understand how HIV/AIDS serves as a queer realm of memory because it is through the specter that participants engage with a presence of the past.

Muñoz's concept of queer community building through past and present affect is of particular interest when one investigates the tension Dreyfus establishes between gay and straight lived sexual experiences. When he states, "Tout le monde admet qu'un jeune hétéro ne songe *jamais au sida*" [Everyone admits that a young straight person never thinks *about AIDS*] (Dreyfus, *Journal* 1204), he reifies the reality that HIV/AIDS is a queer phenomenon, which is not to say that HIV/AIDS uniquely targets gays. Instead, it underscores how the epidemic defined gay temporalities from its onset until its current iteration as endemic. Dreyfus continues to drive the wedge between heterosexual and gay experience when he writes, "Alors qu'un jeune gay se lève avec le sida, aime avec le sida, craint à chaque instant le sida – jusqu'au jour où il le chope" [Whereas a young gay guy wakes up with AIDS, loves with AIDS, fears AIDS at every moment – until the day it nabs him] (1204), testifying to how queerness coincides with and lives parallel with AIDS. It is Dreyfus's final quote here that helps HIV/AIDS materialize as a queer realm of memory: first, as a realm of memory that is constructed as a site of variable meaning. But second, as a queer realm because of how it subverts who can participate and how the participation occurs through the specters of the past.

The dialectic between past and present is uniquely depicted in Constance Joly's *Over the Rainbow* (2021), winner of the Prix Orange, in which she tells the story of her father who died of complications related to AIDS. The novel opens with the visit of her friend Justine, who asks how Constance's father is doing, seemingly having forgotten he had died years earlier. This interaction sends Constance spiraling into a self-reflection, claiming: "Mon histoire commence par quelqu'un qui s'en va" [My story begins with someone's departure] (13). Joly highlights how her presence, this current temporality, the very story she tells in the present, exists through her father's death due to AIDS. The virus and her father's suffering and death become a postmemory, transmitted to Joly as almost her own, memories that define her contemporaneity.[8] Her novel is an example of the past in parallel with the future as she recounts the story of her father while simultaneously sharing that of her childhood and her present.

Future epistemologies of HIV/AIDS

HIV/AIDS embodies a queer realm of memory in two ways: first, it maintains a lethal, socio-sexual connotation despite medical

---

8 See the editors' introduction for how postmemory can help us nuance a deeper understanding of queer realms of memory.

advancements that have changed how people live with AIDS. Françoise Barré-Sinoussi, French virologist and co-discoverer of HIV, even went so far as to state in 2023: "On ne guérit toujours pas du sida" [We still have not found a cure for AIDS] (Gardier), a quote that highlights how HIV/AIDS exists, despite treatment, and how its existence is an artifact of a past we cannot forget, a past that lingers in our present. The negative connotation associated with HIV positivity is a remnant of a historical moment that is displaced to the present day (see Van Bilsen et al.). While treatments exist to render the virus undetectable, the stigmatization that surrounds sero discovery (that is, discovering one's HIV positive or negative status) still negatively permeates French society in the form of anxiety, familial abandonment, or suicidal ideation (see Préau et al.). Second, as was articulated earlier, HIV/AIDS resists the national and homogenizing nature of traditional realms by queering how we remember through the force of a looming specter. It therefore becomes proverbially impossible to imagine the last 40 years of queer history in France without acknowledging the impact HIV/AIDS has had on queer culture and the queer sexual psyche. While contracting the virus may not mean death, there are still multiple discriminations and fears embedded in a seropositive diagnosis. Present diagnoses beg the important question: "What transformations can people living with HIV actually claim in the era of biomedical advancement" (Murray 215). It is important to recall the multiple injustices that intersect with an HIV positive diagnosis: moralistic public health regimes, structural or systemic violence and oppression, and poverty. The AIDS specter is tasked with reminding us that intervention, renegotiation, and advocacy will be needed for decades to come.

Sadly, the virus no longer garners the same activist engagement and passion it once did (Caron 229), and the works studied in this chapter demonstrate that while HIV/AIDS occupies mental, social, and sexual space in the contemporary queer psyche, the fear does not change habits and has not mobilized new generations. Dreyfus, Joly, Garcia, and other contemporary authors acknowledge the presence of a specter – of HIV/AIDS – but the biomedical reality of the disease has diffused or attenuated actual social action. However, by viewing HIV/AIDS as a queer realm of memory, we reinvigorate the cause; we give a place to a mental space; we give an actuality to its reality by ensuring that we do not allow it to be forgotten, nor do we allow medical advancement to convince society that we've found our happy ending in undetectability. By memorializing HIV/AIDS as a queer realm in all its senses, we are responding to a much larger, urgent activist call. France has an obligation to engage its public in recognizing the symbolic history of HIV/AIDS as a way to "understand the complexities and open the possibilities for reforming *les lieux de mémoires*" (Orangias 714). Such an action would create cultural narrative that renders a queer realm of memory visible and participatory within the French Republic. Ultimately, haunting necessitates a social relation between the specters of the past, made peripheral by the violence of modernity (Gordon 5). Thus haunting, I contend, is as a methodology that follows the social remnants of an individual or community and tells a story of absence felt as presence. It is through this logic that HIV/AIDS can be seen as a queer realm of memory because we want to understand its presence through its social and political absence in contemporary life – for, ultimately, the epistemology of haunting is "about conjuring subjects who have been excluded, their histories and subjectivities repressed" (Van Wagenen 290).

The HIV/AIDS epidemic gave birth to, and continues to bear, creative responses in storytelling and images that testify to how French citizens dealt with or deal with the effects of the virus. The specters of AIDS haunt us to remind us to be vigilant against all sorts of queer injustices – police brutality against Arab and Black lives, anti-trans ideologies, homophobia against Black and people of color communities, etc. Queer realms of memory are, like their postcolonial counterparts, urgent attempts to "make visible the invisible thread" (Achille, Forsdick, and Moudileno 1) that has linked the queer, in this case, to the Hexagon. The haunting produced from cultural discourse or literary text is a method that forces us to reconcile the interval between two temporalities. This reconciliation should continue to promote social equity for peripheral populations, resolving the specter's goal – his own ontology. That, in essence, is a queer realm of memory: one that resists normative iterations of national memory, but instead sheds light on those long cast to the shadows.

Works cited

Achille, Étienne, Charles Forsdick, and Lydie Moudileno, eds. *Postcolonial Realms of Memory: Sites and Symbols in Modern France*. Liverpool UP, 2020.

Barad, Karen. "Quantum entanglements and hauntological relations of inheritance: Dis/continuities, spacetime enfoldings, and justice-to-come." *Derrida Today*, vol. 3, no. 2, 2010, pp. 240–68.
Caron, David. "Les spectres d'ACT University Press." *Hybrida*, vol. 3, 2021, pp. 229–40.
Colby, Fred. *T'as pas le sida j'espère*. Librinova, 2020.
Davis, Colin. "Hauntology, spectres and phantoms." *French Studies*, vol. 59, no. 3, 2005, pp. 373–79.
Derrida, Jacques. *Papier Machine*. Galilée, 2001.
———. *Spectres de Marx*. Galilée, 2006.
Dreyfus, Arthur. *Histoire de ma sexualité*. POL, 2014.
———. *Journal sexuel d'un jeune garçon d'aujourd'hui*. POL, 2021.
Evans, Elliot. "Your HIV-positive sperm, my trans-dyke uterus: Anti/futurity and the politics of bareback sex between Guillaume Dustan and Beatriz Preciado." *Sexualities*, vol. 18, no. 1/2, 2015, pp. 127–40.
Garcia, Tristan. *La meilleure part des hommes*. Gallimard, 2010.
Gardier, Stéphany. "Françoise Barré-Sinoussi: 'On ne guérit toujours pas du sida.'" *Le Monde*. March 25, 2023.
Gill-Peterson, Julian. "Haunting the queer spaces of AIDS." *GLQ*, vol. 19, no. 3, 2013, pp. 279–300.
Gordon, Avery F. *Ghostly Matters: Haunting and the Sociological Imagination*. U of Minnesota P, 1997.
Jameson, Frederic. "Marx's purloined letter." Jacques Derrida, Terry Eagleton, Frederic Jameson, and Antonio Negri. *Ghostly Demarcations*. undated.
Joly, Constance. *Over the Rainbow*. Flammarion, 2021.
LCP Assemblé Nationale. "Loïc, séropo indétectable." April 1, 2021.
LeRoy, Yves. "40 ans de sida: 'Je suis vivant, mais une partie de moi est morte', témoigne Maxime, rescapé de l'épidémie." *Le Parisien*. June 4, 2021.
Møller, Kristian, and Chase Ledin. "Viral hauntology: Specters of AIDS in infrastructures of gay sexual sociability." *SocArXiv*, 2020, pp. 147–62.
Muñoz, José Esteban. *Cruising Utopia: The Then and There of Queer Futurity*. New York UP, 2009.
Murray, David B. *Living with HIV in the Post-Crisis Times: Beyond the Endgame*. Lexington Books, 2021.
Nora, Pierre. *Realms of Memory: The Construction of the French Past*, vol. 3, *Symbols*, edited by Pierre Nora and Lawrence D. Kritzman. Translated by Arthur Goldhammer. Columbia UP, 1998.
Orangias, Joseph, Jeannie Simms, and Sloane French. "The cultural functions and social potential of queer monuments: A preliminary inventory and analysis." *Journal of Homosexuality*, vol. 65, no. 6, 2018, pp. 705–26.
Préau, M., A.D. Bouhnik, P. Peretti-Wattel, Y. Obadia, and B. Spire. "Suicide attempts among people living with HIV in France." *AIDS Care*, vol. 20, no. 8, 2008, pp. 917–24.

Slavicek, Marie. "Séropositifs au VIH: 'J'avais 22 ans et, pour moi, c'était quelque chose qui ne touchait pas les jeunes.'" *Le Monde*. June 5, 2021.

Van Bilsen, W.P.H., Hanne M.L. Zimmerman, Anders Boyd, and Udi Davidovich. "Burden of living with HIV among men who have sex with men: A mixed-methods study." *The Lancet*, vol. 7, no. 21, 2020, pp. 835–43.

Van Wagenen, Aimee. "An epistemology of haunting." *Critical Sociology*, vol. 30, no. 2, 2004, pp. 287–98.

V

New Technologies as Archive

CHAPTER TWENTY ONE

Cases Rebelles

The archipelagic and transnational construction of Black queer sites of memory

Michaëla Danjé

Introduction

To come together under the common denominator of dispersion is to position oneself, from the outset, within a terrain fractured by distance and its many ramifications: rupture, disappearance, oblivion, confusion, dilution, illusion. This is the background of Cases Rebelles, our collective born of lineages marked by slavery, colonization, and an unfinished liberation, endless struggles. Born out in narratives shaped by the colonizer's desire to erase, to blur, to obstruct remembrance – to silence the very sites of memory. We stand at the crossroads of the May 1967 massacre in Pointe-à-Pitre, Guadeloupe, and the terror unleashed on the Cameroonian maquis during the war of liberation.

There is a palatable response to these legacies – a response deemed legitimate, official, and promoted by many: to demand that the colonial nation-state and its institutions repair history, restore what can be restored, and commit to transmitting knowledge through its schools and universities, its commemorations – circulating research, findings, and archival material as widely as possible..

But the assumption underlying such a demand is that the State thus called into question is fundamentally free and willing with regard to the histories we wish to shed light on, and that it is fundamentally distinct from the colonial and slave empire project. The regular shirking by successive governments of demands for the acknowledgment of crimes, and the pathological interventionism for the purpose of fabricating a deceitful *roman national* [national narrative], attests to the fact that in France there is, at the very least, a systematic and populist instrumentalization of the issues of memory and history.

Proof of this can be seen in the use made of commissions of inquiry regarding the two aforementioned countries. The report of the Stora Commission, which was launched under the auspices of the administration of President François Hollande to investigate the 1967 massacres in Guadeloupe, was nothing but a smokescreen, and the results bear all the hallmarks of a botched job. As for the joint commission recently launched by Emmanuel Macron on the repression of the war of liberation in Cameroon, it was thrown like a bone to the Cameroonian people, who were demanding justice and reparations from France on deeds that are already well-established and documented by various researchers.

Embracing the full reality of French colonial continuums is liberating. In particular, it allows us to recognize that the historical work is ours to do – through acts of recuperation and (re)discovery, and through counter-memorial projects like those we pursue in Cases Rebelles. Freed from any expectation regarding the institutions that hold power over knowledge production and its dissemination, without any expectations from the totalizing ideology of collective memory.

When Cases Rebelles was founded in 2010, part of our vision included the recovery of Black communities' histories and their reconnection to each other. And then to see how those histories of Black worlds would resonate with each other in a Glissantian archipelagic mode:

> Another form of thought is developing, more intuitive, more fragile, threatened, but in tune with the chaos-world and its unpredictability, perhaps supported by discoveries in the human and social sciences but stemming from a vision of the poetics and the imagination of the world. I call this thought "archipelagic", that is non-systematic, inductive thought that explores the unexpected in the world-totality and reconciles writing with orality and orality with writing. (Glissant 20)

Since Black worlds emerged from this post-catastrophe unpredictability, this intuitive and fragile form of thought would be our way to reconnect with each other. The horizon opened up by the Afrodiasporic perspective, because it is not national, is free from the geographical injunctions of political utilitarianism. This perspective is based on a dual spatialization: transnational in the territories it mobilizes, includes, and connects, as well as global through the virtual space it inhabits since Cases Rebelles was born as a podcast.

Welcoming traces

At the very inception of our collective, we had only a few scattered fragments on what queer Black lives might be. Even though we didn't dedicate a standalone review to her book, Oyèrónkẹ́ Oyěwùmí's *The Invention of Women: Making an African Sense of Western Gender Discourses* (1997) was a critical lead (albeit problematic) to follow in our quest: there weren't that many. As the first Black podcast in France, we had an enormous task ahead of us and few traces available. Yet, we were certain that Black queer and trans realities had always been there, though under different names and modes of expression, integrated into different conceptual divisions, obscured, and pushed to the margins by successive waves of epistemic violence. Therefore, we had to collect, share, and pass on.

It was a matter of going against the diffusionist paradigms, which envision African and Black queerness as something handed down from the West. We also wanted to reinterpret colonial and neo-colonial productions: making imperfect archives speak in order to discern some remnants of long lost Black queer existences. A decade later, in my text, "Je chante l'amour collectif" ["I sing the love collective"], I would return to this blueprint:

> On peut en concevoir d'amers regrets à sentir le réel si proche et pourtant si définitivement perdu dans l'archive qui a tout saisi de travers.
>
> Les concepts, les outils mêmes du récit – les langues – transportent une force normative et une puissance idéologique qui altèrent les réalités sous prise de notes coloniale. C'est une expérience inextricablement ambiguë que l'examen de ces archives erronées et lacunaires. Ces observateurs, qu'ont-ils vu? Et qu'ont-ils compris?
>
> Sans doute pas grand-chose... Mais j'insiste comme celle qui s'acharne à reconnaître des visages familiers sur une photographie diaboliquement floue. (Danjé 91)
>
> [O the bitter regret of feeling realities so close and yet so definitively lost in an archive that has captured everything askew. The very concepts and tools of this narrative – languages themselves – carry a normative force and an ideological power that alters realities under the pen of dutiful

colonial scriveners. What an inextricably ambiguous experience to peruse these erroneous and incomplete archives! What did these observers see? And what did they understand? Probably not much ... But I am the one who persists – persists in trying to make out familiar faces in a diabolically blurred picture.]

In our project, the histories and sites of memory of North America's Black populations clearly occupy an ambiguous, paradoxical place. First, they are the most directly accessible elements of Black queer history. But that's because they benefit from the power of North American dissemination, its normative, exclusionary, and spectacular self-satisfaction. In other words, to embrace African American sites of memory is not only to risk feeling complacent and easily contented, but also to highlight sites of memory that are in great danger of being appropriated and strongly neutralized in France: James Baldwin or Josephine Baker, for example, both reflect the depoliticizing affection people can nurture here for Black Americans. James Baldwin was made a Commandeur de la Légion d'Honneur in 1986, by a so-called socialist government, which at the same time successfully worked to stop the rise of autonomous struggles by Black and Arab youth from working-class neighborhoods. In addition, to this day, Baldwin's views on love are used to chastise any form of anger born of racial oppression. In November 2021, Baker became the first Black woman to be honored in the Panthéon monument in Paris. Like her, a lot of African American artists finding sanctuary from white supremacist terror at home were used to cement the idea that there is no racism in France. The first Black queer people we talked about in our podcasts were indeed Marlon Riggs, Becky Birtha, and Gwendolyn Bennett (Cases Rebelles). It took time to find other fruitful avenues of Black queerness, whether in the Caribbean or Africa.

Is it a historical–geographical coincidence that the first queer organization we interviewed for our podcast was KOURAJ [pronounced like "COURAGE" in French], in Haiti? What place in the world more powerfully embodies Western desires to silence – to distort historical truth through the French *roman national* [national narrative]? Here, silence is understood as the "active and transitive process" conceptualized by Michel-Rolph Trouillot in *Silencing the Past: Power and the Production of History* (1995 48).

Interviewing KOURAJ in 2013 meant collecting the words of the M community – M for *masisi, madivin, miks* (words that could be translated into gay, lesbian, bisexual) – which promotes other ways of naming, understanding, and living in Haitian Creole, a language familiar to some of us. We wanted to bear witness to these realities, to record these current oral histories and understand their sources, their ties with revolutionary Haiti,

Our methods of collecting always include a questioning of origins: what collective, family, or solitary paths led people to take action? Collecting never really ends. It grows out in a starry, archipelagic, rhizomatic way. Past, present, and affinities form the constellation.

Moreover, opening up such conversations means making space for upheavals in our own ways of expressing ourselves and existing. Our transnational approach – combined with our refusal of homogenized, normative queer identities – pushes us toward an ethic of non-resolution. This is not about making some kind of inventory of black worlds through the lens of gender and sexuality. Rather, the task of recording stems from a willingness to welcome trouble – not to trouble gender per se, but to trouble the successive waves of colonization of gender, its grammar, its epistemologies. In 2013, activist Mariam Armisen, founder of the Queer African Youth Network (QAYN) and the online magazine Q-zine, asked these important questions in our podcast no. 35:

> Quand on utilise cette appellation "gay," "lesbienne," "bisexuelle," surtout "trans," en Afrique, qu'est-ce que cela pose comme problèmes? On veut vraiment engager des contributeurs à questionner ces appellations: est-ce que ça nous appartient ou ça nous appartient pas? Comment est-ce que cela contribue au discours comme quoi l'homosexualité a été une importation de l'Occident? (Cases Rebelles 26:45)

> [When we use this label "gay," "lesbian," "bisexual," especially "trans," in Africa, what issues does it raise? We really want to push our contributors to question these namings: Do they belong to us or not? How do they contribute to the discourse that homosexuality was imported from the West?]

KOURAJ in Haiti, which used Haitian words to define the M community, wasn't sure what term to use for transfeminine people. This uncertainty, this absence of words, was indicative of the people involved in the organization at the time. But temporarily accepting that words are lacking, and refusing to assimilate the ready-made Western lexicon by default, seemed especially healthy and courageous to us in the face of globalization. Uncertainty is diametrically opposed to ethnological or anthropological positions. It is a means of resistance to numerous attacks: by NGOs, western activists, social networks, the cultural industry, and so on.

In our podcast *Samy Atsika* (*Between Ourselves*) – a series in Malagasy and French about queer communities in Madagascar – we find, for example, transfeminine people who refer to themselves as transgender women, others as *sarimbavy*, a Malagasy word that could be translated as "image of a woman." One of them said of another woman who defines herself as *sarimbavy*: "If she doesn't define herself as a trans woman, it's because she doesn't know the right words," while the second asserts that if she calls herself *sarimbavy*, it's because she lives in Madagascar, loves its culture, its *traditional* culture, and the words that her people can understand. Our aim here is not to judge, because this is not our place. However, this example does illustrate the harm done by the lexical and conceptual hegemony of the West in the field of non-conforming genders and non-heteronormative sexualities

The European, or more broadly Western, grip on gender construction and its transgressions carries with it its prescriptions and injunctions, even in its most activist garb. The normative, conventional apparatus of Pride Celebrations and International Days is still informed by the arrogance of the Enlightenment. It bears the cultural and political hallmarks of the power of the Center against the margins, the periphery, the subalterns. All of this is combined with a belief in the idea of progress and a claim to scientificity, in its most imperialist sense. We archive personal testimonies that recount lives lived differently, lives thwarting mainstream cultural scripts, lives that are negotiated without the hackneyed prerequisite steps such as "coming out," for instance, and are differently affected by the issue of visibility.

Our work thus moves in a dual way: we collect and archive many points of view, which are more or less conventional, more or less surprising, de facto creating Black and queer sites of memory, in a polyphonic and non-totalizing way. We record the aforementioned multitude while reaffirming the right to opacity and substituting Relation for the absolutism of equivalence or translation.

Collective memories

In the anthology I edited, *AfroTrans* (2021), there are two trans women from Réunion. One pays tribute in a moving poetic text to Leila, a transfeminine trailblazer, who was known for her brashness and her provocative words, broadcast regularly on FreeDom, a local radio station. The other one talks about Leila's "frasques et interventions à scandales" [hijinks and inflammatory comments] while obviously distancing herself and refusing to name her. Being able to unite these two visions of Leila is invaluable. Without idealization, the embarrassing Leila is celebrated, not buried under collective shame for the sake of respectability. However imperfect she may be, she exists, both in reality and in the collective imagination. She must be concealed if we consider that in the name of collective memory, we have to assess her from a moral, intellectual, political point of view. The co-presence of these two women allows the readers to make their own decisions regarding which places Leila could or should occupy in our collective memories.

> L'oubli, et je dirai même l'erreur historique, sont un facteur essentiel de la création d'une nation, et c'est ainsi que le progrès des études historiques est souvent pour la nationalité un danger. (251)
>
> [The act of forgetting, I would even say, historical error, is an essential factor in the creation of a nation, which is why progress in historical studies often constitutes a danger for nationality.]

In his March 11, 1882, lecture, "Qu'est-ce qu'une nation?" [What Is a Nation?], Ernest Renan makes it clear that nation-building is based on fictional narratives, on concealment. This explicit formulation of the function of forgetting in the French national contract casts a harsh light on what Pierre Nora, almost a century later, would call "collective memory," not only in the context of the nation-state, but also of any group fictionalized as a homogeneous community or encouraged to think of themselves as such. The so-called collective memory (the authorized, sanctioned memory) testifies above all to the unequal memorial and epistemic firepower, and therefore to the relations of power – material and symbolic – that lead to the production, upholding, or reassessment of history and memory. This is why "revolutionary Haiti" cannot leave its imprint on the French collective consciousness – let alone in its memory – and is systematically replaced by "Haiti the wretched."

Choosing to embrace a vague and boundless Black queerness in a pan-African, transnational, Afrodiasporic way necessarily implies extricating oneself from uniqueness, from homogenization, and therefore categorically abandoning the production of a consensual memory and consensual sites of memory. As mentioned above, it is extremely tempting to yield to a unified nomenclature of Black transness and queerness inherited from North American history. Iconic figures such as Marsha P. Johnson, Stormé DeLarverie, James Baldwin, Audre Lorde, and Miss Major rightly seem to be part of a counter-narrative. But these byways lead back to the memorial highways – prides, days of visibility, etc. The diversity business has turned the aforementioned people into particularly prized prey.

In 2018, a year after he was elected, French President Emmanuel Macron invited Black queer members of the voguing scene to the Elysée Palace for the *Fête de la Musique* [Music Day], the annual music festival throughout France in late June. In so doing, he capitalized on the *neutralizing effects* of the Atlantic crossing by spectacularly mobilizing an alternative site of memory – the ballroom scene – in the service of an exclusionary, xenophobic, and violent political project. A few selfies with the President and his wife were taken and widely reported in the media, triggering the fury of many reactionary politicians, particularly on the far right. The President stayed quiet, and the media storm and threats hit the Black and queer guests. At no point did the President make any statement against queerphobia or racism, and of course this whole episode wasn't an opportunity to better learn about the history of the ballroom. In fact, many people, regardless of their political stripes, have discovered the virtues of rainbow washing, and are symbolically over-investing in pride celebrations and the fight against homophobia and transphobia, often to racist ends. A lot of nonprofit organizations and individuals seeking recognition and legitimacy are unfortunately complicit in this trend. Queer and trans memory and places of memory are not intrinsically transgressive. Pride parades and discourses on tolerance are easily integrated into the universalizing mishmash that serves as a smokescreen for the rise of the far right, both at the ballot box and in the streets, where racially motivated attacks are becoming increasingly frequent.

It is rather interesting to see politicians who once opposed same-sex marriage now castigating a Senegalese footballer from the prominent Paris Saint-Germain team on social media. Citing personal reasons and health concerns, the player had twice withdrawn from matches where players were expected to wear shirts with rainbow-colored numbers in support of the International Day Against Homophobia (IDAHO). His decision was, in many ways, understandable, given the risks to which it could expose him and his family in Senegal. Yet many politicians and media outlets interpreted his absence as a homophobic act. Some even called for his dismissal from the team, accusing him of betraying French values. In this context, queer sites of memory are being instrumentalized to carry on or reactivate the French civilizing mission.

Moreover, our work of collecting, of passing on, and theorizing developed in a space–time where we have witnessed a phenomenal acceleration in cultural globalization, the massive dissemination of representations – on social networks, in films, television series – and concepts, all in a single *lingua franca*: English. It's another aspect of these cultural wars that we don't have the means to win; but nor do we have the desire to. We don't dream of winning against Netflix's ready-made Black queerness – RuPaul's Drag Race being perhaps the epitome of this trend. But we try to preserve what we can in this threatened, fragile ecosystem. In our work, which is informed by Ngugi Wa Thiongo's and Dany Bébél-Gisler's analyses, we try to promote non-colonial languages: Creole, Malagasy, and so on. We listen to individuals, to anonymous people, to activists, not to the summaries of non-governmental organizations (NGOs) or star activists. We don't show photos, easily digestible images; we value the voices, the recordings, the writings. We proclaim the vital importance of the oxygen from collective memories against the warlike effectiveness of a single collective memory.

The inescapability of Blackness

From the beginning, Cases Rebelles has been queer, pan-African, radical, anticapitalist. And this is what has kept us from being lured by the humanitarian approach or the illusion of inclusion. Mainstream globalized queer sites of memory are distractions, tools of capital. If we condone it on the pretext that we just want to belong, Black queer people can very quickly become pawns in state policies. State anti-Blackness is as much a constant in France's domestic and its foreign policies. Cases Rebelles coined the word *PanAfroRévolutionnaire* [PanAfroRevolutionary] in order to define our positions: our fight against all forms of domination from a Black-centered point of view. We refused to tackle queer and trans issues as if they were discrete from the other issues facing Black people, thus refusing to separate queer Black people from their communities.

Our sites of memory aren't just queer: they're Black, pan-African. For example, several people in the anthology *AfroTrans* talk about police violence even though, as the editor, I gave absolutely no guidelines in that direction. These issues emerge because queer people are not cut off from the rest of the world. And demonstrations against police violence, in tribute to the victims, are as much or even more Afroqueer sites of memory as Pride parades. These demonstrations are also places where our desire to live life to the fullest, in freedom and safety, is strongly asserted.

In countries other than France, such as Haiti and Senegal, activists often remind us that the neo-colonialism of Western religions is a vehicle for homophobic and transphobic violence. We also see how the legitimate anger of populations against autocratic regimes is diverted, under the guise of bogus anti-colonialism, towards gender and sexual minorities.

In a brilliant article on the Luanda Leaks, Régis Samba-Kounzi, a political fellow traveler of the Cases Rebelles collective, made a connection between the corruption of the Angolan regime and the soaring number of HIV/AIDS infections. A former member of Act Up-Paris, Régis is part of the pioneering generation of openly gay photographers and AIDS activists on the African continent. In our 73rd podcast, he recounts how his daughter died of Burkitt's leukemia after failing to obtain a visa to enter France on time, even though he had French nationality. He includes this tragic and cruel story in his reflections on the tight control that the West maintains over the circulation of Black people, their bodies, their health, particularly through drugs and the control of pharmaceutical patents. Our histories and struggles are inextricably intertwined with Blackness. And while many people identify Cases Rebelles as an active Black queer (and also afrofeminist) site of memory, it must be said that we've also done a huge and unique job of memorializing the victims of state violence in France in our project and book, *100 portraits contre l'État policier* (*100 Portraits Against the Police State*), our documentary film, *Dire à Lamine*, and the numerous podcasts with victims and families of victims. All these memories are intertwined in our spaces. There, people meet, recognize, and support each other. Our work strives, as much as possible, to reconnect struggles, individuals, and memories.

Conclusion

Infinite is the collective task. Cases Rebelles as a queer Black site of memory will continue to grow as long as we exist, as long as we record, whether in audio, in writing, on the internet, or in books.

Today, I'm working on a research project that aims to write the history of queer and trans presences in traditional Guadeloupean music. The tracks are thin, but here and there, names and faces surface despite the power of silencing. Each of our projects aims to build sites of queer and Black memory, to nurture collective memories: of human collectivities that are nebulous, ephemeral, contested, but nonetheless real.

On November 25, 2019, in Port-au-Prince, Charlot Jeudy died under mysterious circumstances – foul play being probably at hand. He was the first Black queer person to be interviewed on the Cases Rebelles podcast. He had also kindly introduced us to the lesbian organization Facsdis. Our shock and sadness were immense when we heard the news.

We have no illusions about the very limited impact of our work, but Charlot's voice, his Creole, his words, his fighting spirit, his dreams, crossing the sea by means of a most fragile internet connection are forever floating in our minds and for an indefinite time on our site and our backup hard drives. These are places of Black queer memory.

Works cited

Cases Rebelles. "La fin du silence," *Podcast Cases Rebelles*, episode 9, cases-rebelles.org. February 2011. www.cases-rebelles.org/emission-n9-fevrier-2011/.
———. "Notre poésie au monde," *Podcast Cases Rebelles*, episode 10, cases-rebelles.org. March 2011. www.cases-rebelles.org/emission-n10-mars-2011/.
———. "Notre colère,". *Podcast Cases Rebelles*, episode 16, cases-rebelles.org. September 2011. www.cases-rebelles.org/emission-n16-septembre-2011/.
———. "Q-zine, queer panafricain et indispensable," *Podcast Cases Rebelles*, episode 35, cases-rebelles.org. July 2013. www.cases-rebelles.org/emission-n35/.
———. "Régis Samba-Kounzi, photographe et activiste," *Podcast Cases Rebelles*, episode 73, cases-rebelles.org. September 2017. www.cases-rebelles.org/emission-n73/.
Danjé, Michaëla, ed. *AfroTrans*. Éditions Cases Rebelles, 2021.
Glissant, Edouard. *Introduction to a Poetics of Diversity*. Translated by Celia Britton. Liverpool UP, 2020.
Oyěwùmí, Oyèrónkẹ. *The Invention of Women: Making an African Sense of Western Gender Discourses*. U of Minnesota P. 1997.
Renan, Ernest. *What Is a Nation? And Other Political Writings*. Columbia UP, 2018.
Samba-Kounzi, Régis. "Angola: 'Luanda Leaks', corruption, sida et LGBTphobies" *Komitid*. February 2020. www.komitid.fr/2020/02/11/luandaleaks-corruption-sida-lgbtphobies-regis-samba-kounzi/.

Stora, Benjamin. *Commission d'information et de recherche historique sur les événements de décembre 1959 en Martinique, de juin 1962 en Guadeloupe et en Guyane, et de mai 1967 en Guadeloupe: Rapport à Madame la ministre des outre-mer.* 2016.

Trouillot, Michel-Rolph. *Silencing the Past: Power and the Production of History.* Beacon Press, 1995.

CHAPTER TWENTY TWO

Podcasting as a queer archival method for an intersectional French culture

Thomas Muzart

During the opening sequence of the famous French podcast *La Poudre*, hosted by Lauren Bastide, listeners are greeted with a collection of prominent feminist voices among which Virginie Despentes stands out for her declaration: "*La Poudre*, pour moi, maintenant, ça devient une archive extraordinaire du féminisme de cette dernière décennie" [For me, now, *La Poudre* is becoming an extraordinary archive of feminism from the last decade]. This statement, made by Despentes when she was a guest on the podcast on August 31, 2022, echoes the ideas shared by Sam Bourcier in an earlier episode of *La Poudre* regarding the temporality of the archive that the podcast, as a new medium, ultimately disrupts. Bourcier explains that archives traditionally refer to historical materials used by scholars to generate knowledge about the past. According to him, this approach, which ascribes value to the archive retrospectively, poses a problem for minoritized subjects who may be told that the records of their life experiences are not worth preserving. Bourcier discusses a "force archivale" that such a conventional understanding of the archive often denies to minorities (Bastide 58:07–58:09). To reclaim this power, he calls for a rethinking of the archival process – one in which recordings of contemporary lives and experiences are recognized as intrinsically valuable and are shared widely, almost by default. Drawing on Bourcier's perspective, and returning to Despentes's insight, I argue that podcasts such as *La Poudre* function as "becoming" archives of the present – living archives oriented toward the future. Unlike the ephemeral nature of traditional radio broadcasts, podcasts remain accessible over time and are relatively easy to produce. This makes them powerful tools for minoritized communities to document their own narratives and reinforce a shared sense of belonging.

In this chapter, I will examine the archival potential of podcasting through an analysis of the podcast *Extimité*, created in 2018 and hosted by Douce Dibondo and Anthony Vincent. The uniqueness of Dibondo and Vincent's work lies in how they provide a platform for minority voices – whether marginalized by ability, ethnicity, gender, race, or sexuality. In an interview published in the magazine *Télérama*, Vincent explains that the choice to title their podcast *Extimité*, comes from the research he had previously conducted on gay author Hervé Guibert. Vincent recalls encountering the concept of *extimité*, a psychoanalytical term coined by Jacques Lacan, which he used to explore how Guibert challenged the division between intimate life and public life, the personal and the political. Guibert's raw depiction of his struggle with AIDS in his literary and photographic work conferred political significance upon an illness that had been silenced and marginalized in the public sphere due to its association with the gay community. As a young queer Black man, Vincent draws a connection that updates the notion of *extimité* from gay and AIDS activism to the current context, which is, as his podcast demonstrates, postcolonial and queer. Serge Tisseron's definition of *extimité* as "le processus par lequel des fragments du soi intime sont proposés au regard d'autrui afin d'être validés" [the process by which fragments of one's intimate self are presented to the gaze of others in order to be validated] (84) is also helpful to understand Dibondo and Vincent's approach in their podcast. Each episode consists of what they refer to as "un récit de la construction et de la déconstruction" [a narrative of construction and deconstruction] of a minoritized subject, which entails a simultaneous critical and empowering self-examination and exposure in a welcoming and validating environment.

By rendering "visible the invisible" (or, rather, rendering audible the inaudible) "thread that links the colonial to French culture" (1), *Extimité* represents what Étienne Achille, Charles Forsdick, and Lydie Moudileno have termed a postcolonial realm of memory. As Afro-descendants who invite Afro-descendants and other members of various diasporas in France to their program, Dibondo and Vincent have crafted a soundscape of voices attesting to the existence of hybrid postcolonial identities in contemporary French society. Beyond their ethnic and racial backgrounds, the subjectivities of the guests, which mostly fall outside "heteronormative, and cis-gendered citizenship" (Bouamer, Provencher, and Schroth 7), also allow for the consideration of *Extimité* as a queer realm of memory. The dual marginalization featured in the podcast, sometimes intersecting with other categories such as ableism and religion, challenges the monolithic understanding of what constitutes Frenchness and French *lieux de mémoire*.

Observing the proximities between sexual and racial issues in their relation to trauma, Ann Cvetkovich's book, *An Archive of Feelings* (2003), proves particularly relevant for examining the testimonies expressed by *Extimité*'s guests. Agreeing with her that queer strategies are best suited to remain "alert to the idiosyncrasies of emotional life" (7), I will first analyze Dibondo and Vincent's queer method to interviewing their guests. Building upon Jack Halberstam's insights in *In a Queer Time and Place* (2005), I will then demonstrate how *Extimité*'s intersectional archive, beyond its role as a repository, represents a queer realm of memory by creating a collective knowledge and memorializing activities that enable non-normative subjects to negotiate their positions in French society and respond to the political urgencies of their time.

Emotions and everyday experiences as valuable intersectional testimonies

In *Le génie lesbien* (2020), Alice Coffin criticizes white men for establishing journalistic standards that prioritize neutrality and rationalism at the expense of lived experiences and emotions (59). The dismissal of emotion in news is viewed by Coffin as a racist and sexist weapon that marginalizes intimate discourses, leading to what she calls "la ruée des journalistes minoritaires et féministes vers les podcasts" [the rush of minority and feminist journalists toward podcasts] (59). As part of this media revolution, Dibondo and Vincent openly express their intention to challenge traditional journalism, which often relies on statistics and the expertise of socially dominant subjects (Racque, "Les visages"). Instead, they give voice to minority subjects, whom they regard as experts in their own life stories and as capable of providing nuanced depictions of their complex realities. By using only the first names of their guests as episode titles, the hosts immediately signal to their audience that their podcast promotes self-evaluation as a form of expertise, favoring *extimité* over mere intimacy. In his analysis of *extimité* in contemporary media, Tisseron observes that, while the internet allows individuals to address a broad audience without acknowledging its presence, such a vast network also poses the risk of being ignored while presenting oneself to an audience. However, I argue that the podcast, as a medium, avoids this negative outcome through the mediation of the hosts. In *Extimité*, the validation offered by Dibondo and Vincent is sufficient for their guests to share their life stories as minoritized subjects. Furthermore, they emphasize that since podcast listeners deliberately seek specific content, it is most likely for guests to find a caring and empathetic audience: "on choisit ce qu'on écoute, au moment où l'on est prêt à l'entendre, ce qui garantit une forme de bienveillance" [we choose what we listen to, at the moment when we are ready to hear it, which ensures a form of benevolence] (Racque "'Extimité'").

Beyond these aspects intrinsic to podcasting, *Extimité*'s own approach initiates what Dibondo and Vincent call in each episode "le désir de rendre visible une partie de sa vie intime afin de mieux se l'approprier" [the desire to make visible a part of one's intimate life in order to better take ownership of it]. To establish trust with their guests, the hosts dedicated the first two episodes of the podcast to sharing their own life stories. By engaging in this practice of self-disclosure for self-empowerment, Douce, for example, openly discusses the challenges she faced after moving to France from Congo, including experiences of racism at school and domestic violence in one of her relationships. She then recalls how she found in feminism, and particularly Afrofeminism, the tools to overcome her situation. Vincent, on his part, reflects on his struggle as an effeminate gay Black man. He later reveals how this exposure contributed to his coming out since his sister discovered his homosexuality after some of her friends had listened to the episode about him (Racque, "Les visages"). According to Dibondo and Vincent, hearing their hosts' personal stories in the early episodes helps guests become more familiar with them – and more comfortable sharing their own experiences. The fact that guests come to Dibondo's or Vincent's bedroom to record the episodes further creates a safe and intimate atmosphere, enhancing the sense of connection between hosts and guests. Qualifying this relationship as an "ethos of group solidarity," in her study, "Podcasting Blackness," Sarah Florini compares this type of socialization to the one found in Black spaces, such as barber/beauty shops or churches (156). When considering not only Blackness but also queer and non-gender conforming identities, the choice of the bedroom as the recording location appears to be highly strategic. It represents a safe space in which subjects do not have to conform to any specific social identity. In a manner similar to Virginia Woolf, who valued a room specifically intended for women's reflection and creative production, the bedroom in *Extimité* becomes a space where individuals with identities at the intersection of diverse minority aspects can think and create content about themselves without the imperatives and pressures of social life.

The sense of safety and compassion offered by the podcast also transpires in the way *Extimité*'s hosts conduct their interviews. Viewing speech as both a mode of existence and a form of resistance, Dibondo underscores the importance of attending to every dimension of testimony – including its "aspérités" [rough edges or textural nuances] (Racque "'Extimité'"). According to her, listening beyond what is conventionally expected from a subject is a strategy to "déjouer les schémas sociaux qui [m']assignent à une place, à l'autre, à un imaginaire colonial, sexiste et hétéronormé" [subvert social patterns that assign [me] to a place, to the other, to a colonial, sexist, and heteronormative imaginary] (Racque "'Extimité'"). What Dibondo refers to as "aspérités," Ann Cvetkovich would describe as affects. By focusing on feelings, affects are considered a "raw material" that gives rise to "cultural formations that are unpredictable and varied" (Cvetkovich 48). Listening to an episode of *Extimité* offers a similar experience, as each testimonial unfolds like a stream of consciousness rather than adhering to the order of a preconceived interview. Favoring what Dibondo describes as "un mélange d'écoute active, de questionnements sur un mot, une situation, un silence" [a blend of active listening, questioning about a word, a situation, a silence] (Racque "'Extimité'"), the podcast frames the conversation with ritual questions only at the beginning and end of each episode. These questions are intentionally open-ended and general, enabling the guests to guide the conversation in the direction they choose.

The first emblematic question, asked by Dibondo and Vincent to open the podcast, is: "Quand tu te regardes dans le miroir, qu'est-ce que tu vois?" [When you look at yourself in the mirror, what do you see?]. This question, somewhat reminiscent of the Lacanian mirror stage in which the child learns to become aware of their body and distinguish it from others, encourages guests to reflect out loud on their relationship with themselves and how their singularity influences their interactions with others. It also places them in a position of intimacy and vulnerability from the very beginning, which fosters the expression of affect. For example, Rumi, the guest of episode 20, responds by laughing nervously and remaining somewhat vague when asked what he sees when he looks in the mirror.[1] He asserts that he sees "une grande histoire, très longue, très complexe, difficile à reconstruire, plein de souffrances, plein de chemins, une histoire de migrations" [a great, very long, very complex story, difficult to reconstruct, full of sufferings, full of paths, a history of migrations] (Dibondo and Vincent "Épisode 20: Rumi," 1:48–2:03). Concluding his answer with "c'est tout" [that's all] and another laugh, Dibondo interjects with "ça fait déjà beaucoup" [that's already a lot] and shares a sympathetic laugh with him (2:07–2:11).

Invited to continue his story, starting from his childhood, Rumi recalls the racist gaze he used to receive from others at school, even though he could not articulate it at that young age. He was often the target of comments and jokes that equated him with being Arab. This led him to become aware of his racialization and, consequently, his origins. As Cvetkovich points out, exploring trauma in ordinary events rather than necessarily in accidents proves to be politically significant, as it reveals situations of systemic violence (19). By considering everyday experiences as not only valid but also essential points of inquiry when addressing racial issues, *Extimité* provides guests with a space to express the complexity of their identity. As Rumi explains: "Ce que vous faites avec *Extimité*, c'est nous créer nos propres narrations, arriver à se rencontrer avec d'autres personnes racisées, se rendre compte d'une sorte de richesse pas forcément culturelle mais de vie, d'identité qui nous permet de nous comprendre à travers ce partage" [What you are doing with *Extimité* is creating our own narratives, finding ways to connect with other racialized individuals, realizing a kind of richness not necessarily cultural but of life, of identity that allows us to understand ourselves through this sharing] ("Épisode 20: Rumi," 29:27–29:48). As the son of a Moroccan mother and a Pakistani father, Rumi memorializes the uniqueness of his background, which challenges the tendency to reduce *métissage* (mixed heritage) solely to the interbreeding of Black and white parents.

In line with the racial aspect of his subjectivity, Rumi does not connect his gender identity and sexual orientation to a specific traumatic event. Instead, he describes a long-term process that led to feelings of isolation. He relates his internal struggle to the experiences of trans queer racialized individuals living in France who, like him, have

---

1   The pronouns I use for Rumi and the other guests mentioned in this chapter are the same as those used in *Extimité*'s episode descriptions on the podcast platform Acast.

difficulties finding spaces where they can comfortably be themselves. In a section of the episode (31:44–35:42), Dibondo and Vincent allow their guest to share his thoughts without interruption as he audibly grapples with self-definition. Rumi's silences following the four instances where he says "je me suis rendu compte que…" [I realized that…] illustrate his hesitation in finding the right terms to define his gender and sexuality. Even though Rumi remains somewhat vague and deflective about his self-realization, the hosts display patience, and refrain from filling in the blanks of his sentences or asking pointed questions. They provide him with the time and space to express himself. In the end, Rumi admits: "c'est surtout au lycée et puis surtout en 2015 quand j'ai commencé à fréquenter ces forums communautaires que je me suis rendu compte que… ben que j'étais queer" [it's mainly in high school, and especially in 2015 when I started frequenting these community forums, that I realized… well, that I was queer] (35:33–35:42). While Rumi's struggle to use the term "queer" may reflect a sense of confusion, if not shame, he also explicitly expresses the conflict he has with a term that, by its inherent ambiguity, may obscure certain lived experiences, including those of trans individuals. Despite its imperfections, he nonetheless considers "queer" to be the most suitable word to describe how he embodies his gender and sexuality.

Whether it is Rumi's experience, Vénus's as a transracialized sex worker, Aïcha's as a self-proclaimed dyke Tunisian artist, or that of many others, *Extimité*, with over 39 episodes, has evolved into a repository that welcomes the stories of individuals whose positions at the intersections of various minority identities complicate understandings of ableism, class, gender, race, and sexuality in contemporary France. In alignment with Renée Altergott, who, in her article, "'Elles n'ont pas la voix blanche': Colorblind Listening and the French Podcast" (2023), characterizes podcasts as decolonial counter-archives that reveal the existence of racism despite its denial in French colorblind society (52), I consider that *Extimité* expands on this decolonial work by exposing France's gender and sexuality obliviousness. Thanks to the recording and memorialization of these complex singularities, Dibondo and Vincent have successfully transformed intimate stories into an aggregate that contributes to the development of an intersectional queer realm of memory in France.

Media revolution and revolutionary content: from social media to street activism

In *Podcasting: The Audio Media Revolution* (2019), Lance Dan and Martin Spinelli assert that one of the most significant impacts of podcasts is their ability to offer new ways of generating meaning and forming relationships (1–2). Drawing similar conclusions in their respective studies on Black podcasting, Sarah Florini and Élodie Malanda both observe the use of vernacular specific to the Black community. In French Black podcasts such as *Cases rebelles*, *Piment*, and *Le Tchip*, Malanda identifies the use and discussions of expressions like "mysoginoir" and "afroféminisme" as contributing to the formation of core values against sexism, homophobia, and transphobia within the community (76). In the case of *Extimité*, which, as I demonstrated in the first part, embraces a fluid conversational style, Dibondo and Vincent help their guests speak and come up with words and concepts in their own time. This strategy actively participates in the development of an intersectional culture.

In episode 2, Marie explains her use of the term "Asiatfem" to imbue her queer identity with political meaning. She resists the tendency to associate queerness solely with whiteness and seeks to assert with "Asiatfem" that Asian LGBTQ+ people also exist. Marie's decision to append "fem" to "Asiat" stems from a desire to address explicitly the intersection of anti-Asian racism and discrimination against women, inspired by Afrofeminism, a movement that correlates feminism with the Afro community. Kelsi, in episode 11, explains the distinction between non-binarity and gender fluidity. Non-binarity serves as an umbrella term encompassing gender fluid people as well as those who define themselves, like Kelsi, as gender-neutral or "neutrois" ("Épisode 11: Kelsi," 5:37). In addition to the quest for appropriate terms, some guests challenge established definitions. Mischa, in episode 30, explains that instead of viewing an "intersex" individual as a person whose body does not conform to the typical male or female anatomy, he favors an approach focusing on the social lived experience that he considers less fetishistic: "les personnes intersexes, ce sont surtout des personnes qui ont vécu une invalidation médicale et sociale de leur corps" [intersex people are mainly individuals who have experienced medical and social invalidation of their bodies] ("Épisode 30: Mischa," 3:54–3:59). In doing so, Mischa promotes a perspective on intersexuality that resists the absolute authority of medicine and values the voices of those most directly affected.

Beyond these examples of self-naming and self-definition, the podcast's guests also use terms that identify the aspects that make them targets of violence as minorities. In episode 9, Miguel discusses "whitesplaining" ("Épisode 9: Miguel," 26:00), akin to "mansplaining," which involves white individuals explaining to racialized subjects what is or is not racist, thus effectively discrediting their lived experiences. In a special episode recorded on September 7, 2019, during the *Festival Extimité*, Jean-Victor warns against what he terms the "blantriarcat," a concept at the intersection of patriarchy and whiteness used to describe the oppression of racialized people, including that which occurs within the queer community. Similarly, in episode 5, Yuni seeks to raise awareness about "follophobie," which discriminates against effeminate gay men and drag queen performers like him. By identifying issues both outside and within the LGBTQ+ community, and their impact on individuals at the intersection of multiple minority aspects, *Extimité* contributes to the construction of a culture that simultaneously necessitates self-critique.

Among the features analyzed in Dan and Spinelli's essay, the interweaving of podcasts with other social media platforms, and the increased community engagement it generates, are particularly pertinent to the case of *Extimité*. In addition to its repository quality, the podcast's goal is to share the knowledge presented in its episodes, fostering a collective awareness that empowers non-normative subjects to reconsider their relationship with society. On their Instagram page, which features 186 posts published between September 2018 and May 2022, Dibondo and Vincent not only promote their program by sharing pictures of their guests and quotes from the episodes but also take the time to address issues of terminology and provide cultural recommendations, sourced from themselves or their guests. In this extension of *Extimité*'s archival practice, references to classics from African American intellectuals who pioneered critical race theory and Afrofeminism scholarship, such as bell hooks's *Ain't I a Woman* (1981) and Audre Lorde's *Sister Outsider* (1984), stand alongside contributions by Françoise Vergès and Maboula Soumahoro, who, respectively in *Un féminisme décolonial* (2019) and *Le Triangle et l'Hexagone* (2020), introduced these issues in the context of the French-speaking world. Beyond this geographical connection between the United States and the francophone world, Dibondo and Vincent engage in a dialogue with the past, which includes white feminist and queer figures, among them Virginia Woolf and Monique Wittig. In the same fashion as the podcast's episodes, the intersectional landscape and genealogy created on Instagram promote a free-flowing style to creating and disseminating knowledge. This method further challenges the divide between high and low theory, as initially questioned by Stuart Hall and later by Jack Halberstam in *The Queer Art of Failure* (2011). Whether it is Solange Knowles's music album *A Seat at the Table* (2016) or the television show *Killing Eve* (2018–22), their inclusion, alongside the scholarly works mentioned earlier, invites the podcast's followers to recognize pop culture as a serious and relevant realm that contains messages and micropolitics contributing to the development of a queer intersectional culture.

Having explored the podcast's relationship with social media, it is also crucial to examine its connection with street activism. Dibondo and Vincent address this connection in special episodes like the one recorded during the 2020 Pride March in Paris. Presented on the podcast's platform as a "documentaire qui fait office d'archive" [documentary that serves as an archive], this 75-minute episode captures the vibrant energy of the crowd in the streets, with activists enthusiastically displaying their signs and delivering speeches on behalf of advocacy organizations that had chosen to propose an alternative to the traditional Gay Pride. Indeed, the Pride March organized on July 4, 2020, challenged the conventional format of Pride events, which usually featured floats celebrating capitalistic and conservative groups, accused by Dibondo and other queer activists from the march of sidelining those at the margins of the LGBTQ+ rainbow. Giving up floats and focusing on the political aspect of the march, the 2020 Pride that *Extimité* invites its audience to hear focuses on rights yet to be obtained by the queer community, especially trans people and sex workers. Race also took center stage in this Pride, with the lead of the procession exclusively dedicated to queer racialized people. In her rare interventions during the episode, Dibondo explains the historical and political significance of racial non-mixing, a typically controversial practice in France. She reminds the audience of the instrumental role played by Marsha P. Johnson and Silvia Rivera, two racialized trans women who initiated the 1969 Stonewall riots. By re-politicizing the march, the 2020 Pride aimed to both honor its lineage with Black activism and provide visibility to racialized queer individuals today. This decision may have played a significant role in Dibondo's own participation in a march she admittedly had not attended previously. In her introduction to the episode, she speaks of it as a "baptême qu'[elle] attendai[t] peut-être inconsciemment" [baptism that [she] may have been waiting for, perhaps unconsciously] ("Pride 2020," 0:16–0:18).

Despite the explicit celebration of racialized activists leading to her queer baptism during the march, Dibondo openly shares her disillusionment with some white activists who complained to the police about being excluded from the head of the procession. True to the podcast's approach, Dibondo seizes this discriminatory event as an opportunity for education, highlighting this situation as a clear example of white fragility. The fact that white participants in the march reached out to the police to accuse racialized activists is particularly shocking, given the context in which the Pride event took place. Organized a little over a month after the murder of George Floyd by police officers in Minneapolis, the march aimed to contribute to the global awareness of police brutality against Black lives and to extend this struggle to other marginalized groups facing repressive measures, especially migrants and sex workers. While a representative of the STRASS (Syndicat du TRAvail Sexuel), the union for male, female, and transgender sex workers in France, expressed her joy at having the opportunity to gather for reasons other than mourning the loss of their members, the speeches and chants did not let the murders be forgotten of Vanessa Campos in 2018 and Jessyca Sarmiento in 2020, two immigrant sex workers. Reproaching the lack of emotion and public outcry following their deaths, STRASS and the activists marching in the 2020 Pride chanted their names to ensure that these lives are remembered as significant. *Extimité*'s recording of the memorialization of this traumatic past and its impact on the present aligns with what Heather Love describes as "looking back," in *Feeling Backward: Loss and the Politics of Queer History* (2007). Love suggests that focusing on the negative aspects of the past is a necessary queer response to LGBTQ+ activism's tendency to emphasize the present and positivity, such as pride, while neglecting the historical injuries that have affected non-normative sexual subjects. By doing so, queer criticism utilizes negativity as a catalyst for political action, which, in this case, the podcast serves to amplify.

Conclusion

From the hosts' bedroom to the streets via social media, *Extimité*'s recording and archiving work on the identities, cultures, and practices of minoritized subjects offers a unique lens through which to reconsider minority politics, especially the concept of "convergence des luttes" from an intersectional perspective. As explained in *Le combat Adama*

(2019), written by Geoffroy de Lagasnerie and Assa Traoré, leader of the "Comité Vérité pour Adama," formed in honor of her brother who was killed by the police in 2016, "convergence des luttes" tends to erase the specificity of individual struggles in favor of a universalism that often aligns with the ideas and values of the white middle class (211). Consequently, rather than thinking of social struggles from a general perspective, with abstract categories, Lagasnerie and Traoré advocate for an intersectional approach that recognizes how these categories are deeply embedded in and intertwined with our existence (222). During an episode in which a roundtable discussion questioned the relevance of "convergence des luttes," Dibondo shared a similar analysis, stating, "c'est nos vécus qui nous permettent de rayonner [...]. Je pense que c'est ça qui fait la convergence" [it's our experiences that allow us to shine [...]. I think that's what creates the convergence] ("#FestivalExtimité," 1:15:30–1:15:45). Dibondo emphasizes that individual freedom, far from being an obstacle, forms the very foundation for collaborative and collective commitment. She mobilizes intersectionality to reconcile the notion of "convergence" with the present reality: "On est pluriels et nos luttes sont plurielles" [We are plural, and our struggles are plural] (1:16:43–1:16:45). To reinforce such a statement, she adds that this is not only her personal conviction but also the core objective of *Extimité*.

As this chapter demonstrates, the podcast achieves its aim through an archival process that goes beyond presenting individual stories. It succeeds in bringing intersectional, embodied experiences into conversation, thereby contributing to a form of universalism akin to the one advocated by Mame-Fatou Niang and Julien Suaudeau. Comparing universalism to practices like kintsugi or mosaic-making, Niang and Suaudeau contend that the fragmented nature of contemporary society does not undermine universalism but rather opens up the possibility of reimagining it as a more fluid and inclusive concept. As a queer *lieu de mémoire* of the present, *Extimité* represents one of the sources of inspiration to build this universalism to come, or to enable its "futurity," to use José Esteban Muñoz's term. Like Mari Ruti – who describes Muñoz's investment in futurity as reparative, in that it frames negative emotions such as pain, shame, or despair as opportunities for generating collective political response (174) – I argue that *Extimité*'s focus on affect and trauma offers a promising path for minority activism. It seeks to confront the wound of the present as a way to help shape an emerging intersectional collective society.

Works cited

Achille, Étienne, Charles Forsdick, and Lydie Moudileno, eds. *Postcolonial Realms of Memory: Sites and Symbols in Modern France*. Liverpool UP, 2020.
Altergott, Renée. "'Elles n'ont pas la voix blanche': Colorblind listening and the French podcast." *CFC Intersections*, vol. 2, no. 1, 2023, pp. 45–61.
Bastide, Lauren, host. *La Poudre*, Spotify. 2016–23.
———. "Épisode 87. La revolution transféministe avec Sam Bourcier." *La Poudre, Spotify*. February 10, 2021.
———. "Épisode 120. Virginie Despentes." *La Poudre, Spotify*. September 7, 2022.
Coffin, Alice. *Le génie lesbien*. Grasset, 2020.
Cvetkovich, Ann. *An Archive of Feelings: Trauma, Sexuality, and Lesbian Public Cultures*. Duke UP, 2003.
Dan, Lance, and Martin Spinelli, eds. *Podcasting: The Audio Media Revolution*. Bloomsbury Academic, 2019.
Dibondo, Douce, and Anthony Vincent, hosts. *Extimité*, Acast, 2018–22.
———. "Épisode 0: Douce." *Extimité*, Acast. September 30, 2018.
———. "Épisode 1: Anthony." *Extimité*, Acast. October 14, 2018.
———. "Épisode 2: Marie." *Extimité*, Acast. October 28, 2018.
———. "Épisode 5: Yuni." *Extimité*, Acast. December 9, 2018.
———. "Épisode 8: Vénus." *Extimité*, Acast. January 19, 2019.
———. "Épisode 9: Miguel." *Extimité*, Acast. February 3, 2019.
———. "Épisode 11: Kelsi." *Extimité*, Acast. March 3, 2019.
———. "Épisode 20: Rumi." *Extimité*, Acast. July 7, 2019.
———. "Épisode 21: Aïcha." *Extimité*, Acast. July 21, 2019.
———. "Épisode 30: Mischa." *Extimité*, Acast. January 12, 2020.
———. "#FestivalExtimité – Table Ronde – Vous Avez Dit Convergence Des Luttes?" *Extimité*, Acast. September 22, 2019.
———. "Pride 2020, nos fiertés sont politiques." *Extimité*, Acast. July 12, 2020.
Florini, Sarah. "Podcasting Blackness." *Race and Media. Critical Approaches*, edited by Lori Kido Lopez. New York UP, 2020, pp. 153–62.
Halberstam, Jack. *The Queer Art of Failure*. Duke UP, 2011.
———. *In a Queer Time and Place: Transgender Bodies, Subcultural Lives*. New York UP, 2005.
hooks, bell. *Ain't I a Woman: Black Women and Feminism*. South End Press, 1981.
Knowles, Solange. *A Seat at the Table*. Saint Records and Columbia Records, 2016.
Lagasnerie, Geoffroy de, and Assa Traoré. *Le combat Adama*. Stock, 2019.
Lorde, Audre. *Sister Outsider: Essays and Speeches*. Crossing Press, 1984.

Love, Heather. *Feeling Backward: Loss and the Politics of Queer History*. Harvard UP, 2007.

Malanda, Élodie. "'Rendez-nous le Tchip': Performing a French Black community through podcasts." *CFC Intersections*, vol. 2, no. 1, 2023, pp. 63–79.

Muñoz, José Esteban. *Cruising Utopia: The Then and There of Queer Futurity*. New York UP, 2009.

Niang, Mame-Fatou, and Julien Suaudeau. *Universalisme*. Anamosa, 2022.

Racque, Élise. "'Extimité', le podcast où 'la parole est existence et resistance.'" *Télérama*. February 10, 2021. Web.

———. "Les visages du podcast: Douce Dibondo et Anthony Vincent donnent la parole aux minorités." *Télérama*. October 15, 2021. Web.

Ruti, Mari. *The Ethics of Opting Out: Queer Theory's Defiant Subjects*. Columbia UP, 2017.

Soumahoro, Maboula. *Le Triangle et l'Hexagone*. La Découverte, 2020.

Tisseron, Serge. "Intimité et extimité." *Communications*, vol. 1, no. 88, 2011, pp. 83–91.

Vergès, Françoise. *Un féminisme décolonial*. La Fabrique, 2019.

Waller-Bridge, Phoebe. *Killing Eve*. Television series. BBC America, 2018–22.

CHAPTER TWENTY THREE

Bodies, memories, visibility
Élisabeth Lebovici's digital reinscription of lesbians in the French visual arts

Cristina Johnston

French art historian, Élisabeth Lebovici, describes herself on X as "1/3 art + 1/3 queer + 1/3 both." Her interests span visual, aural, and verbal art forms, approaching them from an intersectional perspective that simultaneously foregrounds the activist and the artistic, the postcolonial and the feminist, the individual and the collective, the lesbian and the queer. She has been posting on her blog "Le Beau Vice" (le-beau-vice.blogspot.com) since 2006, and it is similarly wide-ranging in its gaze, but there Lebovici operates at a different pace, more inclined to allow the detail to unfold, often with a specific interest in reinscriptions of, and reflections on, the place of feminist and *lesbian* artists, activists, and politics within a wider queer landscape.

In spring 2020, over the early months of the Covid pandemic and the lockdowns in metropolitan France, Lebovici used the blog to chart the territory of her "jours et nuits" [days and nights], first "de confinements" [of confinements], then, from May 12, 2020, "de déconfinements" [of openings up]. On March 16, 2020, the first of Lebovici's "jours et nuits de confinements" quickly sets the tone. This first post, subtitled "(To Chantal Akerman)," combines stills from a series of the Belgian filmmaker's works, with both Lebovici's reflections on the lockdown that would be imposed on metropolitan France from March 17 and with the first artistic visual and aural landscape it evokes for her, entwining temporalities and geographies along the way. The entry considers

Akerman's representation of women indoors that is a far remove from "une image des femmes confinées dans un intérieur, dictée par un point de vue patriarcal et qui ne porte, en réalité, aucune attention à ce qui se passe dans ce cadre" [an image of women confined within an interior space, an image determined by a patriarchal perspective that, in reality, pays no attention to what is happening within the frame].[1] Rather, as Lebovici notes, Akerman "fait attention, y compris aux confins les plus brûlants, les plus inquiétants du confinement" [pays attention, including to the most tendentious, the most unsettling confines of lockdown]. In so doing, both Akerman and Lebovici highlight – well before mainstream news outlets began to ponder whether there *might* be differences in individuals' experiences of the pandemic – the value that can be derived by considering such experiences from the perspectives of those who have tended to be peripheral to a framing of events, and memories thereof, in light of their gender, sexuality, ethnicity, or other characteristics. From June 2020 through into late 2021, the posts expanded beyond the "dé/confinement" binary and became "jours et nuits" of everything from the male gaze to fragmentation, mapping out a new queer realm of contemporary memory in the digital sphere.

In his influential *Lieux de mémoire*, Pierre Nora observed that "a process of interior decolonization has affected ethnic minorities, families, and groups that until now have possessed reserves of memory but little or no historical capital" (7). Subsequent scholars and theorists of contemporary France have highlighted *Lieux de mémoire*'s "omissions and blind spots concerning the French Empire" (Achille, Forsdick, and Moudileno 1). Indeed, Achille, Forsdick, and Moudileno's introduction to their volume on *Postcolonial Realms of Memory*, issues a scholarly call to arms, declaring that "we now need a more sustained and collective intervention" (1) and emphasizing "the urgency of asserting the central place of the colonial in the making of modern France, and of anchoring it in a collective memory that has often evacuated traces of empire, as if deemed unworthy of remembrance or simply considered marginal" (2). Achille, Forsdick, and Moudileno, and the contributors to their work, play a crucial role in issuing what the editors of the present collection describe as "an important corrective by expanding realms of memory to include those pertaining to (post)colonial history" (Bouamer, Provencher, and Schroth 1). Other "omissions" have, nevertheless, continued to exist, most notably in

[1] All translations are my own.

relation to the role played by queer remembering, and it is precisely such "omissions" that I argue Élisabeth Lebovici's art criticism and art activism seek to address, specifically by offering perspectives on, and from, the gendered and sexual peripheries. I should note here that, in most instances, in line with the expression as used elsewhere in this volume and in the wider scholarship, I have tended to use "realm" rather than "landscape." However, given Lebovici's determined focus on the reinscription of *lesbian* experiences through her work and the centrality of that reinscription to this chapter, something in the etymology of "realm" sits uncomfortably with me.

None of this should be taken as implying that Lebovici simply looks back over a personally curated digital archive, using the blog and her other social media postings merely to suggest contemporary queer-inflected reinterpretations of static art events, exhibitions, installations, or films. Lebovici's work is not a digital repository of her writings on material objects and events. Rather, the ongoing layering of temporalities and geographies she offers enables the reinscription of perspectives that were always already there in the works, artists, and moments – activist and/or artistic – upon which lockdown, for example, affords her time to reflect. The digital archive created through Lebovici's blog and social media can be understood in line with Jack Halberstam's assertion that the archive is "a theory of cultural relevance, a construction of collective memory, and a complex record of queer activity" (293). And as I argue, we can also see a similar process unfolding across Lebovici's work beyond the digital domain, more often than not demonstrating the ways in which, in the queer landscape being charted, individual and collective experiences necessarily coexist and sustain each other.

Across Lebovici's "Jours et nuits de confinement" posts, there is an explicit acknowledgement that "the practices of private everyday experience [...] are as politically revealing in their own way as any event played out in the public arena" (Hirsch and Smith 12) and, crucially, that acknowledgement encompasses both Lebovici's individual reflections on her *own* "practices of private everyday experience" and the cultural, shared, and collective representations thereof that she has explored and mapped out over the years, demonstrating that "the content, sources and experiences that are recalled, forgotten or suppressed are of profound political significance" (12). In this way, across these posts, Lebovici recalls French Surrealist photographer Claude Cahun's use of masks in her photography of the 1920s and 1930s and draws parallels with lockdown mask-wearing and mask-appropriation, observing that "on ne sait jamais (assez) l'utilité d'une expérience individuelle de la poésie dans la lutte collective" [we can never be aware (enough) of how useful an individual experience of poetry can be in the context of a collective struggle]. Masks have a particular significance in Cahun's work, as is clear, for example, from one of the chapter openings of a 1929/30 work, *Aveux non avenus*, produced by Cahun with her partner Marcel Moore. Alongside a superimposed series of 11 photographic images of Cahun, in many of which she is masked, we can read: "Sous ce masque, un autre masque. Je n'en finirai pas de soulever tous ces visages" [Under this mask, another mask. I will never be done with removing all these faces]. Cahun and Moore's work "explored gender and identity through photographs [... and Cahun] used performance to allude to their many selves and alter egos" (Hessel 153). However, their work remained largely unknown until the 1980s, when it resurfaced, largely thanks to the work of the art historian François Leperlier. This resurfacing "coincide[ed] with an era of feminist interventions in art's discourses" that meant Cahun and Moore's "coupledom, gender nonconformity, and many masked self-portraits readily dovetailed with the era's sexual politics" (Reznick 53).

Similarly, the lockdown experience of endless exchanges via Skype, Zoom, WhatsApp, and other platforms "qui occupe[nt] une grande partie de nos (mes) journées" [which take up a large portion of our (my) days], reminds Lebovici of a 1970s videographic exchange between American artists Lynda Benglis and Robert Morris, through which the duo layer images and sound. For Lebovici, from the perspective of twenty-first-century lockdown, the conversation of Benglis and Morris offers scope for a renewed contemplation of the type of relationship it – and more contemporary forms of communication – reflects and engenders. She interrogates the role that video technology plays in the shaping and framing of the relationship depicted in this way through Benglis and Morris's project but Lebovici also notes, reflecting on her experience during lockdown, that "dans ces conversations où on se voit en même temps qu'on se parle, on peut aussi aimer les moments barbants, les brouillages de communication où tout le monde parle de concert" [in these conversations during which we can see each other as we speak to each other, we can also enjoy the boring moments, the communication mix-ups when everyone speaks at the same time]. Across the "jours et nuits de confinement" posts there is a constant to-ing and fro-ing between contemporary experience and the surfacing of memories prompted by that contemporary experience, between Lebovici's personal, individual reflections on those memories and the collective experiences of which they also form part.

The political significance of such layering of the individual and the collective is at the heart of Lebovici's blog posts from these early months of lockdown onwards, just as it is core to all other aspects of her digital presence. The first lockdown blog post begins with a series of stills from Akerman's films, but its opening sentences that follow on from the stills on the screen read: "Ne pas quitter la chambre. Regarder dehors par la porte-fenêtre" [Not leaving the bedroom. Looking outside through the French window]. Are we to understand this as a description of Lebovici's own experience, or that depicted by Akerman, or both? That individual and collective experiences are enmeshed is fundamental to Lebovici's engagement with queer memory.

In this chapter, I examine the ways in which Lebovici's online presence deftly highlights some of what has previously been overlooked or omitted from the French visual arts landscape. By foregrounding the feminist, the lesbian, the queer artists and activists whose work already exists in those lacunae, I argue that she is seeking to reinscribe their presence, to remap that very landscape, to rename and reclaim its landmarks, to tear down its sculptures and to create others. In this way, Lebovici's work can be understood as contributing to a dynamic and ongoing exploration of the ways in which "the pasts (and presents) of marginalized genders and sexualities have long been marked by erasures, gaps and silences" (Dragojlovic and Quinan 4). While others have productively applied an "actively postcolonial logic" to a process of "mapping the territory, generating the resources and setting the agendas that allow us to prise open France's multidirectional pasts and mobilize their postcolonial afterlives in a more productive way" (Achille, Fordsick, and Moudileno 15–16), Lebovici's actively queer logic seeks to "prise open [...] and mobilise" the afterlives of cultural artifacts, assemblages, events, and spaces within which postcolonial, queer, and lesbian experiences find, and claim, their place. However, she also seeks to demonstrate that, rather than, or in addition to, claiming their place within these "afterlives," in many instances the individual and collective experiences being foregrounded in this way are, in fact, being reinscribed within a queer landscape whose contours are being redescribed to render these experiences more visible, more audible.

While the "jours et nuits de confinement" posts offer a concentrated example of this process at work, its intensity, in many ways, is dictated by the intensity of that initial Covid lockdown period; these reinscriptions and reevaluations have long formed part of Lebovici's work, both in the sense that it has constantly sought to bring to the fore specificities of lesbian experience *and* in the sense that she has often recognized that, in order to foreground previously hidden or silenced experiences, there will be a need to turn to spaces, objects, and events that exist beyond the confines of what she terms a "linéarité hétéro-chronologique" [a heterochronological linearity].

By way of example, in *Femmes/artistes, artistes/femmes, Paris de 1880 à nos jours*, Lebovici and her co-author Catherine Gonnard analyze the work of photographer Claude Cahun. However, as Lebovici reflects in one of the "jours et nuits de confinement" posts, in the context of a study that was already aiming to uncover a history of art that redirected the gaze away from better known male artists to the "femmes/artistes, artistes/femmes" of the title, in fact the authors also wanted to reconsider, to re-evaluate, how individual "femmes/artistes" had previously been viewed, in order to overturn what Griselda Pollock terms "the created invisibility of women as creators" (1). In the case of Cahun, first, Lebovici recalls her own amazement at seeing Cahun's photographs as physical objects for the first time in 1994, not only because of the images themselves, but also because of the coincidence of this encounter "entre l'apparition, toute armée (masquée) de Claude Cahun, et celle de la Queer Nation. Le début des années 1990 ouvrait une actualité du genre à l'invention de la théorie queer" [between the appearance, armed (and masked) of Claude Cahun, and that of Queer Nation. The early 1990s were opening up questions of gender to the invention of queer theory]. In other words, for Lebovici, it is impossible to disentangle her individual encounter with Cahun's photomontages as artworks from her individual engagement with feminist and queer activist movements. The memories that she has of cultural encounters are necessarily political and the political necessarily feeds into her encounters with the cultural, "bringing politically loaded pasts to bear in the present with new intensities" (Chidgey 3–4).

Second, in seeing the photographs, the "autoportraits à deux" [collaborative self-portraits], as she describes them, Lebovici also recognizes that that "collaboration" has thus far been erased or silenced within a particular narrative of art/photo history and it is that silencing to which her work aims to offer a counter-discourse. For Cahun's "autoportraits" to be as they are, someone else, necessarily, has to have been actively involved in their creation:

> Non seulement j'ai été frappée par leur taille, minuscule (c'est à dire privée, intime, non exposable) mais également par le fait que "Claude Cahun" ne pouvait être techniquement l'autrice de ces autoportraits, en tout cas nombre d'entre eux avait certainement demandé le concours d'une seconde personne pour déclencher la prise de vue. On sait, surtout depuis les travaux de Tirza True Latimer, à quel point cette "seconde personne" a pris de l'importance. Claude Cahun et Marcel Moore, ça veut dire couple, mais surtout ça veut dire couple *lesbien*. (Lebovici)
>
> I was struck not only by their size, by the fact that they were minuscule (and thus private, intimate, non-exposable) but also by the fact that "Claude Cahun" could not technically be the author of these self-portraits, in any case a number of them had most certainly required the input of another person to push the button. And, particularly thanks to the work of Tirza True Latimer, we know to what extent this "other person" has grown in importance. To speak of Claude Cahun and Marcel Moore, means to speak of a couple, but above all it means to speak of a lesbian couple.

The multiple entwinements that emerge here are crucial to the approach Lebovici takes to the charting of a queer realm of memory, encompassing the individual, the collective, the political, the activist, and the artistic, but what is also crucial is the diversity of the objects of memory Lebovici brings together. This is not only a lockdown recollection of an exhibition of photographs but rather a reflection on the impact of Queer Nation, both on Lebovici's political and activist trajectory *and* on her political and activist engagement with art history, and a further acknowledgment of the need to bring those experiences to the fore, in order to inscribe them into a queer cultural present. And, perhaps most fundamentally, an explicit commitment to render visible the *lesbian* couple, not only in the specific example of Cahun and Moore, but as silenced contributor to art history and to narratives of cultural memory. As Pollock further notes: "There is no intention of providing names to be neutrally disappeared into an enlarged official story of modern art. Difference becomes an active, creative presence."

A similarly determined desire to actively resist a tendency towards "neutral disappearance," whether of individuals, couples, or groups, can also be found in Lebovici's *Ce que le sida m'a fait. Art et activisme à la fin du XXe siècle*, published in 2017. In the introduction, Lebovici addresses her active choice "pour les entretiens et plusieurs chapitres, de porter l'accent sur les lesbiennes" [in interviews and in several chapters, to highlight lesbians], noting that they were "négligées par les enquêtes socio-épidémiologiques, considérées comme peu exposées aux risques de contamination par le VIH, leurs pratiques sexuelles et sociabilités ont été et sont encore les grandes absentes des politiques de santé" [neglected by socio-epidemiological studies, considered at low risk of HIV infection, and their sexual practices and forms of sociability having been, and continuing to be, largely absent from health policies] (12). Lebovici further observes that it is in large part through their involvement in "différents projets mémoriels et/ou historiques" [a number of memorial and/or historical projects] (13) that the role played by lesbians during the HIV/AIDS epidemic has recently undergone "[des] reconsidérations radicales" [radical reconsiderations] (13). This, in turn, has enabled an acknowledgement of the crucial role played by lesbians in the construction and transmission of HIV/AIDS histories and representations: "Parce qu'elles avaient survécu, elles étaient encore là à témoigner de cette histoire et à la fabriquer aussi, cette histoire" [Because they had survived, they were still there to bear witness to this history and to construct it, too, this history] (13).

What is particularly striking in Lebovici's foregrounding of the role played by lesbians in HIV/AIDS histories and representations is that it simultaneously recognizes the centrality of a more conventional archiving of tangible objects alongside a need to archive, to recall, to re-collect the non-material, the affective, the remembered:

> L'archivage, non seulement des objets matériels et/ou textuels, mais des affects "associés à la nostalgie, à la mémoire personnelle, au fantasme, au traumatisme" [Cvetkovich]. Ce mélange dans une même matérialité nous renvoie à l'objet de ce livre; son objet principal, pourrais-je dire, tant ce livre essaie de faire avec ces choses matérielles que sont les artefacts, mais aussi avec ces choses immatérielles que sont les sentiments – *mes* sentiments – considérés comme "trop personnels et trop éphémères pour qu'on les consigne par écrit" [Cvetkovich]. (Lebovici, *Ce que le sida m'a fait* 13)

> Archiving, not only material and/or textual objects, but the affects "associated with nostalgia, with personal memory, with fantasy, with trauma" [Cvetkovich]. This mixing in one and the same materiality brings us to the object of this book; its primary object, I could say, such is the extent to which this book tries to work with artifacts, as material things, but also with the immaterial, in the form of feelings – my feelings – considered "too personal and too ephemeral to be consigned in writing" [Cvetkovich].

While Lebovici's key focus in *Ce que le sida m'a fait* is on art and activism of the late twentieth century, specifically in the context of a reflection on the impact of HIV/AIDS on that period, on its artists and theorists, the approach adopted is very much in line with the broader mapping of queer realms of memory I argue are to be found throughout Lebovici's online presence, as much as they are in her *physically* published works. The queer realms of memory that emerge from Lebovici's blog posts, from her contributions on X, from her Instagram posts, are an active, considered, and deliberate assemblage of the personal and the political in the digital domain, demonstrating, as Hirsch and Smith observe, that "cultural memory is the product of fragmentary personal and collective experiences articulated through technologies and media that shape even as they transmit memory" (5).

Lebovici's work does not wholly break from the "traditional" spaces and practices of the archive. Galleries, museums, theatres, libraries, all feature as cultural venues in her posts, key sites of encounter, often, with significant artists, performances, happenings, and exhibits. Rather, first, the queer potential of such "traditional" spaces is often underscored through Lebovici's work. Second, though, these spaces often co-exist in her blogs, tweets, and Instagram posts alongside less conventional, less permanent spaces and practices, seeking to bridge the gap between an "official" history of art and/or activism with a "lived" memory thereof. After all, as Silvana Mandolessi has noted: "Digital archives do not threaten the stability or permanence of our representations of the past but on the contrary, they put into practice the mutation and circulation that keeps memory alive" (1515). What we find, in Lebovici, is precisely an attempt to put "mutation and circulation" into practice, to aim not to replace one set of fixed landmarks and established figures with another but rather to recognize, to chart, to celebrate, and to challenge the dynamic nature of queer mappings of cultural memory. And to recognize, chart, and celebrate the challenges this process brings.

In an Instagram post on March 31, 2024, reflecting on an exhibition of a series of works by American photographer Francesca Woodman at the Gagosian in New York, Lebovici describes the figure who is visible in some of the images as follows:

> [U]ne personne nue – on est au courant que c'est souvent elle – est à quatre pattes, est en train de ramper, se pousse derrière un bout de miroir, se range à côté de lui, disparaît presque avec le mur [...]. Elle ne fait pas partie des meubles. De toute façon, il n'y en a pas. « Inhabiter », pourrait-on dire: c'est peut-être ça, expérimenter. Ne pas s'installer. Laisser donc, de la place tout en laissant de la trace. N'habiter que l'image et la hanter.

> A naked figure – we know it is often her – is on all fours, is crawling, squeezes in behind a fragment of mirror, tucks in beside it, almost disappears into the wall [...]. She's not part of the furniture. In any case, there isn't any. We could describe this as "inhabiting": maybe that's what it is, experimenting. Not settling. Leaving space while also leaving traces. To inhabit only the image and to haunt it.

"Laisser de la place tout en laissant de la trace" could almost be the unintentional tagline for the artists and activists whose trajectories Lebovici maps through her ongoing practice of digital curation. She examines the points at which queer bodies come into contact with the world – and the physical, social, and symbolic limits imposed on such contact. The need for queer bodies to carve out space for themselves necessarily reshapes the world around them through that very act of embodiment. Returning to the first lockdown blog post on Chantal Akerman, Lebovici similarly reflects on a female figure's need to create – and locate – a space of her own within a pre-existing landscape, in this case in Akerman's films *La Chambre* and *Je, Tu, Il, Elle*:

> Il me semble que moins l'appartement est grand plus il faut de temps au film pour le décrire (360° pour *La Chambre*), ou pour l'imager. C'est peut-être pour ça que dans *Je, Tu, Il, Elle*, "Je" pousse les meubles. "Vide, la pièce est grande je trouve", dit-elle alors que l'espace est encombré par la commode, le miroir, la table, le fauteuil. On a toujours – moi du moins- l'impression qu'on va se cogner. Dans les meubles. Au coin des lits. Dans la cuisine. Dans le couloir, Etc. (Lebovici)
>
> It seems to me that, the bigger the apartment, the greater the time it takes for the film to describe it (a 360-degree sweep in *La Chambre*) or to show it to us. Perhaps that's why in *Je, Tu, Il, Elle*, "Je" moves the furniture around. "When it's empty, I find the room big", she says, although the space is cluttered by the wardrobe, the mirror, the table, the armchair. We – or at least I – always have the feeling we're going to knock into something. Into the furniture. Into the corner of the beds. In the kitchen. In the corridor. Etc.

Akerman's and Woodman's respective explorations of the place – and plac*ing* – of the female body, the constraints imposed on women by the environments they inhabit, and their efforts to assert ownership over those spaces are powerfully intertwined with Lebovici's reflections on her own contemporary affective and political responses to their representations of embodiment and the traces it leaves behind. Together, these threads remind us – as Hirsch and Smith have observed – that "theorizing cultural memory through the lens of feminism does not merely foreground the dynamics of gender and power. It also applies feminist modes of questioning to the analysis of cultural recall and forgetting" (11).

Writing about the digital turn in memory studies, Silvana Mandolessi identifies two key transformations that, I argue, are central to Lebovici's work: first, "the shift from narrative as a privileged form of collective memory to the cultural form of the database"; and second, "the shift from mnemonic objects to mnemonic assemblages, comprising persons, things, artefacts, spaces, discourses, behaviours and expressions in dynamic relatedness" (1514). In relation to the former, as Mandolessi notes (1519), we should not consider "the narrative and the database [...] as opposing terms but rather as existing in a symbiotic relationship. [...] The symbiosis between the two enables the emergence of new forms of telling that incorporate narrative elements, just as contemporary narratives often incorporate aspects of databases." The very form of Lebovici's work in the digital sphere embodies that "symbiosis," combining, as it so often does, still images with the dates and details of exhibitions, performances, and conferences, as well as theoretical critique and analysis alongside elements of personal history and narrative that are, in turn, intricately imbricated into aspects of late twentieth- and early twenty-first-century political histories of gender and sexuality. In relation to the latter, the "dynamic relatedness" seems absolutely fundamental to Lebovici's engagement with memory, with remembering, with recording, and with giving voice and it is striking that "assemblages" are so often present both in the content of her posts *and* in her own bringing together of objects, people, and practices.

Lebovici does also signal the ways in which the digital context is sometimes not easily adaptable to the recording of significant artist/activist events, as in the case, for example, of a 2024 exhibition at the Palais de Tokyo in Paris. Entitled "Toucher l'insensé" [Touching the Senseless], at the heart of this exhibition is an exploration, through installations and video pieces in particular, of practices of "institutional psychotherapy." For Lebovici, in her Instagram post of March 4, 2024, the exhibition is "non-instagrammable parce que ce médium-ci choisit, isole et glorifie des œuvres, fussent-elles des mochetés, et des noms, fussent-elles de 'grands femmes' [*sic*]" [non-Instagrammable because this medium chooses, isolates, and glorifies particular works, even if they are ugly, and certain names, even if they are those of "great women"], while the aim of "Toucher l'insensé" is to depict an everyday experience ("un quotidien partagé et quotidiennement rediscuté"). While Mandolessi has observed that "the digital turn goes beyond the study of digital objects alone and instead investigates how the digital realm has transformed contemporary mnemonic culture, resulting in the reconfiguration of actors, objects and practices" (1525–26), Lebovici seems ready to accept that there may be limits to the digital realm's usefulness in giving voice to the full range of practices and experiences of the contemporary world.

That Lebovici, in so much of her contemporary practice and activism, presents her curation, her responses, and her reflections across a range of digital domains, entwining the individual and the collective along the way, is all the more significant because it reminds us that "collective memory may be conceived of as a process, mediated and remediated by multiple media with the participation of dynamic communities that perform rather than represent the past" (Mandolessi 1514). However, it also asserts digital spaces as "key waypoints" (Gott 90) in the emergence of a new realm of queer memory – one that resists containment by refusing to offer a single alternative to the existing model, which has largely been grounded in "material and spatially defined place[s]" (Achille, Forsdick, and Moudileno 9). Rather, through Lebovici's extensive art criticism and activism, it seeks to open up the multiple temporalities and geographies that underpin new queer realms of memory, to ensure that lesbian experiences are reinscribed within a queer artistic and activist landscape, and to recognize the value of *lieux* that "transcend the strictly spatial dimension" (9). In this way, Lebovici's work clearly indicates scope for a further extension of the conversation Achille, Forsdick, and Moudileno identify at the "intersection of memory studies and postcolonialism" (15) to incorporate and acknowledge feminist, lesbian, and queer experiences.

Works cited

Achille, Étienne, Charles Forsdick, and Lydie Moudileno. "Introduction." *Postcolonial Realms of Memory: Sites and Symbols in Modern France*, edited by Étienne Achille, Charles Forsdick, and Lydie Moudileno. Liverpool UP, 2020, pp. 1–19.

Bouamer, Siham, Denis M. Provencher, and Ryan K. Schroth. "Introduction: Queering *Lieux de mémoire*." *Queer Realms of Memory: Archiving LGBTQ Sites and Symbols in the French National Narrative*, edited by Siham Bouamer, Denis M. Provencher, and Ryan K. Schroth. Liverpool UP, 2025, pp. 1–23.

Chidgey, Red. *Feminist Afterlives: Assemblage Memory in Activist Times.* Palgrave Macmillan, 2018.
Cvetkovich, Ann. "In the archives of lesbian feelings: Documentary and popular culture." *Camera Obscura*, no. 17, 2002, pp. 107–47. Quoted in Élisabeth Lebovici, *Ce que le sida m'a fait. Art et activisme à la fin du XXe siècle.* JRP/Ringier, 2017.
Dragojlovic, Ana, and C.L. Quinan. "Queering memory: Toward re-membering otherwise." *Memory Studies*, vol. 16, no. 1, 2023, pp. 3–11.
Gott, Michael. "Borders." *Postcolonial Realms of Memory: Sites and Symbols in Modern France*, edited by Étienne Achille, Charles Forsdick, and Lydie Moudileno. Liverpool UP, 2020, pp. 85–100.
Halberstam, Jack. *In A Queer Time and Place: Transgender Bodies, Subcultural Lives.* New York UP, 2005.
Hessel, Katy. *The Story of Art Without Men.* Penguin/Random House, 2022.
Hirsch, Marianne, and Valerie Smith. "Feminism and cultural memory: An introduction." *Signs: Journal of Women in Culture and Society*, vol. 28, no. 1, 2002, pp. 1–19.
Lebovici, Élisabeth. "Le Beau Vice." January–April 2024. https://le-beau-vice.blogspot.com.
———. *Ce que le sida m'a fait. Art et activisme à la fin du XXe siècle.* JRP/Ringier, 2017.
Lebovici, Élisabeth, and Catherine Gonnard. *Femmes/artistes, artistes/femmes, Paris de 1880 à nos jours.* Hazan, 2007.
Mandolessi, Silvana. "The digital turn in memory studies." *Memory Studies*, vol. 16, no. 6, 2023, pp. 1513–28.
Nora, Pierre. "Between memory and history: *Les Lieux de mémoire.*" Translated by Marc Roudebush. *Representations*, vol. 26, 1989, pp. 7–24.
Pollock, Griselda. "Women who are artists, artists who are women." *Critique d'art*, vol. 31, 2008. Web.
Reznick, Jordan. "Through the Guillotine Mirror: Claude Cahun's theory of trans against the void." *Art Journal*, vol. 81, no. 3, 2022, pp. 53–69.

Conclusion

Siham Bouamer, Denis M. Provencher, and Ryan K. Schroth

In this volume, we have both engaged in and enacted an archival practice. We have brought together various realms of queer memory, while at the same time interrogating the very processes of archiving. The chapters collected contribute to this endeavor in different ways: some critically examine existing archives and the ways in which queer archives have been recorded, erased, and contested, while others construct new archives and highlight traces, voices, and narratives that might otherwise remain invisible. Together, these contributions shape *Queer Realms of Memory* as an archive in its own right with a diverse range of experiences, sites, and symbols, including, for example, city streets, neighborhoods, commemorative plaques, novels, movies, and digital exhibits. In the quest to make queer experiences more visible, this volume intervenes in ongoing discussions of various queer spaces of remembrance and the specific processes by which queer memories are produced and recorded. The chapters engage with not only Nora's original conceptualization of *lieux de mémoire*, but also with the existing scholarship that expands these ideas from disciplines such as memory studies, history, and postcolonial studies. To varying degrees, each of these chapters, by cataloging certain queer *lieux de mémoire*, also highlights various strands of queer thought in order to further unsettle the normative ways that realms of memory are created, maintained, and preserved.

Recognizing the potential pain experienced by those whose identities have been systematically invisibilized in memorialization processes, we understand that some readers may regret the absence of specific realms of memory that they consider significant, either as individuals or for their communities. Our deliberate use of the expression "archiving" in our title, rather than "an archive" or "archives," signals our commitment to an ongoing and dynamic process rather than a fixed repository. This choice reflects our understanding that no archive can ever be fully exhaustive, despite our efforts at categorization. Indeed, our aim with this volume was not to comprehensively encompass all facets of queer realms of memory within the field. Instead, our primary objective has been to initiate and advance a dialogue regarding the need to challenge the exclusionary archiving of realms of memory within France's national narrative of republican universalism.

We primarily sought to include contributions that helped us reflect on ways to reimagine new forms and spaces of remembrance for queer lives and history. During our investigation, we faced a significant challenge, namely, the scarcity of scholars in French studies who dedicate their work to this specific area of study. This shortage of researchers is a noteworthy observation and, interestingly, aligns with one of the foundational premises of our volume. It highlights the recurring pattern of queerness being rejected and rendered invisible within both French history and the academic and research landscapes dedicated to this field on both sides of the Atlantic. However, it is imperative to recognize certain other limitations in our approach.

The volume may initially seem to focus on Paris, and rightfully so, as the city has historically been recognized as one of the centers of queer cultures and resistance. Stephen Shapiro's chapter, for example, provides an in-depth analysis of the 2014 plaque in rue Montorgueil that commemorates Bruno Lenoir and Jean Diot, the last two men executed in France for sodomy charges. Jules O'Dwyer's chapter focuses on another Parisian neighborhood, Bonne Nouvelle, and the depiction of its cruising grounds in the filmmaking of Vincent Dieutre. Leslie Choquette's chapter analyzes nineteenth-century queer Paris by focusing on *la tournée des grands-ducs*. James Williams pushes the bounds of the city by examining the queer Maghrebi French experience just beyond the capital's beltway as chronicled in contemporary cinema. However, queer communities and activism can also be found in other cities and regions, each with its unique history. For example, Kory Olson compares the queer maps of Paris and Toulouse in his chapter on new social media technologies. Luke Eildert's study moves our project beyond the French capital by focusing on *La Marche des visibilités gaies, lesbiennes, bisexuelles et transgenres in Strasbourg*. These chapters expand the geographic boundaries of queer *lieux de mémoire* in their cataloging of queer spaces outside of the French capital.

To be sure, a number of chapters move outside of the Hexagon altogether in their transnational analyses of queer spaces. For instance, Denis M. Provencher's chapter on Abdellah Taïa's representation of Genet's tomb looks at this unique queer realm of memory in Morocco and online in globally oriented social media. Maxime Foerster's contribution focuses on Moroccan author Leila Slimani's recent writing, in the trilogy *Le pays des autres*, which records alternative narratives regarding the sexual diversity of the Moroccan nation. In her contribution, Michaëla Danjé shares the work of the collective *Cases Rebelles*, as an Afrodiasporic, Black, digital, and transnational *lieu de mémoire* that aims to disrupt, and liberate itself from, the French colonial context while embracing the power of pan-African collective memories.[1] This more pronounced emphasis on North Africa was the result of our specific research interests and the influence of our network. It should be recognized as a deliberate outcome of our research process and the scope of our scholarly connections.

Another important observation we would like to make is that the majority of our chapters tend to center on men in their discussions of authors, directors, and icons. The authors of *Ecrire à l'encre violette: Littératures lesbiennes en France de 1900 à nos jours* (2022) begin with a valid premise: the exclusion of lesbian voices in literary institutions. They note:

> La mémoire de cette littérature, héritière de décennies d'invisibilisation, est précaire à double titre. Les quelques textes qui nous sont parvenus subissent encore le poids des discours qui ont distordu leur lecture. Surtout, une bonne part est issue d'archives qu'il faut exhumer, ou des souvenirs de celles qui, depuis cinquante ans, se battent pour la faire vivre au grand jour. Mémoire immense, donc, mais enterrée, éclatée, écrite au fil d'articles, de revues, de billets dispersés. L'enjeu que représente le lesbianisme en littérature peine par ailleurs à être reconnu dans les milieux de la recherche littéraire. (15)
>
> The memory of this literature, heir to decades of invisibility, is precarious on two counts. The few texts that have been handed down to us still bear the weight of the discourses that distorted their reading. Above all, a

---

1 We encourage our readers also to consult Danjé's edited collection, *AfroTrans* (2021), which includes a variety of texts – poetry, essays, interviews – exclusively written by Black trans people living in France.

good part comes from archives that must be exhumed, or from memories of those who, for 50 years, have fought to bring it to light. An immense memory, then, but one that is buried, fragmented, written in scattered articles, journals, and notes. The issue that lesbianism in literature represents continues to struggle to be recognized in literary research.

Our volume acknowledges the presence of lesbian memory, however "éclatée" and "dispersée" it may be, through a number of chapters that focus specifically on lesbian *lieux de mémoire*. For instance, Cristina Johnston, in her chapter on the work of lesbian art historian Élisabeth Lebovici, explores the digital, affective, and aesthetic aspects of queer realms of memory. Exhuming the "mémoire enterrée" of English poet Renée Vivien, Melanie Hawthorne examines the symbolic value of gravesites as literal queer realms of memory. Finally, Siham Bouamer, in her chapter on Fatima Daas, employs an intersectional lens to comment on the interlocking – and often exclusionary – discourses of sexuality, ethnicity, nationality, and religion in the constitution of queer citizenship. Each of these chapters works to challenge the various ways women, and specifically lesbians, have been written out of French memory.

We must also address the paucity of scholarly research on trans identities within French and Francophone studies. Following Alexandre Baril, in "Francophone Trans/Feminisms" (2016), we recognize the "difficulty francophone communities seem to face not only in conceptualizing the possibility of moving beyond the rift between transphobic and trans-inclusive feminists but also in simply addressing trans issues within various activist, community, institutional, and academic feminist spaces" (41). In our volume, Todd Reeser demonstrates these difficulties in his chapter on the ways in which the Chevalier d'Eon has simultaneously been remembered and forgotten throughout French history. Expressing a similar scholarly motivation, Blase Provitola, in their chapter on prominent trans activist Giovanna Rincon, archives Rincon's important political contributions to trans and queer activism while drawing attention to the very absences that constitute the French national narrative. Ultimately, by centering trans voices, these chapters further delineate hetero- and homo-normative processes of queer remembering in the production of queer realms of memory.

Returning to the question of archiving that opened this conclusion, we must also acknowledge the complexity and subjectivity involved in the process, which Sara Ahmed acutely articulates in her discussion on her own archival methodology:

> To name one's archive is a perilous matter; it can suggest that these texts "belong" together, and that the belonging is a mark of one's own presence. What I offer is a model of the archive not as the conversion of self into a textual gathering, but as a "contact zone". An archive is an effect of multiple forms of contact, including institutional forms of contact (with libraries, books, web sites), as well as everyday forms of contact (with friends, families, others). Some forms of contact are presented and authorised through writing (and listed in the references), whilst other forms of contact will be missing, will be erased, even though they may leave their trace. (14)

Agreeing with Ahmed, we recognize that compiling an archive involves gathering elements that do not naturally belong together, and that the process is not neutral. This subjectivity is evident through the very acts of categorizing, editing, writing an introduction and conclusion, as well as in the selection of chapters. Ahmed's use of the expression "contact zone" – borrowed from Mary Louise Pratt – to describe the archive particularly resonates with our editorial process. Indeed, this volume became a space where the common and respective influences of both editors and contributors converged, through formal (institutional) and informal (everyday, or "banal") interactions. Some of these interactions are documented in references, citations, and footnotes, while others, though not immediately evident, remain impactful, and must be acknowledged. For example, we are indebted to our contributors for their generous willingness to interact with us and this project, whether via email or exchanges through the comments during the review process. Regrettably, some contributions we had the pleasure of reviewing and wished to include ultimately could not be part of the volume due to unforeseen circumstances. Nonetheless, they have left a trace on the work we have done. We must share that we also invited scholars to contribute whom we thought would absolutely accept given their previously published research in LGBTQ French and Francophone studies. Their reaction to our project, seeing it as a perceived reification of Nora's work that could never accommodate queerness, kept them from engaging in further dialogue with us. Finally, it is important to note that this project began just before the COVID-19 pandemic. The challenges brought about by the pandemic – from the loss of potential contributors to the volume's possible gaps or omissions – have inevitably influenced the shape and outcome of this project.

Despite these challenges, our collaborative efforts as editors to catalog new queer realms of memory have continued. We have engaged in numerous discussions with one another, both in formal meetings and informal interactions. These conversations frequently involved reflections on significant current events and recent news publications. In addition, we often shared anecdotes or photos about moments or locations that reminded us of the presence of queer realms of memory in our everyday lives – the "banal du quotidien" we mentioned in the introduction as central to our framework. For example, we recently discovered a mural of Jean-Paul Gaultier in the 11th *arrondissement*. A fresco by Spanish artist Pepo Moreno, the mural reminds us of the ephemerality of queer *lieux de mémoire* (it was taken down at the end of Pride month) as well as its "transfiliality" (Provencher, *Queer Maghrebi French*): the mural depicts a giant sailor in Gaultier stripes holding bottles of the fashion designer's famous fragrances (*Le male* and *Classique*). Sporting sailor-style tattoos, a nautical hat, and a round hoop earring, the image pays homage to the trope of the sailor in queer French culture (Provencher, *Queer French*). Embedding the image in a certain queer aesthetic, the sailor stands before a rainbow, and the words "Jean Paul is queer and 4ever here" float above him. With its overriding message of celebration, this transient, global queer *lieu de mémoire* nonetheless invites Pride attendees to remember the past while celebrating the present. By choosing it as our cover image, we honor queer memory as both present in the everyday and as form of resilient joy.

For the back cover, we selected a photograph of the street plaque for the Rue des Archives in the Marais; the street name lies over a LGBTQ-themed rainbow background. We sought an image that embodied the "banal du quotidien," an important element of queer *lieux de mémoire*. The street sign, which references the task of working with an archive as well as the queer context of our project, is also a space that all three editors, and many of their students and probably countless contributors, have interacted with. Through this familiarity – not necessarily with the Rue des Archives itself, but with the very object of a street sign – we wished to visually encourage the readers to join us in the contact zone that we have created here. We want to invite you to look up – or sideways, or backwards – as you walk, if only to acknowledge some of the queer realms of memory that we encounter daily and to share these experiences with others. In line with a more "institutional form of contact," we also hope that in areas where we have not fully explored a particular queer realm of memory, other scholars will carry the mantle and continue this critical memorial work of archiving and bringing visibility to these important sites and symbols.

Works cited

Ahmed, Sara. *The Cultural Politics of Emotion*. Routledge, 2004.
Baril, Alexandre. "Francophone trans/feminisms: Absence, silence, emergence." *TSQ: Transgender Studies Quarterly*, vol. 3, no. 1–2, 2016, pp. 40–47.
Pratt, Mary Louise. "Arts of the contact zone." *Profession*, 1991, 33–40.
Provencher, Denis M. *Queer French: Globalization, Language, and Sexual Citizenship in France*. Ashgate, 2007.
———. *Queer Maghrebi French: Language, Temporalities, Transfiliations*. Liverpool UP, 2017.
Turbiau, Aurore, Alex Lachkar, Camille Islert, Manon Berthier, and Alexandre Antolin. *Ecrire à l'encre violette: Littératures lesbiennes en France de 1900 à nos jours*. Éditions Le Cavalier Bleu, 2022.

Index

Acceptess-T 219–21, 223, 225, 227–29, 231–34
Achille, Étienne v, 1, 2, 6–7, 9, 14–15, 56, 131–32, 140, 174, 190, 209, 215, 238, 260, 277, 325, 344, 358, 361, 368
Act Up-Paris 5, 48, 65–67, 297–319, 340
activism 86, 137, 212, 215, 224, 226, 299, 306, 364–65, 368, 372
activists 6, 9, 29, 32–33, 58, 85–88, 94, 133–34, 150–51, 224–25, 227, 230, 299, 302–3, 306–7, 310
adolescent love (queer) 74, 239
aesthetics 64, 66–67, 176, 209
affect 3, 72, 255, 298, 300
Afro-diaspora 332, 373
Afro Trans 336, 339, 341, 373
Ahmed, Sara 12, 21, 72, 132, 141, 231, 233, 293–94, 374–75, 377
AIDS/HIV 36, 48, 61, 63, 65–67, 212, 225, 227, 251, 265, 299, 303–4, 306, 315–27, 326, 344
Akerman, Chantal 258, 357–58, 361, 366
Algeria 137, 238, 241, 268
American remembrance 22, 172, 191, 251
Anamosa 23, 192, 295, 356
anger 299, 301–5, 309, 334
anti-monument 55, 57, 59, 61, 63, 65, 67–69

architecture 51, 191, 255, 264
archive 6, 9, 12, 14, 17–22, 33–36, 38–39, 43, 81, 85–97, 161, 183, 195, 199–200, 203, 235, 237, 238, 250, 309, 353, 371, 374, 376
arrondissement 6, 87, 113, 119, 121–22, 125–25, 376
art 38, 101, 108, 163, 191, 232, 250, 316, 357, 362–65, 369, 377
Artère, le jardin des dessins 55–56, 61–69
artists 5, 60, 62, 67, 109, 140, 162, 197, 293, 357 359, 362, 365–67, 369
Atlantide 240–41, 244–45, 248–49, 251
attacks 9–10, 32, 49, 150, 153, 243, 303, 335, 338

Baker, Josephine 7–8, 171, 334
Baldwin, James 334, 337
banlieue 3, 145–56, 278
Baril, Alexandre 21, 233, 374, 377
bars 30, 103, 105, 109–10, 121, 126, 210, 272
Barthes, Roland 35, 37, 262, 311
Bastille 6, 92, 119, 123, 127
baths 75, 150, 156
bed(s)/bedrooms 75, 77, 247, 273, 301, 308–9, 319, 346–47, 366
Belle Époque 101, 106–7, 112–13, 166
Berlant, Lauren 11–12
Berlin 50, 116, 239, 251

Bersani, Leo 11, 21, 175, 191, 240–41, 250, 254, 264
birth 15, 46, 162, 193, 196–97, 251, 273, 299, 325
bisexual 4, 52, 91, 131, 135, 215, 220, 240, 334–35, 372
black queerness and memory *see* memory
blogs 166, 211, 357, 359, 361, 365
bodies 10, 75–76, 137, 142, 151, 178–79, 184, 193–94, 197, 203, 263, 274, 283, 300–1, 304–5, 308–9, 340, 347, 350, 357, 359, 361, 363, 365, 367, 369
Bonne Nouvelle 256, 258–60, 262–64, 372
Bouchor, Maurice 72, 76–77, 79–80, 82
boulevard 261, 305, 312
Bourget, Paul 72, 74–82
boys 31, 73–75, 77–79, 109, 178, 193, 274, 312
brothel 75, 110–11, 272
brothers 152, 196, 213, 273, 288, 354
businesses 104, 110–12, 123, 127–28

café 123, 151–52, 164, 259
Cahun, Claude 360, 362–63, 369
camera 151, 175, 178, 183–86, 243–45, 248, 260, 304, 307
Campillo, Robin 5, 297–98, 300, 304, 306–7, 310–13
Campos, Vanesa 353
capital 101, 115, 119, 121–22, 125, 127–28, 135, 256–57, 288, 339, 372
Capucines 304–5, 312
Casablanca 270
Cases Rebelles 331–42, 350, 373
casino 244–45, 249
celebration 5, 27, 170, 175, 207, 293, 306, 353, 376
cemeteries and cult graves 159–72, 173–92, 203
centers 87, 99, 123–24, 228, 244, 372
Centre LGBT Paris 121

Chamoiseau, Patrick 13, 293–95
Château Rouge 103–5, 109, 114
Chevalier d'Eon 3, 192–205, 374
children 30, 35, 63, 73, 160, 222, 270, 272
church 73–74, 346
cinema 3, 16, 19–20, 60–61, 148, 155, 177–78, 237–41, 249–51
cisgenderism 7, 120, 194, 204, 225–26, 283, 344
citizenship 2, 7, 11–12, 19, 28, 51, 96, 119, 136, 148, 162, 171, 268
city 41, 50, 59, 101, 103–4, 106, 112, 114, 119–27, 131–33, 135, 137, 139–41, 143, 147, 152, 181, 202, 212, 257, 259, 288, 299
Colette 108–9
Collectif archives LGBTQI 85, 87–88, 90, 93–94, 233
collective memory *see* memory
collèges 71–83
    see also schools
colonial cinema 237–52
colonial past 56, 148, 183, 277
colonies 8, 82, 119, 237, 249
commemoration 4, 10, 19, 44–45, 47–52, 56, 60–61, 64–65, 56, 167, 173, 177, 186, 209, 230, 331
communautarisme 49, 90, 153, 228, 303
community archives 86, 91, 94
conflicts 69, 90, 96, 128, 146, 162, 198, 205, 211, 214, 217, 234, 349
contact zone 92, 375–77
counter-archive 349
Covid 37, 137, 155, 168, 228, 357, 361, 375
cruising 6, 30–31, 36, 126 178, 200, 253–65, 372
cultural memory *see* memory
Cvetkovich, Ann 4, 18, 21, 35, 38, 86, 95, 312, 345, 347, 355, 369

Daas, Fatima 5, 277–95, 374
Dalida, 3, 207–18
dance floor 307–8

danger 73–74, 80, 112, 305, 334, 337
Danjé 15, 19, 331, 341, 373
death 11, 21, 36, 45, 48, 63, 66–67, 75, 105, 152, 159–62, 166–68, 171, 193–94, 197, 216, 219, 229–30, 246, 274, 299, 303–4, 309, 313, 317–18, 320, 322–24, 353
death penalty 44
debts 280, 285–86, 288–91, 293
deceased 8, 61, 161, 170, 207, 230–32, 309
decolonial memory *see* memory
demonstrations 58, 132, 136–37, 141, 299, 339
deportation 56–60, 63, 67
Derrida, Jacques 161, 313, 319–20, 322, 326
descendants 16, 147, 194, 202, 259, 310–11
dessins 50, 60–62, 66, 68
Dieutre, Vincent 256, 258–63
digital media 93, 238, 359, 365
Diot, Jean 41–53
disease 60–61, 65, 299, 301, 303, 306, 317, 320–22, 324
disidentification(s) 10, 14, 190
dissociation 35
doctors 161, 193, 195, 197, 224, 270, 282–83
documentary 33, 148, 155, 178, 181, 186, 318, 352, 369
Dreyfus, Alfred 118, 316–17, 319–20, 322–24, 326

effeminophobia 213, 215
éonisme 195–96
emotional geography 297–319
emotions 18, 86, 89, 191, 271, 281, 294, 297–98, 300–1, 311–12, 345, 353–54, 377
ephemera 15, 19, 88–89, 101, 128, 254–55, 260, 341, 364
epidemic 67–68, 225, 301, 310, 317, 321, 323
essay film 258

everyday 14, 146, 149, 152–53, 193, 209, 214, 223, 229, 345, 348, 359, 367, 375–76
equality 5–7, 32–33, 138, 142, 149
era 34, 37, 43, 47, 52, 116, 180, 197, 237, 324, 360
erasure 28, 45, 47, 112, 160, 215, 255, 267, 361
erotic capital 101, 103–5, 107, 109, 111, 113, 115
Europe 32, 37, 58, 115–16, 152, 229, 239, 251, 258, 270

Facebook 47, 52, 174, 180–89
failure 1, 4, 22, 118, 142, 246, 272, 277, 286, 352, 355
families 10, 13, 16, 23, 32–33, 39, 63, 138–39, 146, 170, 177, 181, 190, 221–23, 231–32, 268, 271–73, 288–89, 293, 322, 335, 338, 340, 358, 375
Farmer, Mylène 3, 193, 207–18
father 21, 35, 128, 141, 193, 197, 222, 273, 323
feminism 343, 346, 350, 355, 367, 369
Festival Extimité 354–55
Feyder, Jacques 238, 240–41, 243
FHAR (*Front homosexuel d'action révolutionnaire*) 4, 133–34, 142
filiation 21, 29, 39, 137, 178, 180, 214
flags 29, 139, 151, 299
flâneur 102, 112, 175, 256
flyers 135, 138–41
Forsdick, Charles v, 1, 2, 7, 9, 14–15, 131–32, 174, 190, 209, 215, 238, 260, 277, 325, 344, 358, 361, 368
Foucault, Michel 12, 28, 35, 45–46, 48, 257, 307
foundations 251, 279, 287, 289, 302, 354
freedom 32, 35, 39, 49, 81, 91, 263, 336, 340, 354
French national narrative 2, 4, 10–11, 13–14, 102, 136, 150, 155, 190, 194, 306–7, 374
fugitive planning 279, 283, 292

Gabin, Jean 112, 244–45, 251, 247, 249
Gaultier, Jean-Paul 376
gaze 244–46, 253–54, 260, 344, 357–58, 362
gender 10, 14, 30, 37, 46, 48, 96, 129, 133, 162, 193–205, 209, 231, 251, 276, 290–93, 335–36, 340, 344, 349, 358, 360–62, 367
generation 15, 36–37, 60, 68, 150, 177, 227, 245, 310–11, 318, 321, 324
Genet, Jean 10, 113, 173–90, 192
gentrification 6, 50, 121–22, 253, 255
Gide, André 239, 262
Glissant, Édouard 13, 293, 332, 341
globalization 22, 129, 142, 192, 264, 335, 377
Grand dukes' tours (*tournées des grands-ducs*) 101–16
graves *see* cemeteries and cult graves
Grémillon, Jean 240, 247–48
Guadeloupe 295, 331–32, 342
guidebooks 101, 103, 106, 110, 170

Halberstam, Jack 13, 16, 18, 34, 38, 132, 142, 209, 221, 233, 279, 311–12, 345, 352, 359, 369
happiness 12, 21, 230–31, 233
haunting 171, 272, 274, 315–27
hauntology 4, 161, 315–27
Hérelle, Georges 72, 76–82
heritage 8, 12, 27, 29, 86–87, 94, 348
heteronormativity 132, 133, 279
high school 72, 170, 201, 283, 285, 349
Hirsch, Marianne 15–16, 22, 161, 171, 177, 191, 359, 365–66, 369
historiography (queer) 18, 64
HIV/AIDS 36, 48, 61, 63, 65–67, 212, 225, 227, 251, 265, 299, 303–4, 306, 315–27, 344
Holocaust 16, 179
homonationalism 12, 23, 53, 150, 152, 219–33
homophobia 30, 31–32, 48–49, 66, 138, 146, 148, 210, 212–13, 271, 292, 325, 338, 340, 350

hotel Marigny 110–12
Hyber, Fabrice 55–56, 60, 62–68

icons 19, 112, 157, 188, 210, 212, 215, 223, 226, 373
identification 92, 107, 110, 169, 196, 211–12, 241, 303
illness 35, 61, 281, 283, 319, 344
immigration 10, 111, 227–29, 256
Instagram 174, 180, 185–89, 351, 365, 367
institutions 13, 18–19, 25, 28, 32, 46, 72, 86–89, 92, 94, 203, 238, 280, 283–84, 293, 332
intersectionality 9, 19, 133, 151, 156, 227, 228, 354
interview 33, 56, 68, 85, 136, 148, 176, 192, 214, 219, 222, 229–30, 268, 278, 281, 285, 288, 299, 321, 344, 347, 363, 373
intimacy 150, 155, 168, 274, 308, 345, 347
invisibility 18, 91, 138, 203, 209, 271, 278, 308, 362, 373
Islam 10, 268, 273, 288–91

jardin 55, 60–62, 66, 68
Jews 49, 56–57, 102, 118, 121, 123, 164, 179, 270
journalists 31, 102, 215, 227, 315, 321
joy 61, 74, 102, 230–31, 273, 300–1, 304, 306–7, 353, 376
justice 27, 35, 168, 229–30, 332
Juvigny, Adrien 72, 74–76, 79, 82

Kalifa, Dominique 101, 103, 115
kisses 74, 76, 108, 163, 169, 246
knowledge 88, 101–2, 171, 177, 279, 284, 293, 310, 321, 343, 345, 351
Kritzman, Lawrence 20, 52, 69, 96, 115, 142, 172, 205, 217, 234, 236

Landsberg, Alison 16, 22, 161–64, 172, 177, 179, 186, 189, 191, 238–39, 240, 251

language 22–23, 39, 46–47, 129, 138, 140, 142, 145, 186, 188, 191–92, 209, 218, 254, 264, 268, 276, 290, 292, 295, 306, 333–34, 377
Larache 173–91, 181
law 5–7, 27–31, 36, 147, 239, 257
Lebovici, Élisabeth 357–69
Lenoir, Bruno 41–53
lesbian/lesbian visibility 5, 9, 30–31, 33, 36, 52, 91, 97, 104, 106–8, 112, 114, 118, 120, 123–24, 126–27, 129, 131, 135, 143, 146, 161–62, 166, 172, 194, 215, 220, 271, 278, 280, 288–89, 292, 334–35
letters 19, 72–82, 87, 111, 116, 133, 195, 199, 280
LGBTQ+ pride *see* pride
literature 17–20, 61, 101, 113, 122, 153, 235, 239, 251, 267–68, 273–74, 274, 278, 285, 294, 298, 300, 317, 320
love 47, 74–82, 86, 101, 105, 116, 167, 173, 179, 181, 184, 188, 241, 249, 268–69, 271–72, 286, 288, 300, 309, 321, 333–34, 353, 356

Maghreb 22, 169, 172, 190, 268, 276
male gaze 358
mapping 21, 117–29, 263, 358, 361, 365
maps, 19, 117–23, 125–27, 170, 297
Marais 5, 21, 50, 63, 117–29, 141, 196, 202, 376
Marche des fiertés 131–33, 148–50, 154–55
Marche des visibilités 131, 135, 138, 372
marriage 6, 10, 13, 21, 27–39, 47, 90, 138, 179, 213, 268, 273–74, 338
martyrs 48, 56–58, 106–7, 110, 113, 180, 192
masculinity 71, 191, 241, 245–46, 249
Masson, Adolphe 73
Mbembe, Achille 12
media 5, 19, 27, 30–31, 149, 152–54, 174, 177, 208–9, 218, 338, 345, 355, 365, 368

memorial 44–45, 47–49, 55–57, 60, 62–63, 65, 160, 169, 251, 364, 376
memory
    black queerness and memory 331, 333–34, 338–39, 341
    collective memory 1–2, 16–18, 42, 44, 51, 117, 119, 121, 123, 125, 127, 129, 131–32, 141, 148, 159, 304, 332, 336–37, 359
    cultural memory 16, 154–55, 363, 365, 367, 369
    decolonial memory 7, 349, 351
    multidirectional memory 1, 23, 191
    noeuds de mémoire 1, 23, 69, 192, 234
    postcolonial realms of memory 1–2, 4, 11, 15, 17–18, 20, 22–23, 49, 52, 82–83, 131, 141, 147, 156, 174, 190–91, 216, 250, 264, 277–79, 292, 294–95, 325, 344, 355, 358, 368–69
    postmemory 15–16, 177, 323
    prosthetic memory 16, 161, 179, 182, 189–90, 238, 240, 249, 250
Merrick, Jeffrey 16, 52, 92, 96
metafilm 243, 249
metaphors 65, 69, 281, 285–86
métissage 269, 348
migration 222, 229, 271, 348
military 57, 240, 242, 244, 272
Montmartre 103–4, 106–10, 113, 123
Morhange 241–43
Moudileno, Lydie v, 1, 2, 6–7, 9, 14–15, 56, 131–32, 174, 190, 209, 215, 238, 260, 277, 325, 344, 358, 361, 368
Morocco 173, 176, 178, 180, 183, 190, 238, 268–72, 275–76, 373
mother 35, 77, 80, 176–77, 182, 193, 214, 223, 289, 291–92, 309
Moulin Rouge 104, 108–9, 112
Muñoz, José Esteban 11–16, 19, 47, 64, 66, 209, 216, 221, 255, 311, 322, 354

museum 87, 202, 365
music 19, 135, 145, 153, 167, 212–13, 245, 308, 338
Muslim 146–47, 150, 181, 269, 278, 280, 285–86, 288–90, 292
myth 22, 46, 52, 101, 110, 114, 192, 210, 218, 250, 275

nation 9–11, 17, 21, 45, 83, 117, 119, 121–22, 124, 132, 138, 171, 190, 267–69, 275–75, 312, 337, 241
national narrative 2–5, 7, 9–10, 33, 43, 49–50, 131, 190, 194, 221, 278, 293, 303, 372
nature 13, 64, 67, 92, 97, 112, 120, 125, 127–28, 159, 195, 198, 238, 270, 279, 354
necropolitics 12, 48, 51
neighborhood 6, 104, 106, 108, 111, 120–22, 124–25, 151, 223–24, 259, 263, 371
Niang, Mame-Fatou 1, 23, 190, 192, 279, 295, 354, 356
North Africa 174, 208, 237–50, 373
nostalgia 105, 112, ,161, 211, 249, 312, 364

ontology 161, 318–19, 322, 325
opposition 32, 73, 118, 120, 132, 148, 150, 274, 293, 310, 315
outrage 49, 101, 276, 300–1, 303–7
Ozouf, Mona 20, 22, 138, 142, 297

Pacte civil de solidarité (PaCS) 6, 28, 30, 32–33, 37–39, 90, 139
Panthéon 334
parade 48, 135–37, 140–41, 306
parents 30, 33, 73, 78, 170, 230, 288, 348
Paris 5–6, 20, 23, 29, 30, 38, 39, 41–42, 48–52, 55, 63, 66, 72, 74, 80–81, 83, 85, 87, 90, 93, 101–5, 107–11, 116, 113–16, 118–19, 121–25, 127, 129, 132–33, 145–46, 148–49, 152–55, 162, 208, 257, 260, 299, 305, 362

performances 11, 15, 19, 22, 32, 214, 360, 365, 367
peripheries 20, 22, 39, 50, 96, 99, 118, 145–56, 245, 251, 316–17, 336
Perreau, Bruno 6, 10, 15–17, 19, 27–39, 90
photographs and photography 8, 29, 35, 155, 163, 166, 181, 185–86, 246–47, 271, 311–12, 359, 360, 362–63, 376
pilgrimage 41, 134, 173, 176, 178–79, 185
place Maubert 104
plaque 41, 45–51, 105, 109, 114, 116, 162, 202, 372
podcasting 19–20, 331–42, 343–56
police 43, 58, 85, 88, 91, 93, 95, 97, 108–9, 114, 161, 227, 253, 274, 340, 353–54
politics 12, 22, 39, 129, 180, 233, 250–51, 262–63, 293, 303, 307, 312, 326, 353, 356–57
popular music 209, 211, 213, 215, 217
postcolonial and postcoloniality 2, 9, 147, 150–51, 174, 183, 209, 256, 277–79, 282, 325, 344, 357, 361, 368, 371
postcolonial realms of memory *see* memory
postmemory *see* memory
pride 36, 131–43, 155, 227, 287, 338, 352–53
prison 80–81, 110, 178, 231, 284
prosthetic memory *see* memory
prostitution 97, 104, 106, 109, 114, 123, 126, 129, 176, 185, 264
Proust, Marcel 41, 102, 110–12, 239
Provencher, Denis 2, 5, 9–12, 15, 19, 35, 71, 118–27, 133, 137, 174–76, 209, 214, 239, 254, 257, 281, 289, 293, 345, 358, 373, 376–77
Puar, Jasbir 11, 12, 23, 48, 53, 150, 226, 234
public sex 47, 123, 253, 256–57

Quatre Fromages 146–48, 154, 156
queens 11, 21, 211, 241
queer archival method 343, 345, 347, 349, 351, 353, 355
queer archives 12, 18, 72, 87, 89, 90, 95, 199, 311, 371
queer communities 37, 47, 88, 104, 118, 128, 155, 169, 239, 286, 301, 303, 336, 351–52, 372
queer history 18, 48, 88–89, 92–94, 104–5, 109, 191, 199, 222, 233, 255–56, 264, 34, 353, 356
queer theory 6, 10–11, 21–22, 27, 39, 52, 96, 141, 208, 218, 251, 362
queer times 3, 12, 22–23, 38, 53, 97, 221, 233–34, 312, 345, 355, 369
queer utopia 15–16, 64

race 14, 21, 46, 97, 151, 191, 209, 229, 256, 260–62, 264, 344, 349, 352, 255
radical archive 86
rainbow and rainbow flags 29, 139–40, 151, 316–17, 323, 326, 376
refusal 58, 220, 231, 279, 283, 292–93, 335
region 58, 120, 122, 140, 175, 177, 183, 372
religion 209, 260, 268, 276, 281, 288–89, 345, 374
remembrance 16–17, 55, 57–58, 102, 115, 195, 199, 230, 358
République 7–8, 21, 137–38, 146, 151, 156
resistance 8, 32, 34, 48, 56–58, 61, 74, 82, 120, 151, 155, 161, 261, 281–82, 293, 301, 335, 347, 372
restaurants 106–7, 109, 123–24, 202
rhetorics 21–22, 52, 171, 205
Rincon, Giovanna 219–34
risk 32, 74, 78, 271, 273, 283, 299, 303, 338, 346, 364

Saint-Avit 241–44, 247
Sainte Barbe 73–75, 77–81

Sainte-Croix-de-la-Bretonnerie 121, 123
same-sex marriage *see* marriage
San Francisco 28, 50, 136–67, 255
Sartre, Jean-Paul 39, 57, 69, 180, 192
scarabée 109–10
schools 73–75, 80, 82, 201, 283–85, 331, 346, 348–49
see also collèges
Seel, Pierre 48, 58–60, 63, 69
sex 14, 23, 39, 43, 88, 91–93, 103, 153, 191, 195–98, 207, 228, 257, 272, 275–76, 313, 319, 327
sex workers 5, 102, 105, 107, 112, 219–20, 224–25, 227, 229, 232, 272, 303, 349, 352–53
sexual citizenship 11, 22, 51, 118, 125, 142, 192, 264, 377
Sibalis, Michael 23, 83, 116, 119, 129, 134, 142, 254, 257, 265
sida *see* AIDS/HIV; HIV/AIDS
Sidaction 62–63, 212
silence 17, 21, 89, 95, 131–32, 137, 147, 176, 178, 233, 238, 255, 281, 331, 334, 347, 349, 361, 377
sins 92, 97, 166, 272, 290–91
Slimani, Leila 267–76, 373
slogans 138, 163
social media 19, 30, 37, 119–20, 126, 128, 140–41, 170, 174, 186, 338, 350–53, 359, 372–73
sodomy 41, 44, 46–47, 52, 92, 239
songs 44, 52, 109, 112, 153, 193, 207–8, 214, 238
space and spatiality 2–3, 6, 8, 9, 11, 13, 15–18, 29, 32, 35–37, 50–51, 62–63, 67, 87, 90–91, 101, 103–4, 112, 117–28, 131–32, 135–40, 145–55, 161, 165, 169, 174–75, 178, 199, 202, 209–10, 223, 226, 228, 232, 238, 245, 249, 253–63, 268, 274, 278–80, 283, 285–88, 290, 291, 293, 297, 297–98, 300–1, 303–4, 307–8, 311, 317, 322, 324, 333, 335, 339, 340, 346–49, 258, 361–62, 365–68, 371–76

spahis 244, 246
specter 47, 222, 230, 259, 262, 308, 315, 317–25
spectators 102, 135, 141, 177–78, 183–84, 186, 238–39, 245–46
  see also viewers
stars 32, 108, 167, 207, 214, 215
stigma 65, 147, 225, 227, 272, 324
Stonewall riots 5, 134, 139–40, 352
Strasbourg 131, 135–36, 138–39, 372
streets 6–7, 27, 44, 48, 59, 119, 121, 123–24, 127, 146, 175, 181, 183, 199, 223, 263, 301, 304–7, 338, 252–53
students 71, 73, 75–76, 79–80, 149, 170, 202, 223, 284–85, 376
Suaudeau, Julien 23, 192, 279, 295, 354, 356
subcultures, gay and lesbian 93, 160–61, 171
suicides 161, 208, 229–30, 232, 271, 326
surveillance 6, 133, 169, 209, 229

Taïa, Abdellah 5, 11, 22, 173–92, 209, 214–16, 218, 281, 289, 292, 373
Tangiers 181, 190
Taubira law 27, 29, 31–32
taphophilia 161
television 177, 191, 225, 352
temporalities 3, 22–23, 37, 39, 142, 177, 192, 214, 218, 221, 295, 308, 317, 320–21, 323, 325, 343, 359, 377
Third Republic 72, 83, 101–3, 112–13, 117–19, 138
threat 36, 61, 65, 135, 171, 254, 275, 307, 308
tomb 57, 162–65, 167, 169–71, 176, 181, 183, 191, 203
  see also cemeteries and cult graves
Tonnerre 113, 123, 194–95, 199–203
Toulouse 59, 69, 119, 126, 128, 288, 372
Toulouse-Lautrec 104–5, 108, 113, 115
traces-mémoires 4, 293–94

trans-
  feminisms 21, 233, 374, 377
  TDOR (Transgender Day of Remembrance) 232–33
  transgender and transgenderism 4, 30–31, 38, 91, 131, 135, 193–94, 198, 203, 219–34, 257, 270, 292, 336, 353–54
  trans people 219–22, 225, 227–32, 303, 352
  transphobia 49, 138, 150, 229–30, 338, 350
  transsexuality 196, 270, 276
  trans voices 232, 374
  trans women 5, 16, 219, 222–24, 228–30, 336, 352
transfiliation 23, 35, 39, 103, 106, 142, 172–73, 177, 190–92, 198, 218, 251, 289, 295, 324, 377
transgressions 2, 102, 112, 120, 207, 279, 301, 336
transmission 35–36, 64, 174, 186, 364
transnational and transnationalism 1, 4, 9, 14, 137, 153–54, 165, 176, 186, 190, 226, 289, 292, 310, 331, 332, 335, 337, 373
trauma 13, 16, 21, 38, 74, 95, 152, 309, 312–13, 316–19, 321, 345, 348, 354–55, 364
tributes 41, 162–63, 165, 167, 170, 336, 339
truth 34, 49, 203, 214, 272, 278

undercommons 277–95
United States 61, 133, 137, 179, 232, 351
universalism 2, 4, 7, 9–10, 14, 73, 90, 137, 151, 190, 210, 228, 279, 302, 303, 305, 354, 372
urban space 101, 122, 125, ,127, 129, 256, 260, 263
  see also space and spatiality

victims 5, 16, 31, 56–57, 65–66, 207, 220, 229, 232, 274–75, 305, 322, 339–40

viewers 131, 151, 164, 177–78, 183–85, 197, 241, 300, 302, 307–8
see also spectators
village 31, 125, 149, 202, 272
violence 5, 11, 31, 37, 147, 152, 171, 222, 227, 229, 231, 302, 305, 351
virus 62, 65, 303, 308–9, 315–19, 321–25
visitors 50, 121–22, 162–67, 169–70, 183, 202
visual arts 357–69
Vivien, Renée 162, 165, 167–68, 171
voices 120, 137, 175, 222, 227, 232, 239, 260, 263, 271, 275, 278–79, 310, 339, 341, 344–45, 350, 357–58, 371

walls 153, 165, 169, 184–85, 247, 285, 366
war 58, 60, 63, 69, 112, 116, 239–40, 268–69, 271–73, 276
see also World War I; World War II
web 21–23, 37–39, 51–52, 68–69, 94–96, 114, 116, 156, 204, 216–18, 233–34, 259, 276, 311–12, 356, 369

websites 9, 19–20, 38, 121, 147, 168, 215, 228, 310
Wilde, Oscar 41, 108, 161–67, 170–71, 203
woman and women 9, 29–30, 46, 82, 102, 105–6, 109–10, 113, 142, 147, 161–63, 168, 171, 185, 193, 195–98, 201–2, 205, 222, 224, 229, 241, 244, 247, 270, 271–73, 275–76, 278, 290–91, 333, 336–37, 341, 350, 351, 358, 355, 362, 366–67
World's Fair 101, 106, 108
World War I 111–12, 239–40
see also war
World War II 8, 35, 50, 55–56, 63, 123, 136, 239–40, 268, 270
see also war

xenophobia 338

youth 43, 178, 318, 320

zaps 299, 302, 307
Zola, Emile 106–7, 114, 116, 165

www.ingramcontent.com/pod-product-compliance
Lightning Source LLC
Chambersburg PA
CBHW072347270226
40387CB00035B/1876